# Java Programming
# Introductory Concepts
# and Techniques
# Third Edition

**Gary B. Shelly**
**Thomas J. Cashman**
**Joy L. Starks**

Contributing Author
Michael L. Mick

## COURSE TECHNOLOGY
CENGAGE Learning

Australia • Brazil • Japan • Korea • Mexico • Singapore • Spain • United Kingdom • United States

## COURSE TECHNOLOGY
### CENGAGE Learning™

**Java Programming**
**Introductory Concepts and Techniques, Third Edition**
Gary B. Shelly, Thomas J. Cashman, Joy L. Starks,
Michael L. Mick

Managing Editor: Alexandra Arnold

Series Consulting Editor: Jim Quasney

Marketing Manager: Dana Merk

Senior Product Manager: Karen Stevens

Product Manager: Reed Cotter

Associate Product Manager: Selena Coppock

Editorial Assistant: Patrick Frank

Print Buyer: Justin Palmeiro

Production Editor: Marissa Falco

Marketing Coordinator: Melissa Marcoux

Quality Assurance: Burt LaFountain, Danielle Shaw

Copy Editor: Lyn Markowicz

Proofreader: John Bosco

Cover Art: John Still

Compositors: Jeanne Black, Pre-Press Company, Inc.

For product information and technology assistance, contact us at
**Cengage Learning Customer & Sales Support, 1-800-354-9706**

For permission to use material from this text or product, submit all requests online at **cengage.com/permissions**
Further permissions questions can be emailed to
**permissionrequest@cengage.com**

ISBN-13: 978-1-4188-5983-1

ISBN-10: 1-4188-5983-4

**Course Technology**
20 Channel Center Street
Boston, MA 02210
USA

Cengage Learning is a leading provider of customized learning solutions with office locations around the globe, including Singapore, the United Kingdom, Australia, Mexico, Brazil, and Japan. Locate your local office at:
**international.cengage.com/region**

Cengage Learning products are represented in Canada by Nelson Education, Ltd.

To learn more about Course Technology, visit **www.cengage.com/coursetechnology**

To learn more about Cengage Learning, visit **www.cengage.com**

Purchase any of our products at your local college bookstore or at our preferred online store **www.cengagebrain.com**

Disclaimer: Course Technology reserves the right to revise this publication and make changes from time to time in its content without notice.

Printed in China
3 4 5 6 7 15 14 13 12 11

# Java Programming
# Introductory Concepts
# and Techniques
# Third Edition

## Contents

## CHAPTER 1

### An Introduction to Java and Program Design

# CHAPTER 4

## Decision Making and Repetition with Reusable Objects

# APPENDIX D

## Compiling and Running Java Programs Using the Command Prompt Window

# APPENDIX E

## Creating Documentation with Javadoc

# Preface

The Shelly Cashman Series® offers the finest textbooks in computer education. We are proud of the fact that our previous *Java Programming* books have been so well received by instructors and students. This latest edition continues with the innovation, quality, and reliability you have come to expect from this series. In particular, this edition has been updated for Java 2 SDK version 5.0, while continuing to cover the fundamentals of Java programming and design. Valuable Java 2 SDK 5 programming tips are interspersed throughout this latest edition. In addition, the end-of-chapter exercises have been enhanced with critical-thinking problems.

Java is one of the *more* popular programming languages. Java is widely used to implement network interfaces, Web servers, and e-commence solutions, as well as standard business applications. Java provides an object-oriented, portable, and robust framework for application development.

In our *Java Programming* books, you will find an educationally sound and easy-to-follow pedagogy that combines a step-by-step approach with corresponding screens. The Other Ways and Tip features offer in-depth suggestions about alternative ways to complete a task and programming techniques. Every programming chapter builds an application from start to finish following a disciplined development cycle defined in Chapter 1. The Shelly Cashman Series *Java Programming* books will make your programming class exciting and dynamic and one that your students will remember as one of their better educational experiences.

## Objectives of This Textbook

*Java Programming: Introductory Concepts and Techniques, Third Edition* is intended for a one-credit course or a full-semester course that includes a survey of programming using Java. No experience with a computer is assumed, and no mathematics beyond the high school freshman level is required. The objectives of this book are:

- To teach the fundamentals of the Java programming language
- To teach the basic concepts and methods of object-oriented programming and object-oriented design
- To emphasize the development cycle as a means of creating applications
- To illustrate well-written and readable programs using a disciplined coding style, including documentation and indentation standards
- To use practical problems to illustrate application-building techniques
- To encourage independent study and help those who are working alone in a distance education environment

# The Shelly Cashman Approach

Features of the Shelly Cashman Series *Java Programming* books include:

- **Building Applications**   Each programming chapter builds a complete application using the six phases of the development cycle: (1) analyze requirements; (2) design solution; (3) validate design; (4) implement design; (5) test solution; and (6) document solution.

- **Step-by-Step, Screen-by-Screen Methodology**   Each of the tasks required to build an application within a chapter is identified using a step-by-step, screen-by-screen methodology. Students have the option of learning Java by reading the book without the use of a computer or by following the steps on a computer and building a chapter application from start to finish.

- **More Than Just Step-By-Step**   This book offers extended but clear discussions of programming concepts. Important Java design and programming tips are interspersed throughout the chapters. When a Java statement is introduced, one or more tables follow showing the general form of the statement and the various options available.

- **Other Ways Boxes for Reference**   Java provides a variety of ways to carry out a given task. The Other Ways boxes displayed at the end of many of the step-by-step sequences specify the other ways to do the task completed in the steps. Thus, the steps and the Other Ways box make a comprehensive reference unit.

# Organization of This Textbook

*Java Programming: Introductory Concepts and Techniques, Third Edition* provides detailed instruction on how to program using the Java SDK. The material is divided into four chapters and five appendices as follows:

**Chapter 1 – An Introduction to Java and Program Design**   Chapter 1 provides an overview of the capabilities of the Java programming language, application development, program development methodology, program design tools, object-oriented design, and object-oriented programming. The chapter introduces the components of the Java 2 Standard Edition (J2SE) and other development tools.

**Chapter 2 – Creating a Java Application and Applet**   Chapter 2 introduces students to the process of creating a simple Java program. The chapter begins with a requirements document for the Welcome to My Day application and shows the process of proper design and analysis of the program. Topics include using TextPad to edit, compile, and run Java source code; using comments; creating a class and main() method; and displaying output. Students then learn how to convert the application into an applet that displays both text and a graphic with a color background.

**Chapter 3 – Manipulating Data Using Methods**   Chapter 3 defines the primitive data types used in storing and manipulating data in Java as students develop the Body Mass Index Calculator. Topics include basic input and output methods, declaring variables, using arithmetic and comparison operators, understanding operator precedence and simple expressions, converting data types, and creating dialog boxes from the Swing class. As students convert the program into an applet, they are introduced to creating and manipulating Labels, TextFields, and Buttons.

**Chapter 4 – Decision Making and Repetition with Reusable Objects**   Chapter 4 presents students with the fundamental concepts of the selection and repetition structures, as well as an introduction to exception handling. Students create a Commission application that calls user-defined methods. The reusable methods accept and return data to the calling method and use if, switch, and while statements to test input. As an applet, the commission program uses a CheckboxGroup to display option buttons to the user.

**Appendices**   This book concludes with five appendices. Appendix A covers program design tools, including flowcharting and the Unified Modeling Language (UML). Appendix B explains how to install the Java2 SDK, TextPad, and Tomcat, including choosing destination folders, setting environmental variables, and starting and stopping Tomcat. Appendix C demonstrates changing screen resolution and setting TextPad preferences to customize the programming desktop. Appendix D describes how to compile and run Java programs using the Command Prompt window, including instructions on setting window properties and changing the path and classpath of the system. Appendix E presents ways to create HTML documentation using the Javadoc command.

## End-of-Chapter Activities

A notable strength of the Shelly Cashman Series *Java Programming* books is the extensive student activities at the end of each chapter. Well-structured student activities can make the difference between students merely participating in a class and students retaining the information they learn. The end-of-chapter activities in the Java books are detailed below.

- **What You Should Know**   A listing of the tasks completed in the chapter in order of presentation together with the pages on which the step-by-step, screen-by-screen explanations appear. This section provides a perfect study review for students.

- **Key Terms**   This list of the key terms found in the chapter together with the pages on which the terms are defined aid students in mastering the chapter material.

- **Homework Assignments**   The homework assignments are divided into three sections: Label the Figure, Short Answer, and Learn It Online. The Label the Figure section, in the chapters where it applies, involves a figure and callouts that students fill in. The Short Answer section includes fill in the blank and short essay questions. The Learn It Online section consists of Web-based exercises that include chapter reinforcement (true/false, multiple choice, and short answer), practice tests, learning games, and Web exercises that require students to extend their learning beyond the material covered in the book.

- **Debugging Assignment**   This exercise requires students to open an application with errors from the Java data files that accompany the book and debug it. Students may obtain a copy of the Java data files by following the instructions on the inside back cover of this book.

- **Programming Assignments**   An average of ten programming assignments per chapter require students to apply the knowledge gained in the chapter to build applications on a computer. The initial programming assignments step students through building the application and are accompanied by screens showing the desired interface. Later assignments state only the problem, allowing students to create on their own.

## Shelly Cashman Series Instructor Resources

The two categories of ancillary material that accompany this textbook are Instructor Resources (ISBN 1-4188-5965-6) and Online Content. These ancillaries are available to adopters through your Course Technology representative or by calling one of the following telephone numbers: Colleges and Universities, 1-800-648-7450; High Schools, 1-800-824-5179; Private Career Colleges, 1-800-648-7450; Canada, 1-800-268-2222; Corporations with IT Training Centers, 1-800-648-7450; and Government Agencies, Health-Care Organizations, and Correctional Facilities, 1-800-477-3692.

## Instructor Resources CD-ROM

The Instructor Resources for this textbook include both teaching and testing aids. The contents of the Instructor Resources CD-ROM are listed below.

- **Instructor's Manual**   The Instructor's Manual is made up of Microsoft Word files. The Instructor's Manual includes detailed lesson plans with page number references, lecture notes, teaching tips, classroom activities, discussion topics, projects to assign, and transparency references. The transparencies are available through the Figure Files described below.

- **Syllabus**   Any instructor who has been assigned a course at the last minute knows how difficult it is to come up with a course syllabus. For this reason, sample syllabi are included that can be customized easily to a course.

- **Figure Files**   Illustrations for every figure in the textbook are available in electronic form. Use this ancillary to present a slide show in lecture or to print transparencies for use in lecture with an overhead projector. If you have a personal computer and LCD device, this ancillary can be an effective tool for presenting lectures.

- **Solutions to Exercises**   Solutions and required files for all the chapter projects, Homework Assignments, Debugging Assignments, and Programming Assignments at the end of each chapter are available.

- **Test Bank & Test Engine**   The test bank includes 110 questions for every chapter (25 multiple-choice, 50 true/false, and 35 fill-in-the-blank) with page number references, and when appropriate, figure references. A version of the test bank you can print also is included. The test bank comes with a copy of the test engine, ExamView. ExamView is a state-of-the-art test builder that is easy to use. ExamView enables you quickly to create printed tests, Internet tests, and computer (LAN-based) tests. You can enter your own test questions or use the test bank that accompanies ExamView.

- **Data Files for Students**   Most of the projects created in this book do not use files supplied by the authors. In the few instances, however, where students are instructed to open a project to complete a task, the files are supplied.

- **PowerPoint Presentation**   PowerPoint Presentation is a multimedia lecture presentation system that provides PowerPoint slides for each chapter. Presentations are based on the chapters' objectives. Use this presentation system to present well-organized lectures that are both interesting and knowledge based. PowerPoint Presentation provides consistent coverage at schools that use multiple lecturers in their programming courses.

## Online Content

If you use Blackboard or WebCT, the test bank for this book is free in a simple, ready-to-use format. Visit the Instructor Resource Center for this textbook at www.cengagebrain.com to download the test bank, or contact your local sales representative for details.

# Shelly Cashman Series — Traditionally Bound Textbooks

The Shelly Cashman Series presents the following computer subjects in a variety of traditionally bound textbooks. For more information, see your Course Technology representative or call 1-800-648-7450. For Shelly Cashman Series information, visit Shelly Cashman Series at course.com/shellycashman.

| COMPUTERS | |
|---|---|
| Computers | Discovering Computers 2006: A Gateway to Information, Complete |
| | Discovering Computers 2006: A Gateway to Information, Introductory |
| | Discovering Computers 2006: A Gateway to Information, Brief |
| | Discovering Computers: Fundamentals, Second Edition |
| | Teachers Discovering Computers: Integrating Technology in the Classroom, Third Edition |
| | Essential Introduction to Computers, Sixth Edition (40-page) |

| WINDOWS APPLICATIONS | |
|---|---|
| Microsoft Office | Microsoft Office 2003: Essential Concepts and Techniques (5 projects) |
| | Microsoft Office 2003: Brief Concepts and Techniques (9 projects) |
| | Microsoft Office 2003: Introductory Concepts and Techniques, Second Edition (15 projects) |
| | Microsoft Office 2003: Advanced Concepts and Techniques (12 projects) |
| | Microsoft Office 2003: Post Advanced Concepts and Techniques (11 projects) |
| | Microsoft Office XP: Essential Concepts and Techniques (5 projects) |
| | Microsoft Office XP: Brief Concepts and Techniques (9 projects) |
| | Microsoft Office XP: Introductory Concepts and Techniques, Windows XP Edition (15 projects) |
| | Microsoft Office XP: Introductory Concepts and Techniques, Enhanced Edition (15 projects) |
| | Microsoft Office XP: Advanced Concepts and Techniques (11 projects) |
| | Microsoft Office XP: Post Advanced Concepts and Techniques (11 projects) |
| Integration | Teachers Discovering and Integrating Microsoft Office: Essential Concepts and Techniques, Second Edition |
| | Integrating Microsoft Office XP Applications and the World Wide Web: Essential Concepts and Techniques |
| PIM | Microsoft Outlook 2002: Essential Concepts and Techniques • Microsoft Office Outlook 2003: Introductory Concepts and Techniques |
| Microsoft Works | Microsoft Works 6: Complete Concepts and Techniques[1] • Microsoft Works 2000: Complete Concepts and Techniques[1] |
| Microsoft Windows | Microsoft Windows XP: Comprehensive Concepts and Techniques[2] |
| | Microsoft Windows XP: Brief Concepts and Techniques |
| | Microsoft Windows 2000: Comprehensive Concepts and Techniques[2] |
| | Microsoft Windows 2000: Brief Concepts and Techniques |
| | Microsoft Windows 98: Comprehensive Concepts and Techniques[2] |
| | Microsoft Windows 98: Essential Concepts and Techniques |
| | Introduction to Microsoft Windows NT Workstation 4 |
| Notebook Organizer | Microsoft Office OneNote 2003: Introductory Concepts and Techniques |
| Word Processing | Microsoft Office Word 2003: Comprehensive Concepts and Techniques[2] • Microsoft Word 2002: Comprehensive Concepts and Techniques2 |
| Spreadsheets | Microsoft Office Excel 2003: Comprehensive Concepts and Techniques[2] • Microsoft Excel 2002: Comprehensive Concepts and Techniques2 |
| Database | Microsoft Office Access 2003: Comprehensive Concepts and Techniques[2] • Microsoft Access 2002: Comprehensive Concepts and Techniques2 |
| Presentation Graphics | Microsoft Office PowerPoint 2003: Comprehensive Concepts and Techniques[2] • Microsoft PowerPoint 2002: Comprehensive Concepts and Techniques[2] |
| Desktop Publishing | Microsoft Office Publisher 2003: Comprehensive Concepts and Techniques[2] • Microsoft Publisher 2002: Comprehensive Concepts and Techniques[1] |

| PROGRAMMING | |
|---|---|
| Programming | Microsoft Visual Basic .NET: Comprehensive Concepts and Techniques[2] • Microsoft Visual Basic 6: Complete Concepts and Techniques[1] • Java Programming: Comprehensive Concepts and Techniques, Second Edition[2] • Structured COBOL Programming, Second Edition • Understanding and Troubleshooting Your PC • Programming Fundamentals Using Microsoft Visual Basic .NET |

| INTERNET | |
|---|---|
| Concepts | Discovering the Internet: Brief Concepts and Techniques • Discovering the Internet: Complete Concepts and Techniques |
| Browser | Microsoft Internet Explorer 6: Introductory Concepts and Techniques, Windows XP Edition • Microsoft Internet Explorer 5: An Introduction • Netscape Navigator 6: An Introduction |
| Web Page Creation | Web Design: Introductory Concepts and Techniques • HTML: Comprehensive Concepts and Techniques, Third Edition[2] • Microsoft Office FrontPage 2003: Comprehensive Concepts and Techniques[2] • Microsoft FrontPage 2002: Comprehensive Concepts and Techniques[2] • Microsoft FrontPage 2002: Essential Concepts and Techniques • JavaScript: Complete Concepts and Techniques, Second Edition[1] • Macromedia Dreamweaver MX: Comprehensive Concepts and Techniques[2] |

| SYSTEMS ANALYSIS | |
|---|---|
| Systems Analysis | Systems Analysis and Design, Sixth Edition |

| DATA COMMUNICATIONS | |
|---|---|
| Data Communications | Business Data Communications: Introductory Concepts and Techniques, Fourth Edition |

[1]Also available as an Introductory Edition, which is a shortened version of the complete book, [2]Also available as an Introductory Edition and as a Complete Edition, which are shortened versions of the comprehensive book.

# To the Student Getting the Most Out of Your Book

Welcome to *Java Programming: Introductory Concepts and Techniques, Third Edition.* You can save yourself a lot of time and gain a better understanding of Java if you spend a few minutes reviewing the figures and callouts in this section.

## 1 Each Chapter Builds an Application

Each programming chapter builds a complete application, which is carefully described and shown in the first figure of the chapter.

## 2 Consistent Presentation

The authors use a disciplined approach to building all chapter applications using the six phases of the development cycle. By the end of the course, you will be building applications using this methodology by habit.

## 3 Pedagogy

Chapter applications are built using a step-by-step, screen-by-screen approach. This pedagogy allows you to build the application on a computer as you read the chapter. Generally, each step is followed by an italic explanation that indicates the result of the step.

## 4 More Than Just Step-by-Step

This book offers extended but clear discussions of programming concepts. Important Java design and programming Tips are interspersed throughout the chapters.

## 5 Review

After successfully stepping through the chapter, a section titled What You Should Know lists the Java tasks with which you should be familiar in the order they are presented in the chapter.

## 6 Test Preparation

The Key Terms section lists the bold terms in the chapter you should know for test purposes.

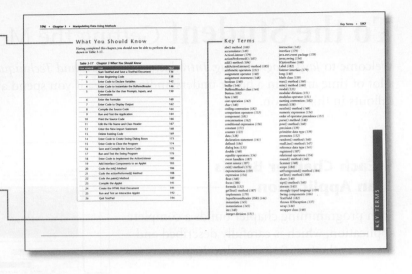

## 7 Reinforcement and Extension

The Short Answer exercises are the traditional pencil-paper exercises. The Learn It Online exercises are Web-based. Some of these Web-based exercises, such as the Practice Test and Crossword Puzzle, are for reinforcement. Others take you beyond the Java topics covered in the chapter.

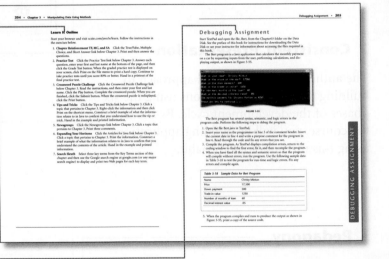

## 8 In the Lab

If you really want to learn how to program in Java, then you must design, program, and debug applications using Java. Every programming chapter includes a Debugging Assignment and several carefully developed Programming Assignments.

# Java Programming, Third Edition CD-ROM

A CD-ROM accompanies this book and can be found on the inside back cover. It includes the following software:

- Sun Java™ SDK, Standard Edition 1.5.0_02
- Sun Java™ SDK, Standard Edition Documentation
- Jakarta Tomcat Server 5.5.7
- Jakarta Tomcat Help
- TextPad 4.7.3 Evaluation
- TextPad Help

# An Introduction to Java and Program Design

## Objectives

You will have
mastered the material in
this chapter when you can:

- Describe characteristics of Java
- Explain the uses of Java and identify types of Java programs
- Identify the phases in the program development life cycle
- Define programs, programming, and applications
- Read, explain, and create a class diagram
- Read, explain, and create an event diagram
- Explain object-oriented programming (OOP) and object-oriented design (OOD)
- Define the terms objects, attributes, methods, and events
- Define and explain encapsulation, inheritance, and polymorphism
- Describe rapid application development (RAD)
- Identify key components of the Java Software Development Kit (SDK)

# Introduction

A computer **program** is a step-by-step series of instructions that tells a computer exactly what to do. **Computer programming** is the process of writing that set of instructions for the computer to follow in order to produce a desired result. A **programming language** is a set of words, symbols, and codes that enables a programmer to communicate instructions to a computer. Computer **programmers**, also called **software developers**, design and write programs using a programming language or program development tools. Programming also is referred to as **coding** because the instructions written by a programmer are called computer **code**.

Just as humans understand a variety of languages, such as English, Spanish, and Japanese, a computer programmer can select from a variety of programming languages or program development tools to code a program that solves a particular problem. In fact, more than 2,000 programming languages exist today. This chapter introduces you to basic computer programming concepts to help you learn about fundamental program design and the tools that programmers use to write programs. You will learn these concepts and tools while working with an object-oriented programming language called Java.

Java is a good general-purpose programming language. Schools, businesses, and software development firms are realizing that Java provides the structured basis necessary to write efficient and economical computer programs, which makes Java skills extremely marketable. Most programmers also realize that using an object-oriented approach results in programs that are easier to develop, debug, and maintain than previously accepted approaches. For beginning programmers, who sometimes are overwhelmed by the complexity of programming languages, or those who become carried away with the bells and whistles of graphical user interfaces, Java provides the structure to develop disciplined programming habits.

# What Is Java?

**Java** is a high-level computer programming language. **High-level languages**, like Java, allow programmers to write instructions using English-like commands and words instead of cryptic numeric codes or memory addresses. Each instruction in a high-level language corresponds to many instructions in the computer's machine language. Machine languages consist entirely of numbers and are the only languages understood by computers. The particular set of rules or grammar that specify how the instructions are to be written is called the **syntax** of the language.

Java was designed in the early 1990s by a team from Sun Microsystems led by James Gosling. Java designers began with the basic syntax of languages like C, C++, and Smalltalk. Java initially was designed for use on devices such as cellular phones; however, within a few years, Sun Microsystems was using Java to provide animation and interactivity on the Web. IBM has adopted Java as its major program development language. Many network interfaces, Web servers, and e-commerce solutions now are Java-based — a trend that will continue in the future as businesses learn to take full advantage of the Java language.

## Characteristics of Java

Java is the fastest growing programming language in the world, due in part to the design team's successful effort to make the language parsimonious, robust, secure, and portable. Computer professionals use the word **parsimonious** to mean that a language has a compact set of commands without numerous versions or adaptations of the same command. While new commands are periodically added, the original Java commands will not change, meaning that older Java programs still will run on newer versions of the software.

Java is an object-oriented programming language. **Object-oriented programming** (**OOP**) is an approach to programming in which the data and the code that operates on the data are packaged into a single unit called an **object**. A software object represents real objects, such as a person or thing, or abstract objects, such as a transaction or an event — for example, a mouse click. **Object-oriented design** (**OOD**) is an approach to program design that identifies how objects must interact with each other in order to solve a problem. You will learn more about object-oriented programming (OOP) and object-oriented design (OOD) later in this chapter and as you apply the concepts throughout this book.

Being **robust** means that programmers can use Java to develop programs that do not break easily or cause unexpected behaviors; and, if a program fails, it does not corrupt data. Java thus is suitable for developing programs that are distributed over a network. Java is a **strongly typed language**, which means that it checks for potential problems with different types of data — a big plus for beginning programmers. Java is considered **secure** because its programs are easy to protect from viruses and tampering.

A computer program is **portable** if it can be run on a variety of platforms other than the one in which it was created, without requiring major rework. A **platform** is the underlying hardware and software for a system. Java is portable because it is **platform-independent**, which means that you can use Java to write and run a program on many platforms, such as a PC running Windows or Linux, an Apple running Mac OS, or a server running UNIX. Java is based on the idea that the same program should run on many different kinds of computers, PDAs, cellular phones, and other devices. From the time of its initial commercial release in 1995, Java has grown in popularity and usage because of its true portability.

## The Java Software Development Kit (SDK)

In addition to being a programming language, Java also is a platform. The Java platform, also known as the **Java Software Development Kit** (**SDK**), is a programming environment that allows you to build a wide range of Java program types. The Java SDK includes programming interfaces, programming tools, and documentation. The Java SDK is described in more detail later in this chapter.

# Java Program Types

The Java platform allows you to create programs and program components for a variety of uses. Figure 1-1 on the next page illustrates the types of programs you can create using the Java platform, including console applications, windowed applications with a graphical user interface, applets, servlets, Web services, and JavaBeans. The following sections describe the types of programs you can develop in detail.

# Java Program Types

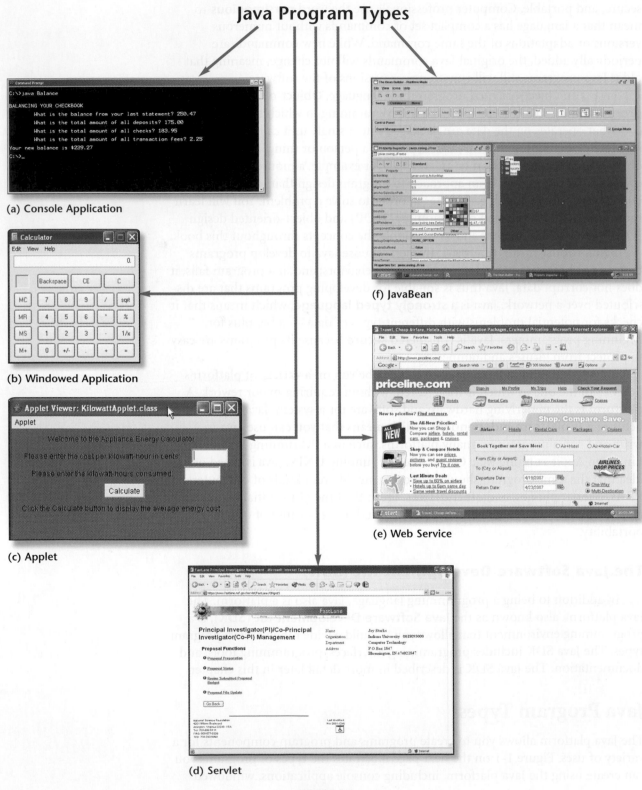

(a) Console Application

(b) Windowed Application

(c) Applet

(d) Servlet

(e) Web Service

(f) JavaBean

FIGURE 1-1

## Console and Windowed Applications

An **application** is a program that tells a computer how to accept input from a user and how to produce output in response to those instructions. Typically, applications are designed to complete a specific task, such as word processing or accounting. Java applications are considered to be stand-alone because they can run independent of any other software.

Stand-alone Java applications can be broken down into two types: console applications and windowed applications. A **console application**, also called a console-mode application, uses a command-line interface, such as a command prompt window, to support character output (Figure 1-2). A **windowed application** uses a graphical user interface (GUI) for user input and program output with on-screen elements such as text boxes, buttons, menus, and toolbars to support user interaction (Figure 1-3).

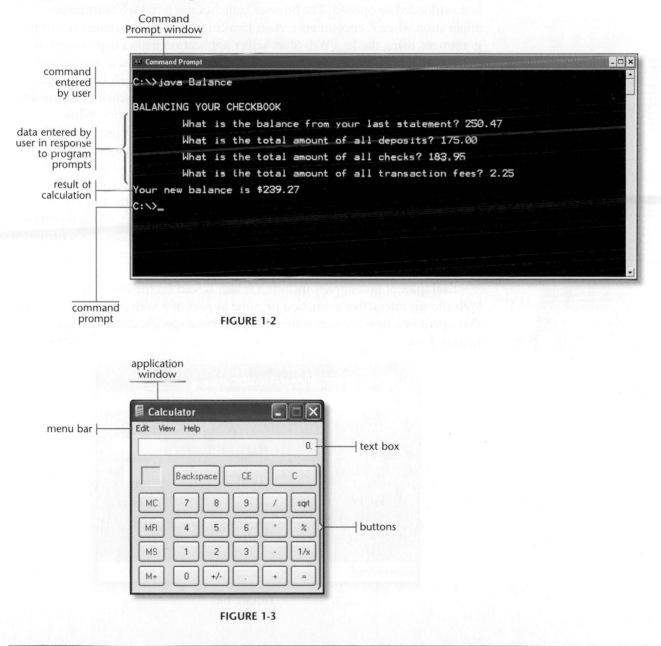

FIGURE 1-2

FIGURE 1-3

## Applets

An **applet** is a small program that can be downloaded and executed as part of a displayed Web page. Applets, which are intended for general use by people browsing the Web, are considered to be **client-side**, which means the applet executes on the client machine. The client program still may rely on the server or host for some resources, however.

Because applets run within a Web browser, they are subject to security restrictions imposed by the browsers: they cannot read or write files on the client system or connect to any computer other than the applet host. These restrictions made it difficult to use applets for advanced programming applications, such as word processing, until Sun Microsystems introduced a client-side helper application. This helper application, called **Java Web Start**, functions much like Windows Media Player and the RealOne Player, which launch when an audio file is downloaded or opened. The browser launches the Java Web Start helper application when it encounters certain Java commands and statements. For programmers, using the Java Web Start helper application makes deployment of full-featured Java applications as easy as the HTML code used to start applets. For users, Java Web Start means they can download and launch Java applications, such as a complete spreadsheet program, with a single click in a browser.

Some people associate Java's Web capabilities with JavaScript. While JavaScript and Java sometimes are combined in an applet, JavaScript is different from Java. **JavaScript** is a scripting tool, created by Netscape, used to insert code statements directly into the HTML of a Web page, to add functionality and improve the appearance of the Web page. **Hypertext Markup Language** (**HTML**) is a set of special codes called tags that specify how the text and other elements of a Web page display. Unlike a JavaScript statement, which is embedded in the HTML document, a Java applet is sent to the browser as a separate file. A special HTML tag tells the browser where to find and execute the applet file.

Examples of Java applets include a splash screen on the home page of a Web site, an interactive animation or game as part of a Web page, or a program that opens in a new browser window to perform a specific client-side function (Figure 1-4).

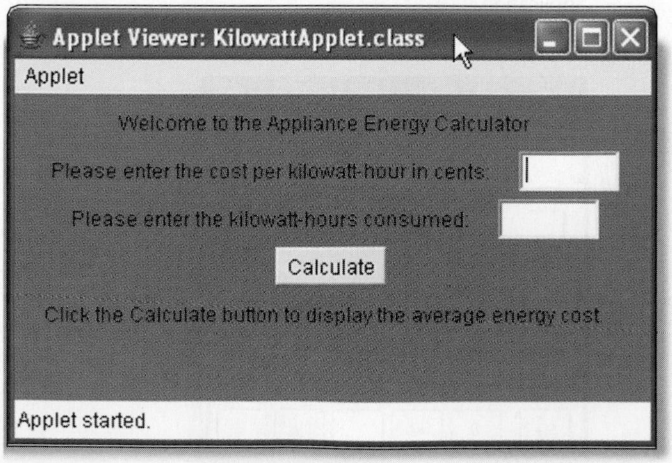

**FIGURE 1-4**

## Servlets

A third use of Java is to create servlets. A **servlet** is a Java program that is hosted and run on a Web server rather than launched from a browser. **Hosting** involves storing Web pages, programs, and other data on a computer that a user connects via a network, intranet, or the Web. A **Web server** is a computer that hosts Web pages, programs, and other files, which it delivers or serves to requesting computers. Web servers use **server software** that responds to incoming requests and serves different forms of data, as well as interfacing with applications and servlets. Thus, servlets are considered to be **server-side**, because the programs are hosted and run on the server and are not executed on the client, as are applets (Figure 1-5).

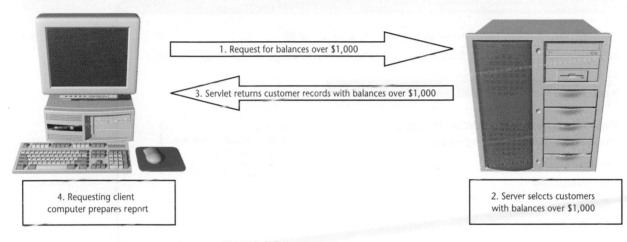

1. Request for balances over $1,000

3. Servlet returns customer records with balances over $1,000

4. Requesting client computer prepares report

2. Server selects customers with balances over $1,000

FIGURE 1-5

Servlets now are widely used to extend Web server and database functionality. Servlets can be used with **Java Server Pages** (**JSP**), a server-side technology that extends the Java servlet technology to provide a way to create sophisticated solutions that run on any platform. JSP, when used with servlets, separates the display logic on the client machine (for example, how a Web page or program displays to a user) from the business logic on the server (the rules that define program calculations, responses, and so on). Upon first use, a JSP page is translated into Java source code, which is then compiled into a class file. From then on, it runs similar to any other servlet unless the original JSP file is changed.

Another common use of Java servlets is to connect to databases using **Java Database Connectivity** (**JDBC**), a Java interface that enables Java applications to execute queries and interact with most databases.

Programmers use JSP and JDBC to develop data-driven Web applications. Experts estimate that 80 percent of the world's computer applications are database applications; therefore, many programmers use Java servlets to develop database applications for a variety of purposes and deploy them over intranets, extranets, and the Web. Whether a company's human resource department needs to deploy an employee benefits application, or a company needs an enterprise-wide solution for customer service, account management, and inventory control, a programmer can use Java servlets to develop programs to meet those needs. Figure 1-6 displays a Web page that uses a servlet to provide functionality.

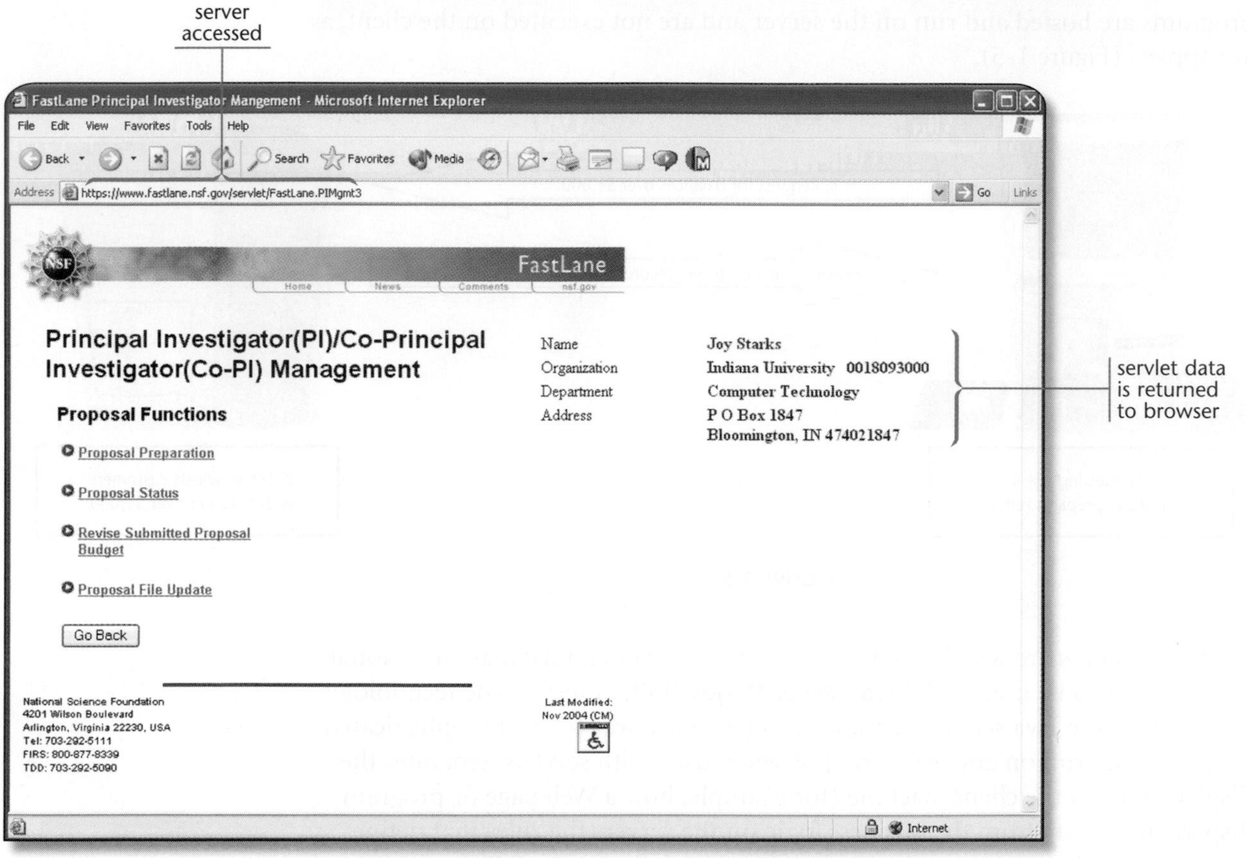

FIGURE 1-6

## Web Services

Another use of Java is to create Web services. A **Web service**, sometimes called an application service, is a program that receives a request for information from another program over the Web and then returns data to the requesting program. Web services usually incorporate some combination of programming and data, but may support user input as well. In a typical Web services scenario, a business application sends a request to a service at a given URL using a special Web-based protocol (Figure 1-7). The Web service receives the request, processes it, and returns a response to the application. A typical example of a Web service is that of an automatic stock quote service, in which the request asks for the current price of a specified stock, and the response returns the stock price. Another example might be a service that maps out an efficient route for the delivery of goods. In this case, a business application sends a request containing the delivery destinations, and a Web service processes the request to determine the most cost-effective delivery route.

FIGURE 1-7

## JavaBeans

Java also can be used to create components for use by other programs. Such a component, called a **JavaBean** or simply a **bean**, is a reusable software component developed in Java, which can be used by any application that understands the JavaBeans format. Beans allow programmers to develop applications visually using standard development tools. Beans provide the benefit of **reusability**, which means they can be used over and over in many programs developed by different programmers. A bean also can store data and retrieve it later. For example, a bank account bean might store an account number and balance. A programmer might write code to display the bean's properties on a secure Web page when the customer requests his or her balance. Figure 1-8 on the next page displays a development tool used to create JavaBeans.

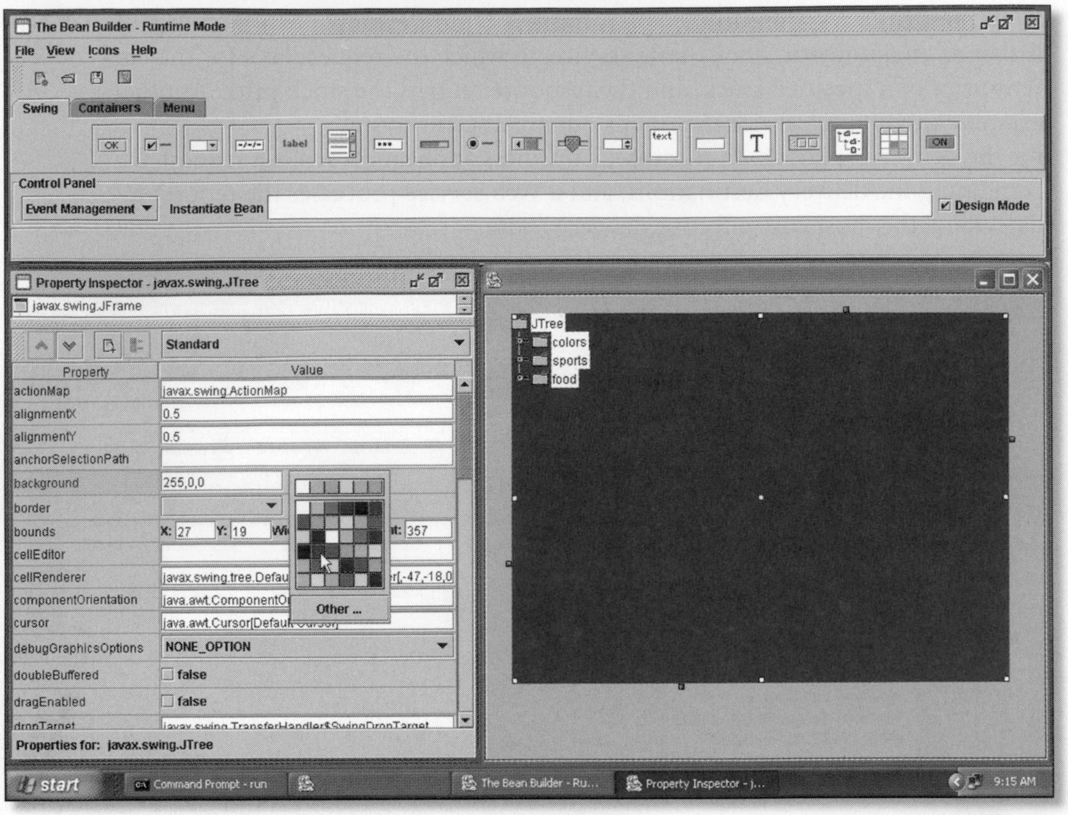

**FIGURE 1-8**

## Programming a Computer

Most computer users do not write their own programs. Programs required for common business and personal applications such as word processing or spreadsheets can be purchased from software vendors or stores that sell computer products. These purchased programs are referred to as **application software packages**.

Even though good application software packages can be purchased inexpensively, software development firms and other companies have a need for developers to build application software packages as well as custom applications. Large companies, for example, need industry-specific software not available in the retail market due to its limited use. Smaller companies want programs that can be adjusted and tailored to fit their needs. Existing programs also need constant maintenance, monitoring, and upgrades. Learning to develop programs, therefore, is an important skill. Learning program development improves logical- and critical-thinking skills for computer-related careers, and it teaches why applications perform as they do. As hardware, networking, and Internet technologies progress and change, developers will be needed to meet the challenge of creating new applications. Programming, a combination of engineering and art, is a very marketable skill.

# The Program Development Cycle

Programmers do not sit down and start writing code right away. Instead, they follow an organized plan, or **methodology**, that breaks the process into a series of tasks. Just as there are many programming languages, there are many application development methodologies. These different methodologies, however, tend to be variations of what is called the **program development cycle**. The cycle follows these six phases: (1) analyze the requirements, (2) design the solution, (3) validate the design, (4) implement the design, (5) test the solution, and (6) document the solution. Table 1-1 describes each phase that a programmer goes through to arrive at a computer application. Figure 1-9 on the next page portrays the program development cycle as a continuing, iterative process or loop. When the maintenance phase identifies change, or the program must meet new requirements, a new iteration of the cycle begins again.

*Table 1-1  The Program Development Cycle*

| | PHASE | DESCRIPTION |
|---|---|---|
| 1 | Analyze the requirements | Precisely define the problem to be solved, verify that the requirements are complete, and write program requirements and specifications — descriptions of the program's inputs, processing, outputs, and user interface. |
| 2 | Design the solution | Develop a detailed, logical plan using tools such as pseudocode, flowcharts, class diagrams, or event diagrams to group the program's activities into modules; devise a method of solution or algorithm for each module; and test the solution algorithms. Design the user interface for the application, including input areas, output areas, and other necessary elements. |
| 3 | Validate the design | Step through the solution design with test data. Receive confirmation from the user that the design solves the problem in a satisfactory manner. |
| 4 | Implement the design | Translate the design into an application using a programming language or application development tool by creating the user interface and writing code; include internal documentation (comments and remarks) within the code that explains the purpose of the code statements. |
| 5 | Test the solution | Test the program, finding and correcting errors (debugging) until it is error-free and contains enough safeguards to ensure the desired results. Implement the solution at the user level. |
| 6 | Document the solution | Review and, if necessary, revise internal documentation; formalize and complete user (external) documentation. |

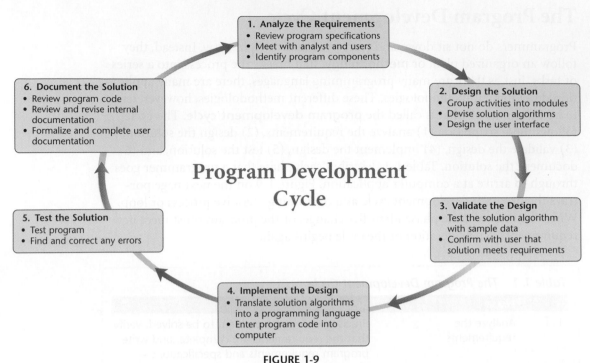

**Program Development Cycle**

1. **Analyze the Requirements**
   • Review program specifications
   • Meet with analyst and users
   • Identify program components

2. **Design the Solution**
   • Group activities into modules
   • Devise solution algorithms
   • Design the user interface

3. **Validate the Design**
   • Test the solution algorithm with sample data
   • Confirm with user that solution meets requirements

4. **Implement the Design**
   • Translate solution algorithms into a programming language
   • Enter program code into computer

5. **Test the Solution**
   • Test program
   • Find and correct any errors

6. **Document the Solution**
   • Review program code
   • Review and revise internal documentation
   • Formalize and complete user documentation

FIGURE 1-9

Program requirements drive the program development cycle. Requirements often are identified by a program's users or a representative of the users when they have a particular problem they believe can be solved by a computer program. Users then submit a **requirements document** that lists the functions and features that the program must provide. The requirements document usually includes a statement of purpose for the requested program (also called a problem definition), the formulas the program must use, and an explanation of how the program should respond to user interaction. Requirements also may specify that a new program be developed or specify updates to an existing program. In addition, requirements indicate how the program will be made available to users; for example, requirements may specify that a stand-alone application must be developed for the program, or they may specify that the program must function over the Web.

Figure 1-10 shows an example of a requirements document. The document specifies the requirements for a new program that must be made available to users as both a console application and an applet. The program's main purpose is to allow users to calculate shipping charges based on the weight of the shipment.

## REQUEST FOR NEW APPLICATION

| | |
|---|---|
| **Date submitted:** | November 11, 2007 |
| **Submitted by:** | Vickie Hefner |
| **Purpose:** | Legal secretaries and clerks need a quick way to calculate shipping charges as they overnight legal documents to clients and other attorneys. |
| **Application title:** | Shipping Charge Calculator |
| **Algorithms:** | Shipping charges are based on the weight of the document package in ounces. The secretaries and legal clerks have scales to weigh the package. If the package is 16 ounces or less, the minimum charge is $12.95, then it is 30 cents an ounce for every ounce over 16.<br><br>Calculations can be summarized as follows:<br>Basic Charge = 12.95<br>Extra Charge = (Ounces – 16) * .30<br><br>If ounces are more than 16<br>      Total Charge = Basic Charge + Extra Charge<br>Otherwise<br>      Total Charge = Basic Charge |
| **Notes:** | 1) Legal clerks frequently work away from the office. A Web interface would allow them to ship from remote locations. Legal secretaries work mainly from their desks or in the copy room; they have access to a computer, but not always the Web.<br><br>2) Employees are accustomed to the terms, shipping charge, and ounces.<br><br>3) The application window should allow users to enter the weight and then click a button to see the calculated charge.<br><br>4) Packages over 5 lbs (80 ounces) are shipped via a different method.<br><br>5) The application should also allow the user to reset the weight, which clears the ounces and charge areas of the screen, so that another calculation can be performed.<br><br>6) Use the words, Calculation, Shipping, and Reset, on the buttons. |

**Approvals**

| | | |
|---|---|---|
| **Approval status:** | X | Approved |
| | | Rejected |
| **Approved by:** | Dennis Louks | |
| **Date:** | November 18, 2007 | |
| **Assigned to:** | J. Starks, Programmer | |

**FIGURE 1-10**

## Analyze the Requirements — Phase 1

When a programmer receives a requirements document or similar assignment, the first step is to make sure that the requirements are clear and complete. If equations are included, they need to be correct and precise. If necessary, the programmer must request that the requirements document be revised to address these issues.

Next, the programmer must evaluate the problem to determine that, indeed, it is solvable with a computer program. One way to do this is for the programmer to make a list of the required input and output data. The programmer must also determine whether input data is available for testing purposes. Figure 1-11 shows a sample list of inputs and outputs, along with test data for the Shipping Charge Calculator application.

**INPUTS AND OUTPUTS**

| INPUTS | OUTPUTS |
| --- | --- |
| Shipment Weight | Shipping Charge |

**SAMPLE DATA**

| INPUTS | OUTPUTS |
| --- | --- |
| 16 ounces | $12.95 |
| 10 ounces | $12.95 |
| 26 ounces | $15.95 |

**FIGURE 1-11**

The next step is for the programmer to verify that the provided information explains how to convert the input data into output data so that a solution, or **algorithm**, can be developed. The requirements document must clearly state the rules that govern how to convert the input into output. The requirements document in Figure 1-10 on the previous page describes the algorithm in words and in mathematical formulas. When writing an algorithm, consider that the goal of computer programming is to create a correct and efficient algorithm that is a clear and unambiguous specification of the steps needed to solve a problem. **Correct** refers to using logical constructs and valid data in an organized way so that the steps will be carried out correctly and the program will make suitable responses to invalid data, such as displaying a warning message for numbers outside a given range. **Efficient** refers to the program's ability to deliver a result quickly enough to be useful and in a space small enough to fit the environment. For instance, if a program to look up a price on a product takes more than a few seconds, customers may become impatient; or if a computer game takes an enormous amount of memory and hard disk space, it will not be marketable. Computer programs should be as straightforward as possible in the certain event that modifications and revisions will need to be made.

The requirements also must state how the user will interact with the program, such as whether the program must be made available in a windowed application with a graphical user interface, as an applet for Web users, or as a

The Program Development Cycle • 15

Web service for use in a larger application. The requirements may include industry-specific terminology with which the user is familiar and which, therefore, must be included in the user interface. These requirements help the programmer determine which technologies to use when designing a solution to the problem. For larger problems, the analysis also should include an initial breakdown of the problem into smaller problems so that programmers can develop solutions gradually and in smaller, more manageable pieces.

The requirements for the Shipping Charge Calculator shown in Figure 1-10 on page 13 specify the input data that should be entered by the user and the algorithm that must be used to calculate the output data. The requirements also explain how users will interact with the program, including the rules that govern valid and invalid input data entered by the user. The end result of the analyze requirements phase is that both the user and the programmer agree in writing that the requirements for the program are clear and complete. At this point, the programmer can begin to design a solution, and the user can begin designing tests to verify that the solution satisfies the program's requirements.

## Design the Solution — Phase 2

Designing a program solution usually involves developing a logical model that illustrates the sequence of steps you will take to solve the problem. Programmers use many tools to think algorithmically and to design their programs correctly and efficiently. Programmers use storyboards, class diagrams, flowcharts, and pseudocode to outline the logic of the program.

**STORYBOARDS**  Because Java often is used to create windowed applications or applets used in Web pages, programmers often create a **storyboard**, or hand-drawn sketch, of how the application window or applet will look and where the user interface elements will be placed in the window. A storyboard also can serve as a reference for the logical names of these elements as you code your program.

The Shipping Charge Calculator may use a similar user interface for both a windowed application and an applet, as shown in the storyboard in Figure 1-12. Although these interfaces may be programmed separately, the user interface is similar, and the same storyboard is useful for both.

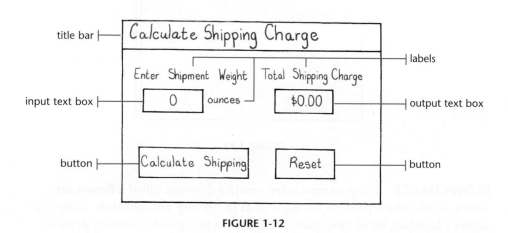

**FIGURE 1-12**

**CLASS DIAGRAMS**   As you have learned, programs can be broken into smaller pieces, called objects, which represent a real person, place, event, or transaction. Object-oriented design is an approach to program design that identifies how groups of objects interact with each other in order to solve a problem. A **class** represents the common structure and behavior shared by the same type of objects. A modeling tool that helps developers visualize how a class works within a program is called a class diagram. A **class diagram** illustrates the name, attributes, and methods of a class of objects. The **attributes** of a class are properties used to define characteristics such as appearance. The **methods** of a class are instructions that the class uses to manipulate values, generate outputs, or perform actions. Many times, classes are individual program modules that often can be reused by other programs.

The Shipping Charge Calculator requires that users access the program in one of two ways: a windowed application or an applet. Rather than creating two completely separate applications for these different users, the algorithm used to solve the problem should be programmed only once. By centralizing the program logic for the two application types, maintenance of the program is easier, and the logic needs to be programmed only once, rather than twice. The algorithm can be placed in a class. The Shipment class has an attribute that corresponds to the input, shipment weight. The class requires one method, getShipping(), that tells the class how to manipulate the input value and generate the required output. Method names typically are represented with an active verb phrase followed by parentheses. The getShipping() method performs the calculation after the attribute, weight, is sent to the object by the program. Figure 1-13 shows a class diagram of the Shipment class. Appendix A includes a more detailed discussion of class diagrams.

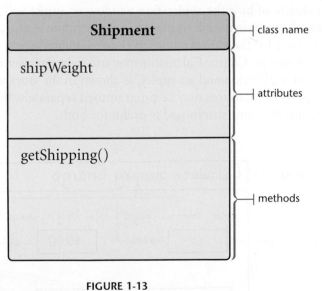

FIGURE 1-13

**FLOWCHARTS**   Programmers often create a diagram called a **flowchart**, which graphically represents the logic used to develop an algorithm. Table 1-2 shows a standard set of flowchart symbols used to represent various steps, or operations, in a program's logic. When you draw a complete flowchart, you must begin with a terminal symbol connected by a flowline to the first logical step in solving the problem. Most of the time, each step in solving a problem is represented by a separate symbol. Most of the flowcharting symbols, except the decision diamond, have one entering flowline and one exiting flowline. Inside the symbol, you write words describing the logical step. Flowcharts typically do not display programming language commands. Rather, they state the concept in English, pseudocode, or mathematical notation. After the last step, you end a flowchart with a final flowline connected to another terminal symbol. Appendix A includes a more detailed discussion of how to develop flowcharts.

**Table 1-2 _Flowcharting Symbols and Their Meanings_**

| SYMBOL | NAME | MEANING |
|---|---|---|
| | Process Symbol | Represents the process of executing a defined operation or group of operations that results in a change in value, form, or location of information; also functions as the default symbol when no other symbol is available |
| | Input/Output (I/O) Symbol | Represents an I/O function, which makes data available for processing (input) or for displaying processed information (output) |
| left to right / top to bottom / right to left / bottom to top | Flowline Symbol | Represents the sequence of available information and executable operations; lines connect other symbols; arrowheads are mandatory only for right-to-left and bottom-to-top flow |
| | Annotation Symbol | Represents the addition of descriptive information, comments, or explanatory notes as clarification; vertical lines and broken lines may be placed on the left, as shown, or on the right |
| | Decision Symbol | Represents a decision that determines which of a number of alternative paths is to be followed |
| | Terminal Symbol | Represents the beginning, the end, or a point of interruption or delay in a program |
| or | Connector Symbol | Represents any entry from, or exit to, another part of the flowchart; also serves as an off-page connector |
| | Predefined Process Symbol | Represents a named process consisting of one or more operations or program steps that are specified elsewhere |

Figure 1-14 shows a flowchart that represents the algorithm used by the getShipping() method to calculate the correct shipping charge. The flowchart includes a **control structure**, which is a portion of a program that allows the programmer to specify that code will be executed only if a condition is met. The control structure in the flowchart, for instance, illustrates how the program decides which shipping rate to use based on the total shipment weight. The breakdown of control structures into sequence, selection, and repetition control structures is explained in detail in Appendix A.

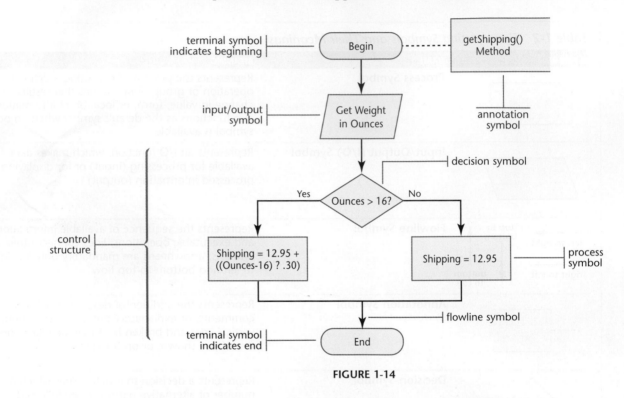

**FIGURE 1-14**

**PSEUDOCODE**   Some programmers use pseudocode to list the actions a computer should perform and to assist in developing the program logic. **Pseudocode** expresses computer actions using keywords and depicts logical groupings or structures using indentation. Figure 1-15 shows the pseudocode for the getShipping() method of the Shipment object. The pseudocode is not program code but an English representation of how the code should be written. The pseudocode serves as an intermediary between the requirements and the final program code.

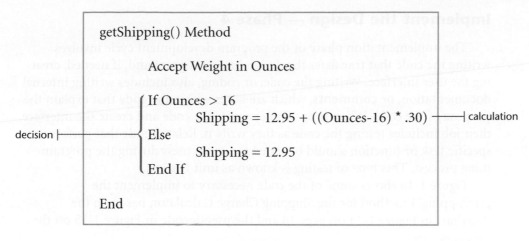

**FIGURE 1-15**

The end result of designing a program solution is the creation of technical documentation that explains how the program will meet the requirements. Any documents that relate to the design of the user interface should be made available to the user, who must verify that the design is correct and that the program's **usability**, which is a measure of a user's ability to interact with a program in a reasonable and intuitive manner, is acceptable.

Most programmers use combinations and variations of these program design tools. Your instructor or supervisor may prefer one type of design tool to another, and you will probably find one or two more useful than others as you develop your own programming style. In addition, companies often have written standards that specify the tools they use to design programs.

## Validate the Design — Phase 3

The third phase in the program development cycle is to **validate** the design, which means that both the programmer and the user must check the program design. The programmer steps through the solution with test data to verify that the solution meets the requirements. The user also must agree that the design solves the problem put forth in the requirements. The validation of the design gives the user one last chance to make certain that all of the necessary requirements were included in the initial requirements document. By comparing the program design with the original requirements, both the programmer and the user can validate that the solution is correct and satisfactory.

The design of the Shipping Charge Calculator can be validated by using a test case for input data and then stepping the test data through both the equation written in the requirements document and the algorithm presented in the program design. The results can be compared to be sure they match.

### Implement the Design — Phase 4

The implementation phase of the program development cycle involves writing the code that translates the design into a program and, if needed, creating the user interface. Writing the code, or coding, also includes writing internal documentation, or **comments**, which are notes within the code that explain the purpose of the code. When programmers write the code and create the interface, their job includes testing the code as they write it. Related code that performs a specific task or function should be tested for correctness during the programming process. This type of testing is known as **unit testing**.

Figure 1-16 shows some of the code necessary to implement the getShipping() method for the Shipping Charge Calculator, based on the flowchart in Figure 1-14 on page 18 and the pseudocode in Figure 1-15 on the previous page.

```
1   // this method accepts an integer named ounces
2   // and returns a double named shipping
3   public static double getShipping(int ounces)
4   {
5       double basicCharge;
6       double shipping;
7
8       // set the basic shipping charge to $12.95
9       basicCharge = 12.95;
10
11      // if the ounces are greater than 16 calculate the
12      // extra charge at 30 cents per extra ounce
13      if (ounces > 16)
14          shipping = basicCharge + ((ounces-16) * .3);
15      else
16          shipping = basicCharge;
17
18      return shipping;
19  }
```

**FIGURE 1-16**

Figure 1-17 shows the user interface developed for the GUI application from the original storyboard design illustrated in Figure 1-12 on page 15.

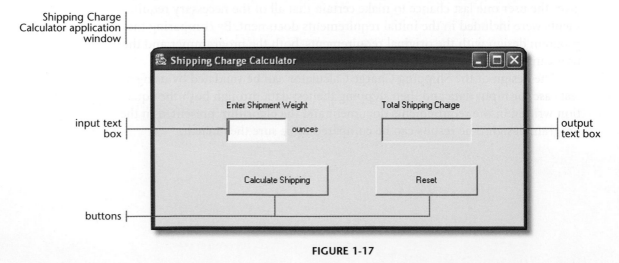

**FIGURE 1-17**

## Test the Solution — Phase 5

Testing the solution is a very important phase in the program development cycle. The purpose of **testing** is to verify that the program meets the requirements from the user's point of view. The program should perform its assigned function correctly under all normal circumstances. If the program includes a user interface, testing should ensure that the user interface also meets requirements. For larger projects, a test plan typically is developed and agreed on during the analyze requirements phase. A **test plan** consists of a collection of test cases. **Test cases** are individual scenarios that include input data and expected output data, and are designed to ensure that the program solves the particular problem indicated in the program requirements.

If a finished application involves several programs or components, **integration testing** must be completed to ensure that all programs and components interact correctly.

The end result of testing the solution includes documentation of any problems with the application. If the user accepts the program as complete and correct, then the user documents this fact, and the program may be put to use. If the testing results are unsatisfactory, then the results are documented and returned to the programmer. The resolution of the problems revealed during testing begins a new iteration of the development cycle, with the outstanding issues serving as requirements.

The Shipping Charge Calculator application requires testing to ensure that all possible cases of valid input data cause the program to calculate the correct result every time. The application must not allow the user to enter values disallowed by the requirements, such as non-numeric data. Test cases also should include input data that would result in the weight being greater than 16 ounces. Based on the requirements, the value of 16 ounces is called a boundary value. **Boundary values** are values that cause a certain rule to become effective. Test cases include the testing of exact boundary values because common logic and programming mistakes occur when boundary values are reached in a problem.

Figure 1-18 shows the Shipping Charge Calculator in the GUI environment being tested with an input value of 24 ounces. Per the requirements, the correct charge should be calculated by adding $12.95 for the first 16 ounces and 30 cents for every ounce thereafter, which results in a total shipping charge of $15.35.

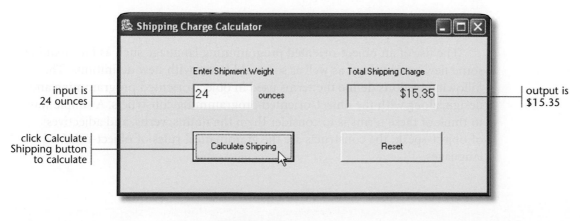

FIGURE 1-18

### Document the Solution — Phase 6

The final phase in the development cycle is to document the completed solution. The **documentation** for a completed programming project includes the requirements documents, program design documents, user interface documents, and documentation of the code. The code should be archived electronically so that it can be accessed in the event that a programmer must fix an error in the code or use the code for other purposes.

Final documentation for the Shipping Charge Calculator consists of all documents generated during the development cycle. This also includes electronic archiving and printing the program code and design. The complete set of documents for the project includes the requirements document, approval of requirements by the user and programmer, program design documents, test cases, program code, and printed proof that the test cases were completed successfully.

## Object-Oriented Programming and Design

The concepts of object-oriented programming and design represent a relatively recent methodology of application development. As you have learned, Java is an object-oriented programming language, meaning that it packages the data and the code that operates on the data together into a single unit called an object. Object-oriented design is an approach to program design that identifies how objects must interact with each other in order to solve a problem.

Structured programs that are not object-oriented are more linear in nature and must define precisely how the data will be used in each particular program. With such a program, if the structure of the data changes, such as when a new field is added to a table in a database, the program has to be changed. With the dynamic nature of data in this information age, traditionally structured programs have limited use-time and high maintenance costs.

Today, object-oriented programming languages like Java are widely used in many industries. Companies like General Motors, for example, now program their assembly line so that cars (objects) on the assembly line can send messages to paint booths asking for an available slot and color (data). The benefit is that programs developed using an object-oriented approach are easier to develop, debug, and maintain.

### Object-Speak

The use of an object-oriented programming language such as Java requires some new terminology, as well as some old terms with new definitions. The following sections define the terms used in object-oriented programming and design, along with the object-oriented programming constructs. A simple way to think of these terms is to consider them the nouns, verbs, and adjectives of object-speak; the constructs are the grammatical rules of object-oriented languages.

**NOUNS**   Recall that an object is anything real or abstract about which you store both attributes (data) and methods (operations) that manipulate the data. You can think of an object as any noun. Examples of objects are an invoice, a file, a record, a form that allows a user to interact with a program, a sales transaction, or an employee. Parts of a graphical user interface such as menus, buttons, and text boxes are also objects. An object may be composed of other objects, which in turn may contain other objects. **Aggregation** is the term used to describe the concept of an object being composed of other objects. An application window, for example, can aggregate a text box, buttons, and a menu bar.

You can think of an object as a closed or black box; this is because an object is packaged with everything it needs to work in a program. The box receives and sends messages and contains code. A user never should need to see inside the box because the object is self-sufficient. Programmers, however, need to know *how* the object works if they are creating or maintaining code for that object, or *what* the object does if writing code to send messages to the object and use it effectively.

You have learned that a class represents an object or a set of objects that share a common structure and a common behavior. A class also can be thought of as a general category of object types, sometimes called an implementation, which can be used to create multiple objects with the same attributes and behavior.

Each class may have one or more lower levels called a **subclass** or one or more higher levels called a **superclass**. For example, a bank has many types of accounts. A savings account is a subclass, or type, of bank account. A savings account can be broken down further into passbook accounts and certificate accounts. In that relationship, a savings account is a superclass of passbook and certificate accounts. Another example might be when developing a windowed application, programmers can use several types of toolbars. A menu bar is a subclass of a toolbar, but it is also a superclass to a drop-down menu. The relationship among the classes, subclasses, and superclasses forms a hierarchy. A **generalization hierarchy** is an object-oriented design tool used to show the relationships among classes (Figure 1-19).

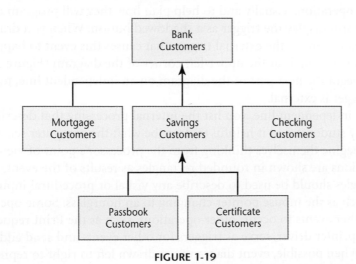

**FIGURE 1-19**

A unique object — a specific use of a class — is called an **instance**. Think of an instance as a proper noun. For example, option buttons are used in a graphical user interface to allow users to choose one option from a list of options. All option buttons belong to the class of option button objects that have the same attributes and the same method of displaying as selected or not selected. The label that accompanies a specific option button, however, has a unique value and signifies a particular instance of an option button. For example, an option button to select a shipping method is a unique instance of the general class of option button objects. Just as a proper noun represents a unique person or place, each instance has a unique name, such as ShippingOptionButton.

**VERBS** An **operation**, or service, is an activity that reads or manipulates the data of an object. You can think of an operation as an active verb. Examples of operations include the standard mathematical, statistical, and logical operations, as well as the input, output, and storage operations associated with computer data. Object-oriented programmers use the term method to refer to code used to perform the operation or service. The Shipment object, for example, performs the operation of calculating shipping charges using the getShipping() method.

For an object to do something, it must receive a message. A **message** activates the code to perform one of the operations. Everything an object can do is represented by the message. The message has two parts — the name of the object to which the message is being sent, and the name of the operation that will be performed. The impetus, or **trigger**, that causes the message to be sent may come from another object or an external user. The entire process of a trigger sending a message that causes an operation to occur is called an **event**. For example, if you click the Calculate Shipping button to determine shipping charges based on weight, clicking the button is the trigger that sends a message to the Shipment object. The Shipment object then uses the getShipping() method to calculate shipping costs, which is the operation. In this example, clicking the Calculate Shipping button is the trigger and the calculation of shipping costs is the operation; together, they make a Calculate Shipping event.

Programmers often draw an **event diagram** to show relationships among events and operations visually and to help plan how they will program events. Event diagrams display the trigger as a shadowed button. When you draw an event diagram, you list the external trigger that causes this event to happen in the shadowed rectangle at the upper-left corner of the diagram (Figure 1-20). Then you begin the next part of the diagram on an independent line, to show that the trigger is external.

On the independent line, you list the internal processing that describes the event. Many students find it helpful to describe what the computer senses at this point or imagine themselves thinking from the processor's point of view.

Operations are shown in rounded rectangles as results of the event. Operation rectangles should be used to describe any visual or procedural inputs and outputs, such as the mouse pointer changing to an hourglass. Some operations cause no other events to occur; other operations, such as the Print request being sent to the printer driver, serve as triggers for other events and send additional messages. When possible, event diagrams are drawn left to right to represent a sequence of events over time.

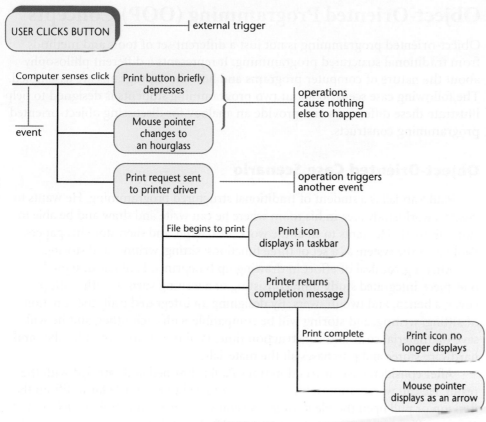

**FIGURE 1-20**

As shown in Figure 1-20, nothing happens unless the trigger sends a message and causes the event to occur. At the conclusion of the operation, the system again will do nothing until another trigger causes an event to occur. This relationship between events and operations is a key feature of object-oriented programming, and programs that are constructed in this way are said to be **event-driven**.

Event diagrams and class diagrams are part of the **Unified Modeling Language** (**UML**), which provides a standardized model for object-oriented design to depict or describe concepts graphically. The UML is a system of symbols used to describe object behaviors and interaction and to represent how a system should behave. The UML is a relatively new language tool, having been developed in the 1990s from a number of object-oriented design tools. Appendix A includes an introduction to the use of the UML.

**ADJECTIVES** In object-oriented terminology, the characteristics of an object are defined by its attributes, or properties. Recall that attributes of an object are values that determine the properties of an individual object, such as its name, size, or background color. Think of attributes as adjectives that describe an object. The attributes of a hyperlink on a Web page might include the font, the color, the font size, and the URL to which it links. Attributes of a bank account object might include a balance and an account number; if the object were an airline flight, the number of passengers would be an attribute. An attribute should not be confused with the data or value assigned to the attribute. Color, for example, is an attribute, while red is the data or value.

# Object-Oriented Programming (OOP) Concepts

Object-oriented programming is not just a different set of tools and methods from traditional structured programming. It represents a different philosophy about the nature of computer programs and how those programs are assembled. The following case scenario about two programming students is designed to help illustrate these differences and provide an analogy for discussing object-oriented programming constructs.

## Object-Oriented Case Scenario

Paul Randall is a student of traditional structured programming. He wants to create a work/study area in his room where he can write and draw and be able to store his work. He wants to sit at the work area, write, and then store his papers. Paul views the system as a set of three functions: sitting, writing, and storing.

After a great deal of effort in drawing up blueprints, Paul has designed a one-piece integrated study unit, consisting of a writing surface with rolltop cover, a bench, and two drawers. By designing an integrated unit, the functions of sitting, writing, and storing will be compatible with each other, and he will save on material costs and construction time. Paul travels to several lumber and hardware stores and purchases all the materials.

After considerable construction time, Paul is finished and satisfied with the result. He can work comfortably and does not need to reach too far to lift up the desktop or pull open the file drawers. Several weeks pass and Paul begins to think about making enhancements to his system. His bench is not as comfortable as he would like, his writing area feels cramped, and his two drawers are full. Paul decides to live with his system's shortcomings, however, because any change would require substantial effort to dismantle and rebuild the entire system.

Mary Carter is a student of object-oriented programming. She would like to have a study area with the same functionality as Paul's study area. Mary, however, views the system as a set of three objects: a sitting object, a writing surface object, and a storage object. Even though they are separate objects, Mary is confident she can make them interoperate for an effective study area. Mary travels to a furniture factory warehouse and begins evaluating the hundreds of different chairs, desks, and file cabinets for their suitability to her needs and their compatibility with each other.

Mary returns to her room after purchasing a matching chair, two-drawer file cabinet, and rolltop desk. When the desk handle is pulled, it activates a hardware mechanism that raises the rolltop. With little effort, Mary's study area is complete.

Although Mary's furniture cost more than Paul's materials, the savings on her labor costs have more than made up the difference. After several weeks, Mary's file cabinet is full. She returns to the furniture store, buys a three-drawer cabinet of the same style, and replaces the one in her study area.

# Encapsulation, Inheritance, and Polymorphism

The conceptual constructs, or building blocks, of object-oriented programming and design include encapsulation, inheritance, and polymorphism. These tools assist programmers with reusing code, and help them create prebuilt objects for rapid application development.

## Encapsulation

**Encapsulation** is the capability of an object to have data (properties) and functionality (methods) available to the user, without the user having to understand the implementation within the object — the closed box concept presented earlier. Traditional structured programming separates data from procedures, which are sections of a program that perform a specific task. In the object-oriented world, an object contains methods as well as its associated data. Encapsulation is the process of hiding the implementation details of an object from its user, making those details transparent. In programming, an action is **transparent** if it takes place without any visible effect other than the desired output. Transparency is a good characteristic of a system because it shields the user from the system's complexity. For example, you do not need to know how the internal parts of a DVD player work in order to view a movie.

This process of making the implementation and programming details transparent to the user sometimes is called **information hiding**. Providing access to an object only through its messages, while keeping the details private, is an example of information hiding. Users know what operations can be requested of an object, but do not know the specifics of how the operations are performed. Encapsulation allows objects to be modified without requiring that the applications that use them also be modified.

In the case scenarios, both Paul and Mary want drawers that cannot be pulled all the way out accidentally. In constructing his system, Paul had to attend to the details of how drawer stops work, which ones to use, and how to build them into the system. For Mary, the safety-stop functionality and behavior is encapsulated within the file cabinet object. As an object-oriented programmer, she does need to understand how her system is constructed. This is not to say that Paul understands his system better than Mary does. From a user's point of view, however, the object-oriented nature of her system means that Mary does not need to concern herself with how the safety stops on her drawers work — only that they *do* work.

## Inheritance

**Inheritance** means that a programmer can use a class, along with its functions and data, to create a subclass, which saves time and coding. A subclass has at least one attribute or method that differs from its superclass, but it inherits functions and data of the superclass. Also known as **subclassing**, this is a very efficient way of reusing code, and provides a way for programmers to define a subclass as an extension of another class without copying the definition. If you let a subclass inherit from a superclass, it automatically will have all the data and methods of the superclass.

In the case scenario, Mary's desk, chair, and cabinet all have similar wood grain, color, and style. If you think of the furniture as a superclass, then Mary's individual pieces are subclasses of that furniture line. Because they are subclasses of the same superclass, they *inherited* the same wood grain, color, and style attributes from the superclass.

## Polymorphism

**Polymorphism** allows an instruction to be given to an object using a generalized rather than a specific, detailed command. The same command will obtain different but somewhat predictable results depending on the object that receives the command. For example, clicking the right mouse button in a windowed environment usually displays a shortcut menu. However, the menu may differ dramatically depending on whether you right-click a folder icon or right-click a toolbar. While the specific actions internal to the object are different, the command, in this case a right-click, would be generally the same.

In the case scenario, when Paul wants to open his desktop, he must perform an open desktop operation. To open his file drawers, he must perform an open drawer operation. Mary's rolltop desk, however, encapsulates the operation of opening within the desk and file cabinet objects. Mary's desk and file cabinet objects are polymorphic with respect to opening, which means Mary can give the same command, opening, to open either object and know that this will result in the same general operation, in which the object opens. As a user, the specific actions internal to the object that cause it to open are not a concern to Mary because the results are generally the same.

Many object-oriented languages, like Java, provide libraries of classes and objects that already have been programmed to work in certain ways. Object-oriented programmers thus can use these classes and objects in programs without knowing the intricacies of the programming behind them. You simply need to know what operations can be requested of a class or object and the results of those operations. Table 1–3 lists 10 object-oriented programming and design concepts in a quick reference format.

**Table 1-3  Ten Object-Oriented Programming and Design Concepts**

| | |
|---|---|
| 1 | An **object** is the basic unit of organization, a combination of a data element and a set of procedures. |
| 2 | A **method** is the code to perform a service or operation, including tasks such as performing calculations, storing values, and presenting results. |
| 3 | A **class** is an object or a set of objects that shares a common structure and a common behavior. A specific occurrence of an object class is called an **instance**. |
| 4 | A **subclass** is a lower-level category of a class with at least one unique **attribute** or method of its own. |
| 5 | A subclass **inherits** the attributes, methods, and variables from its superclass. A **superclass** is a higher-level category of class, from which the subclass inherits attributes, methods, and variables. |
| 6 | The treelike structure showing the relationship of subclasses and superclasses is called a **generalization hierarchy**. |
| 7 | A **message** requests objects to perform a method. A message is composed of the object name and the method. |
| 8 | An **event** occurs when a trigger causes an object to send a message. |
| 9 | **Encapsulation** is the process of hiding the implementation details of an object from its user by combining attributes and methods. |
| 10 | **Polymorphism** allows instructions to be given to objects in a generalized rather than a specific, detailed command. |

## Rapid Application Development (RAD)

**Rapid application development** (**RAD**) refers to the use of prebuilt objects to make program development much faster. Using prebuilt objects is faster because you use existing objects rather than creating new ones yourself. The result is shorter development cycles, easier maintenance, and the ability to reuse objects in other projects. One of the major premises on which industry implementation of OOP is built is greater reusability of code.

As shown in Table 1-4, the adoption of an object-oriented approach to programming and program design has many benefits. First, using OOP means that not all members of a development team need to be proficient in an object-oriented programming language such as Java. Second, OOP provides a practical and economical approach to programming because the task of creating objects can be separated from the task of assembling objects into applications. Some programmers, called **class providers**, can focus on creating classes and objects, while other developers, called **class users**, leverage their knowledge of business processes to assemble applications using OOP methods and tools. The end user, or simply user, is the person who interacts with a Java program.

JAVA UPDATE **Java 2 v5.0**

In 2004, Sun Microsystems came out with a new version of the Java Development Kit (JDK), originally called version 1.5.0. Now commonly called Version 5.0, the new JDK includes a number of new features that can be used to enhance performance and compatibility.

### Table 1-4    The Benefits of Object-Oriented Programming

| BENEFIT | EXPLANATION |
| --- | --- |
| Reusability | The classes are designed so they can be reused in many systems, or so modified classes can be created using inheritance. |
| Stability | The classes are designed for repeated use and become stable over time. |
| Easier design | The designer looks at each object as a black box and is not as concerned with the detail inside. |
| Faster design | The applications can be created from existing components. |

# What Is the Java SDK?

As previously noted, the Java Software Development Kit (SDK) is a programming package that enables a programmer to develop applications in Java using the included programming interfaces, programming tools, and documentation. As part of the **Java 2 Standard Edition** (**J2SE**) version 5.0, the Java SDK is available for download free from Sun Microsystems on the Web at java.sun.com. It also is included on a CD-ROM in the back of this book. Appendix B discusses how to install J2SE from the CD-ROM.

When you install the J2SE, you can install both the Java Development Kit (JDK) and the Java 2 Runtime Environment (JRE). The tools and components in the Java SDK help you develop Java programs; the tools and components in the **Java 2 Runtime Environment** (**JRE**) help you deploy Java programs. Table 1-5 on the next page outlines some of the components in the Java SDK and the JRE. Several of these components are discussed in detail on the next page.

*Table 1-5   Java 2 Standard Edition Components*

| JAVA 2 STANDARD EDITION (J2SE) COMPONENTS |
| --- |
| Java Standard Development Kit (SDK) |
| • Java Compiler |
| • Java Debugger |
| • Other Tools |
| Java 2 Runtime Environment (JRE) |
| • Java Virtual Machine (JVM) |
| • Java APIs and Class Libraries |
| • Java Applet Viewer |
| • Other Tools |

JAVA UPDATE **Java 2 v5.0**

There are many reasons to upgrade to Java 5.0. The new version is completely backward compatible, which means your old programs will work in Version 5.0 without any changes. Version 5.0 has improved performance, advanced monitoring and manageability, and runs faster than previous versions. With improved error checking capability and enhanced looping, developers in Version 5.0 will spend less time writing and testing their code.

## The Java Compiler

A **compiler** is a program that converts a programmer's code into machine-readable instructions. A compiler is like a person who translates large portions of written text; he or she has the luxury of being able to read the entire text to see how it all fits together during translation. A compiler looks at the entire source code during compilation, searching for errors and inconsistencies with what it knows from other parts of the program. The Java compiler, which is implemented with a program called javac.exe, converts the source code for the entire Java program into object code called **bytecode** (Figure 1-21). The Java compiler is part of the Java SDK.

## The Java Virtual Machine

Once the source code is compiled into bytecode, the same bytecode can be run on any computer as long as the computer has an interpreter to execute the Java bytecode. An **interpreter** is a program that executes the machine language instructions to produce results, or answers. An interpreter is like a person who translates orally and dynamically, one sentence at a time, knowing what has been said previously but knowing nothing about future statements.

The language interpreter for Java is included as part of the **Java Virtual Machine** (**JVM**). Execution of Java programs is initiated with the java.exe command; the JVM then interprets or attempts to run commands from the bytecode, one command at a time. For example, once a program is compiled to bytecode, the JVM on any platform — whether Windows, UNIX, or a cell phone — interprets the bytecode (Figure 1-21). The Java Virtual Machine is part of the JRE.

## The Java API

The JRE also includes a set of Java application program interfaces, or APIs. An **application program interface** (**API**) is a standard set of interfaces and classes functionally grouped into packages; these APIs are present in any Java implementation. The APIs contain hundreds of pre-written classes that fall into one of more than 50 predefined class packages. **Class packages**, also called **class libraries**, are accessible by every Java program. By using methods and variables

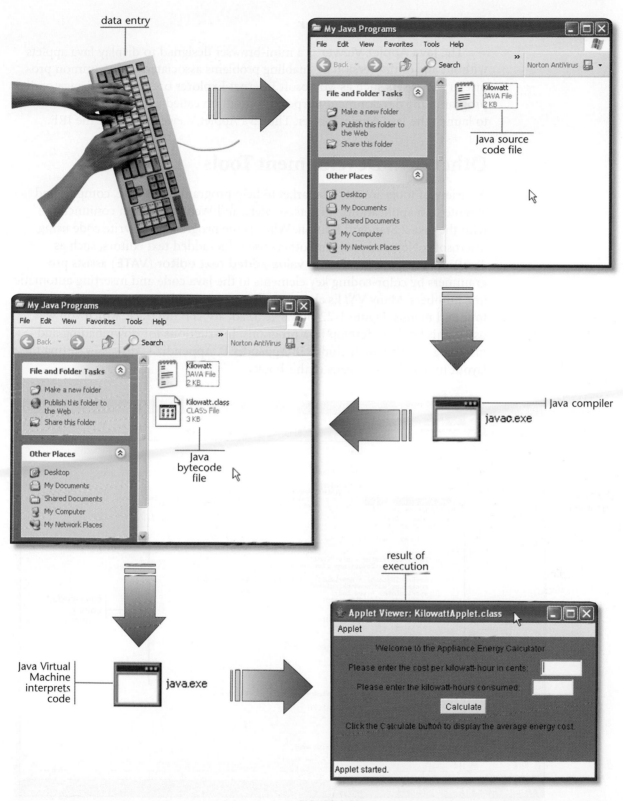

data entry

Java source code file

Java compiler
javac.exe

Java bytecode file

result of execution

Java Virtual Machine interprets code
java.exe

FIGURE 1-21

from these class packages, programmers can reduce the amount of new code they need to develop and test. Documentation for these APIs is available on the Sun Microsystems Web site.

### The Java Applet Viewer

The **Java Applet Viewer** is a mini-browser designed to display Java applets without any of the version or enabling problems associated with common proprietary browsers such as Microsoft Internet Explorer or Netscape Navigator. For programming development purposes, a program called appletviewer.exe is used to launch the Java Applet Viewer. The Java Applet Viewer is part of the JRE.

## Other Java Development Tools

A variety of tools are on the market to help programmers write, compile, and execute Java applications, applets, servlets, and Web services, in conjunction with the Java 2 Standard Edition. While some programmers write code using Microsoft's Notepad program, others use value-added text editors, such as TextPad, JGrasp, or JCreator. A **value-added text editor** (**VATE**) assists programmers by color-coding key elements in the Java code and inserting automatic line numbers. Many VATEs also compile and execute Java programs using buttons and menus. Figure 1-22 shows TextPad, a VATE interface, which you will use in this book to develop Java programs. Instructions for downloading and installing TextPad are included in Appendix B. Appendix C discusses setting the layout to match the screens in this book.

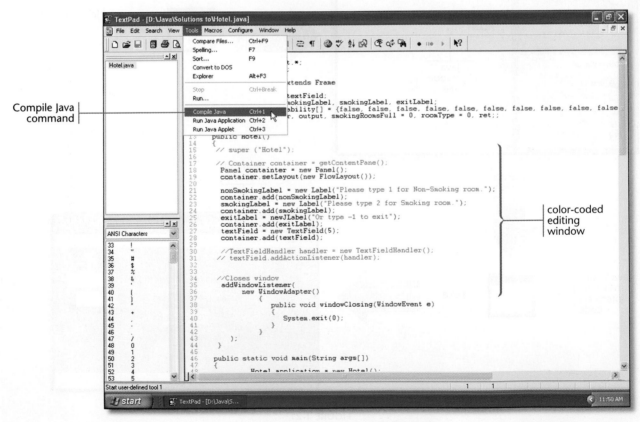

Compile Java command

color-coded editing window

**FIGURE 1-22**

Another tool developed to assist Java programmers is an **integrated development environment** (**IDE**). An IDE, sometimes also called a **builder tool**, assists programmers by displaying toolbars, menus, windows, and dialog boxes that are designed to facilitate coding and debugging (Figure 1-23). Sun Microsystems' ONE Studio software, for example, is an IDE for Java technology developers. Other IDE examples include JBuilder, Visual Age for Java, and Simplicity. While an IDE does assist programmers with the essential steps in developing programs, IDEs are not well suited for beginning programmers, who must learn to use the IDE while learning Java programming.

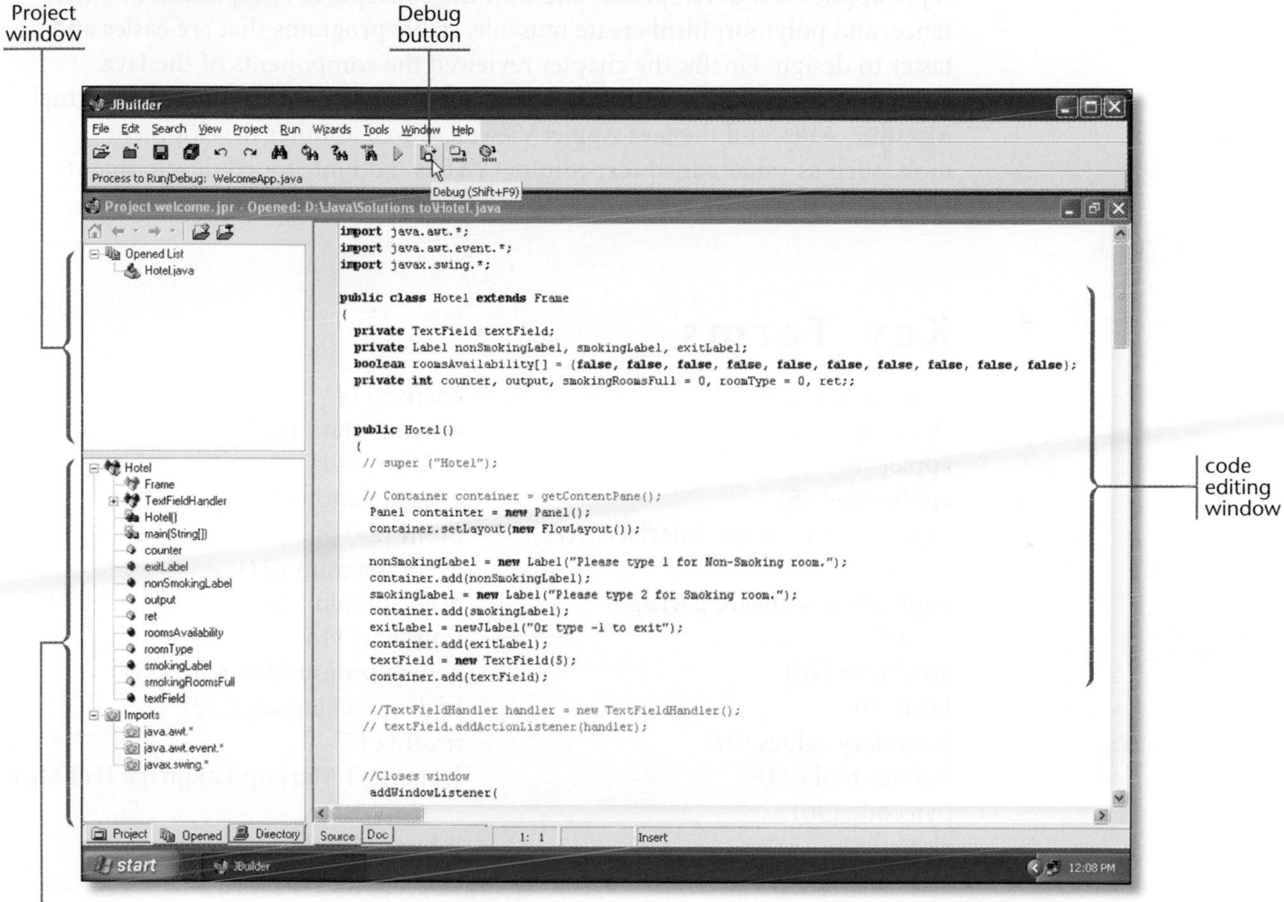

**FIGURE 1-23**

Once you have developed Java programs, such as servlets, you can deploy them using a Web server, such as Tomcat Web server. Tomcat Web server is a free, open-source implementation for Java servlets and Java Server Pages, which will work on a stand-alone computer system. To run Java programs developed in this book, you can install the Tomcat Web server from the CD-ROM in the back of this book or download and install it from the Web. For more information on downloading the Tomcat Web server, see Appendix B. Your instructor or employer also may direct you to use a different server at your school or business.

# Chapter Summary

This chapter provided an overview of computer programming, the Java programming language and its characteristics, and the steps of the program development cycle. The Java platform allows you to build many types of programs, including console applications, windowed applications, applets, servlets, Web services, and beans. The chapter also introduced you to object-oriented programming and design concepts and the use of objects, methods, attributes, and events. You learned how object-oriented programming and design facilitates rapid application development and how the concepts of encapsulation, inheritance, and polymorphism create reusable, stable programs that are easier and faster to design. Finally, the chapter reviewed the components of the Java Software Development Kit (SDK), including the Java compiler, the Java Virtual Machine, APIs, and the Java Applet Viewer, as well as other development tools, such as value-added text editors (VATEs) and integrated development environments (IDEs).

# Key Terms

aggregation *(23)*
algorithm *(14)*
applet *(6)*
application *(5)*
application program interface (API) *(30)*
application software packages *(10)*
attributes *(16)*
bean *(9)*
boundary values *(21)*
builder tool *(33)*
bytecode *(30)*
class *(16)*
class diagram *(16)*
class libraries *(30)*
class packages *(30)*
class providers *(29)*
class users *(29)*
client-side *(6)*
code *(2)*
coding *(2)*
comments *(20)*
compiler *(30)*
computer programming *(2)*
console application *(5)*
control structure *(18)*

correct *(14)*
documentation *(22)*
efficient *(14)*
encapsulation *(27)*
event *(24)*
event diagram *(24)*
event-driven *(25)*
flowchart *(16)*
generalization hierarchy *(23)*
high-level languages *(2)*
hosting *(7)*
Hypertext Markup Language (HTML) *(6)*
information hiding *(27)*
inheritance *(27)*
instance *(24)*
integrated development environment (IDE) *(33)*
integration testing *(21)*
interpreter *(30)*
Java *(2)*
Java Applet Viewer *(32)*
Java 2 Runtime Environment (JRE) *(29)*
Java 2 Standard Edition (J2SE) *(29)*

Java Database Connectivity (JDBC) *(7)*

Java Server Pages (JSP) *(7)*

Java Software Development Kit (SDK) *(3)*

Java Virtual Machine (JVM) *(30)*

Java Web Start *(6)*

JavaBean *(9)*

JavaScript *(6)*

message *(24)*

methodology *(11)*

methods *(16)*

object *(3)*

object-oriented design (OOD) *(3)*

object-oriented programming (OOP) *(3)*

operation *(24)*

parsimonious *(3)*

platform *(3)*

platform-independent *(3)*

polymorphism *(28)*

portable *(3)*

program *(2)*

program development cycle *(11)*

programmers *(2)*

programming language *(2)*

pseudocode *(18)*

rapid application development (RAD) *(29)*

requirements document *(12)*

reusability *(9)*

robust *(3)*

secure *(3)*

server software *(7)*

server-side *(7)*

servlet *(7)*

software developers *(2)*

storyboard *(15)*

strongly typed language *(3)*

subclass *(23)*

subclassing *(27)*

superclass *(23)*

syntax *(2)*

test cases *(21)*

test plan *(21)*

testing *(21)*

transparent *(27)*

trigger *(24)*

Unified Modeling Language (UML) *(25)*

unit testing *(20)*

usability *(19)*

validate *(19)*

value-added text editor (VATE) *(32)*

Web server *(7)*

Web service *(8)*

windowed application *(5)*

# Homework Assignments

## Short Answer

1. A(n) _____ is a set of words, symbols, and codes that enables a programmer to communicate instructions to a computer.

2. The particular set of grammar or rules that specify how the instructions are to be written is called the _____ of the language.

3. List some of the characteristics of Java.

4. Define the differences between a Java application, an applet, and a servlet.

5. _____ is a scripting tool created by Netscape in cooperation with Sun Microsystems to insert code statements directly into the HTML of a Web page, in order to add functionality and improve the appearance of the Web page.

*(continued)*

**Short Answer** (continued)

6. A(n) _____ is a program that receives a request for information from another program over the Web and returns data to the requesting program.

7. Many programmers refer to the entire Java platform as the JDK, which is an acronym for _____.

8. A(n) _____ is a program that converts a programmer's code into machine-readable instructions, whereas a(n) _____ is a program that will execute the bytecode to produce results.

9. The _____ is a standard set of interfaces and classes functionally grouped into packages that are present in any Java implementation.

10. Both _____ and _____ assist programmers by color coding key elements in Java code, as well as inserting line numbers.

11. List the six phases of the program development life cycle in order and briefly describe the purpose of each.

12. List the essential inputs and outputs for a program that calculates and displays sales tax based on a user-supplied dollar amount.

13. List three sets of test data for a program that determines the quotient A/B, where A must be an integer between −1 and 10, and B must be non-zero.

14. Which variable(s) would you test in Figure 1-15 on page 19 to ensure that the entered ounces are a positive integer? Describe the valid range of the variables you select.

15. An employee's weekly gross pay is determined by multiplying the hours worked by the rate of pay. Overtime (hours worked more than 40) is paid at 1.5 times the hourly rate. Answer the following questions:
    a. List the essential inputs and outputs. List sample data that includes boundary values.
    b. Draw a storyboard to label and accept the inputs, and calculate and display the outputs. Identify and label the input and output text boxes, and any buttons on the storyboard.
    c. Draw a class diagram for the Gross Pay object.
    d. Draw a flowchart to calculate the gross pay.
    e. Write the pseudocode that corresponds to the flowchart in Step d above.
    f. Draw an event diagram for the Gross Pay event.

16. Draw a generalization hierarchy chart for a book object. Include a superclass and at least two subclasses. Below the chart, list and label attributes, methods, a trigger, and an instance of a book.

17. Draw a class diagram for a Print button in an application toolbar.

18. Draw an event diagram for an elevator request. Include the user pushing the button as a trigger, the light coming on, and the elevator sensing the request. Follow the event through the elevator arriving at the floor and the doors opening.

19. Write the pseudocode and then draw a flowchart for a program that accepts the age of the user and then tests that value to display one of the following three categories: youth (<18 years), adult (18 to 65 years), or senior (>65 years).

## Learn It Online

Start your browser and visit scsite.com/java3e/learn. Follow the instructions in the exercises below.

1. **Chapter Reinforcement TF, MC, and SA**   Click the Chapter Reinforcement link below Chapter 1. Print and then answer the True/False, Multiple Choice, and Short Answer questions.

2. **Practice Test**   Click the Practice Test link below Chapter 1. Answer each question, enter your first and last name at the bottom of the page, and then click the Grade Test button. When the graded practice test displays on your screen, click Print on the File menu to print a hard copy. Continue to take practice tests until you score 80% or better. Hand in a printout of the final practice test.

3. **Crossword Puzzle Challenge**   Click the Crossword Puzzle Challenge link below Chapter 1. Read the instructions, and then enter your first and last name. Click the Play button. Complete the crossword puzzle. When you are finished, click the Submit button. When the crossword puzzle redisplays, click the Print button.

4. **Tips and Tricks**   Click the Tips and Tricks link below Chapter 1. Right-click the information and then click Print on the shortcut menu. Construct a brief example of what the information relates to in Java to confirm that you understand how to use the tip or trick. Hand in the example and printed information.

5. **Newsgroups**   Click the Newsgroups link below Chapter 1. Click a topic that pertains to Chapter 1. Print three comments.

6. **Expanding Your Horizons**   Click the Expanding Your Horizons link below Chapter 1. Click a topic that pertains to Chapter 1. Print the information. Construct a brief example of what the information relates to in Java to confirm that you understand the contents of the article. Hand in the example and printed information.

7. **Search Sleuth**   Select three key terms from the Key Terms section of this chapter and then use the Google search engine at google.com (or any major search engine) to display and print two Web pages for each key term.

# Programming Assignments

## 1 Using Object Terminology

You are a teller at a bank. A customer has come in asking to open a savings account — just one of the many kinds of accounts that you handle. After determining that the customer wants a passbook savings rather than a certificate of deposit, you remind the customer that all accounts are FDIC insured. You assign a unique account number and accept the customer's initial deposit. You explain that while all accounts earn some form of interest, this specific savings account is compounded quarterly. The interest will appear automatically on the monthly statement. The customer now can deposit and withdraw from the account.

*(continued)*

### 1 Using Object Terminology *(continued)*

If savings account is the object, give an example of each of the following as it relates to that savings account.

1. superclass  _____
2. subclass  _____
3. attribute  _____
4. method  _____
5. instance  _____
6. trigger  _____
7. event  _____
8. inheritance  _____
9. encapsulation  _____
10. polymorphism  _____

### 2 Writing Pseudocode

Write pseudocode to describe the logic illustrated by the flow-chart shown in Figure 1-24. For additional information about pseudocode, see Appendix A.

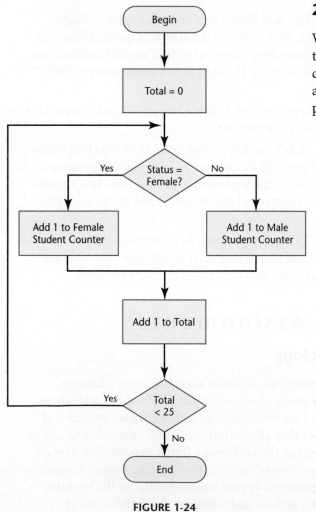

FIGURE 1-24

## 3 Analyzing Requirements

Review the requirements document in Figure 1-25 and then answer the questions on the next page.

### REQUEST FOR NEW APPLICATION

| | |
|---|---|
| **Date submitted:** | September 26, 2007 |
| **Submitted by:** | Ray Lykins |
| **Purpose:** | Cattle ranchers rely on feed grains to feed their cattle, along with hay and grazing land. The ranchers use more feed during the winter and less during spring, summer, and fall, unless there is a drought. A field agent helps ranchers calculate the amount of feed they will need. The distribution manager takes the order over the phone and calculates the cost and the shipping. |
| **Application title:** | Cattle Feed Calculator (CFC) |
| **Algorithms:** | <u>Dietary needs</u>: Each cow consumes 3% of body weight per day in feed (for example, 1,200 lb. cow x 0.03 = 36 lbs. of feed per day). <br> <u>Truck capacity</u>: 2.5 Tons <br> <u>Current market price for dry ration matter</u>: $150 per ton. |
| **Notes:** | 1) The application should allow users to enter values for the number of cows, the number of days — a calculation based on the commonly used Animal Unit Month (AUM) — and the current market price. <br><br> 2) The application should also allow the user to reset all values on the screen to zero (0) so that another calculation can be performed. <br><br> 3) In the near future, we would like to allow the field agents to access the calculator remotely via the Web. <br><br> 4) The application should include the company logo in the interface. The application window should be sizable so that the user can get a better view of the data. <br><br> 5) A common dry ration uses a mixture of the following: <ul><li>grains</li><li>grain by-products</li><li>protein-rich meals</li><li>hays</li><li>straws/stubble</li></ul> 6) The user should be able to exit the application at any time. |

**Approvals**

| | | |
|---|---|---|
| **Approval status:** | X | Approved |
| | | Rejected |
| **Approved by:** | Isaac King | |
| **Date:** | October 18, 2007 | |
| **Assigned to:** | J. Starks, Programmer | |

**FIGURE 1-25**

(continued)

### 3 Analyzing Requirements *(continued)*

1. List at least three relevant requirements necessary to design a complete program that are missing from the requirements document. Use these new requirements when completing the remaining tasks.

2. List the inputs and outputs necessary to solve the problem.

3. Draw a storyboard for a program that would meet the program requirements.

4. Design three sets of test data and step the test data through the algorithm listed in the requirements in order to test the expected output of the problem.

## 4 Understanding Flowcharts

Figure 1-26 shows a flowchart that represents part of a cardiovascular disease risk assessment. The higher the point total, the greater the risk of cardiovascular disease. In the spaces provided, write the point total for the following persons using the logic in the flowchart. For additional information about flowcharting, see Appendix A.

1. A 40-year-old smoker with normal blood pressure who eats a low-fat diet.

   _____

2. A 20-year-old nonsmoker with normal blood pressure who eats a high-fat diet.

   _____

3. A 27-year-old smoker with high blood pressure who eats a high-fat diet.

   _____

4. A 16-year-old nonsmoker with normal blood pressure who eats a high-fat diet.

   _____

5. A 63-year-old nonsmoker with high blood pressure who eats a low-fat diet.

   _____

6. A 50-year-old nonsmoker with high blood pressure who eats a high-fat diet.

   _____

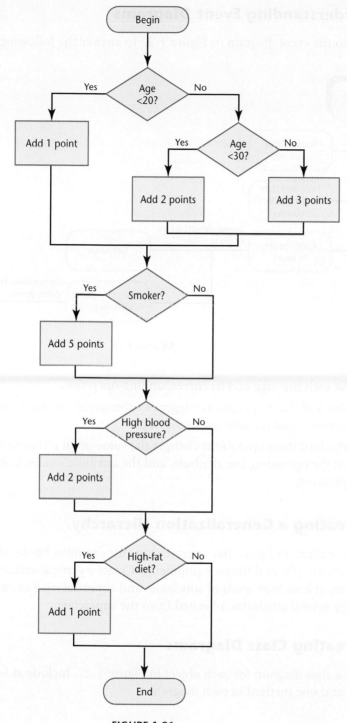

**FIGURE 1-26**

### 5 Understanding Event Diagrams

Refer to the event diagram in Figure 1-27 to answer the following questions:

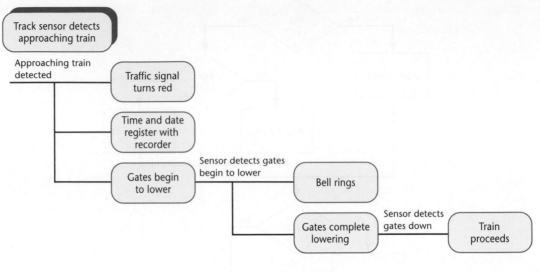

**FIGURE 1-27**

1. List each message and its corresponding operation.
2. Which of these operations triggers a subsequent message? List any such operation and its subsequent message.
3. Which of these operations changes the value of an attribute of an object? List the operation, the attribute, and the attribute's value before and after the operation.

## 6 Creating a Generalization Hierarchy

Pick any class of objects that interests you (for example, books, clothes, musical instruments, physical fitness equipment). Create a generalization hierarchy showing at least four levels of subclasses and superclasses. For each subclass, identify several attributes inherited from the superclass.

## 7 Creating Class Diagrams

Draw a class diagram for each object in Figure 1-27. Include at least two attributes and one method in each diagram.

## 8 Creating an Event Diagram

Using Figure 1-27 as an example, draw an event diagram to raise the gates when the track sensor has detected the train is clear of the intersection. The trigger is the lack of weight on the tracks. The events that happen include the sensor detecting that loss of weight and the gates rising. Possible operations include traffic signal changing, time and date recording, and gate movement.

## 9 Thinking Algorithmically

Take one of the following tasks and write a set of instructions that is sufficiently complete so that another person could perform the task without asking questions. Test your solution by giving it to another class member and having him or her perform the steps. If a step in your task is dependent on a condition, use the words if, then, and else to describe the criteria to be met for that condition and the results. If steps in the task repeat, use the phrases do while, do until, or do a certain number of times to describe the repetition. For more information about conditions and repetitions, see Appendix A.

1. light a candle
2. make a cup of tea
3. send an e-mail
4. walk from the classroom to the bookstore
5. log on to your school's network or intranet

## 10 Identifying Triggers and Events

Figure 1-28 displays a user interface to calculate prices at a movie theater. Notice there is no button labeled Calculate. Using your knowledge of graphical user interfaces, list each object in the window, identify the trigger(s) to select the objects, and then describe the output related to the event and its operations. *Hint*: only one event trigger should cause the price to display.

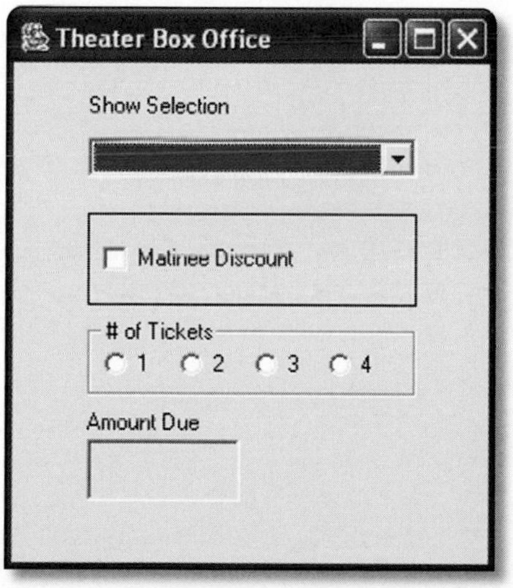

**FIGURE 1-28**

## 11 Understanding Java Components

Create a generalization hierarchy or class diagram of the various JDK components in Java 2 Standard Edition (J2SE), version 5.0. Use information from this chapter and information from the Sun Microsystems Java Web site at java.sun.com. Include such components as the JRE, JVM, and API, among others.

PROGRAMMING ASSIGNMENTS

## 12 Exploring Other Java Technologies

Visit the Sun Microsystems Java Web site at java.sun.com. Choose any one of the listed Java technologies and explore the linked Web pages. Write several paragraphs about your chosen technology. Include a general description of the technology and information on current versions, new enhancements, and compatibility. Describe how the technology interacts with J2SE 5.0.

## 13 Blog about Java Technology

Visit the Sun Microsystems blog site at java.sun.com/developer/blogs/index.html or an other Java technology blog. Search the site for information related to J2SE 5.0. Print out several references and hand them in to your instructor.

# 2

# Creating a Java Application and Applet

## Objectives

You will have
mastered the material in
this chapter when you can:

- Write a simple Java application
- Use TextPad
- Understand the different types and uses of comments
- Use proper naming conventions for classes and files
- Identify the parts of a class header and method header
- Code output
- Use the println() method
- Compile a Java program
- Understand the common types of errors
- Run a Java program
- Edit Java source code to insert escape characters and a system date
- Print source code
- Differentiate between an application and an applet
- Create an applet from Java source code
- Write code to display a graphic, text, color, and the date in an applet
- Create an HTML host document
- Run a Java applet

# Introduction

The way in which a user enters data and instructions into a computer and receives feedback from the computer is called a **user interface**. As discussed in Chapter 1, the Java platform allows you to create programs and program components that have many different user interfaces. In a Java console application, for example, the user interface is a command-line interface that displays character input and output on a black screen. A windowed application, by contrast, has a graphical user interface that is displayed in a window. Another type of Java program, an applet, can use a graphical user interface to display output to a user in a browser window.

In this chapter, you will learn how to use TextPad to write, compile, and execute a stand-alone Java program that runs as a console application. Even though communicating with a computer using a command-line interface may seem tedious when compared with today's highly interactive GUI applications, using commands to interact with a computer is a common, easy place to start. Many networking and server applications, for example, use console applications written in Java; console applications also are useful for testing and system configuration. Next you will learn how to create an applet using TextPad. The applets will run and display in the Applet Viewer window, which is the mini-browser supplied with the Java SDK.

In this chapter, you will learn the basic parts of a Java program as well as the use of proper Java syntax, which is the set of grammar or rules that specifies the spelling of its commands and any required symbols. You will learn to analyze a problem and design a solution. You then will learn how to create a console application, compile and test the application, and run the program. Finally you will learn how to create an applet and its HTML hosting file. The applet will display text and a graphic in Java's Applet Viewer window.

## Chapter Two — The Welcome to My Day Program

The console application developed in this chapter is the Welcome to My Day program, which displays a welcome message, the user's name, and the system date on a splash screen (Figure 2-1a). A **splash screen** is a screen that is displayed before the main program is displayed. The compiled Java source code will cause text output to display on the screen for the user to read. Creating this console application serves as a first step in creating an electronic calendar application for either a desktop or a handheld computer system.

The same electronic calendar application also will need to be accessible to users via the Web. To create a splash screen for the Web-based version of the calendar application, the console application must be converted to an applet that displays text output and a graphic in the Applet Viewer window (Figure 2-1b). As shown in Figures 2-1a and 2-1b, the console application displays white letters on a black screen, while the applet displays black letters on a light blue (cyan) background, beside the graphic. Both the console application and the applet will become part of the electronic calendar application when it is fully implemented.

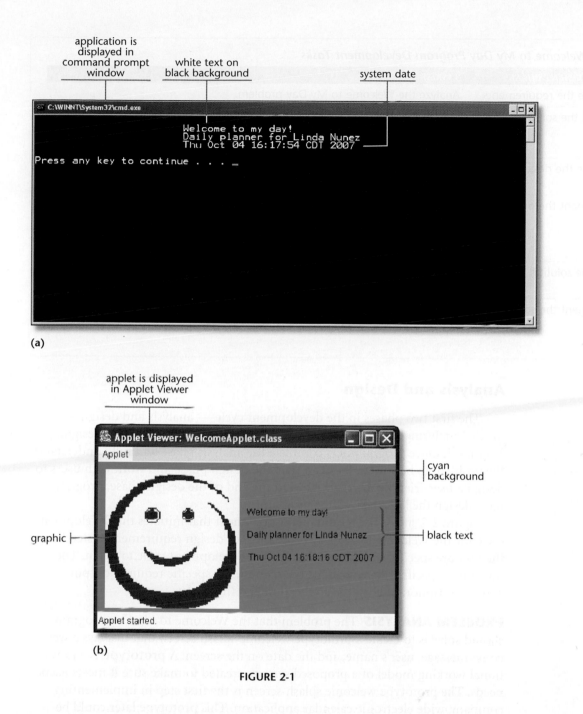

**FIGURE 2-1**

# Program Development

As you learned in Chapter 1, the tasks involved in developing an application follow the series of six iterative phases outlined in the development cycle. The six phases and corresponding tasks of the development cycle for the Welcome to My Day program are shown in Table 2-1 on the next page.

*Table 2-1  Welcome to My Day Program Development Tasks*

| | DEVELOPMENT PHASE | TASK(S) |
|---|---|---|
| 1 | Analyze the requirements | Analyze the Welcome to My Day problem. |
| 2 | Design the solution | Design the user interface for both the application and the applet including output data and placement of the applet graphic. Design the logic to solve the problem. |
| 3 | Validate the design | Confirm with the user that the design solves the problem in a satisfactory manner. |
| 4 | Implement the design | Translate the design into code for both the application and the applet. Include internal documentation (comments and remarks) within the code that explains the purpose of the code statements. Create the HTML file to host the applet. |
| 5 | Test the solution | Test the program. Find and correct any errors (debugging) until it is error-free. |
| 6 | Document the solution | Print copies of the application code, applet code, applet interface, and HTML code. |

## Analysis and Design

The first two phases in the development cycle — analysis and design — involve analyzing the problem to be solved by the program and then designing a solution. Once programmers complete the analysis phase and fully understand the problem to be solved, they can start the design phase and work with users to design a user-friendly interface. Toward the end of the design phase, programmers design the logic behind the program.

Figure 2-2 shows the requirements document that initiates the development cycle for the Welcome to My Day program. The design requirements listed by the user are specific enough to allow for the development cycle to begin. The document specifies the reason for the request, the specific required output, and a description of both the application and the applet.

**PROBLEM ANALYSIS** The problem that the Welcome to My Day program should solve is to create a prototype welcome splash screen that displays a welcome message, user's name, and the date on the screen. A **prototype** is a functional working model of a proposed system, created to make sure it meets users' needs. The prototype welcome splash screen is the first step in implementing a company-wide electronic calendar application. This prototype later could be modified to interface with the database of the electronic calendar application.

The requirements document has outlined the need for a prototype splash screen. Splash screens generally serve two purposes: (1) to let the user know that the program has started, and (2) to provide information that the user may read while waiting for the entire application to load. As outlined in the requirements document, both the application and the applet versions of the splash screen should display output to the user in the form of text. The text displayed includes a welcome message, the user's name, and the **system date**, which is the current date and time generated by the operating system of a computer. Additionally, the requirements document requests that the applet version of the program includes color and a graphic.

**REQUEST FOR NEW APPLICATION**

| Date submitted: | August 28, 2007 |
|---|---|
| Submitted by: | Linda Nunez |
| Purpose: | Our firm has begun the process of implementing an electronic calendar application for each employee. The calendar application needs to run as a stand-alone application on desktop and handheld computers and also be accessible via the Web. The company wants to create a prototype welcome splash screen that displays a welcome message, the user's name, and the system date. This prototype later will be modified to interface with the database of an electronic calendar application purchased from a major software company. |
| Application title: | Welcome to My Day |
| Algorithms: | Text and graphics will display on the screen when the program executes. |
| Notes: | 1) As some of our employees have handheld computing devices with small monochrome screens, the stand-alone console application should display text only. |
| | 2) If employees choose to view their calendar over the Web, the welcome splash screen should display in an applet. |
| | 3) The application and applet should use the system date, so that it is always current. The system date does not have to be formatted in any special way. Our employees are used to reading the system date on printouts and electronic transfer reports. |
| | 4) The applet should use color and display a graphic. A sample graphic file is included on the accompanying Data Disk. |
| | 5) Employees should be able to close the welcome splash screen at anytime by clicking a standard Close button. |

**Approvals**

| Approval status: | X | Approved |
|---|---|---|
| | | Rejected |
| Approved by: | David Reneau | |
| Date: | September 24, 2007 | |
| Assigned to: | J. Starks, Programmer | |

**FIGURE 2-2**

**DESIGN THE SOLUTION** Once you have analyzed the problem and understand the needs, the next step is to design the user interface. Figure 2-3a shows an example of a hand-drawn storyboard for the user interface of the Welcome to My Day application; Figure 2-3b on the next page shows a storyboard for the user interface of the Welcome to My Day applet. The displayed output data, as specified in the requirements document, includes a welcome message, the user's name, and the system date.

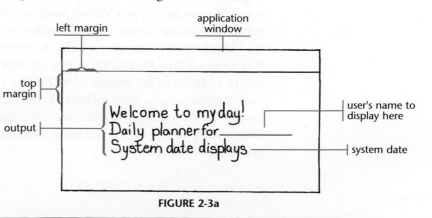

FIGURE 2-3a

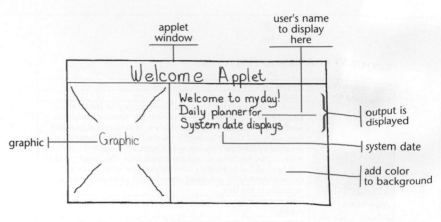

**FIGURE 2-3b**

When designing a console application, programmers typically use text to display the output. Console applications are used when the program must display information such as prompts, simple menus, and input and output data. In the Welcome to My Day application, the program requires no input from the user, so no prompts for data input display. The program displays three lines of output data as left-justified text. As shown in the storyboard in Figure 2-3a on the previous page, the output text is displayed with a top and left margin to provide space between the window's edge and the output text. Design experts agree that adding top and left margins makes the display look less crowded and creates a more visually appealing display of output.

While the system date display may seem cryptic to those unfamiliar with that sort of notation, the requirements document states that the employees are accustomed to seeing the date display in that manner. When designing an application, it is important to adhere to company standards and practices so as to make users comfortable with the user interface.

The output for the applet will include the same text that the application displays, as well as color and a graphic (Figure 2-3b). The smiley face graphic used in this prototype applet is a placeholder graphic submitted with the requirements document and included on the Data Disk that accompanies this book. When the electronic calendar application is implemented, the graphic would be replaced with a company logo.

The requirements document states that the user will click the Close button to exit the program. Both Java console applications and applets automatically display a standard Close button, which is a **default** or preset feature of the command prompt and Applet Viewer windows. When a user clicks the Close button, the active window closes. The close action is encapsulated into the Click event of the Close button — in other words, the operating system automatically tells the Java program how to close the active window when a user clicks the Close button. In addition to the default Close button, the command prompt and Applet Viewer windows also both include Minimize and Maximize buttons. When developing a program, programmers can assume that those button objects and their corresponding events will work as intended. No further design issues apply to exiting the program.

### Exiting a Console Application Using a VATE

Some value-added text editors (VATEs), including TextPad, automatically display a "Press any key to continue" message after displaying all the output in a console application. In most cases, pressing any key exits the program in a manner similar to clicking the Close button.

**PROGRAM DESIGN**   Once you have designed the interface, the next step is to design the logic to solve the problem and create the desired results. The only programming task is to display three lines of output, one after another, on the screen; therefore, the structure of the program will be sequential in nature. The program code will send a print message to an object — in this case, the default display device of your system (Figure 2-1a on page 47). The program code then will be modified so that the program can run on the Web as an applet. The program code for the applet will display the three lines of output in a window of their own, along with a graphic (Figure 2-1b on page 47). Both the application and the applet versions of the program should contain appropriate documentation and be saved for future use.

Figure 2-4a shows a flowchart that outlines the sequence of steps in the program. Figure 2-4b shows an event diagram that illustrates how the execution of the program triggers the Display event.

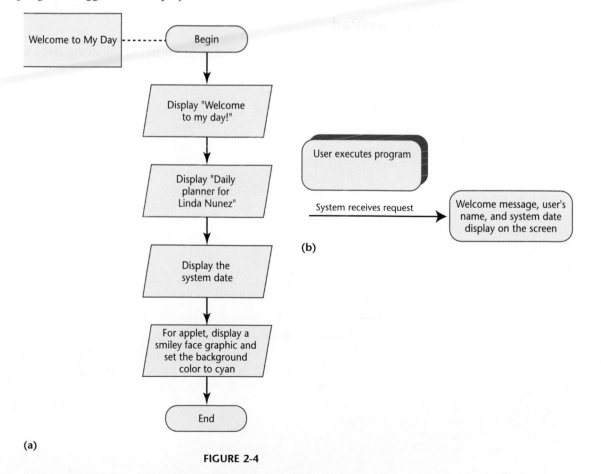

(a)

(b)

FIGURE 2-4

Having analyzed the problem, designed the interface, and designed the program logic, the analysis and design of the application is complete. As shown in Table 2-1 on page 48, the next task in the development cycle is to implement the design using the Java SDK. To complete the steps in this text, you must have downloaded the Java 2 Standard Edition (J2SE) version 5.0 from the Sun Microsystems Web site or installed it from the CD in the back of this book. You also must have downloaded and installed TextPad. This book uses TextPad to edit code, but you can use any text editor available on your system, as indicated by your instructor. For more information on installing the Java SDK and TextPad, see Appendix B.

## Using TextPad

This book uses TextPad to enter Java source code—the English-like statements that represent the step-by-step instructions a computer must execute. **TextPad** is a powerful, value-added text editor (VATE) used to create many different kinds of text-based files, one of which is a Java source code file. Any text-editing program capable of creating a text file can be used to write Java programs; however, TextPad displays line numbers and color coding to assist programmers in writing and testing their programs. Additionally, TextPad contains many programmer-friendly tools, including commands to compile and execute both applications and applets.

### Starting TextPad

With TextPad installed on your computer, perform the following steps to start TextPad.

## To Start TextPad

*1.* With the Windows desktop displayed, click the Start button on the taskbar and then point to All Programs on the Start menu. Point to TextPad on the All Programs submenu.

*The All Programs submenu is displayed (Figure 2-5). Your system may have a different set of menus.*

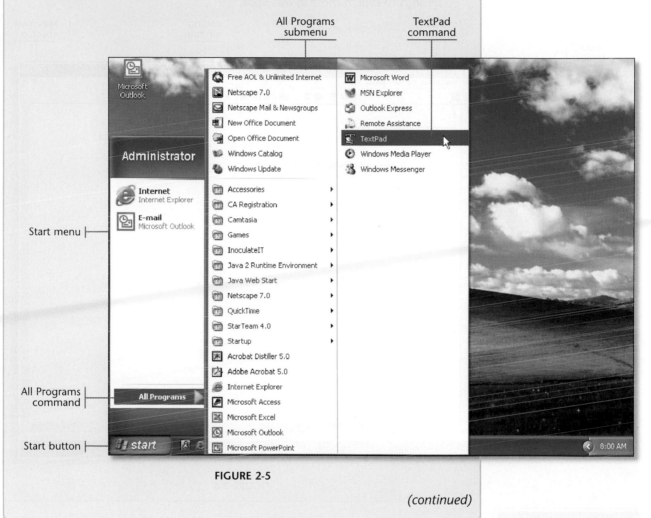

FIGURE 2-5

*(continued)*

> *2.* Click TextPad. When the TextPad window opens, if necessary, click the Maximize button to maximize the screen. If a Tip of the Day dialog box is displayed, click its Close button.
>
> *TextPad starts and displays a blank coding window (Figure 2-6). A Help message box may display briefly. The insertion point and mouse pointer display in the TextPad coding window. Your system may display a shadow or highlight on the line with the mouse pointer. See Appendix C to change your settings to match those in this book.*

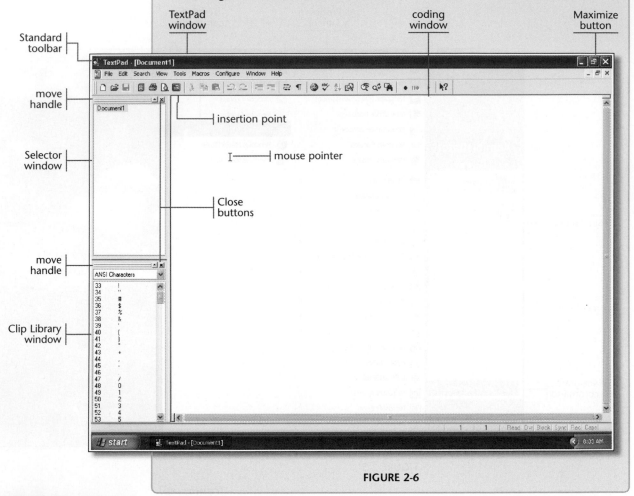

FIGURE 2-6

OTHER WAYS

1. Click TextPad on Start menu
2. Double-click TextPad icon on desktop

## The TextPad Window

The TextPad window consists of several window areas and a Standard toolbar to help you create programs. Depending on the task you are performing or the options you choose, other windows and toolbars will display or replace components shown in Figure 2-6.

The TextPad **coding window** is the area where you can enter and edit lines of Java code (Figure 2-6). Also referred to as a list or listing, the code will be entered and edited later in the chapter.

The window in the upper-left corner of the screen shown in Figure 2-6 is the **Selector window**, which displays a list of open TextPad files. Notice that the default file name, Document1, is displayed. The window below the Selector window is the Clip Library window. The **Clip Library window** displays a list of special codes and tags used by some scripting tools and languages such as HTML. You can double-click any code or tag in the list to insert it into the code in the coding window.

Java programmers customize the display of the TextPad window in a variety of ways. For example, a programmer can move both the Selector window and the Clip Library window to any part of the TextPad window by dragging the respective window's move handle, or resize each window by dragging its border. A programmer also can close the windows by clicking their respective Close buttons, in order to maximize the space in the coding window.

## Displaying Line Numbers in the TextPad Window

Another way you can customize the TextPad window is to display line numbers in the coding window. TextPad allows you to display **line numbers** that begin with one and progress sequentially down the left side of the coding window. Using line numbers not only allows you to keep track of which line you are on while you enter code but also provides a reference for possible errors when you compile Java source code.

Perform the following steps to display line numbers in the TextPad window.

### To Display Line Numbers in the TextPad Window

*1.* With the TextPad window still open, click View on the menu bar.
   *The View menu is displayed (Figure 2-7).*

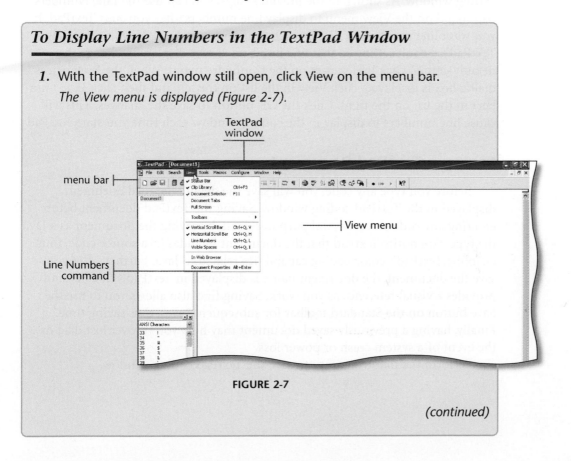

FIGURE 2-7

*(continued)*

2. Click Line Numbers on the View menu.

*Line number 1 is displayed in the coding window (Figure 2-8).*

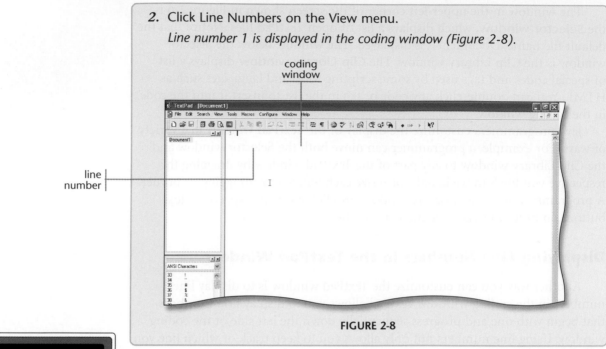

FIGURE 2-8

### OTHER WAYS

1. Press CTRL+Q, press L
2. Press ALT+V, press L

By default, TextPad does not display line numbers automatically in the coding window. As shown in the previous steps, you can use the Line Numbers command on the View menu to display line numbers after you start TextPad. If you want line numbers to display each time you start TextPad, you can change TextPad's default setting so that line numbers always display. To change the default setting, click Preferences on the Configure menu. When the Preferences dialog box is displayed, click View in the list on the left and then click Line numbers in the list on the right. Click the OK button to save the changes. This will cause line numbers to display in the coding window each time you start TextPad.

## Saving a TextPad Document

Before you type any code, you will save the default TextPad document displayed in the TextPad coding window. Saving the TextPad document before entering any code serves several purposes. First, by saving the document as a Java file type, you notify TextPad that the document includes Java source code, thus enabling TextPad's color-coding capabilities related to Java. Further, after you save the document, the document name is displayed in TextPad's title bar and provides a visual reference as you work. Saving first also allows you to use the Save button on the Standard toolbar for subsequent saves, thus saving time. Finally, having a previously saved document may help you recover lost data in the event of a system crash or power loss.

Perform the following steps to save the TextPad coding window.

## *To Save a TextPad Document*

1. Insert the Data Disk in drive A. See the preface of this book for instructions for downloading the Data Disk or see your instructor for information about accessing the files required in this book.

2. With the TextPad window still open, click File on the menu bar.

   *The File menu is displayed (Figure 2-9).*

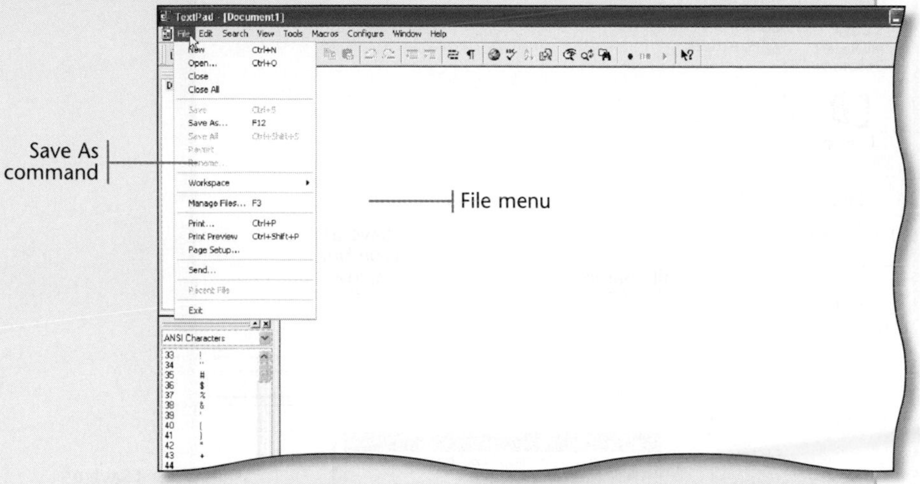

Save As command

File menu

**FIGURE 2-9**

3. Click Save As on the File menu.

   *The Save As dialog box is displayed (Figure 2-10). Your screen may differ.*

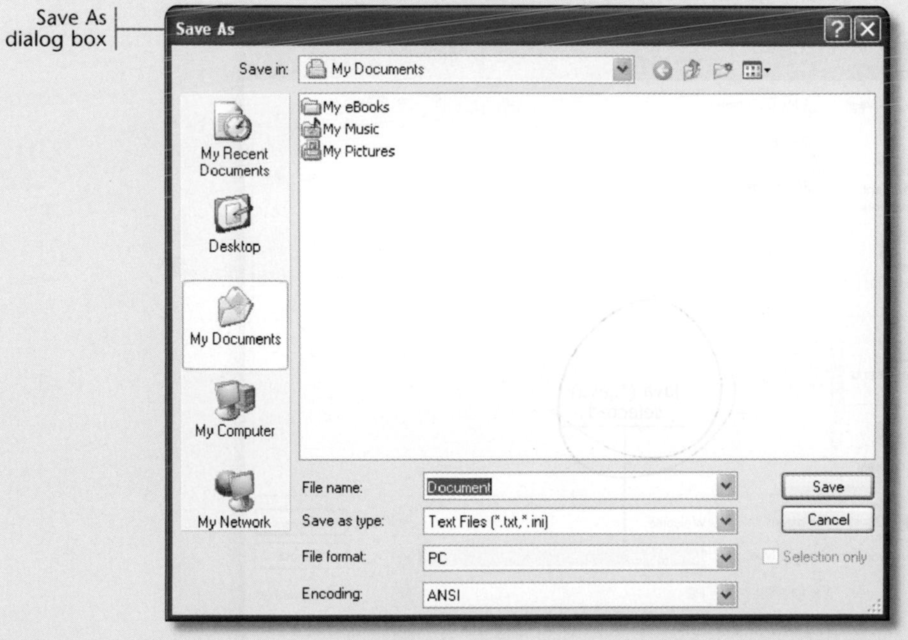

Save As dialog box

**FIGURE 2-10**

*(continued)*

4. Type We1come in the File name text box. Do not press the ENTER key. Click the Save as type box arrow.

*Welcome is displayed in the File name text box as the new file name (Figure 2-11). The Save as type list displays a list of file types supported by TextPad.*

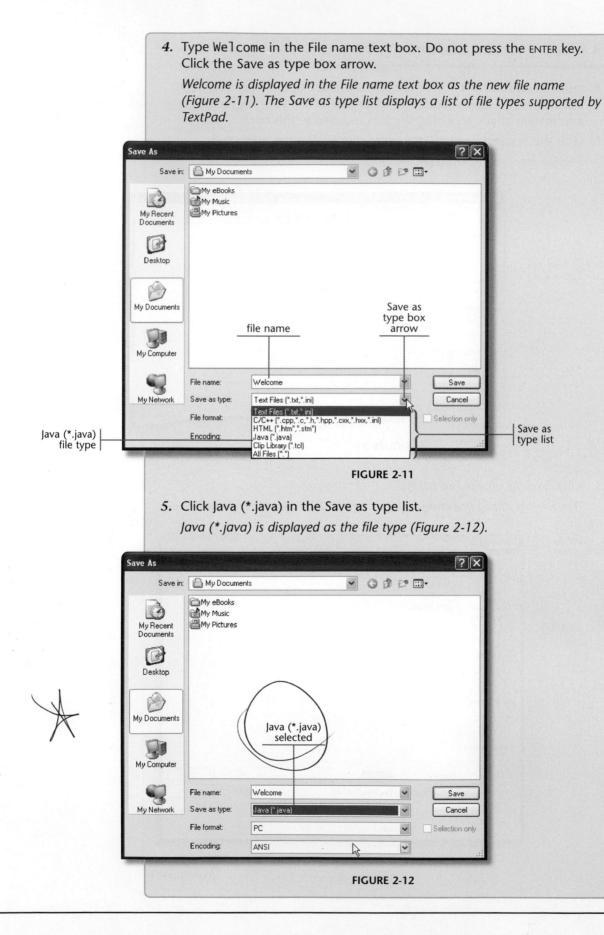

**FIGURE 2-11**

5. Click Java (*.java) in the Save as type list.

*Java (*.java) is displayed as the file type (Figure 2-12).*

**FIGURE 2-12**

**6.** Click the Save in box arrow.

*The Save in list displays the available storage locations (Figure 2-13).*

Save in
box arrow

3½ Floppy (A:)

Save in list
of storage
locations

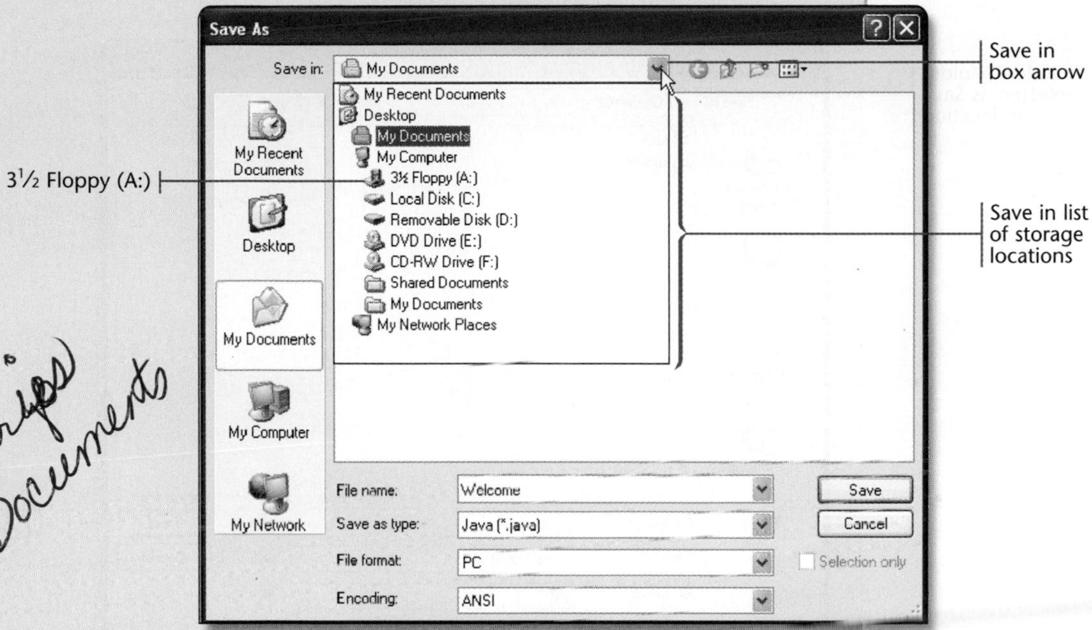

**FIGURE 2-13**

**7.** Click 3½ Floppy (A:) in the Save in list.

*3½ Floppy (A:) is displayed in the Save in box (Figure 2-14).*

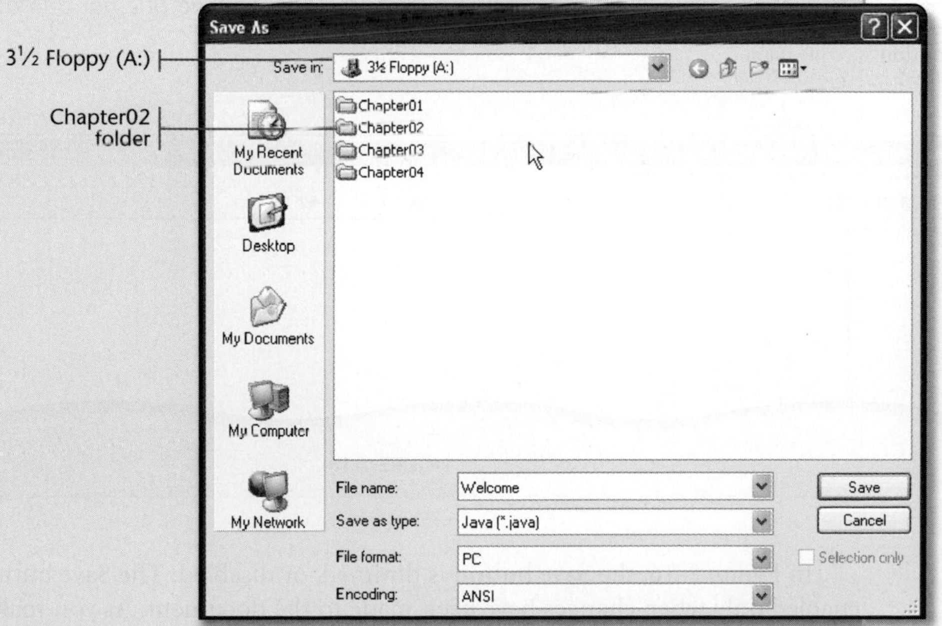

3½ Floppy (A:)

Chapter02
folder

**FIGURE 2-14**

*(continued)*

8. Double-click the Chapter02 folder or other location as directed by your instructor.

*Chapter02 is displayed in the Save in box (Figure 2-15). Your list of files may differ.*

Chapter02 folder selected as Save in location

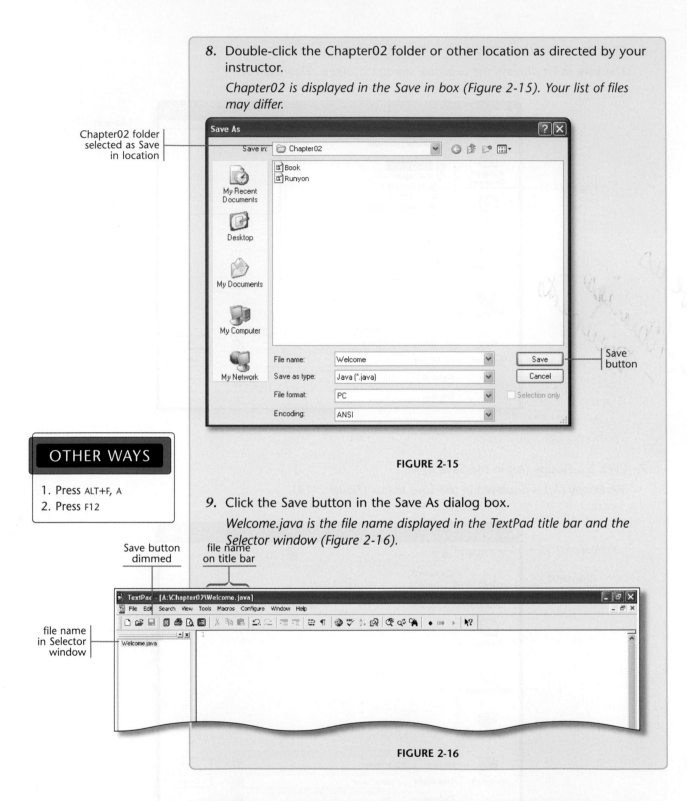

Save button

**FIGURE 2-15**

9. Click the Save button in the Save As dialog box.

*Welcome.java is the file name displayed in the TextPad title bar and the Selector window (Figure 2-16).*

Save button dimmed

file name on title bar

file name in Selector window

**FIGURE 2-16**

In Figure 2-16, the Save button is dimmed, or disabled. The Save button is enabled only when changes have been made to the document. As you make changes to the document by entering code, it is good practice to save the program periodically. To save the program again in the same folder, you can click the Save button on the Standard toolbar, rather than using the Save As command on the File menu.

# Coding the Program

As you have learned, the implementation phase of the program development cycle involves writing the code that translates the design into a program. During program design, a flowchart was used to outline the logic of the program code in the Welcome to My Day application (Figure 2-4a on page 51). As outlined in that flowchart, the task to be performed is to display a welcome message, the user's name, and the system date on the screen. Implementing the code to perform the task, instructing the computer to save that set of instructions, and then learning how to execute those instructions on any computer platform or the Web is a stepping stone to creating larger, more intricate, and more useful programs.

## Coding Comments as Documentation

The process of writing code, or coding, includes adding internal documentation in the form of **comments**, which are notes within the code that explain the purpose of the code. These comments describe the purpose of the program, the name of the programmer, the date, and other important information for the programmer and other users.

When writing code, it is a good programming practice to include comments at the beginning of a program and at the start of every major section of a program. When it is necessary for a programmer to review program source code, these comments provide an immediate description of what the program is going to do. Comments also help the programmer think clearly about the purpose of the upcoming code.

Comments are not executed when the program runs. Comment lines display in the coding window and on printouts of the source code, but they do not cause the computer to perform any task.

In Java, comments can take several different forms. A **block comment** begins with a forward slash followed by an asterisk (/*) and ends with the symbols reversed, an asterisk followed by a forward slash (*/). Block comments can span as many lines as necessary within the beginning and ending marks.

**Tip**

### Comment Placement

Comments provide important program information and remind you and other programmers of the purpose of code. Use comments in the following three ways:
1. Place a comment that identifies the file and its purpose at the top of every class or file that contains code. This type of comment typically is called a **comment header**.
2. Place a comment at the beginning of code for each event and method.
3. Place comments near portions of code that need clarification or serve an important purpose.

Typically, each line within a block comment is indented for ease in reading. Block comments can be placed before or after any line of code. All of the lines in the block, however, must stay together in a block; they cannot be interrupted or separated by commands or other lines of code. Programmers may use a block comment at the beginning of a program to describe the entire program, or in the body of a program to describe the function of a specific method.

A second type of block comment, called a **doc comment**, or a documentation comment, begins with a forward slash followed by two asterisks (/**) and ends with an asterisk followed by a forward slash (*/). Doc comments are meant to provide a concise summary of the code, not to comment on specific lines of code. Doc comments can be extracted to HTML files using the javadoc tool. For more information on the javadoc tool, see Appendix E.

A **line comment**, or single line comment, is a comment that spans only a single line or a part of a line. Line comments begin with two forward slashes (//), which cause the rest of the line to be ignored during compilation and execution. Line comments have no ending symbol. A line comment is useful especially when describing the intended meaning of a single line of code, whereas the block comment generally is more useful when describing larger sections of code. Table 2-2 shows the general form of block, doc, and line comment statements.

---

*Table 2-2* **Comment Statements**

| General form: | /* block comments */<br>/** doc comments */<br>// line comments |
|---|---|
| **Purpose:** | To insert explanatory comments in a program as internal documentation. |
| **Examples:** | 1. `/*Chapter 2:    Anita's Antiques Splash Screen`<br>`   Programmer:   J. Starks`<br>`   Date:         September 3, 2007`<br>`   Filename:     Anita.java`<br>`   Purpose:      This program displays the name, address,`<br>`   and Web site address for a company as a console application.`<br>`   */` |

2. 
```
/**
 * Returns an Image object that can be painted on the screen.
 * The URL argument must specify an absolute {@link URL}.
 * The name argument is a specifier relative to the URL.
 * <p>
 * @param  url  a URL giving the base location of the image
 *                 name and the location, relative to the URL
 * @return       the image at the specified URL
 * @see          Image
 */
```

3. `//   The following section sets the object's properties.`

---

In the code for the Welcome to My Day application, a comment header identifies the application, programmer, date, and purpose of the Welcome to My Day program. Figure 2-17 shows the comment header in block comment format. Later in the code, a line comment will explain the code used to construct the system date.

```
1   /*
2         Chapter 2:   Welcome to My Day
3         Programmer: J. Starks
4         Date:        October 4, 2007
5         Filename:    Welcome.java
6         Purpose:     This project displays a welcome message, the user's
7                      name, and the system date in a console application.
8   */
9
```

**FIGURE 2-17**

The code shown in Figure 2-17 includes **tab characters**, which are entered by pressing the TAB key and are used to indent items on each line. For example, in line 2, the tab characters indent the beginning of the line and separate the words, Chapter 2:, from the words, Welcome to My Day. Line 9 is left blank to separate the comments visually from the rest of the program code.

Perform the following step to enter comments in the coding window.

## *To Code Comments*

*1.* With the insertion point in line 1 in the coding window, type the eight lines of the block comment header as shown in Figure 2-17. Do not type the line numbers. You can insert your own name as the programmer. Press the TAB key at the beginning of lines 2 through 7 and after each colon to indent the text as illustrated in Figure 2-17. You may need to press the TAB key more than once to create the correct indentation, or press the BACKSPACE key if necessary. Press the ENTER key after each line. After typing the comment header, press the ENTER key one more time to create a blank line in line 9.

*The code window displays the comment header for the Welcome to My Day application, as shown in Figure 2-18. The insertion point is displayed in line 10.*

asterisk denotes unsaved
changes to file

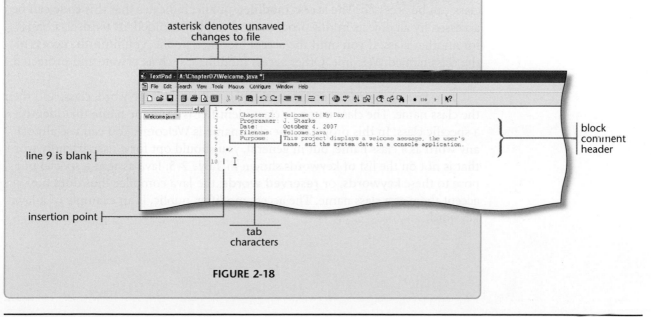

line 9 is blank

insertion point

tab
characters

block
comment
header

**FIGURE 2-18**

Notice that TextPad displays comments in the color green (Figure 2-18 on the previous page). Color coding helps you identify which lines of code are included in the comment and which are not. TextPad allows you to customize the colors used for regular code, comments, line numbers, URLs, and other items using the Preferences dialog box.

> ### Saving Code Files
>
> **Tip**
>
> The Save button on TextPad's Standard toolbar is enabled if the file contains unsaved edits but that is not the only way to determine if the code has been changed. If TextPad displays an asterisk after the file name in its title bar or in the Selector window, the code contains edits that have not been saved (Figure 2-18 on the previous page).

## The Class Header

The first line of code entered after the comment lines is the class header (Figure 2-19). The **class header** identifies how the code will be accessed and specifies the class name. The class header is displayed in line 10 in Figure 2-19.

```
10    public   class   Welcome
11    {
12
```

**FIGURE 2-19**

As you learned in Chapter 1, a class is an object or a set of objects that shares a common structure and a common behavior. In Java, an entire program is considered a class. The word **public** in line 10 is an access modifier. An **access modifier**, also called a scope identifier, specifies the circumstances in which the class can be accessed. The access modifier, public, indicates that this code can be accessed by all objects in this program and can be extended, or used, as a basis for another class. If you omit the access modifier, public, you limit the access to the class named Welcome. Other access modifiers, such as private and protected, are discussed in a later chapter.

In a Java program, an access modifier is followed by the word, class, and then the class name. The class name or class identifier is a unique name that identifies a specific class. In this program, the class name is Welcome. You can use almost any word as a class name, but in general, you should opt for a user-friendly word that is not on the list of keywords shown in Table 2-3. Java assigns a special purpose to these **keywords**, or **reserved words**; the Java compiler thus does not accept them as a class name. The access modifier, public, is an example of a Java keyword.

### Table 2-3   Java Keywords

| | | | |
|---|---|---|---|
| abstract | else | int | super |
| axiom | enum | interface | switch |
| boolean | extends | long | synchronized |
| break | false | native | this |
| byte | final | new | throw |
| byvalue | finally | null | throws |
| case | float | operator | transient |
| cast | for | outer | true |
| catch | future | package | try |
| char | generic | private | var |
| class | goto | protected | void |
| const | if | public | volatile |
| continue | implements | rest | while |
| default | import | return | |
| do | inner | short | |
| double | instanceof | static | |

The Java programming language syntax also sets forth certain rules about class names, which specify that a class name cannot contain spaces and must not begin with a number. It also is customary to begin a class name with an uppercase letter; the names of objects and data items customarily begin with lowercase letters. Table 2-4 displays the naming rules and examples of valid or legal class names, as well as invalid or illegal ones.

### Table 2-4   Java Class Naming Rules

| RULE EXAMPLES | LEGAL EXAMPLES | ILLEGAL |
|---|---|---|
| Class names must begin with a letter, an underscore, or a dollar sign. (Letters are preferred to make class names more user-friendly). It is customary to begin class names with an uppercase letter, but not mandatory. | Employee<br>Anita<br>_MyProgram<br>$myFile | 123Data<br>1Calculator3 |
| Class names may contain only letters, digits, underscores, or dollar signs. Class names may not contain spaces. | Record<br>Record123<br>Record_123 | Record#123<br>Record 123 |
| Class names may not use reserved keywords. (Refer to Table 2-3 for a list of reserved keywords.) | MyClass | class |

When you save a Java source code file, the Java compiler will expect the file name to match exactly the class name assigned at the beginning of your program in line 10 of Figure 2-19 on page 64. Java is **case-sensitive**, which means that the Java compiler considers uppercase and lowercase as two different characters. If you use a class name beginning with an uppercase letter, you also must begin the file name with an uppercase letter. Conventionally, Java programmers use uppercase letters, as opposed to underlines, to distinguish words in the class names, such as MyAddressProgram or OctoberPayroll.

All code entered after the class header is considered to be the body of the class and must be enclosed in **braces { }**. The opening brace is displayed in line 11 in Figure 2-19; the closing brace will display later in the code. Perform the following step to enter the class header and its opening brace.

---

### *To Code the Class Header*

*1.* With the insertion point in line 10 in the coding window, enter the class header and opening brace in lines 10 and 11, as shown in Figure 2-19 on page 64.

*The class header is displayed (Figure 2-20). The keywords, public and class, are displayed in blue, and the opening brace is displayed in red. When you press the* ENTER *key after a brace, TextPad automatically indents the next line.*

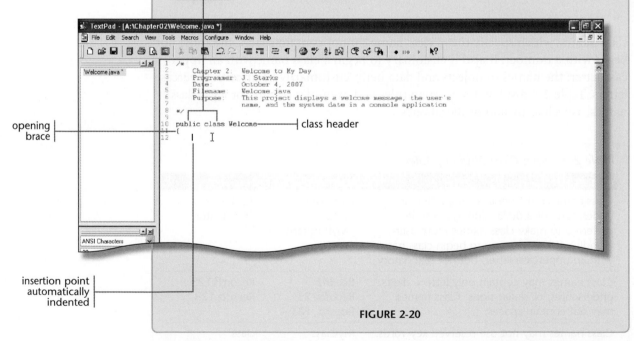

**FIGURE 2-20**

---

In Java, using a pair of opening and closing braces to enclose a portion of code indicates that they form a single, logical unit in the program, such as a class. It does not matter if you place the opening brace on the same line as the access modifier and class name or on the next line. When writing code, it is good programming practice to be consistent in the placement of the opening brace.

## The Method Header

The first line of code inside the Welcome class is the main() method header. As discussed in Chapter 1, a method is the code to perform a service or operation, including manipulating values, generating outputs, or performing actions. Methods are the basic building blocks in Java code and thus are very important. Where other programming languages have functions, Java has methods.

To code a method in Java, you begin with a method header. The **method header** notifies the Java compiler of the method's attributes, the type of data it will generate (if any), the name of the method, and any other information or parameters the method needs to perform a service or operation. Table 2-5 shows the general form of a method header.

*Table 2-5   Method Header*

| | |
|---|---|
| **General form:** | modifier returnDataType methodName(DataType parameter)<br>{<br>         //code to execute when the method is called<br>} |
| **Purpose:** | To notify the compiler of a method, its attributes, the type of data it will return (if any), and to provide a list of parameters the method may need. A method header can have several access modifiers and several parameters, or it can have none. Any parameters follow the method name in parentheses, with each parameter preceded by its data type. Multiple parameters are separated by commas. A method header can have only one return data type. |
| **Examples:** | 1. `public static void main(String[] args)`<br>2. `public void paint(Graphics g)`<br>3. `public void init( )`<br>4. `public double getOvertime(double hours, double rate)` |

Every stand-alone Java application must contain a **main() method**, which is the starting point during execution. The code in the main() method is performed sequentially during execution; however, the main() method may call other methods in the program. The main() method starts with the main() method header, as shown in line 12 of the Welcome to My Day program (Figure 2-21).

```
12      public   static   void  main( String  []   args )
13      {
14
```

**FIGURE 2-21**

A method header usually begins with one or more method modifiers. A **method modifier** is used to set properties for the method. In line 12, the access modifier, public, declares the method's visibility just as it did when used as an access modifier for a class. Because the main() method is public, other programs may invoke or use this method. The modifier, **static**, means that this method is unique and can be invoked without creating a subclass or instance. As shown in line 12 in Figure 2-21 on the previous page, the main() method in the Welcome class of the Welcome to My Day program is both public and static.

A typical method header has three parts after the modifiers: a reference to the data type of the return value, the method name, and a list of parameters. A **return value** is the result or answer of a method. A method can return data — similar to the return value of a function in a spreadsheet application — or it can return no data. A method that returns data lists the expected data type. A method that does not return data uses the keyword, **void**, instead of a data type. The main() method in the Welcome class does not create a return value and thus uses the keyword, void.

The method name is next in the method header. As shown in Figure 2-21, the main() method uses the name main. The method name is followed by parentheses. It is easy to recognize a method name in Java because it always is followed by a set of parentheses.

The parentheses enclose a list of parameters used by the method. A **parameter** is a piece of data received by the method to help the method perform its operation. For example, a method to calculate sales tax would need to know the amount of the sale and the tax rate in order to create a return value. The sales amount and the tax rate would be parameters. Later in the chapter, when you learn how to send data to a method, that data will be called an **argument**. Parameters and arguments are closely related concepts.

In the Welcome class, the main() method has one parameter named args. The word, args, is not a keyword; it is an identifier for a piece of data that the main() method may need. An **identifier** is any word you choose to name an item in a Java program. An identifier is used to name a **variable**, which is a location in computer memory that can change values as the code executes. For example, you might use the identifier, sTax, to name a variable that holds the state tax. Java programmers typically use the identifier, args, to name the parameter for the main() method, although you can use other identifiers. Variable names have the same spelling restrictions as class names (see Table 2-4 on page 65).

Each parameter must be preceded by a data type declaration. A **data type** is a word that describes the type or category of data the method uses. The parameter, args, has a String data type, which indicates a series or string of characters. The String data type is indicated by the notation, **String[]**, in line 12 in Figure 2-21. You will learn more about data types in a later chapter.

When documenting information about the main() method, programmers and language documentation would use the following terminology: Java's main() method is public and static, accepts a String parameter named args, and returns void.

The main() method header is placed before the lines of executable code, or **body**, of the main() method. The body is enclosed in pairs of braces, just as the body of the class is enclosed in braces. Line 13 in Figure 2-21 contains the opening brace of the main() method's body. It is common to indent all lines of code entered after the opening brace to facilitate reading.

Perform the following step to enter the method header for the main() method, along with its opening brace.

## To Code the Method Header

*1.* With the insertion point in line 12, type the main() method header and opening brace as shown in Figure 2-21 on page 67.

*The main() method header is displayed in line 12 in the coding window (Figure 2-22). The keywords, public, static, and void, display in blue and the opening brace is displayed in red. TextPad automatically indents the line after the opening brace of the method.*

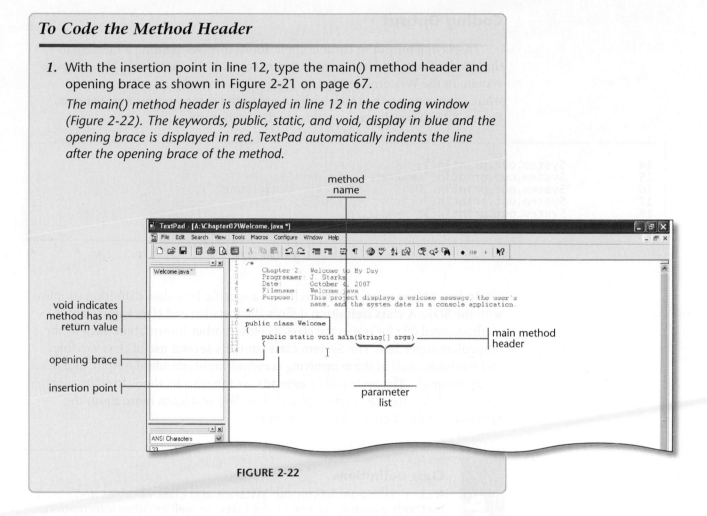

**FIGURE 2-22**

After the code for the class and the main() method is complete, closing braces indicate the end of each method. To make it easier to see what code is included in the body of the class and main() method, the closing brace for each should be indented so that it aligns underneath the respective opening brace. To facilitate entering methods, TextPad automatically reduces the indent after you type a closing brace.

### Tip

**Placement of Braces**

You can place the opening brace on the same line as the class or method header, or on the line below. Each opening brace must be paired with a closing brace. A simple way to avoid forgetting a closing brace is to immediately place the closing brace on a line below the opening brace before writing the code within the braces. Some Java programmers indent the braces; others do not. When writing code, it is good programming practice to be consistent in the placement of the opening brace. Some programmers place a line comment directly after the closing brace to help remember which class or method the brace closes.

### Coding Output

Displaying output in console applications involves sending a message to the standard output device, which in most cases is the monitor of the computer system. In the Welcome to My Day application, the output is displayed as white characters on the black background of the command prompt window. Figure 2-23 shows the code you use to display output.

```
14          System.out.println();
15          System.out.println("Welcome to my day!");
16          System.out.println("Daily planner for Linda Nunez");
17          System.out.println("October 4, 2007");
18          System.out.println();
19
```

**FIGURE 2-23**

In line 14, the word, System, refers to a specific Java class definition supplied with the SDK. A **class definition** defines the instance and class variables and methods available for use in the class, as well as other information, such as the immediate superclass. The **System class** contains several useful class variables and methods, such as those involving standard input, standard output, and other utility methods. The System class **extends**, or inherits, methods from its superclass, which in this case is Java's Object class. You will learn more about the System and Object classes in later chapters.

**Class Definitions**

A class definition defines the instance and class variables and methods available for use in the class, as well as other information, such as the immediate superclass. You can use the Java API to view the hierarchy of individual classes and to look up specific methods used by each class.

The word, **out**, refers to the object representing the default display. Perhaps the most often used object from the System class, out represents the device used to display a standard output of text characters. A period (.) separates or delimits the class, System, and the object, out.

Following another period delimiter, the word, println, identifies the **println() method** from the System class. The println() method returns its value to the System.out device. The println() method is *called* from the Java Object package in this case — the programmer is not writing all of the code to make it work. Calling methods such as println() differs from writing methods such as main(). When coding the main() method, which begins with a method header, the programmer must include the code statements for operations that the main() method must perform. Methods such as println() already have been written, so programmers can use the methods without having to write all of the code that each method must perform. Programmers simply call such methods by the method's name and send data along with it, in the form of arguments enclosed in parentheses. You do not need to specify the argument's data type when calling a method.

In the Welcome to My Day program, the argument for the println() method is the data sent to the monitor at run time. In lines 14 and 18, no argument is displayed in the parentheses, so a blank line with no text will be displayed. In line 15, the string of characters enclosed in quotation marks inside the parentheses will be sent to the monitor for display. The string of characters is called a **literal**, which means the data inside the quotes will be displayed exactly as entered in the code. You will learn how to use the println() method to display stored String data, as well as literal and stored numeric data. When using the println() method to output numbers and variables to the display, you do not need to enclose the argument in quotation marks.

Lines 14 through 18 each end with a semicolon (;). Other than headers and braces, all lines of Java code must end with a semicolon. Line 15 uses the object-oriented components of classes, objects, and methods all in one line. System is the name of the class; out is the object that represents the default display; and println() is the name of a method that accepts a String argument.

After entering the code to display output, you will close the class and the main() method by entering the respective closing braces. You then will save the program. Perform the following steps to enter the code to display output, and then save the Java program file on the Data Disk in drive A.

## To Enter Code to Display Output and Save the Program File

1. With the insertion point in line 14, enter the code as shown in Figure 2-23, keeping in mind that Java is case sensitive.

   *The TextPad window displays the Java source code for the five println() methods (Figure 2-24). Lines 14 and 18 will cause the program to output blank lines.*

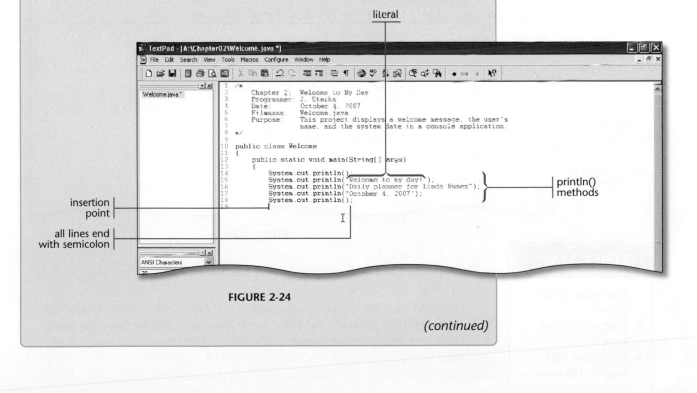

**FIGURE 2-24**

*(continued)*

2. With the insertion point in line 19, type a closing brace and then press the ENTER key.

*The closing brace for the main() method automatically aligns with the opening brace for the main() method (Figure 2-25).*

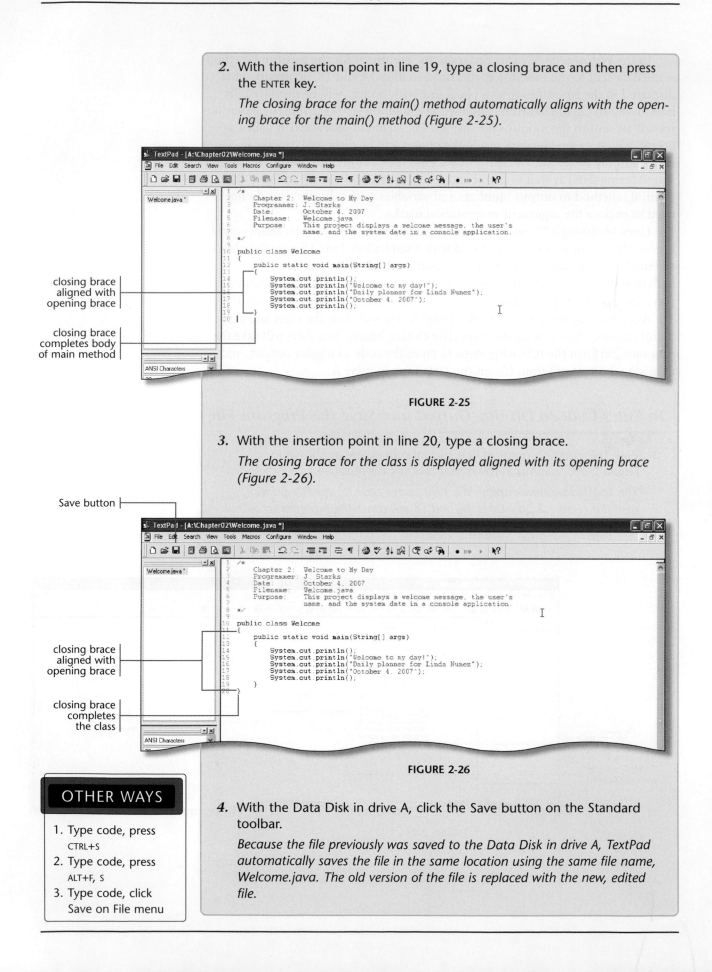

closing brace
aligned with
opening brace

closing brace
completes body
of main method

FIGURE 2-25

3. With the insertion point in line 20, type a closing brace.

*The closing brace for the class is displayed aligned with its opening brace (Figure 2-26).*

Save button

closing brace
aligned with
opening brace

closing brace
completes
the class

FIGURE 2-26

OTHER WAYS

1. Type code, press
   CTRL+S
2. Type code, press
   ALT+F, S
3. Type code, click
   Save on File menu

4. With the Data Disk in drive A, click the Save button on the Standard toolbar.

*Because the file previously was saved to the Data Disk in drive A, TextPad automatically saves the file in the same location using the same file name, Welcome.java. The old version of the file is replaced with the new, edited file.*

Unless you use the Save As command and then choose a different Save as type to change the file extension, TextPad automatically saves the file with the same .java extension. If another application, such as Notepad, is used to create the Java program, the file must be saved in plain text format with the extension .java.

## Testing the Solution

The fifth phase of the development cycle is to test the solution. After the program solution is designed and then implemented in code, it should be tested to ensure that it runs properly. With Java, testing the solution is a two-step process that involves (1) compiling the source code and then (2) executing the bytecode.

### Compiling the Source Code

Java source code must be compiled before it can be executed. TextPad includes a Compile Java command on the Tools menu. The Compile Java command uses the Java compiler command, javac.exe, to translate the Java source code into byte-code that any machine can interpret. The compilation process creates a new file for each class and saves it in the same directory as the source code file.

> **Tip**
>
> **Accessing the Java SDK Compiler**
>
> The Java compiler needs to access certain files from the Java SDK. If you first installed the Java SDK using its setup program and then installed TextPad, the Java compiler will automatically access the necessary SDK files when you execute the Compile Java command in TextPad. If you are compiling Java source code using the command prompt window, you must use operating system commands to designate the location of the SDK files each time you open the command prompt window. See Appendix D for more information on compiling Java source code at the command prompt.

Perform the following steps to compile the Welcome to My Day program.

### To Compile Source Code

1. With the Data Disk in drive A, click Tools on the menu bar.

   *The Tools menu is displayed (Figure 2-27).*

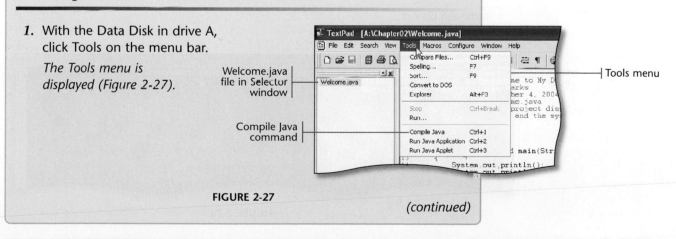

   Welcome.java file in Selector window

   Compile Java command

   Tools menu

   **FIGURE 2-27**

   *(continued)*

**OTHER WAYS**

1. Press CTRL+1
2. At command prompt, type javac Welcome.java

2. Click Compile Java on the Tools menu. If TextPad displays any error messages, click Welcome.java in the Selector window. Fix the errors and repeat Step 1.

*If TextPad finds no errors while compiling the source code, TextPad redisplays the source code. The bytecode for the Welcome to My Day application is saved on the Data Disk.*

During compilation, the compiler saves the source code again and then adds a file to the disk called Welcome.class, which is the actual bytecode.

If your TextPad installation does not display the Compile Java command on the Tools menu, the SDK may have been moved or installed after TextPad. See Appendix C for more information on configuring TextPad. Recall that compiling Java source code with a VATE program such as TextPad allows you to compile using its menu system. Alternately, you can compile by opening a command prompt window and issuing the compile command, javac. If you are compiling at the command prompt, you may need to change to the directory containing your Data Disk. See Appendix D for more information on compiling in the command prompt window.

## Debugging the Solution

If TextPad displays error messages when you compile the source code, you may have a system, syntax, semantic, run-time, or other logic error. The process of fixing errors is called **debugging**. Debugging can be a time-consuming and frustrating process, but it is a skill that will improve as you learn to program.

### System Errors

If your system displays an error such as unrecognized command or cannot read file, you may have a system error (Figure 2-28). A **system error** occurs when a system command is not set properly, software is installed incorrectly, or the location of stored files has changed. System errors usually display in the command prompt window. If you get a system error while compiling using TextPad, you may not have first installed the Java SDK (see Appendix B). If you get a system error compiling the program using the javac command, you may not have set the required path locations properly (see Appendix D).

command prompt window

system error

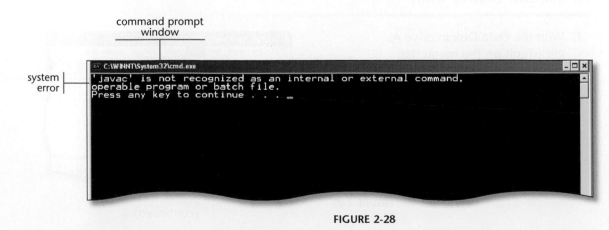

**FIGURE 2-28**

## Syntax Errors

A **syntax error** is an error caused by code statements that violate one or more syntax rules of the Java programming language. Typing mistakes often cause syntax errors. When you compile Java source code, TextPad lists syntax errors in a **Command Results window**, as shown in Figure 2-29.

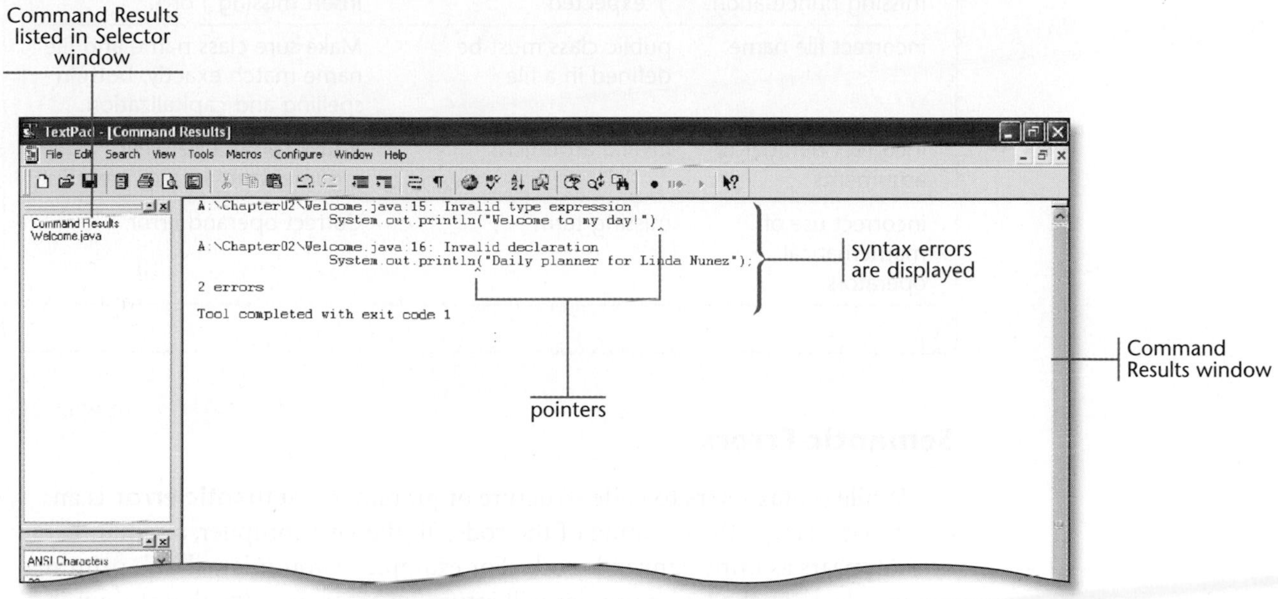

Command Results listed in Selector window

syntax errors are displayed

Command Results window

pointers

**FIGURE 2-29**

When it encounters syntax errors, the compiler attempts to isolate the syntax error by displaying a line of code with pointers pointing to the first incorrect character in that line. The error, however, may not be at that exact point. For instance, if you omit a necessary semicolon at the end of a line, TextPad may display error messages, similar to those shown in Figure 2-29. Both errors are due to the same missing semicolon. Without the semicolon in the first line, the compiler cannot find the end of the first line and thus generates an error message with the file name, the line number, and the error message, Invalid type expression. The compiler then tries to compile the two lines together, which results in a second error message, Invalid declaration. Once the semicolon in the code is corrected, neither error message will display.

A rule of thumb to follow when debugging syntax errors is to correct the first mistake in a long list. Doing so may reduce the total number of errors dramatically and allow you to focus on the cause of the remaining errors.

The most common mistakes that cause syntax errors are capitalization, spelling, the use of incorrect special characters, and omission of correct punctuation. Table 2-6 on the next page lists some common syntax errors, the error messages that indicate the specific syntax error, and the method of correction.

*Table 2-6   Common Syntax Errors*

| SYNTAX ERROR | SAMPLE ERROR MESSAGE | METHOD OF CORRECTION |
|---|---|---|
| missing semicolon | invalid type expression invalid declaration ';' expected | Add a semicolon at the end of the line. |
| missing punctuation | ')' expected | Insert missing ) or }. |
| incorrect file name | public class must be defined in a file | Make sure class name and file name match exactly, both in spelling and capitalization. |
| incorrect number of arguments | invalid argument | Add a comma between arguments in an argument list. |
| incorrect use of mathematical operators | missing term | Correct operand error. |

## Semantic Errors

While syntax refers to code structure or grammar, a **semantic error** is an error that changes the meaning of the code. To the Java compiler, a semantic error appears as unrecognizable code. For example, if you misspell the println() method in code, the Java compiler will return an error message that it cannot resolve the symbol or that the method was not found (Figure 2-30). If you use a variable name that has not been declared properly, the compiler will return an error message that the variable is undefined. Most semantic errors can be fixed by correcting the spelling of keywords or by properly defining variables and methods.

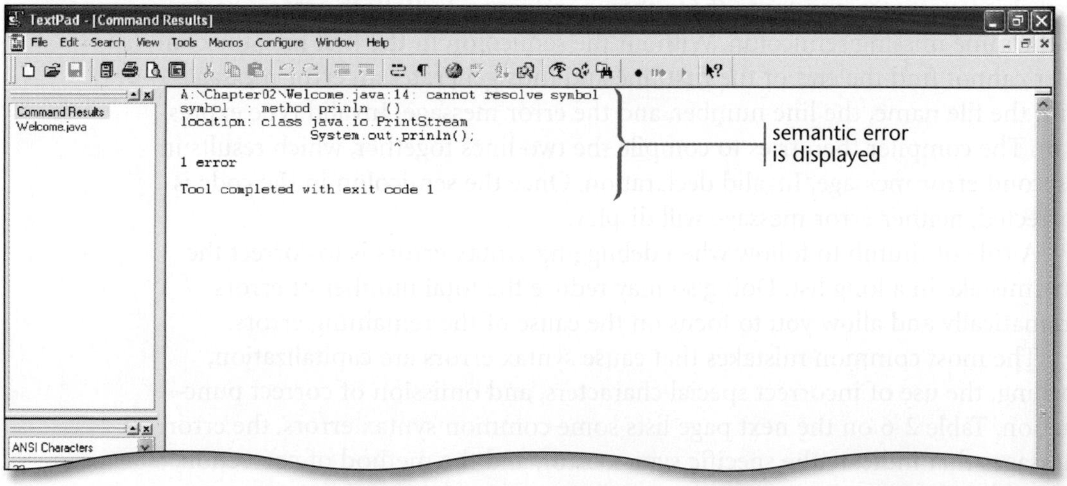

FIGURE 2-30

If TextPad displays error messages when you try to compile a program, click the file name in the Selector window to display the code in the coding window and then correct any syntax or semantic errors. Alternately, you can double-click the first line of the error message itself, and TextPad will open the coding window automatically, placing the insertion point at the beginning of the line in question. Once the errors are fixed, save the file and then compile the program again. If Java still displays error messages after you have corrected all syntax or semantic errors, consult your instructor.

### Logic and Run-Time Errors

A **logic error** occurs when a program does not behave as intended due to poor design or incorrect implementation of the design. A **run-time error**, also called an **exception**, is an error that occurs when unexpected conditions arise as you run or execute the program. Even programs that compile successfully may display logic or run-time errors if the programmer has not thought through the logical processes and structures of the program. Your goal should be to have error-free programs, and by implementing the development cycle correctly, you will achieve that goal.

Occasionally, a logic error will surface during execution of the program due to an action the user performs — an action for which the programmer did not plan. For example, if a user inputs numbers outside of valid ranges or enters the wrong types of data, the program may stop executing if the code cannot handle the input. In later chapters, you will learn how to write code to handle data entry errors based on validity, range, and reasonableness. In this chapter, the user inputs no data into the application, so these types of logic errors should not occur.

Other logic or run-time errors may occur as you run a program. For example, if a programmer typed the wrong data or used an incorrect operator in code, the program would compile and run correctly, but the wrong output would display. No run-time error message would occur. These types of errors can be difficult to identify.

A run-time error message also will display if you are executing the program from the command prompt window and misspell the command, misspell the name of the bytecode file, or add an extension by mistake.

## Running the Application

After a Java program is compiled into bytecode, and syntax and semantic errors are fixed, the program must be run or executed to test for logic and run-time errors. Programmers run the program to display output, receive input from the user if necessary, and interpret the commands to produce the desired result.

### Running the Application

TextPad includes a Run Java Application command on the Tools menu. The Run Java Application command executes the compiled bytecode of the file selected in the Selector window. TextPad automatically looks for the class file with the same name and then executes it. If you are running the application from the command prompt, you type `java` followed by the name of the class file, `Welcome` (no extension). Perform the steps on the next page to run the Welcome to My Day application.

## To Run the Application

1. **Click Tools on the menu bar.**

   *The Tools menu is displayed (Figure 2-31).*

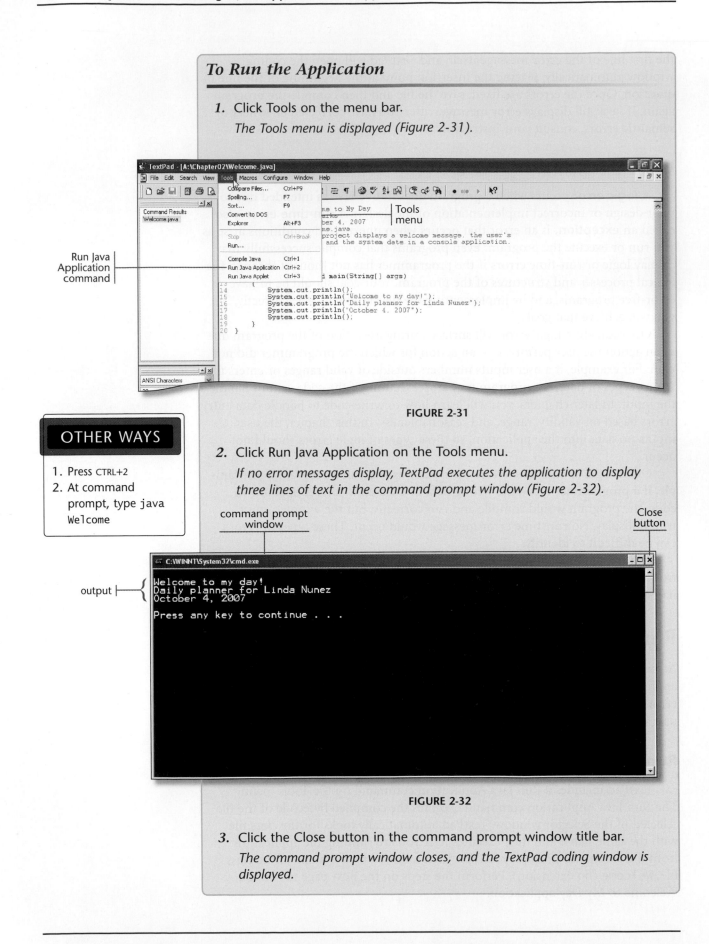

**FIGURE 2-31**

2. **Click Run Java Application on the Tools menu.**

   *If no error messages display, TextPad executes the application to display three lines of text in the command prompt window (Figure 2-32).*

**FIGURE 2-32**

3. **Click the Close button in the command prompt window title bar.**

   *The command prompt window closes, and the TextPad coding window is displayed.*

The println() method of the System.out object causes each output String to display on a new line in the command prompt window. The System.out object supports other output methods in addition to the println() method. For example, the System.out object supports the print() method, which prints output on a single line, without moving the insertion point down to the next line. The print() method is useful when you want the insertion point to display directly after a prompt to the user. You can use the Java API and language documentation on the Sun Microsystems Web site to research other methods supported by the System.out object.

## Editing the Source Code

When you **edit** or modify the source code in any way, you must repeat the steps of saving, compiling, and executing the program. Even if you make a simple change, such as editing the spacing between characters, you should repeat the steps of saving, compiling, and executing the program to ensure that the program runs properly.

The source code of the Welcome to My Day application must be edited so that the application obtains the current date from the operating system, displays the date, and formats the output as requested in the requirements document. Figure 2-33 shows the source code after the edits are complete.

```
1    /*
2         Chapter 2:   Welcome to My Day
3         Programmer:  J. Starks
4         Date:        October 4, 2007
5         Filename:    Welcome.java
6         Purpose:     This project displays a welcome message, the user's
7                      name, and the system date in a console application.
8    */
9
10   import java.util.Date;
11
12   public class Welcome
13   {
14       public static void main(String[] args)
15       {
16           Date currentDate = new Date(); // Date constructor
17           System.out.println();
18           System.out.println("\t\t\tWelcome to my day!");
19           System.out.println("\t\t\tDaily planner for Linda Nunez");
20           System.out.println("\t\t\t" + currentDate);
21           System.out.println();
22       }
23   }
```

**FIGURE 2-33**

TextPad allows programmers to use standard editing techniques, such as those used in a word processing program, to replace and enter new code in the coding window. The Edit menu in the TextPad menu bar displays commands for many standard editing functions, including cut, copy, paste, insert, and delete. For more information on using shortcuts, selecting text, and moving the insertion point through the coding window, see Appendix C.

## Entering Code to Import Packages

The classes and methods needed to display the system date are not immediately available, which means the programmer must tell the compiler to access the storage location in order to use these methods. The SDK includes class packages as part of the standard installation. Recall that class packages, or libraries, contain portable Java bytecode files. Because hundreds of these files are available, Java organizes them, by category, into packages.

Some of the more widely used Java packages and their descriptions are listed in Table 2-7. The Java API contains a complete list of Java packages.

**Table 2-7   Java Packages**

| PACKAGE NAME | DESCRIPTION | EXAMPLES OF CLASSES IN PACKAGE |
|---|---|---|
| java.applet | Provides the classes necessary to create an applet and the classes an applet uses to communicate with its applet context. | Class used to create the applet window and methods to initialize, start, and stop the applet. |
| java.awt | The Abstract Window Toolkit (AWT) provides the classes for creating user interfaces and for painting graphics and images. | Classes to define GUI objects, including Button, Label, TextField, and Checkbox. |
| java.awt.event | Provides interfaces and classes for dealing with different types of events fired by AWT components, such as button clicks and key press events. | Classes to support events, including ActionEvent, WindowEvent, MouseEvent, and KeyEvent. |
| java.io | Provides classes that support system input and output through data streams, serialization, and the file system. | Classes to handle I/O methods, including FileReader, InputStreamReader, and BufferedReader. |
| java.lang | Provides classes that are fundamental to the design of the Java programming language, which facilitate data types, threads, Strings, and others. | Classes such as those related to String, System, Double, Integer, Float, and Thread. |
| java.net | Provides classes used for networking and client/server applications. | Classes related to networks, such as URL, InetAddress, and NetworkInterface. |
| java.util | Provides classes for the date and time facilities, internationalization, and miscellaneous utilities. | Classes related to time (such as Date, Calendar, and Timer) and location (such as Locale and TimeZone). |
| javax.swing | Provides a set of lightweight Java-based components. | Classes to define GUI components such as JApplet, JOptionPane, JLabel, JTextField, and JScrollBar. |

The java.lang package is the only package imported automatically without an explicit command; all other packages need an **import statement** to tell the compiler where to access the classes, fields, and methods of an existing class in the package. The import statement is placed at the beginning of the Java source code, most commonly right after the opening documentation. During compilation, the import statement goes to the location where the SDK is stored, and loads the appropriate class or classes. Typing an asterisk (*) after the package name tells the program to load all the classes within a package; typing an individual class name after the package name tells the program to load an individual class.

**Tip**

**Using the import Statement**

Using the import statement to import all of the classes in a package does not make the bytecode longer because the compiler uses only the classes it needs. Importing numerous packages does slow the compiler, however, as it checks through each package when it needs a class. To keep compile times reasonable, a programmer should use the import statement to import only packages with the tools the compiler needs.

In the Welcome to My Day application, you will import the Date class from the java.util package, as shown in the following steps.

## To Code the Import Statement

1. With the Welcome.java file displayed in the TextPad coding window, click line 9, below the block comment. Press the ENTER key.

   *The insertion point displays in line 10 (Figure 2-34).*

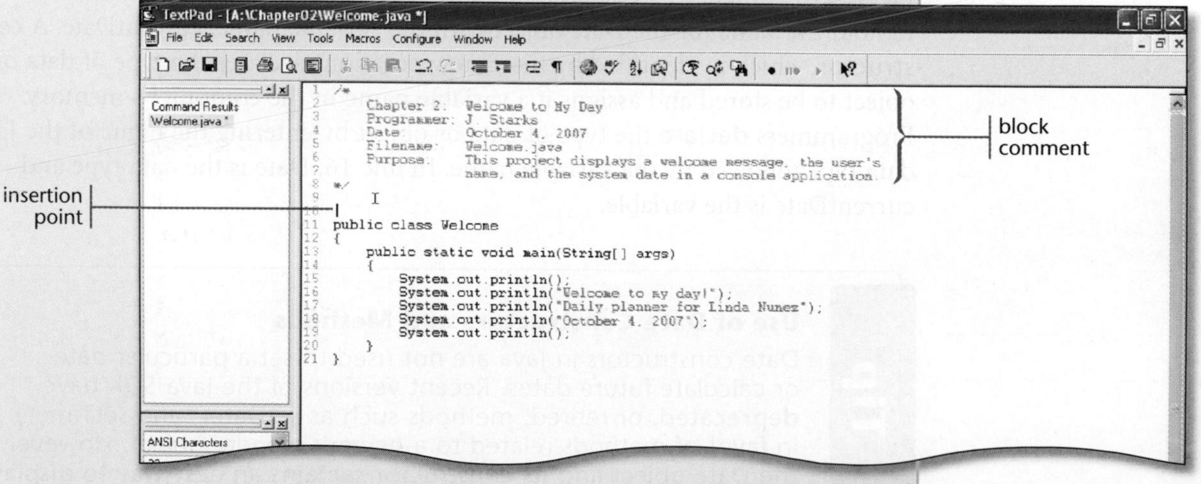

**FIGURE 2-34**

*(continued)*

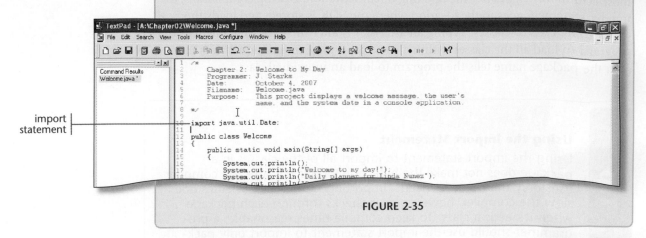

**2.** Enter line 10 from Figure 2-33 on page 79. Press the ENTER key.

*The import statement to import the Date class package from the SDK is displayed in line 10 (Figure 2-35). The Date class from the java.util package will be imported into the Welcome to My Day application. Line 11 is blank.*

import statement

**FIGURE 2-35**

Some programmers place import statements before the block comments rather than after them. Either placement is acceptable, provided that the import statements are placed before the class header.

## Entering Code to Call a System Date Constructor

The operating system running on your computer keeps track of the current date and time. This system date is kept current by a battery inside the system unit on most computers. The **Date class** in Java represents a specific instant in time, measured to the nearest millisecond. Java creates a Date object and initializes it so that it represents the exact date and time it was allocated.

In order for Java to ask the operating system for that system date, a programmer must create a storage location to hold the system date data. Line 16 in Figure 2-33 on page 79 displays the code to construct the storage location to hold the value for the Date object with the variable name, currentDate. A **constructor**, which is identified by the = new notation, declares the type of data or object to be stored and assigns it a variable name in the computer's memory. Programmers **declare** the type of data or object by entering the name of the Java data type followed by the variable name. In line 16, Date is the data type and currentDate is the variable.

**Use of Date Constructors and Methods**

Date constructors in Java are not used to set a particular date or calculate future dates. Recent versions of the Java SDK have **deprecated,** or retired, methods such as setDate() and setTime() in favor of methods related to a newer Calendar object. However, the Date object and its constructor remains an easy way to display the system date on a given computer system.

Perform the following steps to enter code for the Date constructor to construct an instance of the system date.

## *To Code a Call to a System Date Constructor*

***1.*** Click the TextPad coding window, immediately to the right of the main() method's opening brace in line 15.

*The insertion point displays to the right of the brace in line 15 (Figure 2-36).*

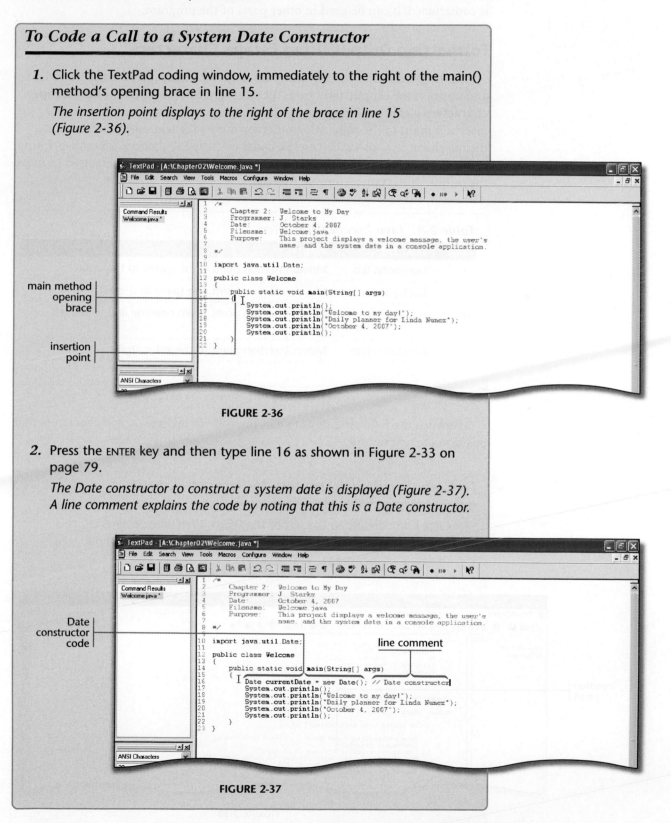

**FIGURE 2-36**

***2.*** Press the ENTER key and then type line 16 as shown in Figure 2-33 on page 79.

*The Date constructor to construct a system date is displayed (Figure 2-37). A line comment explains the code by noting that this is a Date constructor.*

**FIGURE 2-37**

The Date constructor allows the program to request and store the current system date at the time the program is executed. Once the variable currentDate is constructed, it can be used in other parts of the program.

## Formatting Output Using Escape Characters

In the Welcome to My Day program, you will insert special codes to indent and position the output away from the left side of the screen. Java uses **escape characters** inside the String arguments of the println() method to move the insertion point to the right, which thereby moves the text output to the right. Escape characters, also called escape codes or escape sequences, are non-printing control codes. Table 2-8 displays some of the Java escape characters used to move the output of data on a computer screen.

*Table 2-8   Java Escape Characters*

| CODE | CONCEPT | RESULT |
| --- | --- | --- |
| \t | horizontal tab | Moves insertion point eight spaces to the right. |
| \b | backspace | Moves insertion point one space to the left. |
| \n | new line | Moves insertion point down one line and to the left margin. |
| \r | carriage return | Moves insertion point to the left margin. |

Perform the following steps to edit the code to include escape characters that position the text output.

### To Code Escape Characters to Format Output

*1.* Click immediately to the left of the word, Welcome, in line 18.

*The insertion point displays between the quotation mark and the W of Welcome (Figure 2-38).*

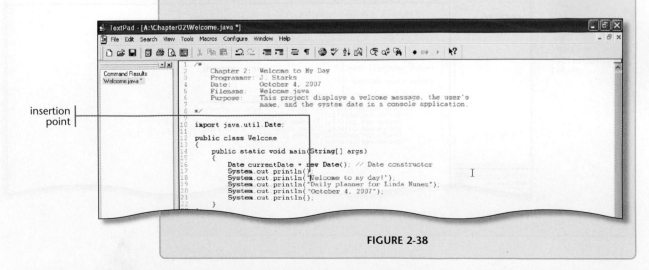

**FIGURE 2-38**

2. Type \t\t\t after the quotation mark in line 18.

*The escape code characters are displayed as part of the String argument (Figure 2-39). The three horizontal tab escape characters will cause the insertion point to move 24 spaces to the right — eight spaces for each escape character — before outputting the words to the screen.*

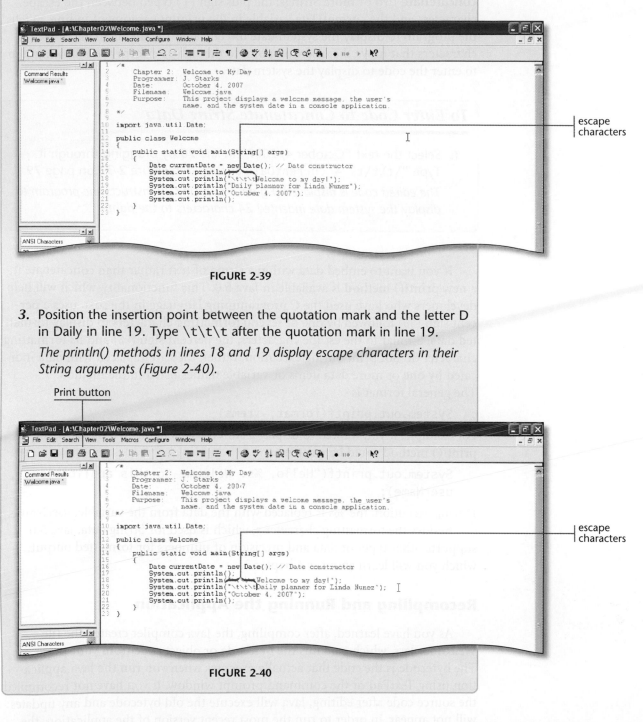

escape characters

**FIGURE 2-39**

3. Position the insertion point between the quotation mark and the letter D in Daily in line 19. Type \t\t\t after the quotation mark in line 19.

*The println() methods in lines 18 and 19 display escape characters in their String arguments (Figure 2-40).*

Print button

escape characters

**FIGURE 2-40**

The final edit is to insert the line of code to display the system date constructed by the Date constructor in line 16. As shown in line 20 of Figure 2-33 on page 79, the code is changed to use the variable currentDate, instead of the previously typed date. Unlike the typed date, the variable currentDate is not enclosed in quotation marks, so it will not literally print the words, currentDate, on the screen. Alternately, it will print whatever value is in the storage location at run time — in this case, the system date.

In the Java programming language, you can use a plus sign (+) to join or **concatenate** two or more Strings: the plus sign (+) typed between the escape characters and the currentDate variable in the println() argument in line 20 tells the program to display the system date directly after the literal String of escape characters that move the insertion point to the right. Perform the following step to enter the code to display the system date.

---

### To Enter Code to Concatenate String Data

---

*1.* Select the text "October 4, 2007" in line 20 by dragging through it. Type "\t\t\t" + currentDate as shown in Figure 2-33 on page 79.

*The edited code is displayed (Figure 2-33). Line 20 instructs the program to display the system date indented 24 characters to the right.*

---

If you want to embed data within a string of text rather than concatenate it, a new **printf() method** is available in Java 5.0. This functionality, which will help developers who have used the C programming language in the past, uses a percent sign (%) followed by one of several formatting characters to display formatted data. Similar to the escape characters, the percent sign (%) and its formatting character do not print during execution; rather, they are replaced with data indicated by one or more data items or variable names listed in the method. The general format is

```
System.out.printf(format, items);
```

For example, if you wanted to display a stored user's name in a message, the printf() method could be written as

```
System.out.printf("Hello, %s. Welcome to this application.",
userName);
```

During execution, the %s is replaced with the data from the variable, userName.

Besides the formatting character s, which is used for String data, Java 5.0 supports other types of data and precision of numbers for formatted output, which you will learn about in Chapter 3.

## Recompiling and Running the Application

As you have learned, after compiling, the Java compiler created the file Welcome.class, which contains the bytecode or object code from your program. The bytecode is the code that actually executes when you run the Java application using TextPad or the command prompt window. If you have not recompiled the source code after editing, Java will execute the old bytecode and any updates will not appear. In order to run the most recent version of the application, the source code first must be recompiled into new bytecode.

Follow these steps to recompile and then run the application.

## To Recompile and Run the Application

1. Click Tools on the menu bar and then click Compile Java on the Tools menu. If TextPad displays any error messages in the coding window, click Welcome.java in the Selector window. Fix the errors and repeat Step 1.

   *The source code is compiled. Clicking the Compile Java command automatically saves the file again.*

2. After TextPad successfully compiles the source code, run the program by clicking Tools on the menu bar and then click Run Java Application on the Tools menu.

   *The program runs and the println() methods send data to the monitor (Figure 2-41). The output is displayed, with all lines indented from the left side of the command prompt window.*

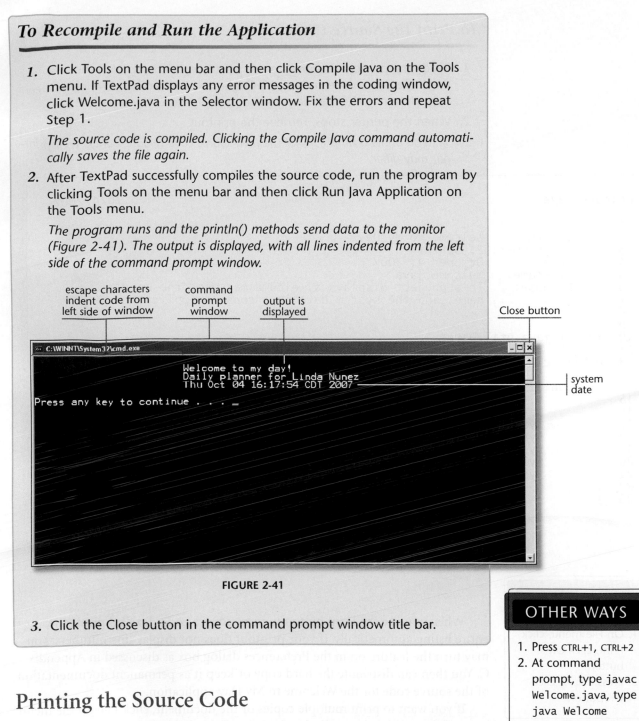

FIGURE 2-41

3. Click the Close button in the command prompt window title bar.

### OTHER WAYS

1. Press CTRL+1, CTRL+2
2. At command prompt, type javac Welcome.java, type java Welcome

## Printing the Source Code

The final step of the development cycle for this application is to document the program by printing the code. A printed version of the source code is called a **hard copy**, or **printout**. Perform the steps on the next page to print the source code.

### To Print the Source Code

1. Ready the printer according to the printer instructions. With the Welcome.java source code displaying in the TextPad window, click the Print button in the Standard toolbar (see Figure 2-40 on page 85).

2. When the printer stops, retrieve the printout.

   *TextPad prints a hard copy of the Java source code (Figure 2-42). Your printout may differ.*

```
Welcome.java                                                        10/4/2007

 1   /*
 2        Chapter 2:   Welcome to My Day
 3        Programmer:  J. Starks
 4        Date:        October 4, 2007
 5        Filename:    Welcome.java
 6        Purpose:     This project displays a welcome message, the user's
 7                     name, and the system date in a console application.
 8   */
 9
10   import java.util.Date;
11
12   public class Welcome
13   {
14       public static void main(String[] args)
15       {
16           Date currentDate = new Date(); // Date constructor
17           System.out.println();
18           System.out.println("\t\t\tWelcome to my day!");
19           System.out.println("\t\t\tDaily planner for Linda Nunez");
20           System.out.println("\t\t\t" + currentDate);
21           System.out.println();
22       }
23   }
```

FIGURE 2-42

### OTHER WAYS

1. On File menu, click Print, click OK button
2. Press CTRL+P, click OK button

When you use the Print button to print source code, TextPad prints the entire listing automatically. If your printout does not display line numbers, you may turn the feature on in the Preferences dialog box as discussed in Appendix C. You then can distribute the hard copy or keep it as permanent documentation of the source code for the Welcome to My Day application.

If you want to print multiple copies of the document, click File on the menu bar and then click Print to display the Print dialog box. The Print dialog box has several printing options, including the option to specify the number of copies to print.

## Quitting TextPad

After you create, save, compile, execute, test, and print the program, you can quit TextPad. To quit TextPad and return control to Windows, perform the following step.

*ting a Java Application and Applet*

---

### *To Quit TextPad*

---

**1.** Click the Close button on the right side of the TextPad title bar.

*If you made changes to the project since the last time it was saved, TextPad displays a TextPad dialog box. If you click the Yes button, you can resave your file and quit. If you click the No button, you will quit without saving changes. Clicking the Cancel button will close the dialog box.*

## Moving to the Web

One of the features that makes Java so useful is that programmers can use it to develop programs that are machine-independent and can run on the Web. Much of Java's portability lies in the use of applets. As you learned in Chapter 1, an applet is a small program that can be downloaded and executed as part of a displayed Web page. When run as part of a Web page, applets often are used to perform interactive animations, immediate calculations, or other simple tasks without having to access the computer that is hosting the Web page.

Other major differences between Java applications and Java applets exist. One difference is that applications run as stand-alone programs with full access to system resources, whereas applets can run only within a browser or viewer and are usually delivered to the local computer via the Web. Another difference is in their scope for data handling. An applet cannot be used to modify files stored on a user's system, while an application can. Finally, unlike applets, applications do not need a memory-intensive browser or viewer in order to execute.

The source code for the Welcome to My Day application is complete and can be edited to convert the application into an applet that can run via the Web. The steps to convert the application into an applet include opening the Welcome file in TextPad, editing the code to import two new packages, changing the class name, and specifying that the class is an applet. Then the class code is edited to include a paint method that draws text in the applet window and displays a graphic and color. Once the changes are complete, the file is saved and the applet is compiled.

### Opening an Existing File in TextPad

Once you have created and saved a file, you often will have reason to retrieve it from disk. For example, you might want to revise the code or print it again. Earlier you saved the Java source code file created in this chapter on a disk using the file name Welcome. The steps on the next page illustrate how to open the file Welcome.java from the Data Disk in drive A using TextPad.

## To Start TextPad and Open an Existing File

**1.** With the Data Disk in drive A and the Windows desktop displayed, click the Start button on the taskbar and then point to TextPad (Figure 2-43). If TextPad does not display on the Start menu, point to All Programs on the Start menu and then point to TextPad on the All Programs submenu.

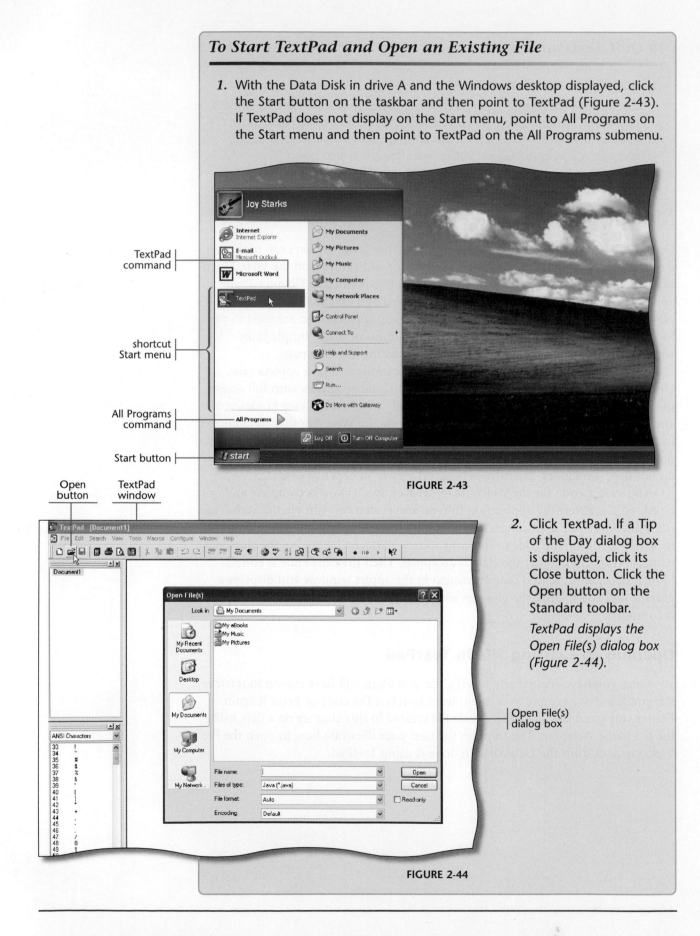

TextPad command

shortcut Start menu

All Programs command

Start button

**FIGURE 2-43**

Open button

TextPad window

**2.** Click TextPad. If a Tip of the Day dialog box is displayed, click its Close button. Click the Open button on the Standard toolbar.

*TextPad displays the Open File(s) dialog box (Figure 2-44).*

Open File(s) dialog box

**FIGURE 2-44**

3. If necessary, click the Files of type box arrow and then click Java (*.java) in the list. Click the Look in box arrow and then click 3½ Floppy (A:) in the list.

   *The Look in box displays 3½ Floppy (A:) (Figure 2-45). The names of folders on the Data Disk in drive A display in the Open File(s) dialog box.*

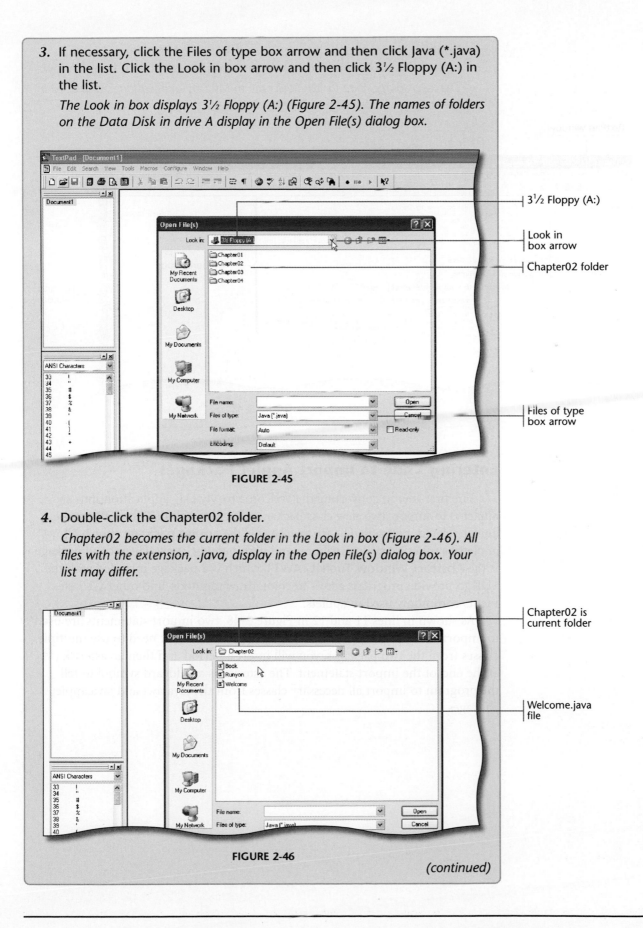

**FIGURE 2-45**

4. Double-click the Chapter02 folder.

   *Chapter02 becomes the current folder in the Look in box (Figure 2-46). All files with the extension, .java, display in the Open File(s) dialog box. Your list may differ.*

**FIGURE 2-46**

*(continued)*

5. Double-click Welcome. If necessary, click View on the menu bar and then click Line Numbers to display line numbers in the coding window.

*The Java source code for the Welcome to My Day application is displayed in the coding window (Figure 2-47).*

TextPad window

```
TextPad - [A:\Chapter02\Welcome.java]
File   Edit   Search   View   Tools   Macros   Configure   Window   Help

Welcome.java
                      1   /*
                      2      Chapter 2:   Welcome to My Day
                      3      Programmer:  J. Starks
                      4      Date:        October 4, 2007
                      5      Filename:    Welcome.java
                      6      Purpose:     This project displays a welcome message, the user's
                      7                   name, and the system date in a console application.
                      8   */
                      9
                     10   import java.util.Date;
                     11
                     12   public class Welcome
                     13   {
                     14      public static void main(String[] args)
                     15      {
                     16         Date currentDate = new Date(); // Date constructor
                     17         System.out.println();
                     18         System.out.println("\t\t\tWelcome to my day!");
                     19         System.out.println("\t\t\tDaily planner for Linda Nunez");
                     20         System.out.println("\t\t\t" + currentDate);
                     21         System.out.println();
                     22      }
                     23   }
ANSI Characters
```

source code

coding window

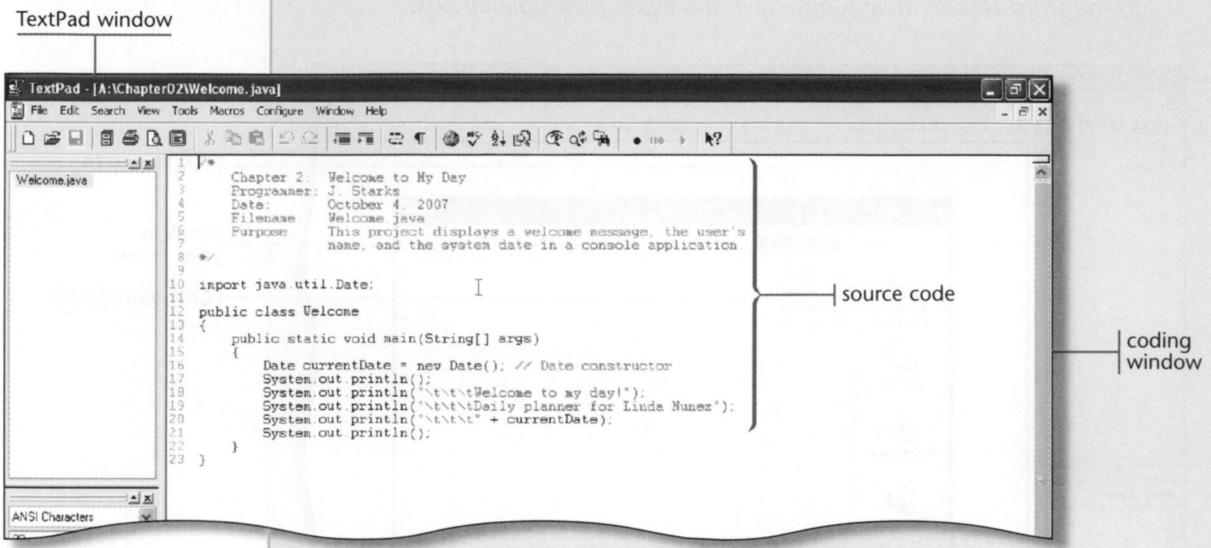

**FIGURE 2-47**

## Entering Code to Import Applet Packages

The first step in converting the Welcome to My Day application into an applet is to import two new class packages that Java will need to support the applet-related methods. The first package is the **applet package**, which allows applets to inherit certain attributes and manipulate classes. The second package is the **Abstract Window Toolkit** (**AWT**), which is a package included with the SDK to provide programs access to color, draw methods, and other GUI elements commonly used in applets.

As shown in lines 11 and 12 in Figure 2-48, two import statements are used to import the applet and AWT packages. Because Java will need to use multiple classes from the two packages, you will insert a period and then an asterisk (\*) at the end of the import statement. The asterisk is a wildcard symbol to tell the program to import all necessary classes from the java.awt and java.applet packages.

```
1   /*
2           Chapter 2:    Welcome to My Day
3           Programmer:   J. Starks
4           Date:         October 4, 2007
5           Filename:     WelcomeApplet.java
6           Purpose:      This project displays a welcome message, the user's
7                         name, the system date, and an image in an applet.
8   */
9
10  import java.util.Date;
11  import java.awt.*;
12  import java.applet.*;
13
14  public class WelcomeApplet extends Applet
15  {
16      public void paint(Graphics g)
17      {
18          Date currentDate = new Date(); // Date constructor
19          g.drawString("Welcome to my day!",200,70);
20          g.drawString("Daily planner for Linda Nunez",200,100);
21          g.drawString(currentDate.toString(),200,130);
22          Image smile; // declare an Image object
23          smile = getImage(getDocumentBase(),"Smile.gif");
24          g.drawImage(smile,10,10,this);
25          setBackground(Color.cyan);
26      }
27  }
```

FIGURE 2-48

Perform the following steps to code the import statements to support the applet.

## To Code Import Statements

1. With the Welcome.java file displayed in the TextPad coding window, click at the end of line 10 and then press the ENTER key.

2. Type lines 11 and 12, as shown in Figure 2-48.

   *The applet will import objects and classes from the applet and awt packages, as well as from the Date package.*

The remaining edits to the source code will incorporate methods and classes that Java uses from the applet and awt packages.

## Changing the Class Name and Extending the Applet Class

Because the purpose of this program now will be to run as an applet on the Web, it is important to change the class name and the file name. The class name is changed to WelcomeApplet in the class header. The file name, which is changed to WelcomeApplet.java, must be updated in the comment header and when the file is saved.

You also will extend the class, which means that this new Java class will be a type or subclass of applet. As shown in line 14 of Figure 2-48 on the previous page, the **extends command** is added to the class header, along with the name of the superclass. Recall that a superclass represents a broader, higher category of a class object, and shares a common structure and behavior with its subclasses. In the Welcome to My Day program, Applet is the superclass you will extend to create the subclass, WelcomeApplet. When a class extends from another class, it inherits attributes and methods from its superclass. The WelcomeApplet subclass will inherit general applet characteristics from the Applet class, such as the ability to run in a browser window.

Perform the following steps to edit the class name and extend the Applet class.

---

## To Edit the Class Name and Extend the Applet Class

1. In the TextPad coding window, click after the word, Welcome, in line 5. Without spacing, type Applet as shown in Figure 2-49.

   *TextPad displays the comment header with the new file name, WelcomeApplet.java, in line 5 (Figure 2-49).*

   new file name

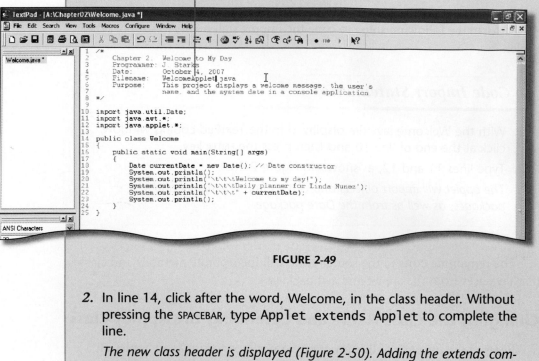

**FIGURE 2-49**

2. In line 14, click after the word, Welcome, in the class header. Without pressing the SPACEBAR, type Applet extends Applet to complete the line.

   *The new class header is displayed (Figure 2-50). Adding the extends command instructs the program to consider WelcomeApplet as a subclass of Applet. You also may change the purpose comment to better reflect the applet.*

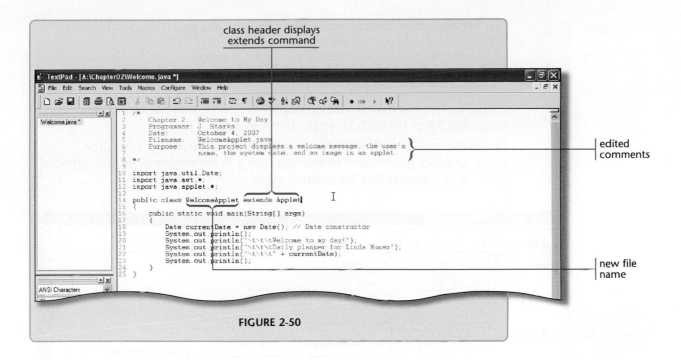

class header displays
extends command

edited
comments

new file
name

**FIGURE 2-50**

The relationship of the SDK to its packages, and the packages to their classes, is a perfect example of the superclass, class, and subclass hierarchy discussed in Chapter 1. In a later chapter, you will learn more about creating subclasses and instances of existing classes.

## The paint() Method

As you have learned, the main() method is the first method called when any stand-alone Java application is executed. With an applet, Java does not look for a main() method because Java does not execute the applet; the applet is executed from a browser or other calling program. Instead, the **init() method** loads the initial setup of the applet when execution begins. Because the code extends the Applet class, init() and all other applet methods are encapsulated in the Applet class, which means they happen automatically without any additional code being added to the program.

In the Welcome to My Day applet, you also will code a **paint() method** to graphically draw text and an image on the applet screen after the applet is initialized. The source code for the beginning of the paint() method is displayed in lines 16 through 21 in Figure 2-51. As shown in line 16, the paint() method accepts a Graphics parameter. It is common practice to identify the Graphics parameter as g, although any variable name can be used. The paint() method returns no value, so it is void.

```
16      public void paint(Graphics g)
17      {
18          Date currentDate = new Date(); // Date constructor
19          g.drawString("Welcome to my day!",200,70);
20          g.drawString("Daily planner for Linda Nunez",200,100);
21          g.drawString(currentDate.toString(),200,130);
```

**FIGURE 2-51**

Perform the following step to enter code for the paint() method header.

---

### To Code the paint() Method Header

*1.* Replace the main() method header in line 16 with the code shown in line 16 of Figure 2-51 on the previous page.

*The paint() method header is displayed in line 16 (Figure 2-52). The Graphics parameter is represented by a g in the parameter list; the keyword, void, indicates that the paint() method returns no return value.*

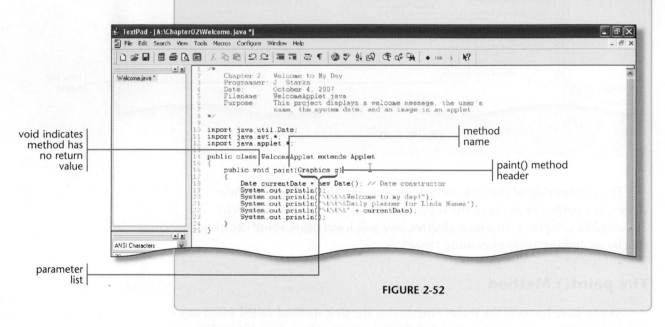

void indicates method has no return value

method name

paint() method header

parameter list

**FIGURE 2-52**

---

Some method arguments, like the one used with the println() method, contain data. Other methods, such as the paint() method, refer to a specific instance of an object. When a method refers to an instance of an object, such as Graphics g, the g is called a **reference variable**. Other methods that use a reference variable include those that draw shapes, set colors, and set fonts. You will learn more about reference variables in a later chapter.

## The drawString() Method

To instruct the program to display text output, the applet uses the drawString() method instead of println(). The **drawString() method**, which is taken from the awt package, draws text in the applet window. The drawString() method accepts three arguments: the String data to display, the horizontal (X-axis) position or coordinate at which to display the String, and the vertical (Y-axis) coordinate at which to display the String. As shown in lines 19 through 21 in Figure 2-51 on the previous page, the code for the drawString() method uses the identifier g from the method header, followed by a dot, followed by the method name. The three arguments are enclosed in parentheses, with each of the multiple arguments separated by commas.

**Setting Horizontal and Vertical Coordinates**
The horizontal and vertical coordinates required by the drawString() method are measured in pixels. A **pixel,** or picture element, is the basic unit of programmable color on a computer display or in a computer image. Think of a pixel as a dot of light; the dots grouped together form characters and images. The physical size of a pixel depends on the resolution of the computer screen. For instance, if your screen resolution is 800 by 600 pixels, a horizontal (X-axis) coordinate of 400 would display approximately halfway across the screen.

The drawString() method must use a String as its first argument. However, the system date object, currentDate, in line 21 is not a String. The **toString() method** can be used to convert currentDate to a String; the code takes the form of the variable currrentDate, followed by a period, followed by toString(). The code is inserted as the first argument of the drawString() method. The toString() method has no arguments in this applet.

Perform the following step to enter three drawString() methods.

## To Code the drawString() Methods

*1.* Replace lines 19, 20, and 21 in the TextPad coding window with the code shown in lines 19, 20, and 21 of Figure 2-51 on page 95. Delete the println() methods in lines 22 and 23. Leave line 22 blank.

*The drawString() methods replace the println() methods in lines 19 through 21 (Figure 2-53). The horizontal and vertical coordinates following each string of characters set the position of the output display and replace the horizontal tab escape characters.*

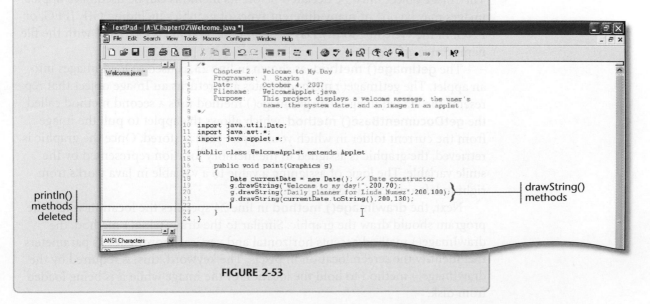

FIGURE 2-53

The drawString() methods instruct the program to display text output in the positions defined by the coordinate parameters. The toString() method in line 21 is an example of polymorphism. As you learned in Chapter 1, polymorphism allows a program to use the same command while obtaining different but somewhat predictable results, depending on the object that receives the command. The toString() method is polymorphic in that the same method name is used to refer to methods that handle many different data types, but the result is always a String conversion. You will learn more about data type conversions in the next chapter.

## Entering Code to Draw an Image and Set the Background Color

The final step in editing the source code is to insert the commands necessary to display a graphic in the applet and change the background color of the window. As shown in Figure 2-54, the edited source code will declare an Image object, use a method named getImage() to retrieve a graphic file from the disk, use the drawImage() method to draw the graphic in the applet window, and then use the setBackground() method to change the color of the window.

```
22          Image smile; // declare an Image object
23          smile = getImage(getDocumentBase(),"Smile.gif");
24          g.drawImage(smile,10,10,this);
25          setBackground(Color.cyan);
26      }
27  }
```

**FIGURE 2-54**

The **Image object** will have a variable name of smile, as declared in line 22. The Image object must be declared before its methods can be used. Java applet images may be one of many different types of graphics including GIF, JPEG, or PNG. In the Welcome to My Day program, the graphic is a GIF file with the file name Smile.gif.

The **getImage() method**, as shown in line 23, is used to load images into an applet. The getImage() method creates and returns an Image object that represents the loaded image. The getImage() method uses a second method called the **getDocumentBase() method**, which allows the applet to pull the image from the current folder in which your applet class is stored. Once the graphic is retrieved, the graphic is assigned to the memory location represented by the smile variable. The logic of assigning a value to a variable in Java works from right to left and uses an equal sign.

Next, the **drawImage() method** in line 24 specifies the location where the program should draw the graphic. Similar to the drawString() method, the drawImage() method accepts horizontal and vertical coordinates as parameters that identify the screen location in pixels. The keyword, this, is required by the drawImage() method to hold the location of the image while it is being loaded from disk.

Notice that the drawString() and drawImage() methods both have a g. in front of the methods. The g refers to the Graphics object that is drawn when the applet initializes. In Java, the period (.) after the g separates an object and its method, or an object and its attribute.

Finally, the **setBackground() method** in line 25 takes a Color object and its attribute, Color.cyan, to change the background color of the applet window. Common color words used by the setBackground() method display are show in Table 2-9.

### Table 2-9  Colors Used with the Color Object

| | |
|---|---|
| black | magenta |
| blue | orange |
| cyan | pink |
| darkGray | red |
| gray | white |
| green | yellow |
| lightGray | |

The setBackground() method does not start with the reference variable, g. The object in this case is understood to be the background of the applet window and does not have to be painted or drawn in a certain place, like the graphic. Other related methods, such as setForeground(), setFont(), and setSize(), also can be used to set characteristics of the applet window.

Perform the following step to enter code to declare, retrieve, and draw an image in the applet, as well as to set the background color to cyan.

### To Enter Code to Draw an Image and Set the Background Color

1. With the insertion point in line 22, type lines 22 through 25, as shown in Figure 2-54.

   *The edited code is displayed (Figure 2-55).*

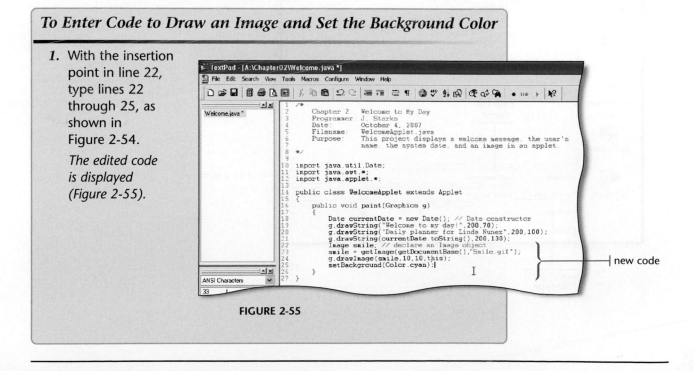

FIGURE 2-55

The source code for the applet now is complete. Lines 22 through 25 of the code declare an Image object and use the getImage() method to retrieve the Smile.gif image file from disk. The drawImage() method then draws the graphic in the applet window. Finally, the setBackground() method changes the background color of the window to cyan.

## Saving a Source Code File with a New Name

Once the editing to convert the application to an applet is complete, the file should be saved with a file name that matches the class name, WelcomeApplet, as shown in the following steps.

### To Save the Source Code File with a New File Name

OTHER WAYS

1. Press ALT+F, A
2. Press F12

*1.* If necessary, insert the Data Disk in drive A. With the TextPad coding window open, click File on the menu bar and then click Save As on the Tools menu.

*2.* Type WelcomeApplet in the File name text box. Do not press the ENTER key. If necessary, click the Save as type box arrow and then click Java (*.java) in the list. If necessary, click the Save in box arrow, click 3½ Floppy (A:) in the list, and then double-click the Chapter02 folder.

*The file name, WelcomeApplet, is displayed in the File name text box (Figure 2-56). Java (*.java) is displayed in the Save as type box. Chapter02 is displayed in the Save in box.*

*3.* Click the Save button in the Save As dialog box.

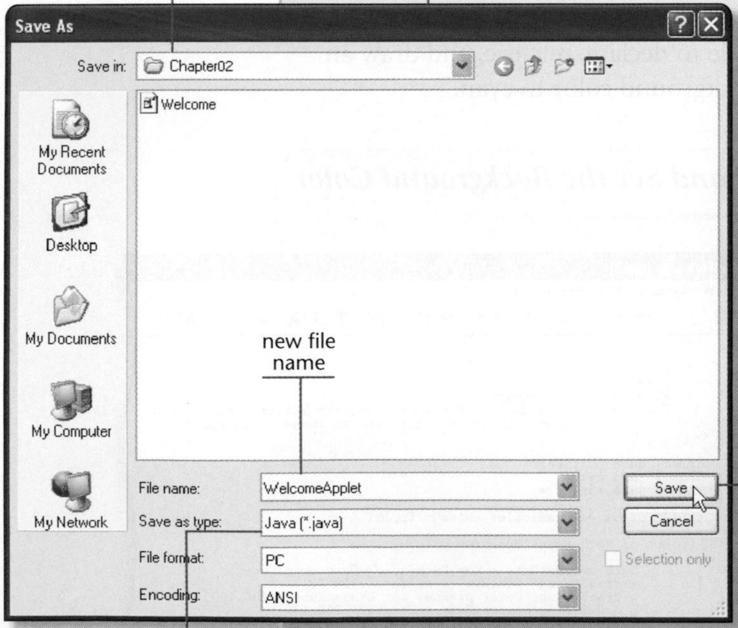

Chapter02 is current folder

Save As dialog box

new file name

Java (*.java) file type

Save button

**FIGURE 2-56**

### Compiling the Applet

When you compile the applet, the compiler looks for the image file in the same directory as the source code file. The image file, Smile.gif, is included in the Chapter02 folder of the Data Disk that accompanies this book. See the preface for instructions on downloading the Data Disk, or see your instructor for a copy of the graphic. The following steps assume that the Smile.gif file is located in the Chapter02 folder on the Data Disk in drive A.

Perform the following steps to compile the applet.

---

*To Compile the Applet*

1. With the Data Disk in drive A, click Tools on the menu bar. Click Compile Java on the Tools menu.
2. If any error messages display in the Command Results window, click WelcomeApplet.java in the Selector window, fix the errors, and then repeat Step 1.

*TextPad compiles the applet.*

---

**OTHER WAYS**

1. Press CTRL+1
2. At command prompt, type javac
   `WelcomeApplet.java`

---

As when the Java application was compiled, possible errors that will be generated while compiling the applet include an incorrect location for the Java compiler, typing mistakes, omitting special characters, case-sensitive errors, and file name errors. If you cannot determine and fix a coding error based on the error messages and the information about errors on pages 74 through 77, consult your instructor.

## Creating an HTML Host Document

Because an applet is initiated and executed from within another language or run as part of a Web page, you must identify a **host**, or reference program, to execute the applet. The applet for this chapter is run as part of a Web page created in HTML.

As you learned in Chapter 1, Hypertext Markup Language (HTML) is a set of special codes called tags that specify how the text and other elements of a Web page display. Unlike a programming language such as Java, HTML mainly is used to display information; it is not suited to support user interaction to accept input and generate output. A Java applet is thus ideal for adding that interactivity and functionality to a Web page.

An extensive understanding of HTML is not needed to build an HTML host document for an applet. A few simple HTML tags to tell the browser where to find and execute the applet file are all that are necessary to create a host for a Java applet.

### Coding an HTML Host Document

In HTML, a **tag**, or markup, is a code specifying how Web page content should display or link to other documents. Each tag actually has two elements: a **start tag**, which is enclosed in angle brackets < >, and an **end tag**, which uses a forward slash and also is enclosed in angle brackets. The tags enclose content or other HTML code to define a section of content or apply a color, style, or other format.

The tag at the beginning and end of the source code for a typical Web page is an example of an HTML tag. At the beginning of the HTML code for a Web page, programmers insert the start tag <HTML>. In order to end the code, programmers need to insert the end tag </HTML>. Figure 2-57 displays the code for the HTML host document for the WelcomeApplet.

```
1  <HTML>
2  <APPLET CODE = "WelcomeApplet.class" WIDTH = "400" HEIGHT = "200">
3  </APPLET>
4  </HTML>
```

FIGURE 2-57

When an HTML host document is loaded in the browser, the Java applet is sent to the browser as a separate file. A special HTML tag, <APPLET>… </APPLET> tells the browser the name of the applet file. In the following series of steps, you will create a simple HTML file to serve as the host document for the applet named WelcomeApplet.

---

## To Code an HTML Host Document

*1.* With the TextPad coding window open, click File on the menu bar. *The File menu is displayed (Figure 2-58).*

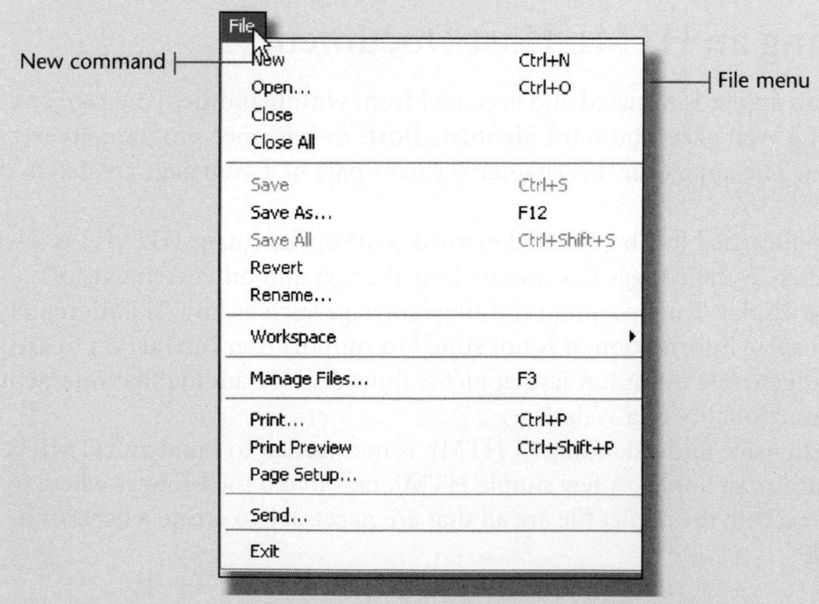

FIGURE 2-58

2. Click New on the File menu. When the new coding window is displayed, if necessary, click View on the menu bar and then click Line Numbers. Click File on the menu bar and then click Save As on the File menu. When the Save As dialog box is displayed, type `WelcomeApplet` in the File name text box. Do not press the ENTER key. Click the Save as type box arrow and then click HTML (*.htm*,*.stm*) in the list. If necessary, click the Save in box arrow, click 3½ Floppy (A:) in the list, and then double-click the Chapter02 folder in the list.

*HTML (*.htm*,*.stm*) displays as the file type (Figure 2-59). The file, Welcome Applet.html, will be saved in the Chapter02 folder on the Data Disk in drive A. Your file name extension may be .htm.*

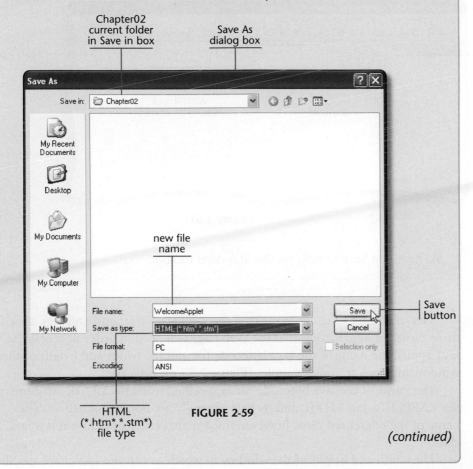

Chapter02
current folder
in Save in box

Save As
dialog box

new file
name

Save
button

HTML
(*.htm*,*.stm*)
file type

**FIGURE 2-59**

*(continued)*

3. Click the Save button in the Save As dialog box.

*TextPad saves the file on the Data Disk in drive A. The file name is displayed in the title bar of the TextPad window.*

4. In the TextPad coding window, type the HTML code as shown in Figure 2-57 on page 102.

*The code for the HTML host document is displayed in the TextPad coding window (Figure 2-60).*

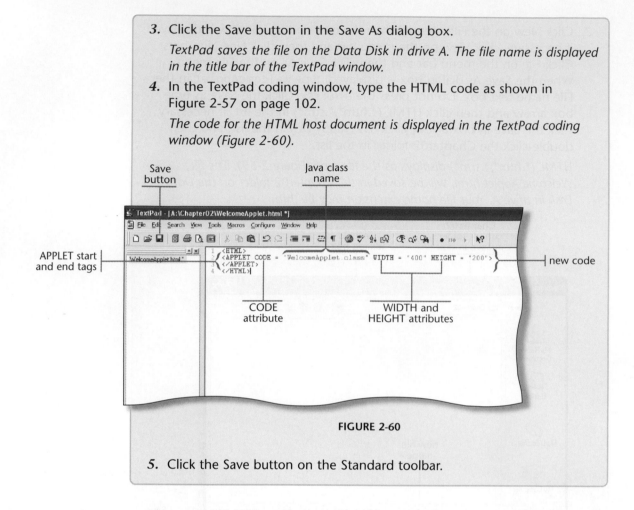

**FIGURE 2-60**

5. Click the Save button on the Standard toolbar.

The <APPLET> tag, nested within the <HTML> start and end tags, specifies three pieces of information that the Web page will need in order to access the Java applet: the name of the Java bytecode file and the width and height of the window in which to run the applet (Figure 2-57 on page 102).

The name of the Java bytecode file is specified using the CODE attribute of the <APPLET> tag. HTML and its tags generally are not case-sensitive. The name of the referenced class, however, must match exactly because it is a Java class.

The width and height of the window in which to run the applet are specified using the WIDTH and HEIGHT attributes of the <APPLET> tag. The values specified for the width and height are measured in pixels.

## Running an Applet

As you have learned, an applet is run by first running the HTML host document. TextPad includes a Run Java Applet command, which opens the HTML host document and executes Java's appletviewer.exe command to display the Applet Viewer window. If you are compiling and running the Java applet from the command prompt, you type appletviewer, followed by the name of the host document.

Applet Viewer provides advantages over a browser for viewing an applet. First, Applet Viewer ignores any HTML that is not immediately relevant to launching an applet. If the HTML host document does not include a correct reference to an applet or similar object, Applet Viewer does nothing. Additionally, Applet Viewer does not have to be Java-enabled, as do some browsers, in order to correctly display the applet. Finally, Applet Viewer uses less memory than does a browser, which makes it a good tool to test that the applet's code works properly before attaching the applet to a Web page.

The following steps show how to run an applet using TextPad.

## To Run an Applet

1. **Click Tools on the TextPad menu bar.**
   *The Tools menu is displayed (Figure 2-61).*

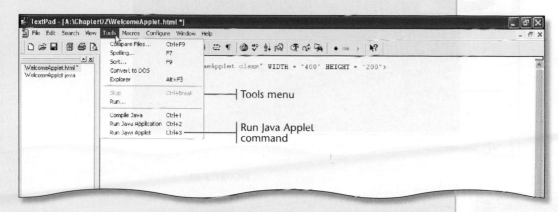

**FIGURE 2-61**

2. **Click Run Java Applet on the Tools menu. If necessary, click the drop-down box arrow and click WelcomeApplet.html in the list.**
   *The Choose File dialog box is displayed (Figure 2-62).*

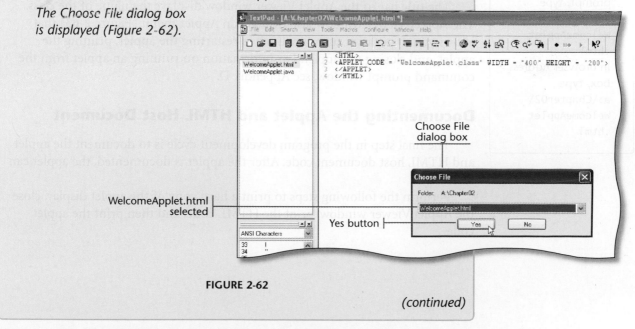

**FIGURE 2-62**

*(continued)*

**3.** Click the Yes button.

*After a few seconds, the applet is displayed in the Applet Viewer window, 400 pixels wide and 200 pixels tall, as defined in the HTML code (Figure 2-63).*

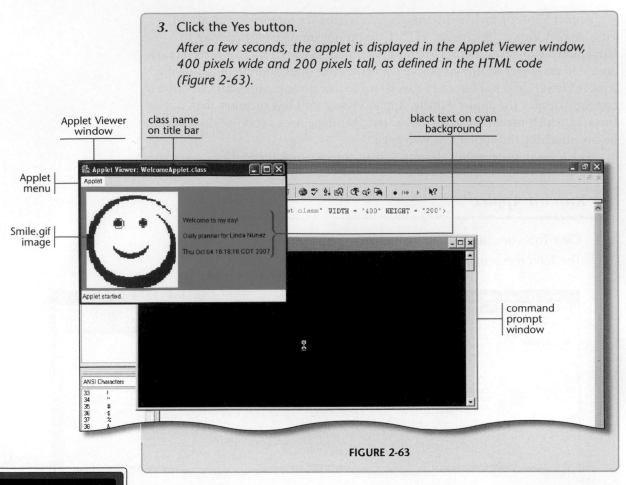

FIGURE 2-63

**OTHER WAYS**

1. Press CTRL+3, click Yes
2. At command prompt, type appletviewer WelcomeApplet .html
3. In browser Address box, type a:\Chapter02\ WelcomeApplet .html

When the applet is displayed in the Applet Viewer window, the Smile.gif image displays to the left, and black text on a cyan background displays to the right. The command prompt window is displayed in the background.

The title bar of the Applet Viewer window displays the name of the class. The Applet Viewer window also displays an Applet menu (Figure 2-63) that allows you to perform such functions as restarting the applet, printing the applet, and closing the applet. For information on running an applet from the command prompt window, see Appendix D.

## Documenting the Applet and HTML Host Document

The final step in the program development cycle is to document the applet and HTML host document code. After the applet is documented, the applet can be closed.

Perform the following steps to print a hard copy of the applet display, close the Applet Viewer window, print the HTML code, and then print the applet code.

## To Document the Applet and HTML Host Document

**1.** Ready the printer according to the printer instructions. Click Applet on the Applet Viewer menu bar.

*The Applet menu is displayed (Figure 2-64).*

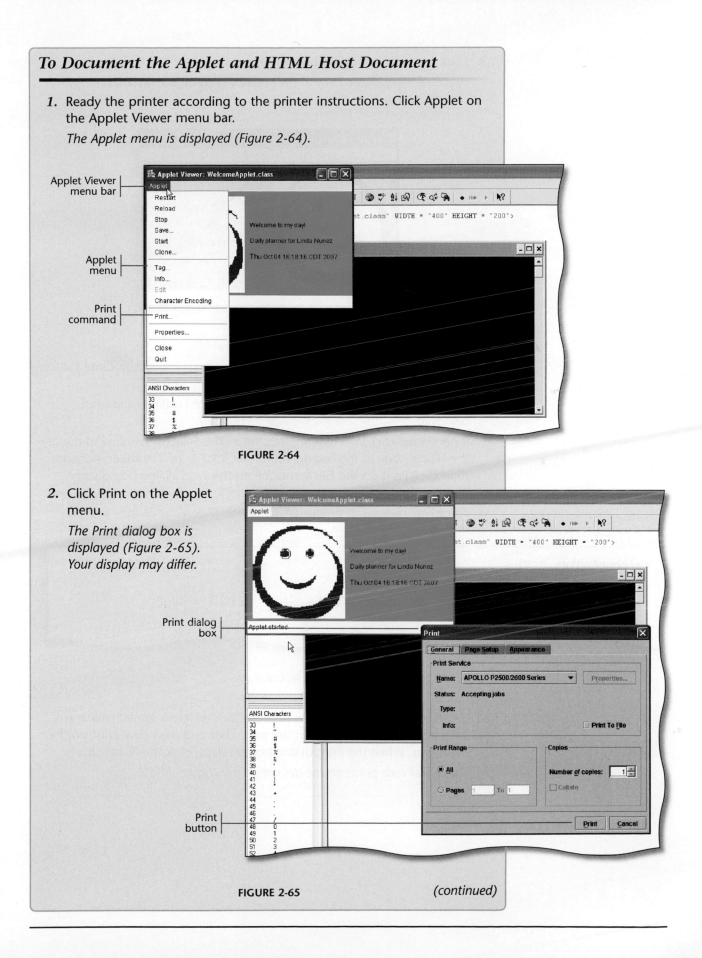

**FIGURE 2-64**

**2.** Click Print on the Applet menu.

*The Print dialog box is displayed (Figure 2-65). Your display may differ.*

**FIGURE 2-65**

*(continued)*

3. Click the Print button in the Print dialog box.

*Applet Viewer prints a copy of the applet display on the default printer (Figure 2-66).*

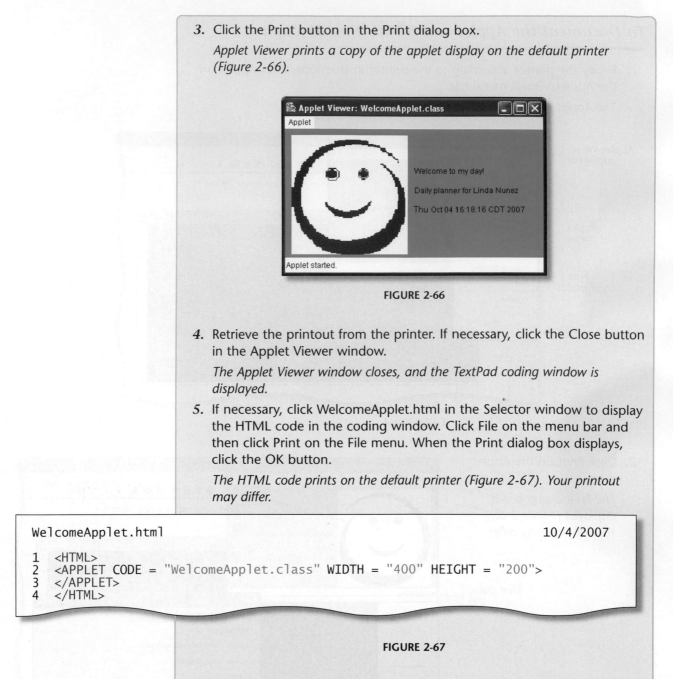

FIGURE 2-66

4. Retrieve the printout from the printer. If necessary, click the Close button in the Applet Viewer window.

*The Applet Viewer window closes, and the TextPad coding window is displayed.*

5. If necessary, click WelcomeApplet.html in the Selector window to display the HTML code in the coding window. Click File on the menu bar and then click Print on the File menu. When the Print dialog box displays, click the OK button.

*The HTML code prints on the default printer (Figure 2-67). Your printout may differ.*

```
WelcomeApplet.html                                              10/4/2007

1  <HTML>
2  <APPLET CODE = "WelcomeApplet.class" WIDTH = "400" HEIGHT = "200">
3  </APPLET>
4  </HTML>
```

FIGURE 2-67

6. Retrieve the printout from the printer. Click WelcomeApplet.java in the Selector window. Click File on the menu bar and then click Print on the File menu. When the Print dialog box displays, click the Print button.

*The applet code prints on the default printer (Figure 2-68).*

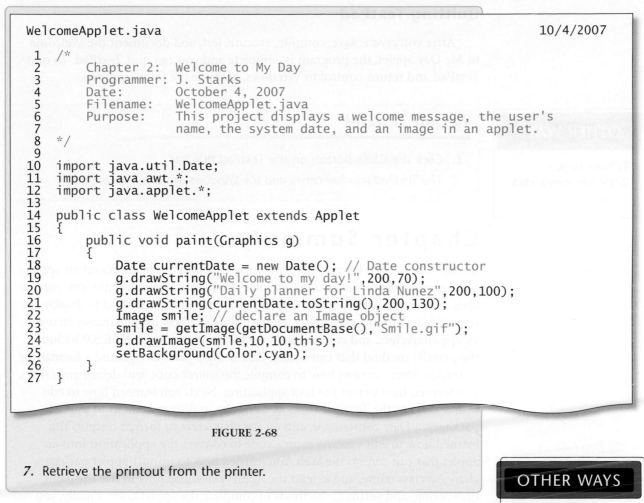

```
WelcomeApplet.java                                                    10/4/2007
 1  /*
 2        Chapter 2:   Welcome to My Day
 3        Programmer:  J. Starks
 4        Date:        October 4, 2007
 5        Filename:    WelcomeApplet.java
 6        Purpose:     This project displays a welcome message, the user's
 7                     name, the system date, and an image in an applet.
 8  */
 9
10  import java.util.Date;
11  import java.awt.*;
12  import java.applet.*;
13
14  public class WelcomeApplet extends Applet
15  {
16      public void paint(Graphics g)
17      {
18          Date currentDate = new Date(); // Date constructor
19          g.drawString("Welcome to my day!",200,70);
20          g.drawString("Daily planner for Linda Nunez",200,100);
21          g.drawString(currentDate.toString(),200,130);
22          Image smile; // declare an Image object
23          smile = getImage(getDocumentBase(),"Smile.gif");
24          g.drawImage(smile,10,10,this);
25          setBackground(Color.cyan);
26      }
27  }
```

FIGURE 2-68

7. Retrieve the printout from the printer.

OTHER WAYS

1. On Standard toolbar, click Print button
2. Press CTRL+P, click OK button

## Tip

### Text Pad Settings

In TextPad version 4.7 and above, current line highlighting may be enabled to delineate the line of code containing the insertion point. The highlight is not the same as a selection highlight. Rather, it is a slight shadow behind the text to assist programmers in following the line of code across the screen. This new feature may be turned on or off in the Preferences dialog box, as discussed in Appendix C.

### Quitting TextPad

After you create, save, compile, execute, test, and document the Welcome to My Day applet, the program is complete and you can quit TextPad. To quit TextPad and return control to Windows, perform the following step.

---

**OTHER WAYS**

1. Press ALT+F, X
2. On File menu, click Exit

---

### To Quit TextPad

*1.* Click the Close button on the TextPad title bar.
*The TextPad window closes and the Windows desktop is displayed.*

---

# Chapter Summary

In this chapter, you learned the basic form of a Java application and an applet. You learned how to use TextPad to enter comments as documentation, enter a class header and a method header, and use the println() method to display output in a console application. The println() method uses character strings, escape characters, and concatenated data to format output. J2SE 5.0 includes the printf() method that can embed data using a percent sign and a formatting character. After learning how to compile the source code and debug any errors, you learned how to run the Java application. Next, you learned how to edit source code in the TextPad window using the import statement to import packages, a Date constructor, and escape characters to format output. You learned how to edit existing source code to convert the application into an applet that can run on the Web. You learned how to import applet packages, change a class name, and extend the Applet class, and how to use the paint, drawString, and getImage methods to complete the applet code. Finally, you created an HTML host document to display the applet and run it using Applet Viewer.

# What You Should Know

Having completed this chapter, you should now be able to perform the tasks shown in Table 2-10.

**Table 2-10   Chapter 2 What You Should Know**

| TASK NUMBER | TASK | PAGE |
|---|---|---|
| 1 | Start TextPad | 53 |
| 2 | Display Line Numbers in the TextPad Window | 55 |
| 3 | Save a TextPad Document | 57 |
| 4 | Code Comments | 63 |
| 5 | Code the Class Header | 66 |
| 6 | Code the Method Header | 69 |
| 7 | Enter Code to Display Output and Save the Program File | 71 |
| 8 | Compile Source Code | 73 |
| 9 | Run the Application | 78 |
| 10 | Code the Import Statement | 81 |
| 11 | Code a Call to a System Date Constructor | 83 |
| 12 | Code Escape Characters to Format Output | 84 |
| 13 | Enter Code to Concatenate String Data | 86 |
| 14 | Recompile and Run the Application | 87 |
| 15 | Print the Source Code | 88 |
| 16 | Quit TextPad | 89 |
| 17 | Start TextPad and Open an Existing File | 90 |
| 18 | Code Import Statements | 93 |
| 19 | Edit the Class Name and Extend the Applet Class | 94 |
| 20 | Code the paint() Method Header | 96 |
| 21 | Code the drawString() Methods | 97 |
| 22 | Enter Code to Draw an Image and Set the Background Color | 99 |
| 23 | Save the Source Code File with a New File Name | 100 |
| 24 | Compile the Applet | 101 |
| 25 | Code an HTML Host Document | 102 |
| 26 | Run an Applet | 105 |
| 27 | Document the Applet and HTML Host Document | 107 |
| 28 | Quit TextPad | 110 |

# Key Terms

Abstract Window Toolkit (AWT) *(92)*
access modifier *(64)*
applet package *(92)*
argument *(68)*
block comment *(61)*
body *(68)*
braces { } *(66)*
case-sensitive *(66)*
class definition *(70)*
class header *(64)*
Clip Library window *(55)*
coding window *(54)*
Command Results window *(75)*
comment header *(61)*
comments *(61)*
concatenate *(86)*
constructor *(82)*
data type *(68)*
Date class *(82)*
debugging *(74)*
declare *(82)*
default *(50)*
deprecated *(82)*
doc comment *(62)*
drawImage() method *(98)*
drawString() method *(96)*
edit *(79)*
end tag *(101)*
escape characters *(84)*
exception *(77)*
extends *(70)*
extends command *(94)*
getDocumentBase() method *(98)*
getImage() method *(9)*
hard copy *(87)*
host *(101)*
identifier *(68)*
Image object *(98)*
import statement *(81)*

init() method *(95)*
keywords *(64)*
line comment *(62)*
line numbers *(55)*
literal *(71)*
logic error *(77)*
main() method *(67)*
method header *(67)*
method modifier *(67)*
out *(70)*
paint() method *(95)*
parameter *(68)*
pixel *(97)*
printf() method *(86)*
println() method *(70)*
printout *(87)*
prototype *(48)*
public *(64)*
reference variable *(96)*
reserved words *(64)*
return value *(68)*
run-time error *(77)*
Selector window *(55)*
semantic error *(76)*
setBackground() method *(99)*
splash screen *(46)*
start tag *(101)*
static *(68)*
String[] *(68)*
syntax error *(75)*
System class *(70)*
system date *(48)*
system error *(74)*
tab characters *(63)*
tag *(101)*
TextPad *(52)*
toString() method *(97)*
user interface *(46)*
variable *(68)*
void *(68)*

# Homework Assignments

## Label the Figure

Identify the elements shown in Figure 2-69.

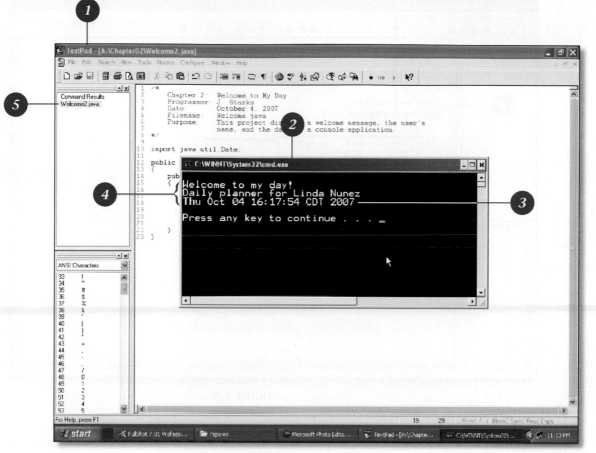

**FIGURE 2-69**

1. _____     4. _____

2. _____     5. _____

3. _____

## Identify Code

Identify the code elements shown in Figure 2-70.

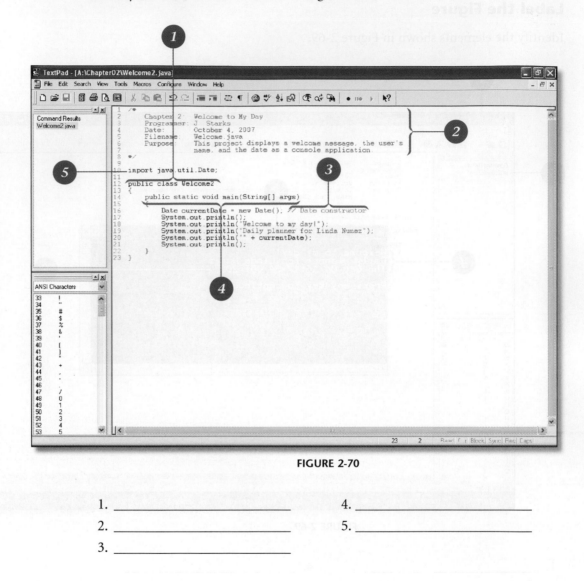

**FIGURE 2-70**

1. _____          4. _____

2. _____          5. _____

3. _____

## Understanding Error Messages

Figure 2-71a displays a Java program that prints a student's name and address on the screen. Figure 2-71b displays the compilation error messages. Use TextPad or a text-editing software to rewrite the code and correct the errors. Print a hard copy of your program.

(a)

(b)

**FIGURE 2-71**

## Using the Java API

The Java API is a good tool to look up information about a class with which you may be unfamiliar or to check the syntax of commands and methods you wish to use in your programs. While connected to the Internet, open a browser, type `http://java.sun.com/j2se/1.5.0/docs/api/` in the Address window, and then press the ENTER key to view the Java API Specification on the Sun Web site. The Java API is organized by packages, hierarchically, but many programmers click the Index link located at the top of the page to display the entire list alphabetically.

With the Java API Specification open in the browser window, perform the following steps.

1. Use the scroll down arrow in the top left frame of the Web page to display the java.lang link. Click the java.lang link.

2. When the Package java.lang page is displayed, scroll down to display the Class Summary table. Click the System link in the left column of the table.

3. When the Class System page is displayed, scroll down to display the Field Summary table and click the out link in the right column.

4. When the out definition is displayed (Figure 2-72), select the definition by dragging through it. Click File on the menu bar and then click Print. When the Print dialog box is displayed, click the Selection option button and then click the Print button in the Print dialog box to print the definition.

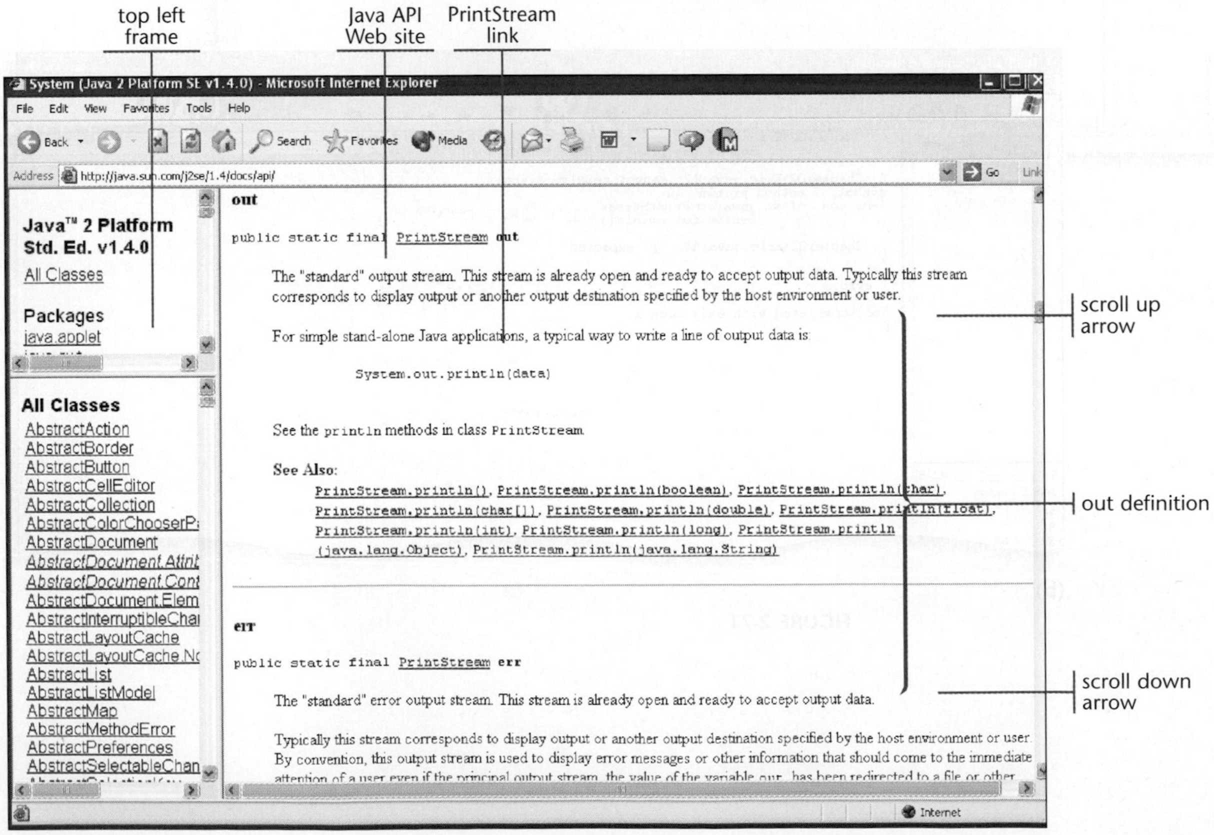

**FIGURE 2-72**

5. Click the PrintStream link. When the Class PrintStream page is displayed, scroll to the Method Summary table. Choose any five methods and then click the links and read their descriptions. Make a list of the five methods, their return values, and their argument data types.

6. Write a paragraph explaining why you think some of the methods are listed more than once in the Method Summary table.

## Short Answer

1. The keyword public is an example of a(n) _____.

2. In Java, every line of code, other than headers and braces, must end with a(n) _____.

3. Line comments begin with _____; block comments begin with _____ and end with _____.

4. _____ is/are collections of classes, sometimes called libraries, which contain portable Java bytecode files.

5. A misspelled method most likely would result in a(n) _____ error.

6. The _____ command is placed at the beginning of Java source code to load the appropriate class package.

7. When you extend the Applet class, you are creating a(n) _____ of the Applet class.

8. The _____ is a current date and time generated by the operating system of a computer.

9. The println() method takes a String _____ in parentheses.

10. The keyword void means the method returns _____.

11. Java looks for the _____ as the usual starting point for all stand-alone applications.

12. A(n) _____, which is easily identified by the = new notation, both declares the type of data or object to be stored and assigns it a variable name in the computer's memory.

13. Describe the difference between the println() and drawString() methods.

14. Describe the code differences between applications and applets.

15. Describe the execution differences between applications and applets.

16. Explain why a Date object cannot be used with the drawString() method.

17. List the three-step process to save, compile, and execute a program.

18. Explain why an HTML host document is needed along with an applet.

19. Write a line of code to declare and construct a Date object named curDate.

20. Write a line of code to assign an image from the current folder to the variable name grandma.

21. Write a line of code that will change an applet's background color to red.

22. Write a line of code to print each of the following in the command prompt window:
   a. your name
   b. a previously declared String named lastName

*(continued)*

**Short Answer** *(continued)*

c. a blank line

d. the name of your instructor tabbed 24 characters to the right

23. Write a line of code to print each of the following in an applet. The numbers represent pixel locations.

a. your name (100, 75)

b. a previously declared and assigned image named grandma (50, 50)

c. a previously declared Date named myDate (200, 300)

d. a previously declared String named firstName (150, 250)

24. Give an example of three valid class names and three invalid class names.

25. Write a line of code that uses the printf() method to display a previously declared String named myName.

## Learn It Online

Start your browser and visit scsite.com/java3e/learn. Follow the instructions in the exercises below.

1. **Chapter Reinforcement TF, MC, and SA**    Click the Chapter Reinforcement link below Chapter 2. Print and then answer the questions.

2. **Practice Test**    Click the Practice Test link below Chapter 2. Answer each question, enter your first and last name at the bottom of the page, and then click the Grade Test button. When the graded practice test is displayed on your screen, click Print on the File menu to print a hard copy. Continue to take practice tests until you score 80% or better. Hand in a printout of the final practice test.

3. **Crossword Puzzle Challenge**    Click the Crossword Puzzle Challenge link below Chapter 2. Read the instructions, and then enter your first and last name. Click the Play button. Complete the crossword puzzle. When you are finished, click the Submit button. When the crossword puzzle is displayed, click the Print button.

4. **Tips and Tricks**    Click the Tips and Tricks link below Chapter 2. Click a topic that pertains to Chapter 2. Right-click the information and then click Print on the shortcut menu. Construct a brief example of what the information relates to in Java to confirm that you understand how to use the tip or trick. Hand in the example and printed information.

5. **Newsgroups**    Click the Newsgroups link below Chapter 2. Click a topic that pertains to Chapter 2. Print three comments.

6. **Expanding Your Horizons**    Click the Expanding Your Horizons link below Chapter 2. Click a topic that pertains to Chapter 2. Print the information. Construct a brief example of what the information relates to in Java to confirm you that you understand the contents of the article. Hand in the example and printed information.

7. **Search Sleuth**    Select three key terms from the Key Terms section of this chapter and then use the Google search engine at google.com (or any major search engine) to display and print two Web pages for each key term.

# Debugging Assignment

Start TextPad and open the file Runyon.java from the Chapter02 folder on the Data Disk. See the preface of this book for instructions for downloading the Data Disk or see your instructor for information about accessing the files required in this book.

The Runyon program is a Java application that displays a splash screen for the Runyon Company, listing its name, address, and Web site address. The desired output is shown in Figure 2-73.

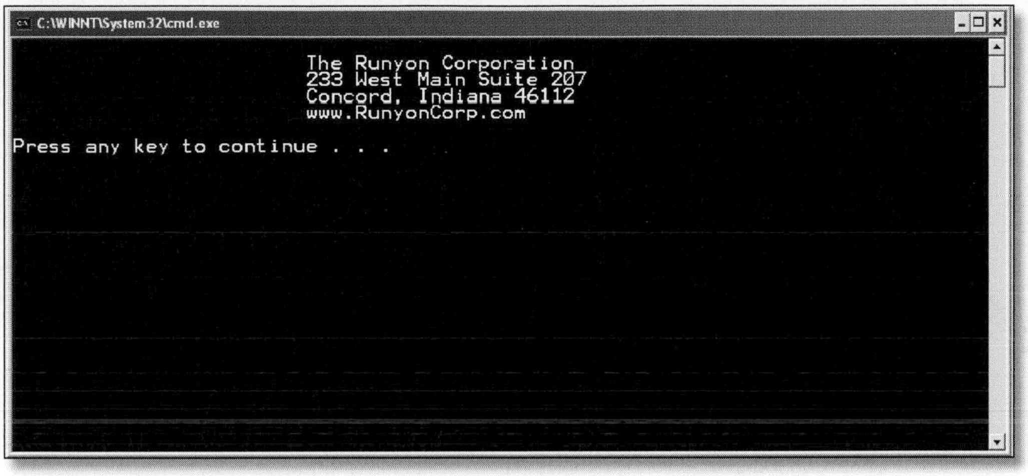

```
C:\WINNT\System32\cmd.exe

                    The Runyon Corporation
                    233 West Main Suite 207
                    Concord, Indiana 46112
                    www.RunyonCorp.com
Press any key to continue . . .
```

**FIGURE 2-73**

The Runyon program has several syntax, semantic, and logic errors in the program code. Perform the following steps to debug the program.

1. Open the file Runyon.java in TextPad.
2. Read through the code and fix any errors that you see. Insert your name as the programmer in the comment header. Insert the current date.
3. Save the program.
4. Compile the program. As TextPad displays compilation errors, fix the first error, then recompile.
5. When you have fixed all the syntax and semantic errors so that the program will compile without errors, run the program and look for run-time and logic errors. Fix any errors and compile again.
6. When the program compiles and runs to produce the output as shown in Figure 2-73, print a copy of the source code.

# Programming Assignments

## 1 Writing Java Code from a Flowchart

Start TextPad. Open the file Book.java from the Data Disk. See the preface of this book for instructions for downloading the Data Disk or see your instructor for information about accessing the files required in this book. Using the techniques you learned in this chapter, write the lines of code inside the main() method to print the bibliographic entry as outlined by the flowchart in Figure 2-74.

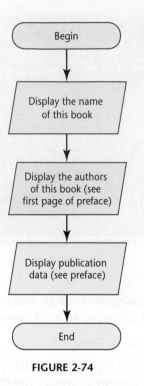

**FIGURE 2-74**

1. With the Book.java source code displayed in the TextPad coding window, locate the access modifier and class name, Book. Change the class name to Biblio. Change the name to Biblio in the comment header, and enter your name as the programmer.

2. Click inside the main() method braces.

3. After studying the flowchart in Figure 2-74, enter the lines of code necessary to produce the output.

4. Save the file on the Data Disk with the name Biblio. Make sure you choose Java (*.java) in the Save as type box.

5. Compile the program. If errors occur, fix them in the TextPad coding window and compile again.

6. Run the program. If the program runs correctly, return to TextPad and print a copy of the source code. Otherwise, return to Step 3 and correct the errors until the program runs error-free.

## 2 Analysis and Design

Figure 2-75 shows a requirements document for a new application, as requested by a small business owner. Using the six phases of the development cycle as shown in Table 2-1 on page 48, perform the following steps.

**REQUEST FOR NEW APPLICATION**

| Date submitted: | September 10, 2007 |
|---|---|
| Submitted by: | Donna Van Krimpen |
| Purpose: | Our small business would like to start thinking about adding e-commerce to our current Web site. As a first step, we need a small window that would open from our current home page. The window would display "coming soon" information as detailed below. |
| Application title: | Donna's Dutch Doilies |
| Algorithms: | A three line message will display. |
| Notes: | 1) We would like the following information to display in an applet:<br><br>Coming soon…<br>Order doilies online at<br>www.DonnasDutchDoilies.com<br><br>2) We would like black letters on a yellow background.<br><br>3) If possible, have the applet display in a perfect square.<br><br>4) The text should be centered as closely as possible.<br><br>5) No graphic is necessary. |

**Approvals**

| Approval status: | X | Approved |
|---|---|---|
| | | Rejected |
| Approved by: | | Doug McMann, programmer<br>We Can Do That on the Web<br>A Web Site Consulting Firm |
| Date: | | September 14, 2007 |
| Assigned to: | | |

**FIGURE 2-75**

1. Analyze the requirements. Read the requirements document carefully. Think about the requester, the users, the problem, and the purpose of the application.
2. Design the solution. Draw a storyboard for the applet. Pay careful attention to the size and spacing request. Write either pseudocode or draw a flowchart to represent the sequence of events in your program.

*(continued)*

**2 Analysis and Design** *(continued)*

3. Validate the design. Have a classmate or your instructor look over your storyboard and make suggestions before you proceed.

4. Implement the design. Translate the design into code for the applet. Create an HTML document to host the applet.

5. Test the solution. Test the program, finding and correcting errors (debugging) until it is error-free.

6. Document the solution. Print a copy of the source code, the HTML code, and a copy of the applet interface.

7. Hand in all documents to your instructor.

## 3 Coding Your Own Splash Screen

In order to practice writing, compiling, and running Java, you decide to create a Java application that displays your name and address on the screen. Perform the following steps.

1. Start TextPad. Save the file on the Data Disk with your first name as the file name. Make sure you choose Java (*.java) in the Save as type box. Click the Save in box arrow to save the file on drive A in the folder named Chapter02.

2. Type the block comments to include your name, the date, the program's name, the course number, and the program's purpose. Press the TAB key as needed to align the comments. Remember to use /* to begin the block comment and */ to end it.

3. Type the class header. Use your first name as the name of the class. Do not forget to enter the keywords, public and class, before your name. On the next line, type an opening brace.

4. Type the main() method header, using the keywords public, static, and void. The main() method takes a String[] parameter named args. As you type, remember that Java is case-sensitive. On the next line, type an opening brace.

5. Type three lines that begin System.out.println(" and then include your name, address and city each on a separate line. Do not forget to close the quotation mark and parentheses. Place a semicolon at the end of each line.

6. Type a closing brace for the main() method.

7. Type a closing brace for the class.

8. Compile the program by clicking Compile Java on the TextPad Tools menu. If necessary, fix any errors in the coding window and then compile the program again.

9. Once the program compiles correctly, run the program by clicking Run Java Application on the TextPad Tools menu. After viewing your output, click the Close button in the command prompt window title bar.

10. In the TextPad window, use the Print command on the File menu to print a copy of the source code.

11. Close the TextPad window.

## 4 Converting an Application to an Applet

After completing the splash screen in Programming Assignment 3, you decide to convert the application into an applet. Perform the following steps.

1. Change the file and class name to SplashApplet every time it displays in the code.
2. Add the words, extends Applet, to the class header.
3. Change the main() method header to a paint() method header.
4. Change each println() method to a drawString() method. Remember to reference the Graphics object (g) as you did on pages 96 and 97.
5. Save the program with the new file name, SplashApplet.
6. Compile the program. If there are errors, fix them in the SplashApplet coding window and then compile again.
7. Create an HTML host document that calls the SplashApplet class. Set the attributes of the applet to have a width of 400 and a height of 300 when it displays in the Applet Viewer window.
8. Run the program.
9. Print a copy of the applet interface by using the Applet menu in the Applet Viewer window. Using TextPad, print a copy of the source code for the Java applet and the HTML code for the host document.
10. For extra credit, edit the program to include a system date.

## 5 Formatting Output Using Escape Characters

Computer applications typically display a splash screen for users to view while waiting for the entire application to load. The Computer Science department at Middle Illinois College wants to display a splash screen with the school's initials, MIC, as each application loads. The display should use text characters to make large versions of the letters M, I, and C, as shown in Figure 2-76.

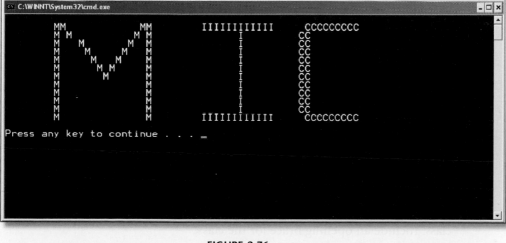

**FIGURE 2-76**

*(continued)*

**5 Formatting Output Using Escape Characters** (continued)

1. Start TextPad.

2. Save the program as Java source code with the file name MIC on your Data Disk.

3. Type block comments to include your name, the date, the program's name, the course number, and the program's purpose. Press the TAB key as needed to align the comments. Remember to use /* to begin the block comment and */ to end it.

4. Enter the code from Figure 2-77 in the TextPad window, using the escape code sequence \t as indicated. *Hint:* Eleven spaces separate the Ms in line 5; each successive line has 2 less spaces.

```
 1   public  class  MIC
 2   {
 3       public  static  void  main( String  []  args )
 4       {
 5           System.out.println ("\tMM            MM\tIIIIIIIIIIIII\t        CCCCCCCC);
 6           System.out.println ("\tM  M          M M\t      I          \tCC" );
 7           System.out.println ("\tM  M          M M\t      I          \tCC" );
 8       //Add new code here
 9       }
10   }
```

**FIGURE 2-77**

5. Add three or four more lines of code to complete the school's initials.

6. Compile your program.

7. If no compilation errors occur, run the program.

8. Using TextPad, print a copy of the source code.

## 6 Creating an Applet with a Background Color

In preparation for creating your own personal Web page, you would like to view some possible background colors that will be easy to read with black text. You decide to write a Java applet that displays black words on a colored background. You will use the setBackground() method, which accepts a color argument in applets.

1. Start TextPad. Save the file as Java source code with the file name MyColorApplet.

2. Type a block header with the information about you and the assignment.

3. Import the java.awt.* and java.applet.* packages.

4. Write the class header for MyColorApplet. Remember to extend the Applet class. Include an opening brace for the class.

5. Write a method header for the paint() method. Include an opening brace for the method.

6. Set the background color to yellow.

7. Use the drawString() method to print the words "This is a color test" at the coordinates 25 and 30.

8. Enter closing braces to close the method and class.

9. Compile the program. Fix errors as necessary.

10. On the TextPad menu bar, click File and then click New. Type the HTML code to reference the MyColor.class with a width of 400 and a height of 200. Be sure to include the start and end <HTML> tags.

11. Save the HTML document with the filename MyColorApplet. Make sure you specify the HTML (*.htm*,*.stm*) file type.

12. Run the program.

13. Edit the program several times and change the color to red, blue, cyan, and orange. Compile and then run the program after each color change.

## 7 Rick's Riding Rodeo

Rick's Riding Rodeo plans to market its line of saddles on the Web next year. In preparation for Rick to begin e-commerce, write a Java application to display the name of the store on the screen. Use appropriate documentation lines. Compile the program and execute it. Once the program executes with no errors, edit the program to include Rick's e-mail address (RideWithRick@rodeo.com). Save, compile, and execute the program again. Convert the program to display as an applet, and add an appropriate logo (your instructor may supply you with a graphic, or you may download a graphic from the Web). When the applet is complete and generates no compilation errors, write the HTML code to run the applet.

## 8 Accessing the System Date

Your school would like to print out the programmer's initials and the system date on all printouts from the mainframe computer. As a prototype, write a Java program to print your initials and the system date on a splash screen. Use the escape characters and spacing to print the letters in the correct locations. Compile and execute your program. Print the source code.

## 9 Looking at Applets

The Web contains many sites that have free Java applets that you may download. Use a search engine to search for Java applets on the Web. When you find a Web page with some applets, use your browser's View Source command to look at the coding. Within that code, look for tags such as <APPLET CODE = >. Print three examples to submit to your instructor.

### 10 Your School Logo

Companies sometimes use a splash screen on the Web to give the user something to look at while the longer, graphic intensive Web page downloads. Write a splash screen applet that displays the name of your company or school, the address, the Web address, and your school's logo. Ask your instructor for the location of the graphic file. Position the lines using the g.drawString() method with the x and y coordinates. Position the graphic beside the text. Compile and run the applet using TextPad. Then run the applet using a browser such as Internet Explorer or Netscape by typing the path and file name of the HTML file in the browser's Address text box. Compare the two results. Print both the source code for the applet and the HTML file.

### 11 Creating a Splash Screen

In preparation for future Java programs, create a Java program, called Center, that displays an opening screen with text information about your program centered in the middle of the screen. Include the name of your program, your name, your instructor's name, the date, and any other necessary information. When maximized, the command prompt window displays approximately 25 lines that are 80 characters across. To center vertically, divide the number of lines of text into 25 (dropping any remainder) to determine how many blank lines (\n) to insert before each text line. To center horizontally, count the characters in the line of text, divide that by 2 (dropping any remainder), and then subtract that from 40 to determine how many spaces you should indent from the left margin. Remember that each escape character (\t) moves the text approximately eight characters to the right. Use the SPACEBAR to insert fewer than eight spaces. Compile and execute your program. Save your program on the Data Disk.

### 12 Creating New Colors

Use the Java API (http://java.sun.com/j2se/1.5.0/docs/api) to research possible colors for use with applets. When the API displays, click the java.awt package. Then click the class, Color. Look at the Field Summary table for possible colors. Then look at the Method Summary table for ways to change those colors. Write an applet that uses some of the methods you found to set both the background and foreground colors in an applet. If necessary, use the Java API Index at the top of the Web page to look up and review the syntax for the setBackground() and setForeground() methods.

CHAPTER

3

# Manipulating Data Using Methods

## Objectives

You will have
mastered the material in
this chapter when you can:

- Identify, declare, and use primitive
  data types
- Use the System class to create data streams
- Instantiate the BufferedReader class in code
- Use the readLine() method to handle user input
- Convert strings to numbers using the parse() method
- Use assignment statements to store data with proper identifiers
- Use operators and parentheses correctly in numeric and conditional
  expressions
- Round an answer using the round() method of the Math class
- Use Swing components to build the GUI for a Swing program
- Use the exit() method to close a Swing program
- Implement an ActionListener to handle events
- Add interface components to an applet
- Use the init() and paint() methods to load the applet interface
- Use the actionPerformed() method
- Run and test an interactive applet
- Manage Java source code files and Java class files

# Introduction

Manipulating data is integral to creating useful computer programs. Programmers must know how to retrieve and store different kinds of data efficiently. **Data** are collections of raw facts or figures, such as words, text, or numbers, which are used in reasoning or calculations (datum is the singular form of the word, data). A computer program performs operations on input data to produce output in the form of information The data used by a program can come from a variety of sources, such as the program itself, from users of the program, or from external files. When developing programs, programmers often embed certain kinds of data, such as constant values that will not change, within the program. Other kinds of data, such as current rates or prices that can change, are input to the program from external files or by users.

In this chapter, you will learn about the numerous ways Java can accept, retrieve, and manipulate data. You will learn how to write code that assigns values to variables, which Java uses to store data temporarily for processing. You also will learn to use classes and methods to set fields to specific values and create instances of classes. As you develop an interactive console application, you will learn to write code to accept a stream of character input from a keyboard, read the line, and then process it. In addition, you will learn how to code formulas with mathematical operators and create a single line of output on the display. In the process of modifying the console application to accept data from a dialog box, you will learn to add Java's Swing components, such as JOptionPane, to an interface to display messages and accept user input via dialog boxes. In converting the application to an interactive applet, you will learn to use an ActionListener to handle events, as well as to call constructors to add Labels, TextFields, and a Button component to the interface, along with an Image. Finally, you will create an HTML host file and then run the applet in the Applet Viewer window.

# Chapter Three — The Body Mass Index Calculator

The programs developed in this chapter create a Body Mass Index Calculator for a health club and its staff of trainers to use as they work with health club customers to establish exercise and diet regimens. Body mass index (BMI) is one way to gauge the total body fat in adults by measuring the relationship of weight to height. Studies have shown that adults should strive to maintain a BMI between 20 and 24. The fitness center wants to measure improvement in its customers by taking a before and after measurement of the customer's BMI. The Body Mass Index Calculator will allow the trainers to input data and generate accurate and consistent computerized calculations. To make it easily accessible from any location in the fitness center, the Body Mass Index Calculator will be available on a notebook computer, over the Web, or via a personal digital assistant (PDA).

The compiled Java source code for the Body Mass Index Calculator will cause prompts to display and will accept user input. The program then will calculate the body mass index. Three versions of the Body Mass Index Calculator are developed in this chapter: (1) a console application with input and output displayed in a command prompt window (Figure 3-1a); (2) a console application with input and output facilitated by dialog boxes (Figure 3-1b); and (3) an applet that provides input and output in a Web environment (Figure 3-1c).

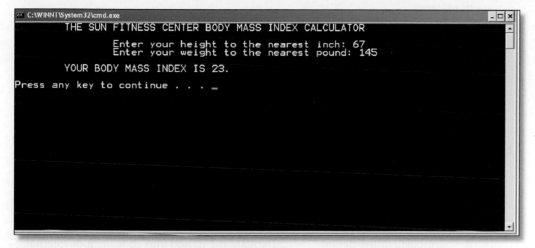

(a) console application accepts input and displays output in a command prompt window

(b) console application accepts input and displays output using dialog boxes

(c) applet accepts input and displays output in a Web environment

FIGURE 3-1

# Program Development

The program development cycle for the Body Mass Index Calculator program consists of tasks that correspond to the six development cycle phases, as shown in Table 3-1.

*Table 3-1    Body Mass Index Calculator Program Development Tasks*

| | DEVELOPMENT PHASE | TASK(S) |
| --- | --- | --- |
| 1 | Analyze the requirements | Analyze the Body Mass Index Calculator problem. |
| 2 | Design the solution | Design the user interface for both console applications and the applet, including output data and placement of the applet graphic. Design the logic to solve the problem. |
| 3 | Validate the design | Confirm with the user that the design solves the problem in a satisfactory manner. |
| 4 | Implement the design | Translate the design into code. Include internal documentation (comments and remarks) within the code that explains the purpose of the code statements. Create the HTML file to host the applet. |
| 5 | Test the solution | Test the program. Find and correct any errors (debug) until it is error-free. |
| 6 | Document the solution | Print copies of the application code, applet code, applet interface, and HTML code. |

## Analysis and Design

Figure 3-2 shows the requirements document that initiates the development cycle for the Body Mass Index Calculator program. The requirements document specifies the reason for the request, lists the required inputs and outputs, and shows the algorithm used to compute the BMI based on a person's height and weight.

**REQUEST FOR NEW APPLICATION**

| | |
|---|---|
| **Date submitted:** | October 9, 2007 |
| **Submitted by:** | Sun Fitness Center, Helen Sun - Office Manager |
| **Purpose:** | Our staff would like an easy-to-use program that calculates the body mass index of our customers. We measure customers when they first enter our program and then again after several weeks. The body mass index is a metric calculation; thus, our employees have had to convert the height and weight and then calculate the body mass index. |
| **Application title:** | Body Mass Index Calculator |
| **Algorithms:** | The body mass index is calculated as follows:<br>$$kilograms / meters^2$$<br><br>To convert inches to meters, divide by 39.36<br>To convert pounds to kilograms, divide by 2.2<br><br>Example: A 5'7" adult that weights 145 pounds has a body mass index of 23 as calculated in the following formulas:<br><br>$1.70$ meters = 67 inches / 39.36<br>$65.91$ kilograms = 145 pounds / 2.2<br>$23$ body mass index = 65.91 kilograms / 1.70 meters$^2$ |
| **Notes:** | 1. The fitness center staff is accustomed to taking measurements using inches and pounds.<br><br>2. The program should allow the user to enter values for the height in inches and the weight in pounds. We do not use decimals or fractions when measuring customers. Please remind program users that they should round the input to the nearest inch or nearest pound.<br><br>3. The calculated index can be rounded to the nearest integer.<br><br>4. Some of our trainers have PDAs, others have notebook computers. Not all of our locations have Web access in the training room.<br><br>5. As we want to distribute this program to all of our locations, please use "THE SUN FITNESS CENTER BODY MASS INDEX CALCULATOR" at the top of the display.<br><br>6. In the Web version, please use our Sun Fitness Center logo. |

**Approvals**

| | | |
|---|---|---|
| **Approval status:** | X | Approved |
| | | Rejected |
| **Approved by:** | Tyler Gilbert | |
| **Date:** | October 15, 2007 | |
| **Assigned to:** | J. Starks, Programmer | |

FIGURE 3-2

**PROBLEM ANALYSIS** The problem that the Body Mass Index Calculator program should solve is the calculation of a health-related measurement of body fat, called the body mass index (BMI). The BMI is based on the relationship between a person's weight and height. To complete the calculation and generate output for the user, the Body Mass Index Calculator program requires the user to input two values: the height in inches and the weight in pounds.

A **formula** is a mathematical sentence that contains values and operators. As stated in the requirements document in Figure 3-2 on the previous page, the Body Mass Index Calculator program must use the following formulas:

**meters = inches / 39.36**
**kilograms = pounds / 2.2**

to convert pounds and inches to the metric measurements of meters and kilograms, respectively. The converted values then are used in the following formula:

**index = kilograms / meters$^2$**

to calculate the BMI.

As noted on the previous page, the formulas require two inputs. The first formula divides the first input, inches, by 39.36 to calculate meters. The second formula divides the second input, pounds, by 2.2 to calculate kilograms. The program then uses the converted values in a third formula, which divides kilograms by the square of the meters to produce the output value for body mass index. In the third formula, the word, index, represents the body mass index value. Figure 3-3 displays a list of inputs and outputs, as well as sample data.

### INPUTS AND OUTPUTS

| INPUTS | OUTPUTS |
| --- | --- |
| inches | body mass index |
| pounds | |

### SAMPLE DATA

| INPUTS | OUTPUTS |
| --- | --- |
| 67 inches 145 pounds | 23 |
| 62 inches 110 pounds | 20 |
| 72 inches 200 pounds | 27 |

**FIGURE 3-3**

**DESIGN THE SOLUTION**   Once you have analyzed the problem, the next step is to design the user interface. There are three versions of the Body Mass Index Calculator program with three different kinds of interfaces: (1) a console application with prompts at the command line; (2) a console application with dialog box prompts; and (3) an applet with windowed input and output controls.

Figure 3-4a shows a storyboard for the Body Mass Index Calculator as a console application. As stated in the requirements document, the program will display the title, THE SUN FITNESS CENTER BODY MASS INDEX CALCULATOR, at the top of the window. Two prompts then will be displayed, allowing the user to enter the input values for inches and pounds. The calculated BMI will be displayed below the prompts. An advantage of creating this program as a console application is that a user does not need a GUI-based operating system or a mouse to enter data or view the resulting output. The console application thus is ideal for use on a personal digital assistant (PDA). Another advantage of creating a console application is that a programmer can validate the program logic before designing and creating a GUI version of the program.

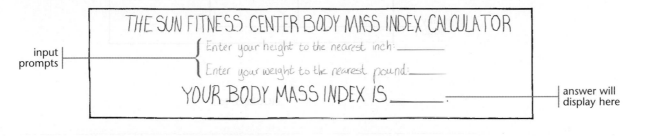

input prompts

answer will display here

**FIGURE 3-4a**

dialog box

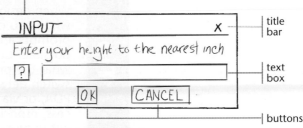

title bar

text box

buttons

**FIGURE 3-4b**

Even though a console application will allow you to edit, backspace, and even cut and paste as you enter data, many users feel more comfortable entering data into a text box or text field. Therefore, a second version of the Body Mass Index Calculator is developed as a console application that will accept input via dialog boxes.

A **dialog box** is a small window that displays messages and can accept user input. Figure 3-4b shows a storyboard for a dialog box. To accept user input, a dialog box may include a text box to accept input data, as shown in Figure 3-4b, or it may include option buttons, lists, or other items that allow a user to select from several preset choices. A dialog box has at least one button and may contain an icon. The title bar of a dialog box displays a caption and has a Close button.

A dialog box may be displayed as a result of a user action, such as clicking a button, or it may display as a result of logic in the program. When a dialog box is displayed, it is displayed in front of the application in which it is running. When the user finishes entering information or clicks an appropriate button in the dialog box, the dialog box closes. The program that called the dialog box, however, does not necessarily close when the dialog box closes.

Dialog boxes that require the user to complete a specific action, such as entering data, clicking the Cancel button, or choosing yes or no before returning to the program's interface, are called **modal**. Modal dialog boxes give the programmer control over how the user interacts with the program.

The third version of the Body Mass Index Calculator — an applet with a Web interface — also will accept user input; however, the applet user will type data into text boxes and then click a Calculate button in the applet window. As shown in the storyboard in Figure 3-4c on the next page, the applet window displays the title of the program, two input prompts with associated text boxes for data entry, and a Calculate button that causes the program to calculate body mass index and display the results. The company logo will display as a graphic in the lower portion of the applet window.

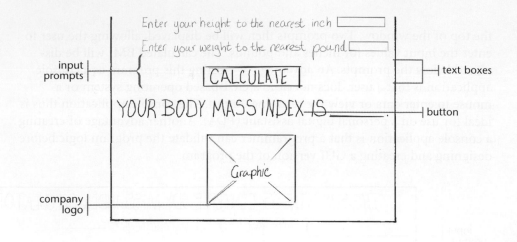

Enter your height to the nearest inch ☐

Enter your weight to the nearest pound ☐

CALCULATE

YOUR BODY MASS INDEX IS _____.

Graphic

input prompts

text boxes

button

company logo

FIGURE 3-4c

**Tip**

**Consistent Wording in Applications and Applets**

When designing different versions of the same program, as you do when you convert console applications to applets, be sure to code prompts and output messages so that the wording is as similar as possible. Consistent wording will allow users to interpret easily what the program is asking and make it easier if they have to switch between program versions running on a desktop, on a PDA, or via the Web. It also will simplify the programming process, especially if you are editing existing code to create a different version of the program.

**PROGRAM DESIGN**    Once you have designed the interface, the next step is to design the logic to solve the problem and create the desired results. The only programming task is to calculate the BMI based on input. The user can execute the program code to calculate BMI by answering the prompts in any version of the application program. The applet requires the additional step of clicking the Calculate button.

The program code for the first console application will allow user input, perform calculations, and display an answer, in that order, so the structure of the program will be sequential in nature. Input prompts and output will display using the System.out object, which is the default display device of your system (Figure 3-1a on page 129).

The program code then will be modified to use dialog boxes. This second version of the application will call on a special Java package named **javax.swing**, which provides a set of Java-based GUI components (Figure 3-1b on page 129).

Finally, the program code will be modified to create a third version of the program that can run over the Web as an applet. The program code for the applet will display text, text boxes, a button, and a graphic in an applet window (Figure 3-1c on page 129). Both the application and applet versions of the program should contain appropriate documentation and be saved for future use.

Figure 3-5a shows the pseudocode that represents the logic of the program requirements. The structure of the program will be sequential in nature, meaning that the computer will perform one action after another without skipping any steps or making any decisions that would affect the flow of the logic. Figure 3-5b shows an event diagram that illustrates how the click of the Calculate button in the applet window triggers the calculation and displays the answer in the applet window.

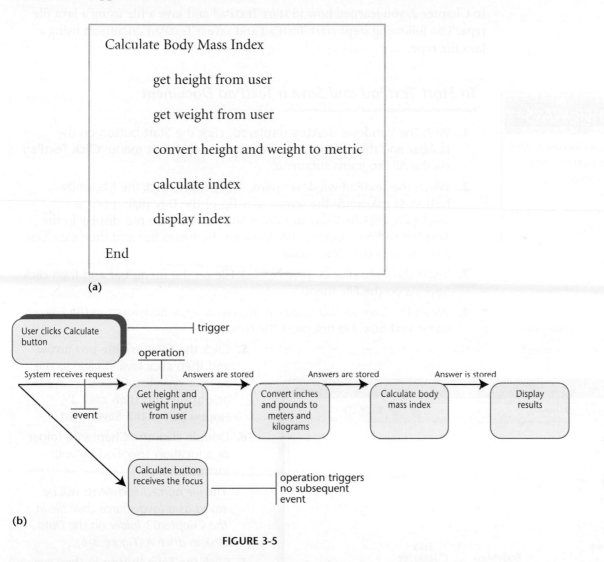

(a)

(b)

**FIGURE 3-5**

**VALIDATE DESIGN** Once you have designed the program, you can validate the design by stepping through the requirements document and making sure that the design addresses each requirement. If possible, you also should step through the solution with test data to verify that the solution meets the requirements. The user also should review the design to confirm that it solves the problem outlined in the requirements. By comparing the program design with the original requirements, both the programmer and the user can validate that the solution is correct and satisfactory.

Having analyzed the problem, designed the interface, and designed and validated the program logic, the analysis and design of the application is complete. As shown in Table 3-1 on page 130, the next task in the development cycle is to implement the design by creating a new Java program using TextPad.

## Starting a New Java Program in Textpad

In Chapter 2, you learned how to start TextPad and save a file using a Java file type. The following steps start TextPad and save a TextPad document using a Java file type.

### To Start TextPad and Save a TextPad Document

**1.** With the Windows desktop displayed, click the Start button on the taskbar and then point to All Programs on the Start menu. Click TextPad on the All Programs submenu.

**2.** When the TextPad window opens, if necessary, click the Maximize button to maximize the screen. If a Tip of the Day dialog box is displayed, click its Close button. If line numbers do not display in the TextPad coding window, click View on the menu bar and then click Line Numbers on the View menu.

**3.** Insert the Data Disk in drive A. Click File on the menu bar and then click Save As on the File menu.

**4.** When the Save As dialog box is displayed, type BodyMass in the File name text box. Do not press the ENTER key.

**5.** Click the Save as type box arrow and then click Java (*.java) in the Save as type list. Click the Save in box arrow and then click 3½ Floppy (A:) in the Save in list.

**6.** Double-click the Chapter03 folder or a location specified by your instructor.

*The file named BodyMass will be saved as a Java source code file in the Chapter03 folder on the Data Disk in drive A (Figure 3-6).*

**7.** Click the Save button in the Save As dialog box.

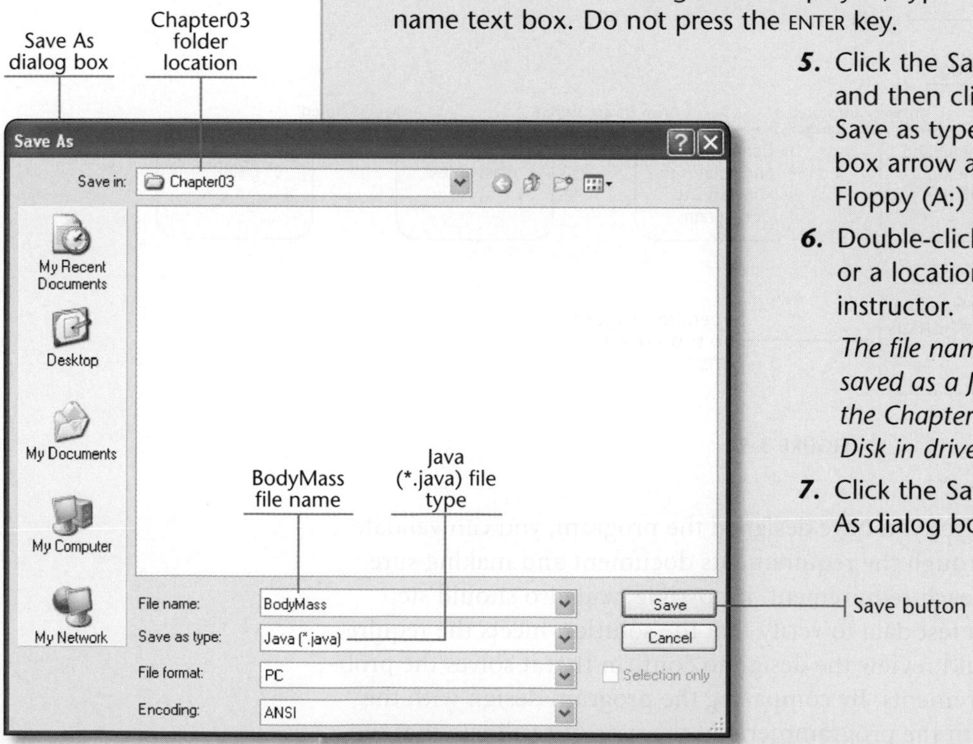

Save As dialog box

Chapter03 folder location

BodyMass file name

Java (*.java) file type

Save button

**FIGURE 3-6**

Recall that saving the program before entering any code causes TextPad to display Java-related color coding as you begin to enter code. It also causes the file name to display on the title bar, on the Windows taskbar, and in the Selector window, which provides a visual reference as you enter code. Finally, after the file is saved once, you can click the Save button on the Standard toolbar to resave the file to the same folder. TextPad also automatically resaves the file each time the program is compiled.

# Coding the Program

As you have learned, the implementation phase of the development cycle involves writing the code that translates the design into a program. During program design, pseudocode was used to outline the logic of the program code in the Body Mass Index Calculator application (Figure 3-5a on page 135). As outlined in that pseudocode, the task to be performed is to accept two inputs of height and weight, convert the input values to metric, calculate body mass index using a given formula, and then display the BMI value as output. The coding process starts with entering the beginning program code.

## Entering Beginning Code

Similar to the console application program in Chapter 2, the code for the Body Mass Index Calculator program will include comments, a class header, and a main() method. The code for the Body Mass Index Calculator also will use an import statement to import the java.io package. Recall from Chapter 2 that the java.lang package is the only package imported automatically without an explicit command; all other packages need an import statement to tell the compiler where to access the classes, fields, and methods of an existing class in the package. In this program, the java.io package is imported to provide classes to support system input and output.

When you use certain methods from the java.io package, you must warn the compiler that the possibility of errors exists. For instance, a user might not have authority to open a file, a disk might not be located in the proper disk drive, or the system might be busy with other input. An easy way to keep the program from aborting prematurely due to these kinds of errors is to add the code, throws IOException, to the end of the main() method header. The code, **throws IOException**, gives the program a way to acknowledge and handle potential input or output errors and still compile correctly.

Figure 3-7 on the next page displays the code for the comment header, import statement, class header, and main() method header used in the Body Mass Index Calculator program.

```
 1    /*
 2          Chapter 3:    The Body Mass Index Calculator
 3          Programmer:   J. Starks
 4          Date:         October 20, 2007
 5          Filename:     BodyMass.java
 6          Purpose:      This project calculates the body mass index based
 7                        on a person's height and weight.
 8    */
 9
10    import java.io.*;
11
12    public class BodyMass
13    {
14            public static void main(String[] args) throws IOException
15            {
```

**FIGURE 3-7**

The following step enters beginning code in the coding window.

## To Enter Beginning Code

**1.** With the insertion point on line 1 in the coding window, type the code as shown in Figure 3-7. In the comment header, insert your own name as the programmer and enter the current date.

*TextPad displays the beginning code in the coding window (Figure 3-8). The insertion point displays after the opening brace on line 15.*

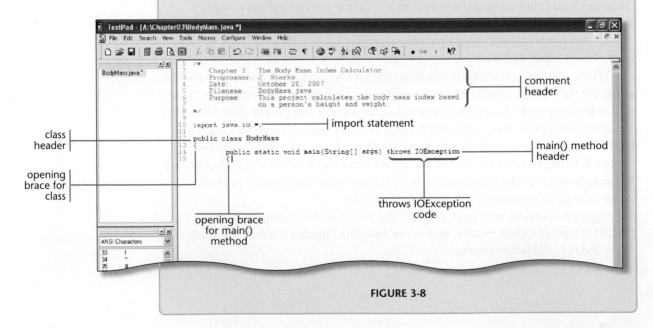

**FIGURE 3-8**

Comments and commands related to packages, such as the import statement, are the only code allowed outside the class header and its braced block of code. Recall that during compilation, the import statement loads the appropriate class or classes from the location where the SDK is stored. Typing an asterisk (*) after the package name tells the program to load all the classes within a package; typing an individual class name after the package name tells the program to load an individual class.

# Storing Data

For a computer program to make use of data, the data must be stored in the memory of the computer. Java makes efficient use of memory by requiring programmers to declare the kind of data they want to store. Java then allocates just enough memory for that data. It is a good programming practice to store data in the smallest location possible while still maintaining the precision and integrity of the data. **Precision** refers to the amount of storage allocated to hold the fractional part of a number. If a greater amount of storage is allocated, a more precise number with additional decimal places can be stored. Thus, the more precision a system uses, the more exactly it can represent fractional quantities.

Before a Java program can manipulate data, the program must identify the types of data to be used, declare a variable identifier, and put actual data into the storage location that the program can access later.

## Java Data Types

As you learned in Chapter 2, a data type classifies the data into a particular category of information and tells the computer how to interpret and store the data. Humans easily can distinguish between different types of data. For example, you usually can tell at a glance whether a number is a percentage, a time, or an amount of money by the use of special symbols, such as %, :, or $, which indicate the data type. Similarly, a computer uses special internal codes and words to keep track of and identify the different types of data it processes.

Java is a **strongly typed language**, which means it enforces a set of rules about how you use the objects you create, especially when using different types of data. For instance, every variable must have a data type, which determines the values that the variable can contain and the operations a program can perform on the data. Java programmers thus cannot declare a variable location as an integer and then try to insert a string of characters into that variable location. There would not be enough room because each data type has internal sizes associated with it.

Java supports two categories of data types: primitive and reference. A **primitive data type** is a data type that is structured by Java to hold single data items, such as integer, character, floating point, and true or false values. Java supports eight primitive data types, which help programmers by restricting the kind of data allowed in the declared variable location. If you try to store some other type of value in that variable location, Java displays an error message during compilation. The eight primitive data types, their descriptions, and examples of each are listed in Table 3-2 on the next page.

*Table 3-2   Java Primitive Data Types*

| TYPE | DESCRIPTION | EXAMPLES |
|---|---|---|
| boolean | stores data in only one of two states, as a logical value of true or false | true<br>false |
| byte | stores whole number values in 8-bit signed locations from –128 to +127 | 75<br>–14 |
| char | stores any one of the 65,436 single characters of the Unicode set, which includes characters and symbols from many languages | 'a'<br>'M' |
| double | stores numbers with up to 14 or 15 decimal places as double-precision, floating-point values | 87.266975314<br>100D |
| float | stores numbers with up to 6 or 7 decimals as single-precision, floating-point values | 349.135<br>954F |
| int | stores whole number values in 32-bit signed locations from $-2^{31}$ to $+2^{31}-1$ | 29387<br>–86421 |
| long | stores whole number values in 64-bit signed locations from approximately $-9 * 10^{18}$ to $+9 * 10^{18} -1$ | 13579286740<br>7362L |
| short | stores whole number values in 16-bit signed locations from –32,768 to +32,767 | 619<br>–530 |

As you learned in Chapter 2, when an actual number or character displays as data in code, it is called a literal. Generally speaking, a literal numeric value with no decimal point is treated by the compiler as an int data type. Programmers can specify that the data be treated as a long integer by putting an uppercase L or lowercase l after the number, which overrides the default int storage. An uppercase L is preferred, as it cannot be confused with the digit 1. In the same way, an uppercase D or lowercase d after the literal forces that number to be considered a double. The compiler considers a literal containing digits and a decimal point as a double. Programmers may override that storage to specify a float by putting an F or f after the number.

The two boolean literals are true and false. Programmers use the boolean data type to store a comparative result or one that has only two states — such as true or false, yes or no, 1 or 0 — as a logical value of true or false. A literal char value is any single character between single quote marks.

**Tip**

**Primitive Data Types Are Platform-Independent**

In other programming languages, the format and size of primitive data types may depend on the platform on which a program is running. In contrast, the Java programming language specifies the size and format of its primitive data types. Therefore, primitive data types are platform–independent, which means programmers do not have to worry about system dependencies.

Note that the char data type is a primitive and is restricted to storing a single character. When programmers want to store more than one character, they often use the non-primitive String class, which can store more than a single character. Classes such as String, Date (which you accessed in Chapter 2), and arrays (which you will learn about in a later chapter) are considered reference data types or object types. A **reference data type** is a data type whose value is an address. Like a primitive data type, a reference data type is declared with an identifier name, but that identifier references the location of the data rather than the actual data.

## Declaring Variables

A **declaration statement** is a line of Java code that identifies, or declares, the data type and names the identifier or variable. Programmers also can use the declaration statement to assign an initial value or call a constructor method to declare an instance of a class as they declare their variables. Table 3-3 shows the general form of declaration statements.

| Table 3-3   Declaration Statements | |
| --- | --- |
| **General form:** | 1. dataType identifier; //simple declaration<br>2. dataType identifier, identifier, identifier; //multiple declarations<br>3. dataType identifier = initialValue; //declaration and initialization<br>4. dataType identifier = new constructorMethod(); //declaration<br> and construction |
| **Purpose:** | To allocate a storage location and specify the type of data or object it will hold. |
| **Examples:** | 1. int userAge;<br>2. boolean flag, done, membership;<br>3. double taxRate = .05;<br>4. Date currentDate = new Date(); |

Figure 3-9 displays the declaration statements that declare the variables used in the Body Mass Index Calculator program. If you want to declare variables with different data types, you must use a separate declaration statement for each data type. If, however, you have several variables of the same data type, you can list the data type once and then include each variable on the same line separated by commas, as shown in lines 18 and 19 in Figure 3-9. You must declare a variable before you can use it in a program; however, you can combine the declaration of a variable with its first value or assignment, as shown in example 3 in Table 3-3.

```
16              // declare and construct variables
17              String height, weight;
18              int inches, pounds;
19              double kilograms, meters, index;
```

**FIGURE 3-9**

**Tip**

**Using Prefixes in Variable Names**

Sun Microsystems has no suggested naming convention for Java variables. It is customary to begin variable names with lowercase letters. Some programmers use single character prefixes in front of their variable names to denote the data type. For example, a double value for sales tax might be named dSalesTax. For non-primitive data types, programmers sometimes use a three-letter prefix, similar to the standard Visual Basic notation for objects. For example, a Label component might be named lblFirstName. Regardless of the convention you follow, it is important to use mnemonic, user-friendly variable names. Naming and coding conventions will be covered in more detail later in the chapter.

The following step enters code to declare variables.

## To Enter Code to Declare Variables

**1.** With the insertion point on line 16 in the coding window, type the line comment and declaration statements, as shown in Figure 3-9 on the previous page.

*A line comment in line 16 explains that the following code declares and constructs variables (Figure 3-10). Three declaration statements are displayed in lines 17 through 19. No assignment of values is made.*

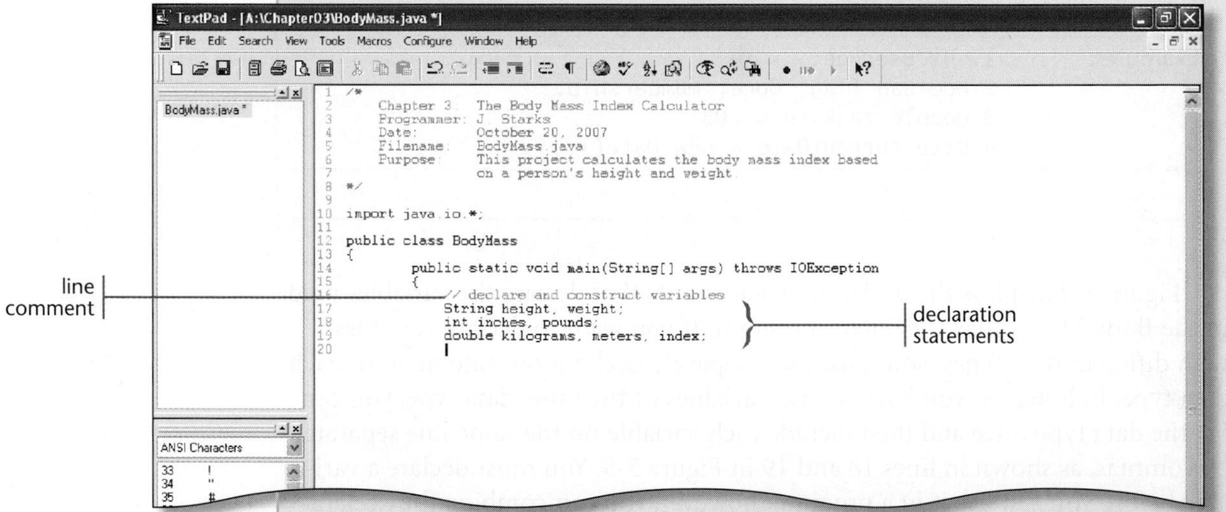

FIGURE 3-10

It may be helpful to remember that the integer data type, as declared in line 18, represents whole numbers, whereas the double data type represents a double-precision, floating-point value. Table 3-2 on page 140 describes a double as a number that is precise up to 14 or 15 decimal places. The word, floating, comes from scientists who refer to large numbers in scientific notation. For instance, 1,200,000 can be notated as 1.2 times 10 to the power of 6. The decimal point *floated* six places to the left.

> ## Performing Math with Floats and Doubles
>
> Programmers must pay particular attention to data types when multiplying or dividing numbers with decimal places. A rule of arithmetic states that when two numbers are multiplied, the number of decimal places in the answer equals the sum of each number's decimal places. For example, if two numbers with four decimal places each are multiplied together, the answer has eight decimal places. Thus, while you might declare the numbers as floats because they have only four decimal places, you would have to declare the answer as double because it has eight decimal places. Another example is that literal data not specified with an L or F is considered double by the Java compiler. Therefore, you must declare the result of any mathematical operation with a nonspecified literal value as a double. If you try to store the answer in a float location, you will receive an error that states, possible loss of precision found, and the program will not compile.

*Tip*

# User Input

Programmers who want to use timely data or data that changes on a regular basis usually do not code literal data into their programs. Instead, programmers code programs to reference an external data source, such as data input by a user. For example, in the banking industry, a programmer must rely on a bank customer to enter data such as a personal identification number (PIN) using the ATM keyboard. In fact, it is more common to rely on data from external sources than it is to include data in the program itself. Using external data allows for flexibility in programming and tailoring of the program to fit the company's or the user's needs.

**Interactive** is the term used with programs that allow the user to interact with the program by making choices, entering data, and viewing results. Interactive input and output in Java usually involves a user of the program entering data using a mouse and keyboard and viewing results on the screen.

## Streams and the System Class

In Java, the act of data flowing in or out of a program is called a **stream**. Examples of streams include data being input from a keyboard or output to a display. Recall that the System class, which was introduced in Chapter 2, contains several useful methods, including those involving standard input and output streams. The System class creates three different streams when a program executes: System.in, System.out, and System.err. Table 3-4 on the next page describes these three System streams or classes. Each has many associated methods; several examples of these methods are listed in the table.

*Table 3-4*   *System Classes*

| CLASS | FUNCTION | EXAMPLES OF ASSOCIATED METHODS | DEFAULT DEVICE | CODE EXAMPLE |
|-------|----------|-------------------------------|----------------|--------------|
| System.in | Accepts input data from the keyboard buffer, wrapped in the InputStreamReader (ISR) | readLine() used with constructed variable | keyboard buffer | String custName = dataIn.readLine(); |
| System.out | Sends output to the display or redirects output to a designated file | print() println() flush() | monitor or other display | System.out.println("Anita's Antiques"); |
| System.err | Sends output to the monitor; used for prompts and error messages | print() println() flush() | monitor or other display | System.err.println("Thread started"); |

Recall from Chapter 2 that System.out sent a stream to the standard output device, which usually is the monitor. System.out implemented the method, println(), to transfer the stream of characters. When the System.out.println() method executed, the program sent a literal string argument to the display. In the code example in Table 3-4, the text, Anita's Antiques, would appear on the display.

While the Java SDK provides the println() method for output, the SDK contains no simple method for input. System.in actually refers to a buffered input stream. As a user types data into a program interface, the keystrokes are sent to a buffer. A **buffer** is a data area shared by hardware devices or programs, where data are held until they are needed by the processor. Buffering ensures that if a user presses the BACKSPACE key to delete a character, the deleted characters are not sent when the program retrieves the characters from the input buffer.

The java.io package contains several classes used to receive input typed by the user. One of these classes is the InputStreamReader, which is a special reader used to read the input buffer. The **InputStreamReader (ISR)** is a Java class or object that serves as an intermediary between the input buffer and the Java program. Java programmers use the word, **wrap**, to describe how the ISR envelops the stream from the input buffer. The Java code necessary to reference the buffer uses the form

**InputStreamReader(System.in)**

in which the InputStreamReader() method uses System.in as the argument.

One more step must be completed before a program can use the data from the ISR. The data must be stored and named in an accessible way, as described in the next section.

## The BufferedReader Class

The **BufferedReader class** is used to store, or buffer, the input received from another object or class, such as the InputStreamReader class. The BufferedReader class, which is part of the java.io package, is used to increase the efficiency of character input. Input devices, such as a keyboard, typically are much slower than the computer's CPU; buffering the data reduces the number of times the CPU has to interact with the device to obtain the input data.

Recall that an instance is a unique object or a specific occurrence of a class of objects. **Instantiation** is the process of constructing an instance of a data type or object from a previously defined class. As discussed in Chapter 2, you use a special method called a constructor to create an instance of a class of objects. All Java classes have constructors that are used to initialize a new object of that type; the constructor method has the same name as the class.

Line 20 in Figure 3-11 calls a constructor to **instantiate**, or declare an instance of, the BufferedReader class. The resulting line of Java code may seem a bit cryptic; Table 3-5 breaks down and explains the purpose of the constructor code to declare the BufferedReader class.

```
20          BufferedReader dataIn= new BufferedReader(new
            InputStreamReader(System.in));
21
```

FIGURE 3-11

**Table 3-5   The BufferedReader Constructor Code**

| CODE COMPONENTS | TERMINOLOGY | EXPLANATION |
|---|---|---|
| BufferedReader | a class from the java.io package | A class that reads text from a character input stream, buffering characters so as to provide for the efficient reading of characters, arrays, and lines. |
| dataIn | identifier (variable) to hold the inputted data | Variable name assigned by the programmer. |
| = new | constructor notation | The standard notation to instantiate or construct an instance of a class. |
| BufferedReader() | method | A constructor or method used to instantiate or construct an instance of the BufferedReader class. |
| InputStreamReader() | a class from the java.io package | An InputStreamReader is a bridge from byte streams to character streams; it reads bytes and decodes them into characters. It usually is wrapped inside a BufferedReader. |
| System.in | an object representing input from a buffer | An object representing the standard input device on a computer system, usually the keyboard. |

The argument of the BufferedReader() method, on the right side of the constructor notation, instantiates a new InputStreamReader class. The InputStreamReader acts as a bridge to read the stream of bytes from the keyboard buffer and decode the bytes into characters. The BufferedReader() method returns a reference to the input data from the System.in.

Most programmers use a variable identifier such as myIn or dataIn to hold the input data read by the BufferedReader class. As shown in Figure 3-11 on the previous page, line 20 uses the identifier dataIn. When assigned by one of several readLine() methods, dataIn will contain the new data from System.in wrapped in the InputStreamReader. Figure 3-12 shows the flow of the data stream.

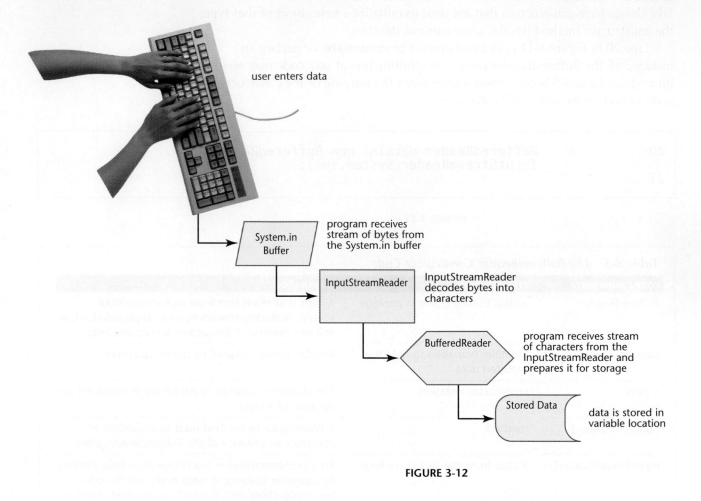

user enters data

System.in Buffer

program receives stream of bytes from the System.in buffer

InputStreamReader

InputStreamReader decodes bytes into characters

BufferedReader

program receives stream of characters from the InputStreamReader and prepares it for storage

Stored Data

data is stored in variable location

**FIGURE 3-12**

The following step enters code to instantiate the BufferedReader.

### To Enter Code to Instantiate the BufferedReader

**1.** With the insertion point on line 20 in the coding window, enter lines 20 and 21, as shown in Figure 3-11 on the previous page.

*The BufferedReader code is displayed in line 20 (Figure 3-13). Line 21 is a blank line.*

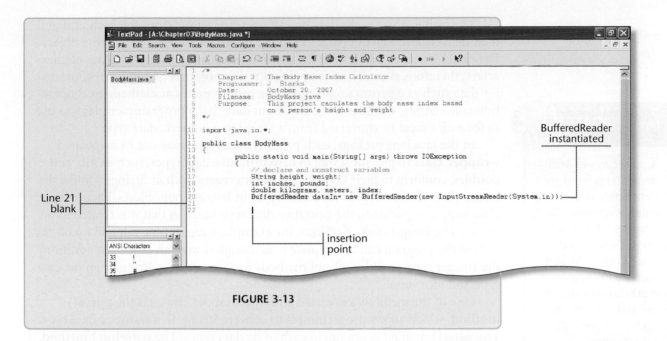

**FIGURE 3-13**

The BufferedReader could be declared and constructed with two separate lines, but it is more common to perform both actions in one line. Later you will learn that the BufferedReader can be used to efficiently read text and numbers from files as well as from the InputStreamReader (ISR).

Many users and textbooks create their own classes for input and output to simplify the process of reading from the buffer. It is exactly this BufferedReader capability, however, that makes Java easy to adapt to all kinds of input, such as strings, numbers, special characters, and foreign language symbols. It aids in Java's platform independence.

## User Prompts, Inputs, and Conversions

As defined during program design, users of this program will respond to prompts on the screen in order to enter the input data for height and weight. The prompts will take the form of questions displayed with the System.out.println() and System.out.print() methods, as shown in lines 23, 24, 25, and 28 of Figure 3-14.

After the user enters text, the **readLine() method** from the BufferedReader class reads the line of inputted text and returns a String containing the contents of the line. Lines 26 and 29 each include a readLine() method that accepts the response from the buffer and stores it in the location named dataIn.

```
22              // print prompts and get input
23              System.out.println("\tTHE SUN FITNESS CENTER BODY MASS INDEX CALCULATOR");
24              System.out.println();
25              System.out.print("\t\tEnter your height to the nearest inch: ");
26                  height = dataIn.readLine();
27                  inches = Integer.parseInt(height);
28              System.out.print("\t\tEnter your weight to the nearest pound: ");
29                  weight = dataIn.readLine();
30                  pounds = Integer.parseInt(weight);
31
```

**FIGURE 3-14**

The buffer stores input data one character at a time from the keyboard and then delivers a stream of characters to the program wrapped as a String object. Data read from the buffer with the method, readLine(), thus is a string of characters; therefore, it must be declared as a String object. A String is appropriate for data such as a person's name, but Java cannot perform mathematical operations on a String. Consequently, any input data that a programmer plans to use in formulas must be converted from a String to a numeric data type.

In the java.lang package, each primitive data type may use its associated **wrapper class** to provide a way to help primitive data types, such as ints and doubles, conform to their Object class counterparts, such as Strings. Unlike the String class of objects, primitive data types in Java are not objects. Each wrapper class wraps, or packages, the primitive data type value so that it is treated as an object. The Integer class of objects, for example, wraps an int value in an object so that the program can manipulate it as though it were an object. In addition, the Integer class provides several methods for converting a String to an int data type and vice versa.

One of the methods associated with the wrapper classes is the **parse() method**, which allows programmers to convert Strings to a numeric data type. The parse() method is unique to each of its data types. The parseInt() method, as shown in lines 27 and 30 of Figure 3-14 on the previous page, belongs to the Integer class of objects, while the parseDouble() method belongs to the Double class of objects. The basic syntax of any parse() method is to list the object class followed by a period, followed by the specific method name, such as parseInt() or parseDouble(). The String variable to be converted is placed inside the method's parentheses.

For each of the parse() methods, the end result is the same: a String is converted to a number. The difference is the data type of the converted number and the object name listed before the parse method.

Note that lines 27 and 30 are indented below the lines of code that include the println() and print() methods used to display input prompts to the user. Typically, the lines of code that accept and manipulate data in response to user input are indented to show their relationship to the prompt.

## Assignment Statements

The parseInt() methods in lines 27 and 30 assign the parsed value on the right of the **assignment operator** (=) to the String variable on the left. An **assignment statement** is a line of code beginning with a location, followed by the assignment operator (=), followed by the new data, method, or formula.

---

**JAVA UPDATE** Java 2 v5.0

A new class of Scanner objects used for data entry is available in version 5.0. A Scanner object can accept user input from System.in and then call predefined methods to extract the data. Methods such as **nextInt()**, nextDouble(), and nextBoolean() allow direct assignment to the corresponding variable without parsing.

The **Scanner** class is part of the java.util package that must be imported in programs that use Scanner.

If you want to amend the BodyMass program to incorporate Scanner, replace lines 11, 20, 27, and 30, then comment out lines 26 and 29 as shown in the following code.

```
11   import java.util.*;

20   Scanner scannerIn= new Scanner(System.in);

26   //height = dataIn.readLine();
27   inches = scannerIn.nextInt();

29   //weight = dataIn.readLine();
30   pounds = scannerIn.nextInt();
```

Table 3-6 displays the general form of an assignment statement. Note that the assignment operator, which looks like an equal sign, never is used to represent equality in Java. The equality operator (= =) will be discussed later in the chapter.

---

**Table 3-6  Assignment Statements**

| General form: | 1. identifier = value; //simple assignment |
| | 2. dataType identifier = value; //declaration and assignment |
| | 3. identifier = formula; //assigning the result of a formula |
| | 4. identifier = differentIdentifier; //copying data between identifiers |
| | 5. identifier = object.method(); //assigning the result of a method call |
| | 6. identifier = identifier + value; //accumulator |
| Purpose: | To assign a value to a storage location |
| Examples: | 1. `userAge = 21;` |
| | 2. `boolean flag = false;` |
| | 3. `totalCharge = sales + tax;` |
| | 4. `newLocation = oldData;` |
| | 5. `inches = Integer.parseInt(height);` |
| | 6. `counter = counter + 1;` |

---

Programmers sometimes declare their data and assign it at the same time, as shown in example 2. When using this type of assignment statement, the literal data must match the data type of the identifier. When a formula is used for assignment, as in example 3, the formula is placed on the right side of the assignment operator and the location to store the result is on the left. In example 4, the assignment is a reference to another storage location; therefore, its data is copied from one location to another. In example 5, the assignment is the result of a method call.

Because Java evaluates the code on the right side of the assignment operator before assigning the result to the left side, a special case may arise in which a value is manipulated and then stored back in the same storage location, as shown in example 6. For instance, if you want to track the number of hits on a Web page, you might write code to add 1 to the current counter value each time the page is downloaded from the Web server. The code then stores the updated counter value back in the original counter storage location. The result is an accumulated total called an **accumulator,** or **counter**. Every time Java executes the line of code, a value of 1 will be added to the current counter total. You will learn more about accumulators and counters in a later chapter.

The step on the next page enters code to prompt the user, accept input, and then parse the String responses. If your code runs over to two lines in the TextPad coding window, let the text wrap to the next line; do not press the ENTER key to split the code into two lines. Even if the code wraps to two or more lines in the coding window, Java looks for the semicolon (;) to indicate the end of the line.

### To Enter Code for the User Prompts, Inputs, and Conversions

**1.** With the insertion point on line 22 in the coding window, enter the code from Figure 3-14 on page 147.

*The System.out.println(), print(), readLine(), and parseInt() methods are displayed (Figure 3-15). Line 31 is a blank line.*

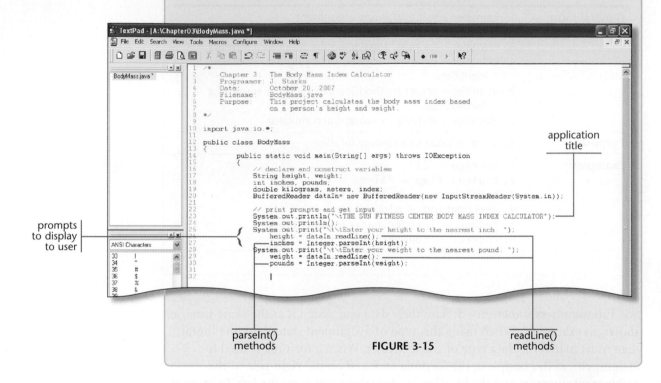

**FIGURE 3-15**

In line 26, the readLine() method takes the value from the dataIn variable location and assigns or copies it to the String location named height. The parseInt() method then converts height to an integer and assigns it to a variable location named inches. Java does not allow two variables with the same name in the same procedure.

## Operators

To complete a program task, a Java program may need to manipulate values mathematically, such as adding or subtracting values, or it may need to evaluate values logically, such as testing to see if the hours worked are greater than 40. The Body Mass Index Calculator, for example, must divide the input value for inches by 39.36 to convert it to meters. Performing mathematical or logical operations in Java is similar to other programming languages and uses two basic types of operators: arithmetic and comparison.

## Arithmetic Operators

**Arithmetic operators** manipulate two or more numeric values. Table 3-7 lists seven arithmetic operations, the operator symbols, an example, and example results.

### Table 3-7   Arithmetic Operators in Java

| OPERATION | OPERATOR SYMBOL | EXAMPLE | RESULT |
|---|---|---|---|
| Cast | (data type) literal or variable | (int) 20.3 | 20 (conversion to integer results in loss of precision) |
| Multiplication | * | 20 * 3 | 60 |
| Division | / | 20.0/3.0 | 6.6666667 for float 6.666666666666667 for double |
| Integer Division | / | 20 / 3 | 6 (the remainder is dropped because the operands both are integers) |
| Modular Division | % | 20 % 3 | 2 (only the integer remainder is stored) |
| Addition | + | 20 + 3 | 23 |
| Subtraction | - | 20 - 3 | 17 |

Table 3-7 lists the arithmetic operators in the order of operator precedence. **Order of operator precedence** is a predetermined order that defines the sequence in which operators are evaluated and resolved when several operations occur in an expression. You may be familiar with most of the arithmetic operators, as operator symbols in Java are similar to regular algebraic symbols. Commonly used arithmetic operators are the plus sign (+), used to add or sum two numbers, and the asterisk (*), used to multiply two numbers.

The less familiar operations, with respect to Java, are integer and modular division. **Integer division** is performed when both the dividend and the divisor are integers. When performing integer division, Java forces the result to be an integer because it is a primitive data type; it then drops any remainder. **Modular division**, or remainder division, is used to store any truncated remainder value from integer division. The **modulus operator** (%), which also is called the remainder operator, is entered between two integers and performs modular division. Modular division is common to many programming languages.

The type of division used in a program can return different results. For example, if you wanted to convert 168 minutes to hours and minutes, regular division using double data types would result in 2.8 hours:

**decimalAnswer = 168D / 60D;**
**decimalAnswer = 2.8;**

On the other hand, using integer or modular division would return a result that separates hours and minutes, rather than the decimal result returned when using regular division. First, integer division would drop the remainder, to result in 2 hours:

**integerAnswer = 168 / 60;**
**integerAnswer = 2;**

Modular division, however, would keep only the remainder minutes, to result in 48 minutes:

**modulusAnswer = 168 % 60;**
**modulusAnswer = 48;**

The operations of addition, subtraction, multiplication, and division shown in Table 3-7 on the previous page can manipulate any data type. Dividing float or double numbers will yield decimal results. If the operands in a division problem are of different data types, Java **promotes** the integers to floating point values before evaluating the expression.

The integer and modular division operations can manipulate only integers. As previously noted, Java performs integer division only on integer values and drops the remainders in the resulting value. Java performs modular division only on integers and stores the resulting remainder as an integer value. You will learn about other special operators that involve single value arithmetic in a later chapter.

A seventh operation, cast, also is listed in Table 3-7 because it performs a kind of arithmetic on numbers. Sometimes programmers want to force data to convert to a different data type. For example, for calculation or storage purposes, an integer value might be forced to become a double, or the other way around. The **cast operation** converts data from one primitive data type to another by entering the new data type in parentheses before a literal or variable, as shown in Table 3-7.

The ability to cast or convert primitive data types has some advantages. For example, the program in Figure 3-16 calculates the average miles per gallon. The user is asked to input miles and gallons. The input values are parsed in lines 16 and 20 to values that have been declared to be integers in line 9. The average then is calculated by dividing the miles by the gallons (line 23). Normally Java would return an int value because both values in the equation are integers. The average variable, however, has been declared to be a double value. Without the cast, the program would perform the operation on the right side first and would store an integer value in average. With the cast (double) in line 23, the program converts the total to a double before it performs the calculation, which increases the precision of the answer. When Java performs math on mixed data types, the result is always the larger data type. Therefore, when the program divides the casted double named total by the integer named count, the result is a double that subsequently is stored in the variable location named average.

```
1   import java.io.*;
2
3   public class Average
4   {
5           public static void main(String[] args) throws IOException
6           {
7                   // declare and construct variables
8                   String miles, gallons;
9                   int total, count;
10                  double average;
11                  BufferedReader myIn= new BufferedReader(new InputStreamReader(System.in));
12
13                  // print prompts and get input
14                  System.out.print("Enter the total number of miles ");
15                      miles = myIn.readLine();
16                      total = Integer.parseInt(miles);
17
18                  System.out.print("Enter the total gallons of gas ");
19                      gallons = myIn.readLine();
20                      count = Integer.parseInt(gallons);
21
22                  // calculations
23                  average = (double) total / count;
24
25                  // output
26                  System.out.println("The average is " + average);
27          }
28  }
```

**FIGURE 3-16**

Occasionally, programmers use casting in order to truncate decimal places. If, however, a programmer chooses to cast to a smaller data type, he or she then has to assume responsibility for any loss of precision in the operation.

## Comparison Operators

**Comparison operators** involve two values, as do arithmetic operators; however, they compare the numbers rather than perform math on them. As shown in Table 3-8 on the next page, comparison operations include greater than, less than, equal to, or not equal to, or any combination of those operations. While the result in arithmetic formulas evaluates to a numeric value, the result in a comparison operation evaluates to either true or false. Programmers use the boolean data type to store a comparative result of true or false. As an example, the statement

**boolean isOvertime = ( hours > 40 )**

would declare a boolean variable, isOvertime, and store a true value if the variable, hours, is greater than 40. The comparison operation is enclosed in parentheses. The identifiers for boolean variables are more easily recognized if a form of the verb, to be, is used as part of the variable name, as in the example above, which uses the variable isOvertime.

Table 3-8 lists the six comparison operations, the operator symbols, and examples of true and false expressions.

*Table 3-8    Comparison Operators in Java*

| OPERATION | OPERATOR SYMBOL | TRUE EXPRESSION | FALSE EXPRESSION |
|---|---|---|---|
| less than | < | (2 < 9) | (9 < 2) |
| greater than | > | (5 > 1) | (1 > 5) |
| less than or equal to | <= | (3 <= 4) | (5 <= 4) |
| greater than or equal to | >= | (8 >= 6) | (3 >= 7) |
| equal to | == | (9 == 9) | (5 == 9) |
| not equal to | != | (4 != 2) | (2 != 2) |

The first four comparison operators sometimes are referred to as **relational operators** because they compare the relation of two values; the last two sometimes are called **equality operators**. The double equal sign, ==, is used to differentiate the equal to operation from the assignment operator (=) used in Java. Spaces are not included between comparison operator symbols.

## Expressions

When using operators in code, it is important to understand their functions, order of precedence, and purpose in the statement expression. In Java and other programming languages, an **expression** can perform a calculation, manipulate characters, call a method, or test data. Expressions can be divided into two basic categories: numeric and conditional.

### Numeric Expressions

A **numeric expression** is any expression that can be evaluated as a number. A numeric expression can include arithmetic operators, values, and variables, as well as methods. The data type of any value in an arithmetic expression must be one of the numeric primitive data types from Table 3-2 on page 140. A numeric expression cannot contain String variables, String literals, or objects.

The values, variables, and methods in a numeric expression often are separated from each other by parentheses and arithmetic operators. A programmer must be concerned with both the form and the evaluation of an expression. It is necessary to consider the purpose of the expression as well as the rules for forming a valid expression before you start to write expressions in Java statements with confidence.

### Forming Valid Numeric Expressions

The definition of a numeric expression dictates the manner in which a numeric expression can be validly formed. For example, the following statement formed to assign the identifier, response, twice the value of myAnswer is invalid:

**response = 2myAnswer; //Invalid statement**

Java will reject the statement because a value (2) and a variable (myAnswer) within the same expression must be separated by an arithmetic operator. The statement can be written validly as:

**response = 2 * myAnswer; //Valid statement**

It also is invalid to use a String variable or String literal in a numeric expression. The following are invalid numeric expressions:

**response = 72 + "BALANCE" / myValue;**
**response = "45" / myValue + "answer" – 19;**

## Evaluation of Numeric Expressions

As you form complex numeric expressions involving several arithmetic operations, it is important to consider the order in which Java will evaluate the expression. For example, in evaluating the expression:

**answer = 16 / 4 / 2**

would the result assign 2 or 8 to the identifer, answer? The answer depends on how you evaluate the expression. If you complete the operation 16 / 4 first, and only then 4 / 2, the expression yields the value 2. If you complete the second operation, 4 / 2, first, and only then 16 / 2, it yields 8.

Java follows the normal algebraic rules to evaluate an expression. The normal algebraic rules that define the order in which the operations are evaluated are as follows: unless parentheses dictate otherwise, reading from left to right in a numeric expression, all multiplications and/or divisions are performed first, then all integer divisions, then all modular divisions, and finally all additions and/or subtractions. Following these algebraic rules, Java would evaluate the expression 16 / 4 / 2 to yield a value of 2.

> **Tip**
>
> **Order of Operator Precedence**
>
> Unless parentheses dictate otherwise, Java evaluates expressions and performs all operations in the following order:
>
> 1. multiplication and/or division
> 2. integer division
> 3. modular division
> 4. addition and/or subtraction
>
> When multiple operations of the same kind exist, Java performs the operations left to right.

This order of operator precedence, which defines the order in which operators are evaluated, sometimes also is called the rules of precedence, or the hierarchy of operations. The meaning of these rules can be made clear with some examples.

For example, the expression 18 / 3 − 2 + 4 * 2 is evaluated as follows:

18 / 3 − 2 + 4 * 2
6 − 2 + 4 * 2
6 − 2 + 8
4 + 8
12

If you have trouble following the logic behind this evaluation, use the following technique. Whenever a numeric expression is to be evaluated, read or scan, the expression from left to right four different times and apply the order of operator precedence rules outlined above each time you read the expression. On the first scan, moving from left to right, every time you encounter the operators, * and /, perform the required operation: multiplication or division. Hence, 18 is divided by 3, yielding 6, and 4 and 2 are multiplied, yielding 8.

On the second scan, from left to right, perform all integer division. On the third scan, from left to right, perform all modular division. This example includes no integer division or modular division, so no operations are performed.

On the fourth scan, moving again from left to right, every time you encounter the operators, + and −, perform addition and subtraction. In this example, 2 is subtracted from 6 resulting in 4. Then it is added to 8 for a total of 12.

The following expression includes five arithmetic operators and yields a value of −3.

5 * 3 % 2 + 7 / 2 − 7
15 % 2 + 7 / 2 − 7       **<-end of first scan – multiplication performed**
15 % 2 + 3 − 7          **<-end of second scan – integer division performed**
1 + 3 − 7               **<-end of third scan – modular division performed**
−3                      **<-end of fourth scan – addition and subtraction performed**

In later chapters, you will add to the hierarchy of operations as you learn about operators that manipulate single operands.

## Conditional Expressions

A **conditional expression** is any expression that can be evaluated as true or false. A conditional expression can include comparison operators, values, and variables, as well as methods. The resulting data type after a conditional expression is evaluated is boolean. A conditional expression may contain String variables and String literals. Table 3-8 on page 154 displays examples of conditional expressions.

Conditional expressions are governed by validity and operator precedence rules that are similar to those used with numeric expressions. Valid conditional expressions that use two operands must separate the operands with a comparison operator. Unless parentheses dictate otherwise, conditional expressions are evaluated from left to right. When multiple comparison operators exist in the same statement, relational operators take precedence over equality operators. For example, in the following expression, the operations are performed left to right, resulting in a value of false:

**10 < 5 = = true**
**false = = true**          <-first scan, less than operator evaluated
**false**                   <-second scan, equality operator evaluated

If you have trouble following the logic behind this evaluation, use the following technique. Whenever a conditional expression is to be evaluated, scan the expression from left to right two different times and apply the order of operator precedence rules outlined above each time you read the expression. On the first scan, moving from left to right, every time you encounter the operators <, >, <=, or >=, perform the required operation: less than, greater than, less than or equal to, greater than or equal to. Hence, 10 < 5 evaluated to false.

On the second scan, moving again from left to right, every time you encounter the operators == and !=, evaluate for equality and nonequality. In the above example, false does not equal true, which results in a false expression. You will learn more about conditional expressions in later chapters.

## Using Parentheses in Expressions

Parentheses may be used to change the order of operations. In Java, parentheses normally are used to avoid ambiguity and to group terms in a numeric or conditional expression. The order in which the operations in an expression containing parentheses are evaluated can be stated as follows: when parentheses are inserted into an expression, the part of the expression within the parentheses is evaluated first, then the remaining expression is evaluated according to the normal rules of operator precedence.

> **Tip**
>
> **Use of Parentheses in Expressions**
> When parentheses are inserted into an expression, the part of the expression within the parentheses is evaluated first, then the remaining expression is evaluated according to the normal rules of operator precedence.

If the first numeric expression example were rewritten with parentheses as 18 / (3 − 2) + 4 * 2, then it would be evaluated in the following manner:

**18 / (3 − 2) + 4 * 2**
**18 / 1 + 4 * 2**
**18 + 4 * 2**
**18 + 8**
**26**

Evaluating numeric expressions with parentheses should be done as follows: make four scans from left to right within each pair of parentheses, and only after doing this make the standard four passes over the entire numeric expression.

Evaluating conditional expressions with parentheses should be done as follows: make two scans from left to right within each pair of parentheses, and only after doing this make the standard two passes over the entire conditional expression.

When coding a numeric expression, use parentheses freely when in doubt as to the valid form and evaluation of a numeric expression. For example, if you wish to have Java divide 6 * D by 5 * P, the expression may be written correctly as 6 * D / 5 * P, but it also may be written in the following manner:

(6 * D) / (5 * P)

> **Tip**
>
> **Using Parentheses When Coding Numeric or Conditional Expressions**
>
> When coding numeric or conditional expressions, use parentheses freely if you are unsure about operator precedence and the form of a valid expression. Using parentheses helps to provide clarity when the expression is evaluated.

For more complex expressions, Java allows parentheses to be contained within other parentheses. When this occurs, the parentheses are said to be **nested**. In this case, Java evaluates the innermost parenthetical expression first, then goes on to the outermost parenthetical expression. Thus, 18 / 3 * 2 + (3 * (2 + 5)) is broken down in the following manner:

$$18 / 3 * 2 + (3 * (2 + 5))$$
$$18 / 3 * 2 + (3 * 7)$$
$$18 / 3 * 2 + 21$$
$$6 * 2 + 21$$
$$12 + 21$$
$$33$$

When coding expressions, be sure to avoid two common errors. First, check that you have surrounded the correct part of an expression with parentheses. Second, check that you have balanced the parentheses by verifying that the expression has as many close parentheses as open parentheses.

## Construction of Error-Free Expressions

If you have written an expression observing the order of precedence rules, Java can translate the expression without generating any error messages. This, however, is no guarantee that Java actually will be able to evaluate it. In other words, although a numeric expression may be formed in a valid fashion, Java may not be able to evaluate it because of the data type of the numbers involved or some other logic error. In situations where error conditions arise during compilation, Java will display an error message.

Applying the following rules when coding expressions should help you avoid such hazards:

1. Do not attempt to divide by zero.
2. Do not attempt to determine the square root of a negative value.
3. Do not attempt to raise a negative value to a non-integer value.

4. Do not attempt to compute a value that is greater than the largest permissible value or less than the smallest permissible nonzero value for the data type.

5. Do not try to compare different data types in a conditional expression.

## The Math Class

Numeric expressions in formulas are the most common use of operators in Java, although some math functions cannot be performed with operators alone. Figure 3-17 displays the formulas used in the Body Mass Index Calculator program. While the first two formulas can be written with operators, the third one needs a special method to calculate the answer.

```
32          // calculations
33          meters = inches / 39.36;
34          kilograms = pounds / 2.2;
35          index = kilograms / Math.pow(meters,2);
36
```

**FIGURE 3-17**

In the first formula, inches are converted to meters by dividing them by 39.36 (line 33). Pounds are converted to kilograms by dividing by 2.2 (line 34). When int variables, such as inches and pounds, are divided by double values such as 39.36 and 2.2, Java stores the answer as the larger data type. Meters and kilograms thus were declared to be double in line 19 (Figure 3-9 on page 141).

The final formula for BMI is calculated by dividing kilograms by the meters squared, which calls for an exponent. The process of raising a number to the power of an exponent is called **exponentiation**. In some math notations, a caret sign ($\wedge$) is used to denote an exponent. For example, $4 \wedge 2$ is the same as $4^2$ and is equal to 16, and $3 \wedge 4$ is the same as $3^4$ and is equal to 81. Even though Java has no exponentiation operator, it easily is accomplished by using a prewritten method from the Math class. The **Math class**, which is part of the java.lang package, contains methods for a number of useful functions, such as rounding, exponentiation, randomizing, and square roots. Methods from the Math class have the general form shown in Table 3-9 on the next page. The table displays only some of the many methods from the Math class; a complete listing is available in the Java API.

Table 3-9   Methods from the Math Class

| General form: | Math.method(arguments) | | |
|---|---|---|---|
| Purpose: | The Math class contains methods for performing basic numeric operations such as the elementary exponential, logarithm, square root, and trigonometric functions. | | |

Examples:

| METHOD | DESCRIPTION | EXAMPLE CODE | RESULT |
|---|---|---|---|
| abs() | Absolute value | Math.abs(-75) | 75 |
| max() | Higher of two numbers | Math.max(99,41) | 99 |
| min() | Lower of two numbers | Math.min(99,41) | 41 |
| pow() | Exponentiation | Math.pow(2,5) | 32 |
| random() | Random number generator | Math.random() | 0< value >1 |
| round() | Rounding to an integer | Math.round(27.59) | 28 |
| sqrt() | Square root | Math.sqrt(144) | 12 |

Recall that the values inside the parentheses are the arguments — the pieces of information the method needs to perform its task. The arguments in most Math methods can be literals (as in the table examples), variables, or calls to other methods. The **pow() method**, used to express exponentiation as in meters squared, requires two arguments: the base number and the exponent. A comma separates the arguments.

Perform the following step to enter the formulas.

## To Enter the Formulas

*1.* With the insertion point on line 32 in the coding window, enter the code from Figure 3-17 on the previous page.

*The formulas to convert input values to metric and to calculate the BMI are entered (Figure 3-18). Line 36 is a blank line.*

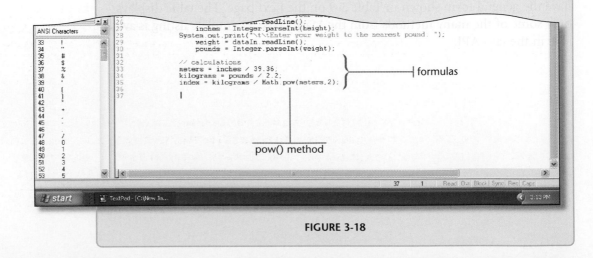

FIGURE 3-18

In general, you invoke Java methods by typing the class name followed by a period followed by the method name. As you have learned, classes must be imported before they can be used. Because the Math class is part of the java.lang default package, it needs no previous import statement.

# Program Output

After all calculations are performed, the program should display appropriate output to the user. The output for the Body Mass Index Calculator program is a message indicating the user's calculated BMI.

## Using Variables in Output

The println() method commonly displays a string of characters, but it also can display values from variable locations. Table 3-10 displays some forms of the println() method.

---

*Table 3-10    The println() Method*

| | |
|---|---|
| **General form:** | 1. System.out.println("literal");<br>2. System.out.println(String variable);<br>3. System.out.println(numeric variable);<br>4. System.out.print("literal");<br>        System.out.println(variable);<br>5. System.out.println("literal" + variable);<br>6. System.out.println(Class.method(arguments));<br>7. System.out.println(""); |
| **Purpose:** | To display output on the standard output device |
| **Examples:** | 1. `System.out.println("Anita's Antiques");`<br>2. `System.out.println(firstName);`<br>3. `System.out.println(dSalesTax);`<br>4. `System.out.print("The answer is ");`<br>        `System.out.println(answer);`<br>5. `System.out.println("The answer is " + answer);`<br>6. `System.out.println(Math.round(answer));`<br>7. `System.out.println(""); //prints a blank line` |

---

Remember that System.out refers to the default output device, usually the monitor. The println() method can display a literal string of characters, using code such as that in example 1. For Java to display the values from variable locations to users, the program code must use a variable identifier as the argument of the println() method, as shown in examples 2 and 3.

If you want to combine strings of characters and variables on the same line, the code can take one of two forms. First, you can use the print() method followed by println() method, as in example 4. The print() method does not force a new line after displaying, so any output following a print() method will display in the same line.

A second way, as shown in example 5 on the previous page, combines Strings and variables in the same line using concatenation. Using a plus sign (+), Java allows a **concatenation**, or joining, of these types of data in a single output line of code. In both example 4 and 5, leaving a space after the word, is, keeps the message and the answer from running together.

Additionally, programmers may invoke methods in their output, as shown in example 6. The Math.round() method rounds the answer to the nearest integer; the println() method then prints the answer.

The output code for the Body Mass Index Calculator program is shown in Figure 3-19. Line 39 begins with an escape character tab, followed by text. Then the index value from the previous calculation is rounded to an integer with the Math.round() method and concatenated to the text, YOUR BODY MASS INDEX IS. Finally, a period is concatenated to complete the output sentence. Lines 38 and 40 print blank lines before and after the output message. Lines 41 and 42 are the closing braces for the main() method and class blocks, respectively.

```
37            // output
38            System.out.println();
39            System.out.println("\tYOUR BODY MASS INDEX IS " + Math.round(index) + ".");
40            System.out.println();
41        }
42    }
```

FIGURE 3-19

The following step enters the code that uses variables, concatenation, and the Math.round() method to produce output on the display.

### To Enter Code to Display Output

*1.* With the insertion point on line 37 in the coding window, type the code from Figure 3-19.

*The output code is displayed in the coding window (Figure 3-20). The calculated BMI will display as a rounded integer value in the same line as the output message. Depending on your TextPad settings, the closing brace in line 42 may display in a different column.*

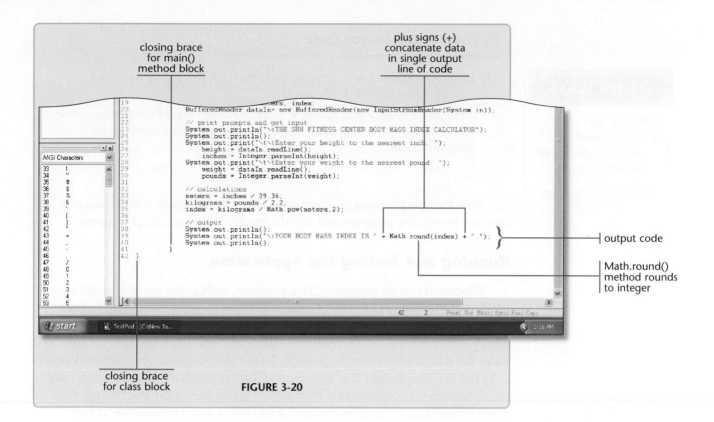

**FIGURE 3-20**

The program now is complete. You coded the documentation; the opening class and method headers; the declaration of variables; the prompts, inputs, and conversions; the calculations; and the output. Check the code to ensure that the syntax, spelling, capitalization, and indentations are correct. When you are confident everything is correct, you are ready to save and compile your program.

# Compiling, Running, and Documenting the Application

The Java source code for the Body Mass Index Calculator program must be compiled before it can be executed and tested. Once the program is running correctly, it is a good idea to print a copy of the source code for documentation.

## Compiling the Source Code

Recall that the compiler automatically saves the program and then translates the source code into Java bytecode. To compile the program, you will use the Compile Java command on TextPad's Tools menu, as shown in the step on the next page.

### *To Compile the Source Code*

**1.** With your Data Disk in drive A, click Tools on the menu bar. Click Compile Java on the Tools menu.

*TextPad compiles the program. If TextPad notifies you of compilation errors, fix the errors in the BodyMass coding window and then compile the program again.*

**OTHER WAYS**

1. Press CTRL+1
2. At command prompt, type `javac BodyMass.java`

Now that the program has been compiled into bytecode, you are ready to execute, or run, the program and test the results of the coded calculations.

## Running and Testing the Application

When you run an interactive Java program, such as the console application version of the Body Mass Index Calculator, prompts will be displayed in the command prompt window. The bytecode runs in the command prompt window, pausing every time the readLine() method is executed, to allow the user to enter the data requested in the prompt. To test the program, programmers typically use the sample data that they created during program design and any sample data from the requirements document. During execution and testing, the programmer acts as the user, entering data from a user's perspective as the program runs.

The following steps execute and test the application.

### *To Run and Test the Application*

**1.** If necessary, click BodyMass.java in the Selector window in TextPad. Click Tools on the menu bar and then click Run Java Application on the Tools menu. Type 67 in response to the first prompt.

*The command prompt window displays the first prompt and user response (Figure 3-21).*

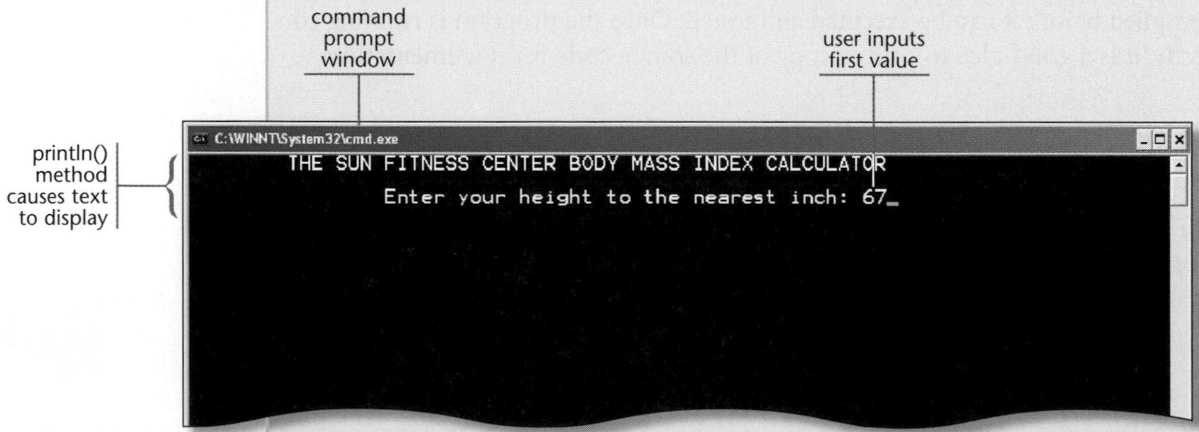


FIGURE 3-21

**2.** Press the ENTER key. Type 145 in response to the second prompt.

*The command prompt window displays the second prompt and user response (Figure 3-22).*

user inputs
second value

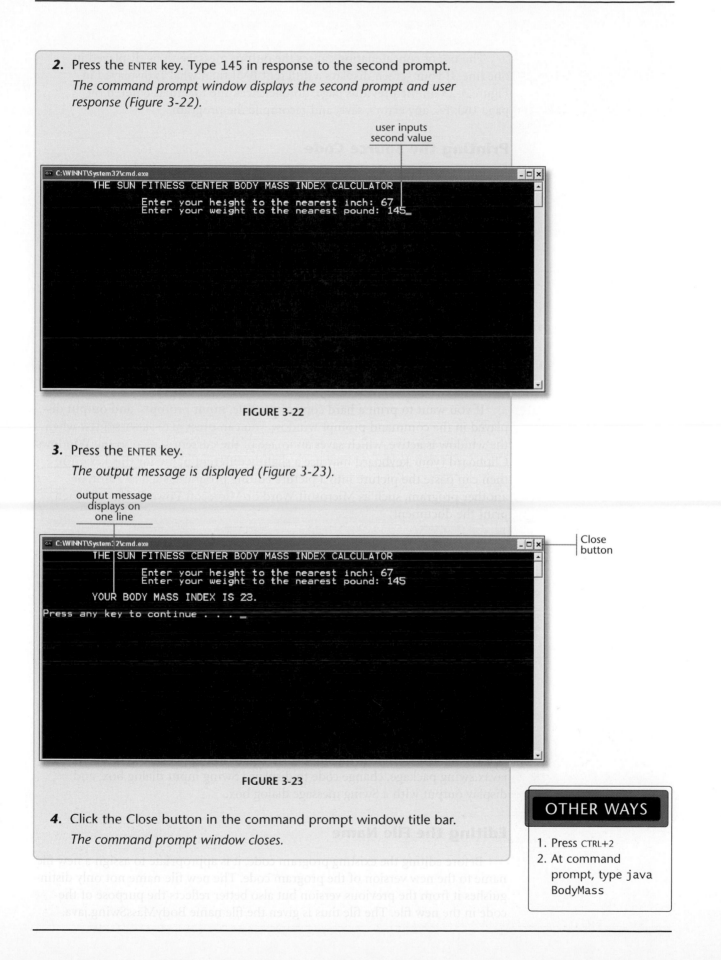

**FIGURE 3-22**

**3.** Press the ENTER key.

*The output message is displayed (Figure 3-23).*

output message
displays on
one line

Close
button

**FIGURE 3-23**

**4.** Click the Close button in the command prompt window title bar.

*The command prompt window closes.*

**OTHER WAYS**

1. Press CTRL+2
2. At command prompt, type java BodyMass

The use of concatenation causes the output message to be displayed in one line. If your screen displays a different BMI than what is displayed in Figure 3-23 on the previous page, double check the formulas entered on page 160. Fix any errors, save, and recompile the program.

### Printing the Source Code

You may want to print a copy of the BodyMass source code for documentation purposes or for reference, as you modify the program to create different versions of the program. The following steps print a copy of the source code.

---

*To Print the Source Code*

**1.** Click the Print button on the Standard toolbar in the TextPad window.
*The source code prints on the printer.*
**2.** Retrieve the printout from the printer.

---

If you want to print a hard copy of the title, input prompts, and output displayed in the command prompt window, you can press ALT+PRINT SCREEN when the window is active, which saves an image of the current screen to the Windows Clipboard (your keyboard may use a slightly different name for this key). You then can paste the picture into a picture editing program, such as Paint, or another program, such as Microsoft Word or Microsoft PowerPoint, and then print the document.

## Using Swing Components

In 1997, Sun Microsystems introduced a new set of GUI components commonly referred to as **Swing components**. As a part of the newer Java Foundation Classes (JFC) that encompass a group of features to help people build graphical user interfaces, Swing components are implemented with no native code. Because Swing components are not restricted to the least common denominator — that is, the features that are present on every platform — they can have more functionality than Abstract Window Toolkit (AWT) components.

As defined during program design, a second version of the Body Mass Index Calculator must be developed as a console application that will accept input via dialog boxes. As you modify the Body Mass Index Calculator program, you will edit the file name, change the import statement to import classes in the javax.swing package, change code to display a Swing input dialog box, and display output with a Swing message dialog box.

### Editing the File Name

Before editing the existing program code, it is appropriate to assign a new file name to the new version of the program code. The new file name not only distinguishes it from the previous version but also better reflects the purpose of the code in the new file. The file thus is given the file name BodyMassSwing.java.

Using a file name such as BodyMassSwing.java instead of BodyMassVersion2 .java more closely represents the purpose of the program and is easier to remember. To change the file name in the program code, you can use TextPad's search and replace function, which makes global changes to text easy.

The following steps edit the file name and class header to reflect the new file name.

### To Edit the File Name and Class Header

**1.** With the TextPad coding window displaying the BodyMass source code, click Search on the menu bar.

*The Search menu is displayed (Figure 3-24).*

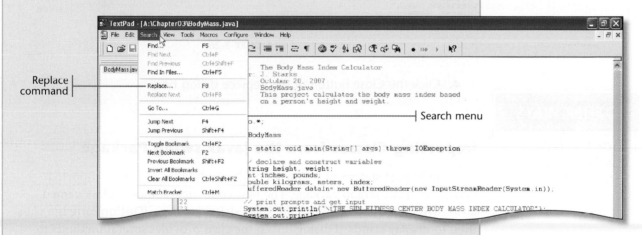

**FIGURE 3-24**

**2.** Click Replace on the Search menu. When the Replace dialog box is displayed, type BodyMass in the Find what text box. Press the TAB key. Type BodyMassSwing in the Replace with text box.

*TextPad will find and then replace every occurrence of the text, BodyMass, with the text, BodyMassSwing (Figure 3-25).*

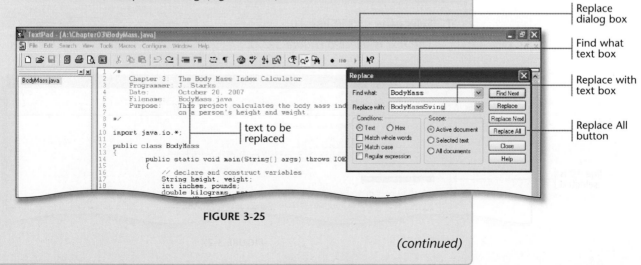

**FIGURE 3-25**

*(continued)*

**3.** Click the Replace All button.

*TextPad replaces the text, BodyMass, with the text, BodyMassSwing, in lines 5 and 12 (Figure 3-26).*

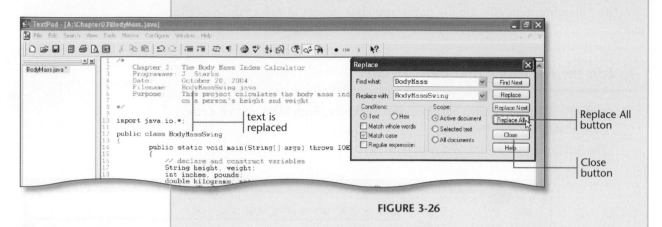

**FIGURE 3-26**

**4.** Click the Close button in the Replace dialog box.

## Importing Classes from the javax.swing Package

The import statement in line 10 of the BodyMass.java code imported classes from the java.io package. The new code must import a class named javax.swing.JOptionPane from the javax.swing package. **JOptionPane** is a class used to display standard dialog boxes; the class provides several methods to create and display dialog boxes that prompt users for an input value, that prompt users to confirm an action, or that display messages.

To replace a line of code in TextPad, double-click the line number and then type the new code. The following steps enter the new import statement.

### To Enter the New import Statement

**1.** Select the text in line 10.

*The text is selected (Figure 3-27).*

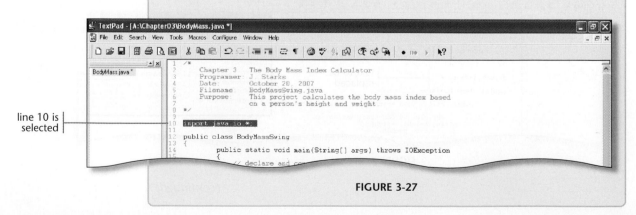

**FIGURE 3-27**

**2.** Type import javax.swing.JOptionPane; to replace the text. Press the ENTER key if necessary, to maintain a blank line 11.

*The JOptionPane class from the javax.swing package will be imported (Figure 3-28).*

import statement
to import
JOptionPane class

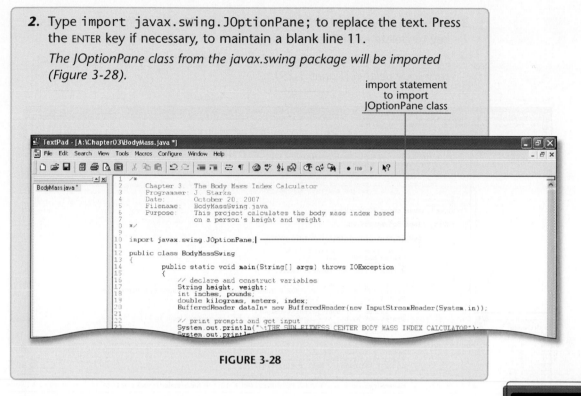

FIGURE 3-28

## Deleting Existing Code

In the Swing version of the Body Mass Index Calculator, the Swing dialog boxes will take care of buffering the data from the user and handling IO errors so that classes and methods from the java.io package, such as the BufferedReader class in line 20, are no longer necessary. Additionally, the Swing version of the Body Mass Index Calculator no longer needs blank lines to print in the command prompt window. While these lines do not affect the output or calculations of the program, they are unnecessary.

The following steps remove unnecessary code. To select an entire line, you can double-click the line number or triple-click the line itself.

### To Delete Existing Code

**1.** Drag through the text, throws IOException, in line 14 to select it. Press the DELETE key.

*(continued)*

**OTHER WAYS**

1. To select line, triple-click line

**2.** One at a time, select lines 40, 38, 24, and 20 and then press the DELETE key to delete each line.

*The TextPad coding window displays the program code, with the unnecessary code deleted (Figure 3-29).*

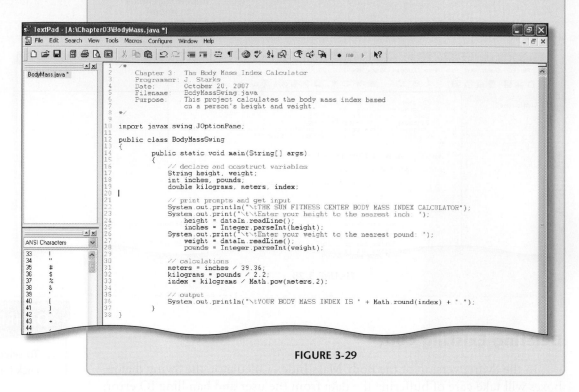

**FIGURE 3-29**

## Creating Swing Dialog Boxes

The Swing JOptionPane class provides many methods that make it easy for programmers to display standard dialog boxes, including methods to show a confirmation, input, or message dialog box. Table 3-11 shows the basic syntax of any JOptionPane method. Table 3-12 displays some of the show methods associated with the JOptionPane class of dialog boxes.

*Table 3-11  JOptionPane Methods*

| | |
| --- | --- |
| **General form:** | JOptionPane.method(arguments) |
| **Purpose:** | To create a dialog box on the screen |
| **Examples:** | 1. `String answer = JOptionPane.showInputDialog("What is your name?");`<br>2. `JOptionPane.showMessageDialog(null, "It's been a pleasure to serve you", "Thank You Box", JOptionPane.PLAIN_MESSAGE);`<br>3. `JOptionPane.showConfirmDialog(null, "Please choose one", "Confirm Box", JOptionPane.YES_NO_OPTION);` |

**Table 3-12  JOptionPane show Methods**

| METHOD | PURPOSE | EXAMPLE |
|---|---|---|
| 1. showInputDialog() | Prompts for input | JOptionPane.showInputDialog(null, "message"); |
| 2. showMessageDialog() | Displays information to the user | JOptionPane.showMessageDialog(null, "message", "title bar caption", messageType); |
| 3. showConfirmDialog() | Asks a confirming question, like yes/no/cancel | JOptionPane.showConfirmDialog(null, "message", "title bar caption", messageType); |

In the first example shown in Table 3-11, the showInputDialog() method displays a dialog box with a message and a text box for user input. The showInputDialog() method actually is assigned to a String variable with an assignment statement. Figure 3-30 shows a typical input dialog box that displays when the JOptionPane.showInputDialog() method is used.

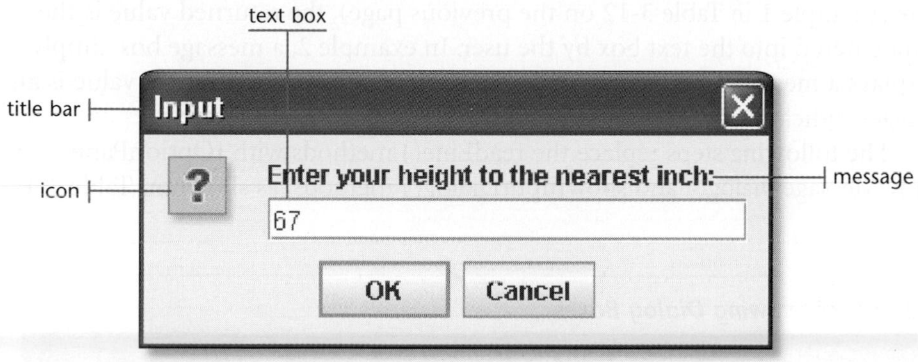

**FIGURE 3-30**

The second and third examples in Table 3-12 each use four method arguments. The first argument indicates the placement of the dialog box on the screen. The Java keyword, null, instructs the program to display the dialog box centered within the program's active window. The second argument represents the display area inside the dialog box and can be an object, icon, component, or String. The third argument indicates the caption that appears on the title bar. The fourth argument refers to one of various constants defined in the JOptionPane class. A **constant** is a value that Java understands to have a certain, intrinsic meaning. In the case of JOptionPane dialog boxes, the argument refers to one of several styles of dialog boxes with displayed icons, as shown in Table 3-13 on the next page.

**Table 3-13   Constant Message Types**

| MESSAGE TYPE | DISPLAYED ICON |
|---|---|
| ERROR_MESSAGE | |
| INFORMATION_MESSAGE | |
| WARNING_MESSAGE | |
| QUESTION_MESSAGE | |
| PLAIN_MESSAGE | no icon display |

JOptionPane dialog boxes can return a value. In the case of an input dialog box (example 1 in Table 3-12 on the previous page), the returned value is the data entered into the text box by the user. In example 2, a message box simply displays a message and has no return value. In example 3, the return value is an integer indicating the option selected by the user.

The following steps replace the readLine() methods with JOptionPane showMessageDialog() and showInputDialog() methods, as shown in Table 3-14.

**Table 3-14   Replacing Code to Create Swing Dialog Boxes**

| LINE | DELETE OLD CODE | REPLACE WITH NEW CODE |
|---|---|---|
| 36 | System.out.println("\tYOUR BODY MASS INDEX IS " + Math.round(index) + "."); | JOptionPane.showMessageDialog(null, "YOUR BODY MASS INDEX IS " + Math.round(index) +".", "Body Mass Calculator",JOptionPane.PLAIN_MESSAGE); |
| 26, 27 | System.out.print("\t\tEnter your weight to  the nearest pound: "); weight = dataIn.readLine(); | weight=JOptionPane.showInputDialog(null, "Enter your weight to the nearest pound: "); |
| 23, 24 | System.out.print("\t\tEnter your height to the nearest inch: "); height = dataIn.readLine(); | height=JOptionPane.showInputDialog(null, "Enter your height to the nearest inch: "); |

## To Enter Code to Create Swing Dialog Boxes

1. Select line 36. Type the new code from Table 3-14.
2. Select lines 26 and 27. Type the new code from Table 3-14.
3. Select lines 23 and 24. Type the new code from Table 3-14.

*The code to create Swing dialog boxes is displayed (Figure 3-31). Your code may wrap differently.*

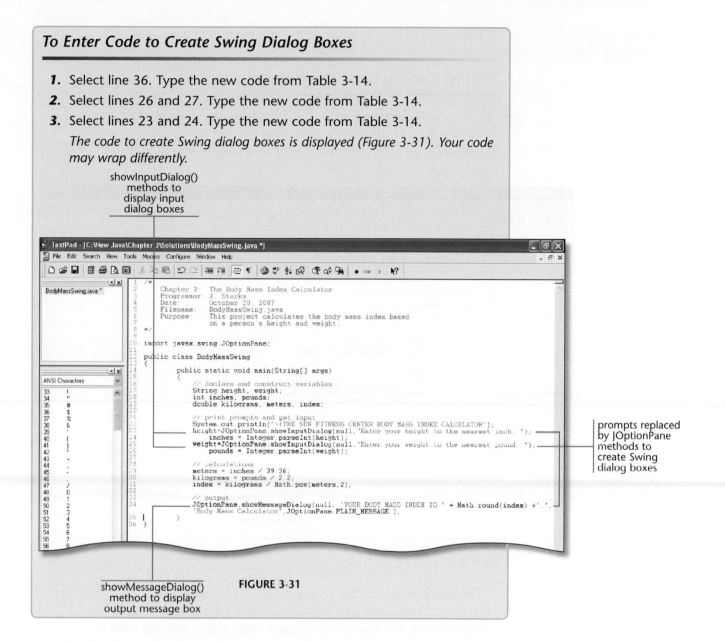

showInputDialog()
methods to
display input
dialog boxes

prompts replaced
by JOptionPane
methods to
create Swing
dialog boxes

showMessageDialog()
method to display
output message box

**FIGURE 3-31**

## Closing Programs That Use Swing

One more line of code is necessary in order to close programs that use Swing dialog boxes, after the program ends. The System class provides an **exit() method**, which is used to terminate an application that displays a graphical user interface, such as a dialog box. The method accepts an integer argument that serves as a status code. A 0 (zero) indicates that the application has terminated successfully. A value of 1 typically indicates abnormal termination. If you do not include a System.exit(0); statement at the end of the program code, the command prompt window will not close at the end of the program.

The following step enters code to close the program.

### To Enter Code to Close the Program

**1.** Click at the end of line 34. Press the ENTER key twice. Type System.exit(0); as the new code.
*The code for the System.exit() method is entered (Figure 3-32).*

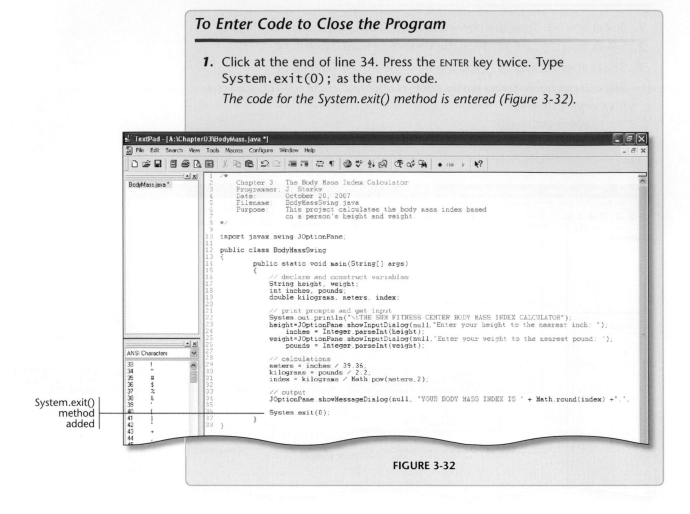

**FIGURE 3-32**

The Swing version of the program now is complete. The code shown in Figure 3-32 includes a new import statement; the new class name, BodyMassSwing; and has no unnecessary code. It also includes code to prompt the user and to accept a String answer using dialog boxes. Finally, the code includes a System.exit() method, so that the program will terminate properly.

Once the code is complete, check for syntax, proper spelling, capitalization, and indentations. When you are confident everything is correct, you are ready to save and compile your program.

# Saving, Compiling, and Running the Swing Version

The Java source code for the Swing version of the Body Mass Index Calculator program must be saved with a new file name and then compiled before it can be executed and tested. Once the program is running correctly, a copy of the source code can be printed for documentation.

## Saving and Compiling the Swing Version

As you have learned, Java program names must be the same as the class statement at the beginning of the code. The program thus must be saved by using the Save As command and indicating the new file name, BodyMassSwing, before it can be compiled. The following steps save the source code file on the Data Disk with a new file name and then compile the source code.

### To Save and Compile the Source Code

1. With the Data Disk in drive A, click File on the menu bar and then click Save As.
2. When the Save As dialog box is displayed, type BodyMassSwing in the File name text box.
3. If necessary, click the Save as type box arrow and then click Java (*.java) in the list.
4. If necessary, click the Save in box arrow and then click 3½ Floppy (A:) in the list. Double-click the Chapter03 folder.
5. Click the Save button in the Save As dialog box.
6. Click Tools on the menu bar and then click Compile Java.

   *The program is saved with a new file name on the Data Disk and then compiled. If TextPad notifies you of compilation errors, fix the errors in the BodyMassSwing coding window and then compile the program again.*

**OTHER WAYS**

1. To Save As, press F12
2. To compile, press CTRL+1
3. To compile, at command prompt, type javac BodyMassSwing .java

## Running and Testing the Swing Program

When testing different versions of the same program, it is a good idea to use the same sample data for each test. That way you can compare output results to ensure that they are consistent for all versions of the program. The steps on the next page run and test the interactive program BodyMassSwing.

## To Run and Test the Swing Program

**1.** Click Tools on the menu bar and then click Run Java Application on the Tools menu. When the height Input dialog box is displayed, type 67 in the text box.

*The command prompt window displays the program name (Figure 3-33). The height Input dialog box, which is displayed in front of the command prompt window, includes a text box for input.*

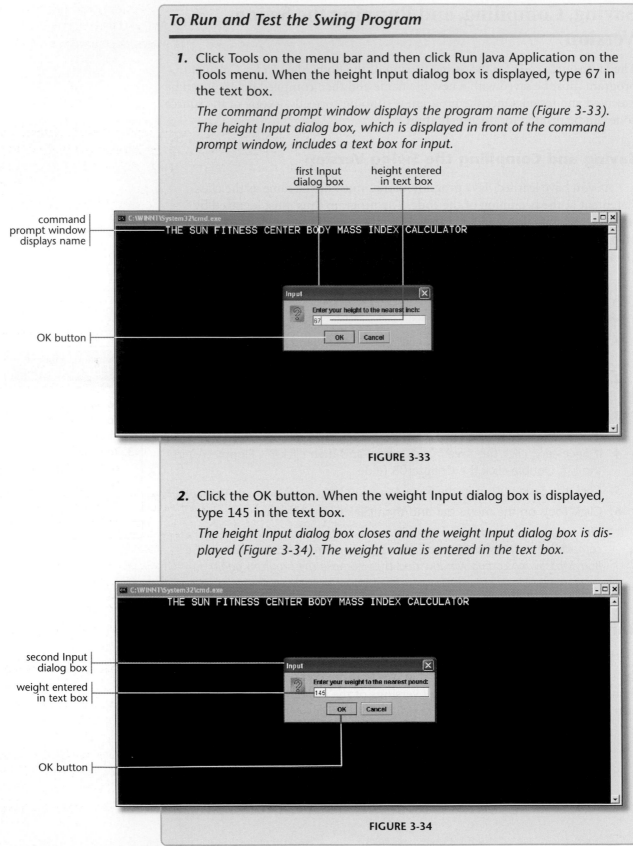

FIGURE 3-33

**2.** Click the OK button. When the weight Input dialog box is displayed, type 145 in the text box.

*The height Input dialog box closes and the weight Input dialog box is displayed (Figure 3-34). The weight value is entered in the text box.*

FIGURE 3-34

**3.** Click the OK button.

*The message box showing the user the Body Mass Index is displayed (Figure 3-35). The calculated BMI value displayed should be 23, the same value calculated by the previous version of the program.*

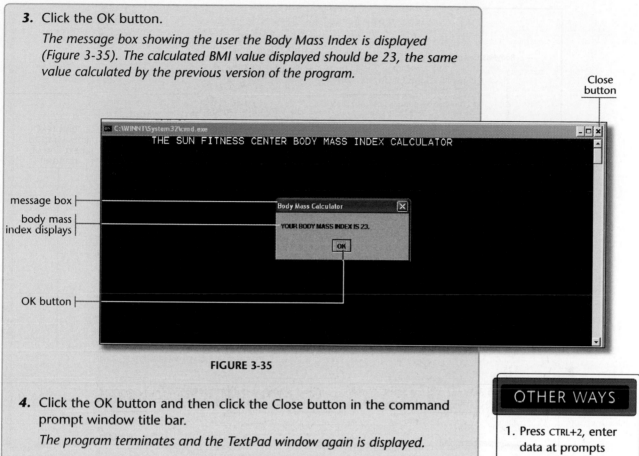

FIGURE 3-35

**4.** Click the OK button and then click the Close button in the command prompt window title bar.

*The program terminates and the TextPad window again is displayed.*

OTHER WAYS

1. Press CTRL+2, enter data at prompts
2. At command prompt, type java BodyMassSwing, enter data at prompts

Interactive programs allow programmers the flexibility of testing the program by running it many times using various sets of sample data, without having to recompile. As users begin using the program and entering the data, many things could go wrong, such as entering incorrect information or unrealistic data. This chapter does not attempt to account for all of the possible errors that might occur; errors and exception handling are covered in more detail in later chapters. If, however, the program is run with data that makes sense, and the data is entered correctly, the correct answer will display.

Once you have determined that the program runs correctly, you should print a copy of the BodyMassSwing source code for documentation purposes. You can print a copy of the program code from the TextPad coding window by using the Print command on the File menu. A printout of the program code will be sent to the default printer. Figure 3-36 on the next page shows the printout of the program code for the Swing version of the Body Mass Index Calculator. As shown in Figure 3-36, long lines of code sometimes wrap to the next line on hard copies.

Your printout may not display line numbers. To print line numbers, see Appendix C, pages APP 50 through APP 52.

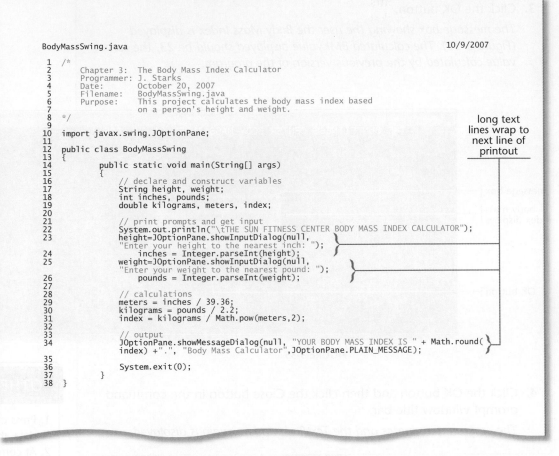

```
BodyMassSwing.java                                                    10/9/2007

 1  /*
 2       Chapter 3:   The Body Mass Index Calculator
 3       Programmer: J. Starks
 4       Date:        October 20, 2007
 5       Filename:    BodyMassSwing.java
 6       Purpose:     This project calculates the body mass index based
 7                    on a person's height and weight.
 8  */
 9
10  import javax.swing.JOptionPane;
11
12  public class BodyMassSwing
13  {
14          public static void main(String[] args)
15          {
16              // declare and construct variables
17              String height, weight;
18              int inches, pounds;
19              double kilograms, meters, index;
20
21              // print prompts and get input
22              System.out.println("\tTHE SUN FITNESS CENTER BODY MASS INDEX CALCULATOR");
23              height=JOptionPane.showInputDialog(null,
                    "Enter your height to the nearest inch: ");
24                  inches = Integer.parseInt(height);
25              weight=JOptionPane.showInputDialog(null,
                    "Enter your weight to the nearest pound: ");
26                  pounds = Integer.parseInt(weight);
27
28              // calculations
29              meters = inches / 39.36;
30              kilograms = pounds / 2.2;
31              index = kilograms / Math.pow(meters,2);
32
33              // output
34              JOptionPane.showMessageDialog(null, "YOUR BODY MASS INDEX IS " + Math.round(
                    index) +".", "Body Mass Calculator",JOptionPane.PLAIN_MESSAGE);
35
36              System.exit(0);
37          }
38  }
```

long text lines wrap to next line of printout

**FIGURE 3-36**

# Moving to the Web

The final version of the program for the Body Mass Index Calculator is to create an applet. Recall that an applet is a program called from within another environment, usually a Web page. In order to convert the Body Mass Index Calculator from a console application that runs in the command prompt window to an applet that will display as part of a Web page, you will need to create four kinds of objects: an Image, Labels, TextFields, and Buttons.

In Chapter 2, you learned that an applet uses different Java packages than an application and thus must import the java.awt and java.applet class packages needed to support the applet-related methods. Recall that applets also must extend the Applet class in the class header in order to inherit attributes from the applet package.

### Implementing an ActionListener to Handle Events

Because the Body Mass Index Calculator applet will be interactive, the program must have the ability to handle events. Every time the user clicks a button, presses a key on the keyboard, or opens a program window, for example, an event occurs. The event classes are included in the **java.awt.event package**, which provides interfaces and classes for dealing with different types of events triggered by AWT components. (The java.awt.event package is not a subset of java.awt; it is a different package.) Table 3-15 lists several classes in the java.awt.event package, an example of an event represented by the class, and an associated listener interface.

**Table 3-15   java.awt.event Classes**

| CLASS | EXAMPLE OF EVENT | ASSOCIATED LISTENER INTERFACE |
|---|---|---|
| ActionEvent | User clicks a button, presses the ENTER key, or chooses a menu item | ActionListener |
| ItemEvent | User selects or deselects an item such as a checkbox or an option button | ItemListener |
| KeyEvent | User presses a key | KeyListener |
| MouseEvent | User performs a mouse action, such as select, drag, or enter MouseMotionListener | MouseListener |
| TextEvent | User changes text in text box | TextListener |
| WindowEvent | Window changes status by opening, closing, or performing some other action | WindowListener |

As shown in Table 3-15, every event class has one or more associated listener interfaces. A **listener interface** — sometimes called simply an **interface** — monitors, or listens, for events during execution of an interactive program. The listener interface used in the applet version of the Body Mass Index Calculator is ActionListener. **ActionListener** is a listener interface that listens for any events that occur during execution of the program, such as when a user clicks a button, double-clicks an item, selects a menu item, or presses the ENTER key. The ActionListener tells the program that some response to the user's action should occur. The keyword, **implements**, is used in the class header to specify which listener interface a programmer wants to use. If more than one listener interface is implemented, those are separated by commas.

Figure 3-37 on the next page shows the comments, import statements, class header, and declarations for the applet. As shown in line 5, the new name of the program will be BodyMassApplet. The applet will import three packages, extend the Applet class, and implement the ActionListener. The BodyMassApplet will declare the same int and double variables that were declared in the BodyMass and BodyMassSwing programs. It also will declare an Image named logo.

```
 1   /*
 2          Chapter 3:    The Body Mass Index Calculator
 3          Programmer:   J. Starks
 4          Date:         October 20, 2007
 5          Filename:     BodyMassApplet.java
 6          Purpose:      This project calculates the body mass index based
 7                        on a person's height and weight.
 8   */
 9
10   import java.applet.*;
11   import java.awt.*;
12   import java.awt.event.*;
13
14   public class BodyMassApplet extends Applet implements ActionListener
15   {
16          //declare variables
17          Image logo; //declare an Image object
18          int inches, pounds;
19          double meters, kilograms, index;
20
```

FIGURE 3-37

As you learned in Chapter 2, programmers sometimes edit existing application code to create applet code. When the required edits are extensive, however, it sometimes is more convenient to start a new document in the coding window. The following steps will start a new document in TextPad in which to code the applet version of the Body Mass Index Calculator. The steps then enter code for comments, import statements, the class header that extends the Applet class and implements the ActionListener, and variable declarations for the applet.

## To Enter Code to Implement the ActionListener

*1.* Click the New Document button on the Standard toolbar in the TextPad coding window. If line numbers do not display, click Line Numbers on the View menu.

*2.* With the Data Disk in drive A, click File on the menu bar and then click Save As on the File menu.

*3.* When the Save As dialog box is displayed, type BodyMassApplet in the File name box. If necessary, click Java (*.java) in the Save as type list. If necessary, click the Save in box arrow, click 3½ Floppy (A:) in the list, and then double-click the Chapter03 folder.

*4.* Click the Save button in the Save As dialog box.

*5.* Enter the code, as shown in Figure 3-37.

*The new code is entered (Figure 3-38). The class header displays the new class name, extension of Applet class, and implementation of the ActionListener. Lines 17 through 19 declare the variables for the program. Line 20 is blank intentionally, in order to separate sections of code.*

file name
displayed on
title bar

file name
displayed in
Selector
window

variables
defined after
class header
have class
scope

new code
entered

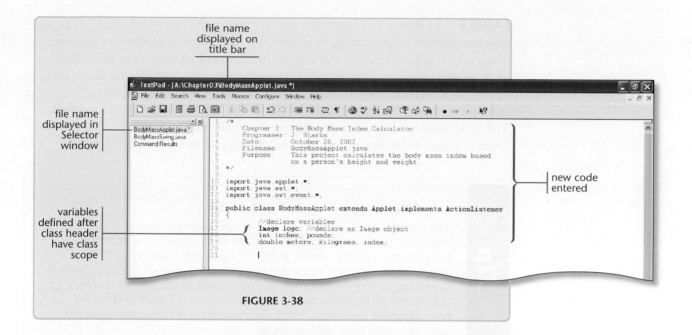

**FIGURE 3-38**

Declaring variables at the beginning of the program, after the class header, creates data that can be accessed by the entire program; that is, the variables are not limited to use by certain methods. The **scope** of an identifier for a variable, reference, or method is the portion of the program that can recognize and use the identifier. The variables in Figure 3-38 have class scope, which means all of the methods defined in this program will be able to utilize these variables.

## Adding Interface Components to an Applet

The java.awt package contains components or object data types that you can use to build a user interface for applets. Each **component**, sometimes called a control, is a Java class with methods to construct, add, and manipulate the object. Java AWT components, such as Checkbox, List, or MenuItem, begin with an uppercase letter for each word in the name — referred to as title case. In the applet version of the Body Mass Index Calculator, you will use three components for the java.awt.package: Labels, TextFields, and Buttons. Figure 3-39 shows the code to add the Labels, TextFields, and Button component to the applet window interface.

```
21      //construct components
22      Label companyLabel = new Label("THE SUN FITNESS CENTER BODY MASS INDEX CALCULATOR");
23      Label heightLabel = new Label("Enter your height to the nearest inch: ");
24          TextField heightField = new TextField(10);
25      Label weightLabel = new Label("Enter your weight to the nearest pound: ");
26          TextField weightField = new TextField(10);
27      Button calcButton = new Button("Calculate");
28      Label outputLabel = new Label("Click the Calculate button to see your body mass index.");
29
```

**FIGURE 3-39**

**LABELS**   A **Label** is an object that displays text in the applet window. Labels are assigned a string of characters, or a text value, by the programmer. A common usage is to use a constructor that assigns the string of characters to the component, as shown in line 22 in Figure 3-39 on the previous page. Recall that a constructor is a method used to create an instance of a class, and that the constructor has the same name as the class — in this case, the Label() method. The Label instance is constructed during compilation. During execution, the Label is added to the applet window and displays its message text.

> ## Tip
>
> ### Label Data Type vs. Label() Method
> The word, Label, on the left of the assignment operator before the identifier is a reference data type. In that capacity, it is a declaration for the variable name that will hold the Label object. The word Label, with its argument on the right side of the assignment operator, is a constructor or method used to create an instance of the class and add the caption. Java considers Label and Label() as two different concepts. Most constructors use a similar concept with the data type and method.

**TEXTFIELDS**   A **TextField** is an object that displays a text box in which users enter text. Like the Label components, a TextField component displays inside the applet window. The code calls the constructor or method TextField(), which has a width argument to define the character width of the text box during execution, as shown in line 24 of Figure 3-39.

**BUTTONS**   A **Button** is an object that displays a command button for users to click. Most computer users are very familiar with command buttons and know to click a command button to trigger an event. Typically, Buttons inherit their characteristics, such as color and shape, from the operating system, but programmers can define the caption on the Button, as well as the actions to be performed when it is clicked. As shown in line 27 of Figure 3-39, the code calls the constructor or method Button(), which has a caption argument to define the string of characters that displays on the face of the button during execution. The constructor code for a Button is similar to a Label constructor.

## Programming Conventions

Component identifiers must follow the same Java naming rules as variable identifiers, but programmers differ in their specific naming conventions. A **naming convention** is the way you use words, case, prefixes, and underscores to name the identifiers in your program. The main reason for using a consistent set of naming conventions within a given program is to standardize the structure and coding style of an application, so that you and others may read and understand the code more easily.

Some programmers name their applet components with a three-letter prefix similar to the ones used in the Visual Basic programming language, such as lblTitle or txtName. Others use few, if any, component-specific prefixes, simply calling their components label, title, or name. This convention makes it difficult to remember and identify what kind of component is being used in longer programs.

In this program, the naming convention utilized is to have a word beginning with a lowercase letter to identify the purpose of the component, followed by the component name in title case. A Label, for example, might be named costLabel; a TextField might be named amountField. The naming conventions for a Button use a verb or a response caption, such as OK. The verb or response will be followed by the word Button. For example, a button might be named calcButton or okButton. Whatever naming convention you decide to use in your own programs, it should provide for easy reading and consistency.

Recall in the previous versions of the Body Mass Index Calculator program you indented related lines of code, such as the lines following the user prompt that read and parsed input data. This kind of indentation rule is part of a programmer's **coding convention**. The program code for the Body Mass Index Calculator applet follows the same coding conventions, indenting the component constructors for TextFields associated with prompt Labels. Java currently provides no specific rules about coding conventions; as Java takes a firmer hold in application development, a system of standardized indentations and spacing will follow. For now, as with naming conventions, coding conventions should provide for easy reading, logical grouping, and consistency.

Perform the following step to construct Label, TextField, and Button components in the applet.

## To Add Interface Components to an Applet

**1.** With the insertion point on line 21, enter the code as shown in Figure 3-39 on page 3.55 to construct the components.

*The code to construct the components is displayed in the coding window (Figure 3-40).*

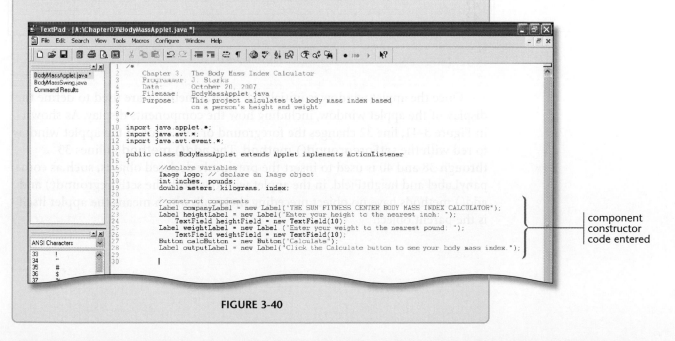

FIGURE 3-40

With the widespread use of graphical user interfaces, users have certain expectations of how they should interact with GUI components. They expect to enter text into text boxes and expect to click buttons to trigger an action or event. Java takes advantage of those expectations and provides the prebuilt classes for typical GUI components. Programmers have these kinds of tools at their fingertips, with many ways to implement them.

## The init() Method

The constructors for Labels, TextFields, and Buttons are merely storage locations until the applet actually is displayed on the screen. To display on the screen, the components must be added to the applet interface using the init() method. As you learned in Chapter 2, the init() method loads the initial setup of the applet when execution begins. In the Welcome to My Day applet created in Chapter 2, the init() method automatically was invoked or initialized by the use of the paint() method to graphically draw text and an image on the applet screen.

When the init() method is **defined**, or coded, as it is in line 30 of the Body Mass Index Calculator applet code, the programmer takes control over what attributes and components are added to the applet window when it is initialized (Figure 3-41).

```
30          public void init()
31          {
32              setForeground(Color.red);
33              add(companyLabel);
34              add(heightLabel);
35              add(heightField);
36              add(weightLabel);
37              add(weightField);
38              add(calcButton);
39              calcButton.addActionListener(this);
40              add(outputLabel);
41              logo = getImage(getDocumentBase(), "logo.gif");
42          }
43
```

**FIGURE 3-41**

Once the applet window is initialized, several methods are used to define the display of the applet window, including how the components display. As shown in Figure 3-41, line 32 changes the foreground or text color of the applet window to red with the **setForeground() method**. The **add() method** in lines 33 through 38 and 40 is used to insert the previously declared objects, such as companyLabel and heightField, in the applet window. Both the setForeground() and add() methods have no object preceding their call, which means the applet itself is the parent object.

Line 39 uses a Button method called the addActionListener() method. Recall that the ActionListener, which was implemented in the class header, is a listener interface that listens for events. If an application is expected to perform some action based on an event from a specific component, such as a Button, the code must (1) implement ActionListener, as it did in line 14 in the class header, and (2) register ActionListener to receive events from the Button, by calling the component's addActionListener() method.

Each component has an **addActionListener() method** that registers, or assigns, an ActionListener to receive action events from that component. In the Body Mass Index Calculator applet, the addActionListener() method for a Button is used to associate the specific Button component, calcButton, with ActionListener. When a user clicks the calcButton, the calcButton sends an action event to ActionListener.

As shown in line 39 of Figure 3-41, the addActionListener() method has only one argument, which is used to assign the specific instance of the Button class that will send action events to the ActionListener. In line 39, the addActionListener() method uses the keyword, this, as the argument for the method. The keyword, this, refers back to the component itself — in this case, the calcButton instance of the Button class. The calcButton thus is the object monitored by the listener interface, ActionListener. In summary, you can think of the ActionListener as telling the applet to listen for the click on the calcButton, and the keyword, this, as identifying which click event code to execute after the user clicks the calcButton.

In line 41, the image for the applet is retrieved from storage and placed in the applet. As in Chapter 2, the getImage() method is used to load an image into an applet. The getImage() method calls a second method called the getDocumentBase() method, which allows the applet to pull the image from the current folder in which your applet class is stored. The getImage() method creates and returns the image object to the variable, logo, which represents the loaded image.

The step on the next page codes the init() method, which adds the components to the applet window, sets the addActionListener() method for the button, and gets the image to display in the applet window.

## To Code the init() Method

1. With the insertion point on line 30, enter the code as shown in Figure 3-41 on page 184.

*The init() method is entered in the coding window (Figure 3-42).*

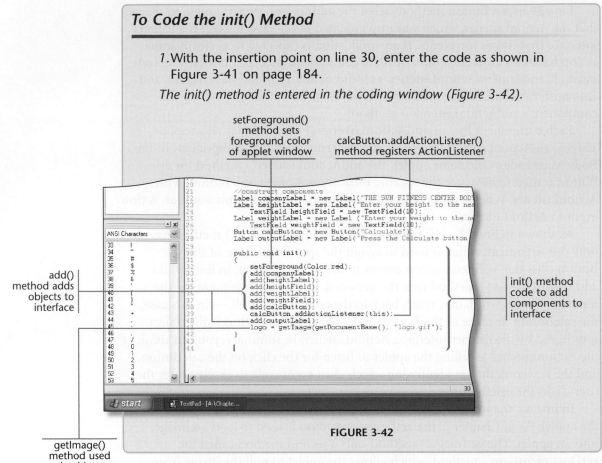

setForeground()
method sets
foreground color
of applet window

calcButton.addActionListener()
method registers ActionListener

add()
method adds
objects to
interface

init() method
code to add
components to
interface

getImage()
method used
to load image

**FIGURE 3-42**

Because the components were constructed before the init() method, the compiled bytecode contains the implementation of those components even before the applet window is initialized. Constructing the components before coding the init() method will speed processing during execution, as the init() method quickly can access and add the constructed components to the applet on the screen. Also, if you try to add a component at the class level, the compiler sometimes interprets it as a new method without a return data type, and will not compile the code.

As you enter code to add components to a user interface, remember that the components will display in the applet window in the order they are entered in the init() method. To the user, the components thus will display as the applet title (companyLabel), followed by the height label and text box (heightLabel and heightField), the weight label and text box (weightLabel and weightField), the Calculate button (calcButton), and the results message (outputLabel).

**Focus and Applet Text Boxes**

When applets use components to display text boxes, the first text box has the **focus**, which means the insertion point displays in that text box. Users may press the TAB key to move to subsequent text boxes. Java programmers should pay close attention to the order in which they add TextFields to applets, as that sets the default tab stop sequence.

## The actionPerformed() Method

The final set of code will create the event behind the Calculate button. Once a user clicks the Calculate button and the click is received, a Java applet must perform a task; in this case, it must calculate the Body Mass Index just as it did in the previous two versions of the program.

When an object such as the calcButton causes an event to happen, the object is called an **event source**. Each event source can have one or more listener interfaces, which become **registered**, or paired, with the event source at compile time. In the Body Mass Index Calculator applet, the ActionListener interface is registered with the calcButton using the addActionListener() method.

A listener interface has methods that specify what will happen when an event is sent to the listener interface. These methods are called **event handlers**. ActionListener has one event handler or method, called **actionPerformed()**, which is executed when the click event occurs. The actionPerformed() method takes the general form shown in line 44 of Figure 3-43. It is common practice to identify the ActionEvent parameter as e, although any variable name can be used.

```
44          public void actionPerformed(ActionEvent e)
45          {
46
47              inches = Integer.parseInt(heightField.getText());
48              pounds = Integer.parseInt(weightField.getText());
49              meters = inches / 39.36;
50              kilograms = pounds / 2.2;
51              index = kilograms / Math.pow(meters,2);
52              outputLabel.setText("YOUR BODY MASS INDEX IS " + Math.round(index) + ".");
53          }
54
```

**FIGURE 3-43**

In lines 47 and 48, the data entered by the user in the text box created by the TextField component are retrieved using the getText() method. The **getText() method** is used to retrieve text from a Label, TextField, or other AWT or Swing component that uses text. Table 3-16 displays the general form of the getText() method.

| *Table 3-16  getText() Method* | |
| --- | --- |
| **General form:** | object.getText(); |
| **Purpose:** | To retrieve text from a Label, TextField, or other AWT or Swing component that uses text. It returns a String composed of the Label's caption or the user-supplied data from a TextField. |
| **Examples:** | 1. heightField.getText();<br>2. myLabel.getText(); |

In lines 47 and 48 of Figure 3-43 on the previous page, the result of the getText() method is wrapped inside the parseInt() method, which means that after Java gets the text from the TextField, it immediately is converted to an integer. The formulas are calculated in lines 49 through 51, and then the answer is sent back to the applet via the setText() method. The **setText() method** does just the opposite of the getText() method: it assigns the caption or String to an object. In line 52, for example, the setText() method assigns the output message to the outputLabel component. The getText() and setText() methods can be used with both Labels and TextFields, as well as with other text-based objects in the java.awt and javax.swing packages.

The following step enters the code for the actionPerformed() method used to handle the click event.

### To Code the actionPerformed() Method

**1.** With the insertion point on line 44, enter the code as shown in Figure 3-43 on the previous page.

*The actionPerformed() method code is entered (Figure 3-44).*

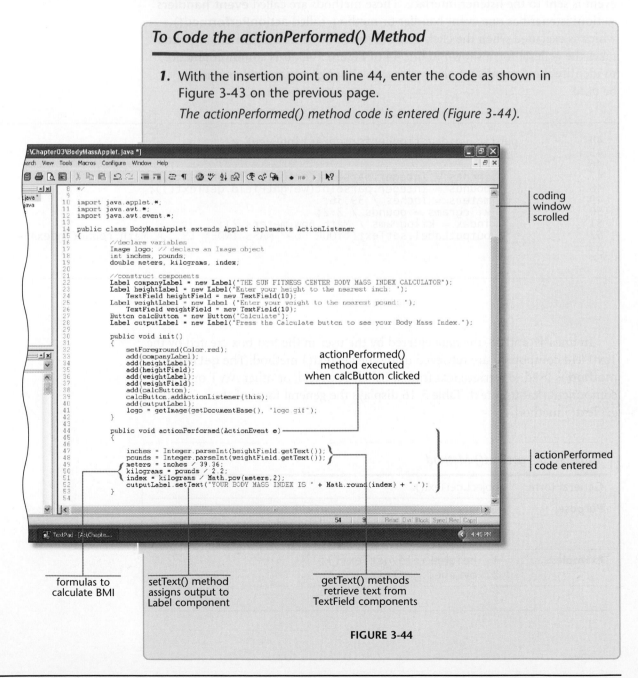

formulas to calculate BMI

setText() method assigns output to Label component

getText() methods retrieve text from TextField components

**FIGURE 3-44**

When the user clicks the calcButton, it triggers the actionPerformed() method. The actionPerformed() method includes the getText() method to retrieve the input values, formulas to calculate BMI, and the setText() method to display output to the user. Anytime you use a TextField component in Java, you can use the getText() and setText() methods to transfer data back and forth easily from the user to the applet, just as you did with the ISR when the program was a console application.

## The paint() Method

The final step in coding the Body Mass Index Calculator applet is to enter the code for the paint() method that draws the image in the applet after it is initialized. As shown in Figure 3-45, line 57 will draw the Sun Fitness Center logo image at a location of 125 pixels from the left side of the applet and 160 pixels from the top. The brace in line 58 closes the block of code for the paint() method. Line 59 displays the closing brace for the entire BodyMassApplet class.

```
55          public void paint(Graphics g)
56          {
57              g.drawImage(logo,125,160,this);
58          }
59   }
```

**FIGURE 3-45**

The following step enters the paint() method.

## To Code the paint() Method

**1.** With the insertion point on line 55, enter the code as shown in Figure 3-45.

*The paint() method is entered (Figure 3-46). Line 59 displays the closing brace for the BodyMassApplet class.*

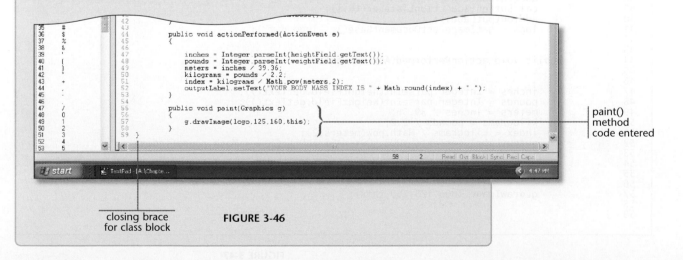

closing brace
for class block

**FIGURE 3-46**

paint()
method
code entered

The applet version of the Body Mass Index Calculator now is complete. You added the import statements, changed the name of the class to BodyMassApplet, and constructed the applet components. You then entered code for the init() method. Next, you included the actionPerformed() method to convert the text to numbers, calculate, and display the answer. Finally, you coded the paint() method to display the company logo in the Applet Viewer window.

Figure 3-47 shows the applet code in its entirety. Check your own code for syntax, proper spelling, capitalization, and indentations. Your lines may wrap differently. When you are confident that everything is correct, you are ready to save and compile your program.

```
1   /*
2       Chapter 3:   The Body Mass Index Calculator
3       Programmer:  J. Starks
4       Date:        October 20, 2007
5       Filename:    BodyMassApplet.java
6       Purpose:     This project calculates the body mass index based
7                    on a person's height and weight.
8   */
9
10  import java.applet.*;
11  import java.awt.*;
12  import java.awt.event.*;
13
14  public class BodyMassApplet extends Applet implements ActionListener
15  {
16      //declare variables
17      Image logo; //declare an Image object
18      int inches, pounds;
19      double meters, kilograms, index;
20
21      //construct components
22      Label companyLabel = new Label("THE SUN FITNESS CENTER BODY MASS INDEX CALCULATOR");
23      Label heightLabel = new Label("Enter your height to the nearest inch: ");
24          TextField heightField = new TextField(10);
25      Label weightLabel = new Label("Enter your weight to the nearest pound: ");
26          TextField weightField = new TextField(10);
27      Button calcButton = new Button("Calculate");
28      Label outputLabel = new Label(
        "Click the Calculate button to see your body mass index.");
29
30      public void init()
31      {
32          setForeground(Color.red);
33          add(companyLabel);
34          add(heightLabel);
35          add(heightField);
36          add(weightLabel);
37          add(weightField);
38          add(calcButton);
39          calcButton.addActionListener(this);
40          add(outputLabel);
41          logo = getImage(getDocumentBase(), "logo.gif");
42      }
43
44      public void actionPerformed(ActionEvent e)
45      {
46
47          inches = Integer.parseInt(heightField.getText());
48          pounds = Integer.parseInt(weightField.getText());
49          meters = inches / 39.36;
50          kilograms = pounds / 2.2;
51          index = kilograms / Math.pow(meters,2);
52          outputLabel.setText("YOUR BODY MASS INDEX IS " + Math.round(index) + ".");
53      }
54
55      public void paint(Graphics g)
56      {
57          g.drawImage(logo,125,160,this);
58      }
59  }
```

**FIGURE 3-47**

## Compiling the Applet

The following step compiles the BodyMassApplet source code.

### To Compile the Applet

*1.* With the Data Disk in drive A, click Tools on the menu bar and then click Compile Java on the Tools menu.

*TextPad automatically saves and then compiles the BodyMassApplet source code. If TextPad notifies you of compilation errors, fix the errors in the BodyMassApplet coding window and then compile the program again.*

**OTHER WAYS**

1. Press CTRL+1
2. At command prompt, type javac BodyMassApplet .java

**Correcting Errors**

In TextPad's Command Results window, you can double-click the first line in an error message to move the insertion point to that error in the coding window, thus eliminating the searching and scrolling necessary to locate the referenced line number.

# Creating an HTML Host Document for an Interactive Applet

You may remember that, because an applet is initiated and executed from within another language or run as a part of a Web page, you must identify a host, or reference program, to execute the applet. The interactive Body Mass Index Calculator applet will run as part of an HTML host document that tells the browser, through the use of tags, the name of the applet and the size of the window. HTML hosts may contain other tags as well.

## Creating the Host Document

You will use the <HTML> tag and the <APPLET> tag in the host document. The following steps create the HTML host document using TextPad.

### To Create the HTML Host Document

*1.* With the TextPad window open, click the New Document button on the Standard toolbar. If line numbers do not display, click Line Numbers on the View menu.

*2.* In the TextPad coding window, type the code as shown in Figure 3-48 on the next page.

*(continued)*

**3.** Click File on the menu bar and then click Save As on the File menu. When the Save As dialog box is displayed, type BodyMassApplet in the File name text box. Do not press the ENTER key. Click the Save as type box arrow and then click HTML (*.htm*,*.stm*) in the list. If necessary, click the Save in box arrow, click 3½ Floppy (A:) in the list, and then double-click the Chapter03 folder in the list.

**4.** Click the Save button in the Save As dialog box.

*TextPad saves the HTML file on the Data Disk in drive A. The file name is displayed on the title bar of the TextPad window and in the Selector window.*

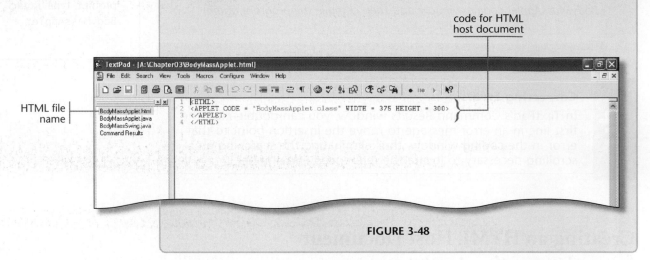

FIGURE 3-48

As you learned in Chapter 2, the <APPLET> tag nested within the <HTML> beginning and ending tags specifies three pieces of information that the Web page needs to access the Java applet: the name of the Java bytecode file, the width of the window, and the height of the window in which to run the applet (Figure 3-48).

## Running and Testing an Interactive Applet

You now are ready to run the applet by using TextPad's Run Java Applet command. The Run Java Applet command automatically executes Java's appletviewer.exe command to display the Applet Viewer window.

When testing the applet version of the same program, you again should use the same sample data for testing each version. That way you can compare output results to ensure that they are consistent for all versions of the program.

### To Run and Test an Interactive Applet

**1.** Click Tools on the menu bar and then click Run Java Applet on the Tools menu.

**2.** If necessary, when the Choose File dialog box is displayed, click the box arrow and choose BodyMassApplet.html in the list. Click the Yes button.

**3.** When the applet is displayed, type 67 in the inches text box. Press the TAB key.

**4.** Type 145 in the pounds text box.

**5.** Click the Calculate button.

*The applet is displayed in the Applet Viewer window (Figure 3-49). The calculated body mass index (BMI) is displayed, along with an output message.*

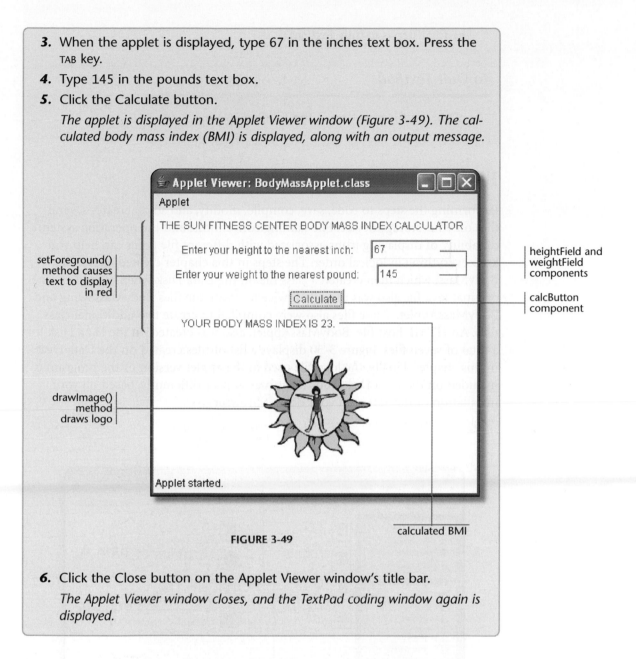

setForeground() method causes text to display in red

heightField and weightField components

calcButton component

drawImage() method draws logo

calculated BMI

**FIGURE 3-49**

**6.** Click the Close button on the Applet Viewer window's title bar.

*The Applet Viewer window closes, and the TextPad coding window again is displayed.*

To enter different data in the applet, you must close the Applet Viewer window and then execute the program again. In a later chapter, you will learn how to write a clear event that will clear the sample data for the next person, without having to close and execute the program again.

Once you have determined that the program runs correctly, you should print a copy of the BodyMassApplet source code and the HTML host document code for documentation purposes. You can print a copy of the program code from the TextPad coding window by selecting the appropriate document in the Selector window and then using the Print command on the File menu. A printout of the program code will be sent to the default printer. Figure 3-47 on page 190 shows the printout of the program code for the applet version of the Body Mass Index Calculator. As previously noted, the longer lines of code wrap to the next line in the printout.

The final step is to quit TextPad.

---

**To Quit TextPad**

**1.** Click the Close button in the TextPad title bar.

---

## File Management

Performing the steps to code, save, compile, modify, and so on creates several files on your storage device. File naming conventions and the operating system's capability of displaying icons associated with different file types can help you keep everything in logical order. The steps in this chapter created a Java file, BodyMass, which then created a class file on the Data Disk when compiled. The original Java file also was modified twice to create the files BodyMassSwing and BodyMassApplet. These files also were compiled to create two additional class files. An HTML host file, BodyMassApplet, also was created on the Data Disk for a total of seven files. Figure 3-50 displays a list of files created on the Data Disk in this chapter. Finally, the logo file used in the applet version of the program is included on the Data Disk. Your icons may appear differently, based on your installation of the SDK and your default browser.

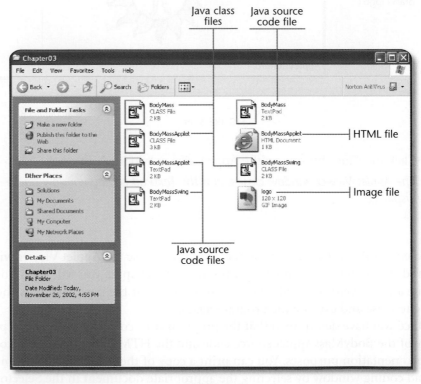

**FIGURE 3-50**

# Chapter Summary

In this chapter, you learned to create a console application to calculate body mass index (BMI). In creating the application, you leaned how to declare variables and write assignment statements to store data with proper identifiers. You also learned to create an instance of a BufferedReader to store, or buffer, the input received from the InputStreamReader (ISR) and to use assignment statements to assign the input data to variables. You learned how to use the readLine() method to make the program pause and wait for user input. In addition, you learned how to code formulas with arithmetic operators, including the use of two methods from the Math class, round() and pow(). You learned to write code that uses variables and concatenation to produce output on the display. You learned to modify the console application to accept data from a dialog box using a Java Swing component called JOptionPane and its associated methods. Finally, you learned how to convert the application to an interactive applet. You learned to use ActionListener to handle events, as well as to use constructors to add Labels, TextFields, and a Button component to the interface. You learned to use the init() method to add components to the applet interface and to use the paint() method to display an image in the Applet Viewer window. After you created an HTML host document to display the applet and run it using the Applet Viewer, you learned about file management and looked at the types of files created by TextPad and the Java SDK.

# What You Should Know

Having completed this chapter, you should now be able to perform the tasks shown in Table 3-17.

*Table 3-17    Chapter 3 What You Should Know*

| TASK NUMBER | TASK | PAGE |
| --- | --- | --- |
| 1 | Start TextPad and Save a TextPad Document | 136 |
| 2 | Enter Beginning Code | 138 |
| 3 | Enter Code to Declare Variables | 142 |
| 4 | Enter Code to Instantiate the BufferedReader | 146 |
| 5 | Enter Code for the User Prompts, Inputs, and Conversions | 150 |
| 6 | Enter the Formulas | 160 |
| 7 | Enter Code to Display Output | 162 |
| 8 | Compile the Source Code | 164 |
| 9 | Run and Test the Application | 164 |
| 10 | Print the Source Code | 166 |
| 11 | Edit the File Name and Class Header | 167 |
| 12 | Enter the New import Statement | 168 |
| 13 | Delete Existing Code | 169 |
| 14 | Enter Code to Create Swing Dialog Boxes | 173 |
| 15 | Enter Code to Close the Program | 174 |
| 16 | Save and Compile the Source Code | 175 |
| 17 | Run and Test the Swing Program | 176 |
| 18 | Enter Code to Implement the ActionListener | 180 |
| 19 | Add Interface Components to an Applet | 183 |
| 20 | Code the init() Method | 186 |
| 21 | Code the actionPerformed() Method | 188 |
| 22 | Code the paint() Method | 189 |
| 23 | Compile the Applet | 191 |
| 24 | Create the HTML Host Document | 191 |
| 25 | Run and Test an Interactive Applet | 192 |
| 26 | Quit TextPad | 194 |

# Key Terms

abs() method *(160)*
accumulator *(149)*
ActionListener *(179)*
actionPerformed() *(187)*
add() method *(184)*
addActionListener() method *(185)*
arithmetic operators *(151)*
assignment operator *(148)*
assignment statement *(148)*
boolean *(140)*
buffer *(144)*
BufferedReader class *(144)*
Button *(182)*
byte *(140)*
cast operation *(142)*
char *(140)*
coding convention *(182)*
comparison operators *(153)*
component *(181)*
concatenation *(162)*
conditional expression *(156)*
constant *(171)*
counter *(123)*
data *(128)*
declaration statement *(141)*
defined *(184)*
dialog box *(133)*
double *(140)*
equality operators *(154)*
event handlers *(187)*
event source *(187)*
exit() method *(173)*
exponentiation *(159)*
expression *(154)*
float *(140)*
focus *(186)*
formula *(132)*
getText() method *(187)*
implements *(179)*
InputStreamReader (ISR) *(144)*
instantiate *(145)*
instantiation *(145)*
int *(140)*
integer division *(151)*

interactive *(143)*
interface *(179)*
java.awt.event package *(178)*
javax.swing *(134)*
JOptionPane *(168)*
Label *(182)*
listener interface *(179)*
long *(140)*
Math class *(159)*
max() method *(160)*
min() method *(160)*
modal *(133)*
modular division *(151)*
modulus operator *(151)*
naming convention *(182)*
nested *(158)*
nextInt() method *(148)*
numeric expression *(154)*
order of operator precedence *(151)*
parse() method *(148)*
pow() method *(160)*
precision *(139)*
primitive data type *(139)*
promotes *(152)*
random() method *(160)*
readLine() method *(147)*
reference data type *(141)*
registered *(187)*
relational operators *(154)*
round() method *(160)*
Scanner *(148)*
scope *(184)*
setForeground() method *(184)*
setText() method *(188)*
short *(140)*
sqrt() method *(160)*
stream *(143)*
strongly typed language *(139)*
Swing components *(166)*
TextField *(182)*
throws IOException *(137)*
wrap *(144)*
wrapper class *(148)*

# Homework Assignments

## 1 Label the Figure

In the spaces provided, identify the various parts of the Java applet shown in Figure 3-51.

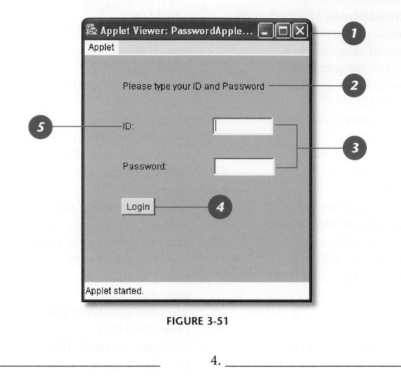

**FIGURE 3-51**

1. _____     4. _____
2. _____     5. _____
3. _____

## 2 Identify Code

In Figure 3-52, arrows point to sections of Java code. Identify the code in the spaces provided using the appropriate word from the following list.

- comment
- calculation
- declaration section
- input from buffer
- class name

- constructor
- concatenation
- conversion
- output section
- package name

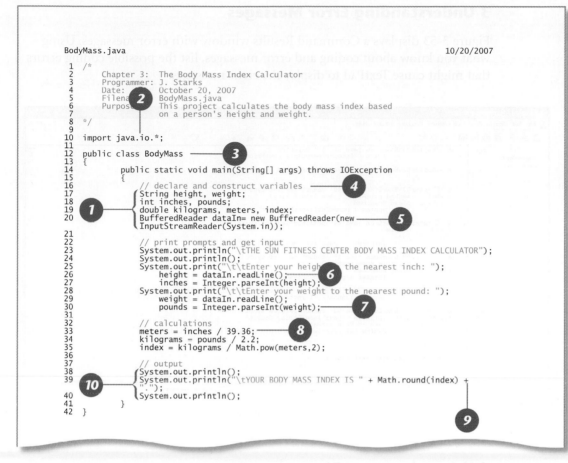

```
BodyMass.java                                                    10/20/2007
 1  /*
 2      Chapter 3:   The Body Mass Index Calculator
 3      Programmer: J. Starks
 4      Date:        October 20, 2007
 5      Filena       BodyMass.java
 6      Purpose      This project calculates the body mass index based
 7                   on a person's height and weight.
 8  */
 9
10  import java.io.*;
11
12  public class BodyMass
13  {
14          public static void main(String[] args) throws IOException
15          {
16                  // declare and construct variables
17                  String height, weight;
18                  int inches, pounds;
19                  double kilograms, meters, index;
20                  BufferedReader dataIn= new BufferedReader(new
                    InputStreamReader(System.in));
21
22                  // print prompts and get input
23                  System.out.println("\tTHE SUN FITNESS CENTER BODY MASS INDEX CALCULATOR");
24                  System.out.println();
25                  System.out.print("\t\tEnter your heigh      the nearest inch: ");
26                      height = dataIn.readLine();
27                      inches = Integer.parseInt(height);
28                  System.out.print("\t\tEnter your weight to the nearest pound: ");
29                      weight = dataIn.readLine();
30                      pounds = Integer.parseInt(weight);
31
32                  // calculations
33                  meters = inches / 39.36;
34                  kilograms = pounds / 2.2;
35                  index = kilograms / Math.pow(meters,2);
36
37                  // output
38                  System.out.println();
39                  System.out.println("\tYOUR BODY MASS INDEX IS " + Math.round(index) +
                    ".");
40                  System.out.println();
41          }
42  }
```

**FIGURE 3-52**

1. _Declaration Section_   6. _Constructor_
2. _Package Name_          7. _Concatenation_
3. _Class Name_            8. _Calculation_
4. _Comment_               9. _Conversion_
5. _Input from Buffer_     10. _Output Section_

## 3 Understanding Error Messages

Figure 3-53 displays a Command Results window with error messages. Using what you know about coding and error messages, list the possible coding errors that might cause TextPad to display the error messages.

**FIGURE 3-53**

## 4 Using the Java API

The Java API is a good tool to look up information about a class with which you may be unfamiliar or to check the syntax of commands and methods you wish to use in your programs. While connected to the Internet, start a browser, type `http://java.sun.com/j2se/5.0/docs/api/` in the Address text box and then press the ENTER key to view the Java API Specification on the Sun Web site. The Java API Specification is organized by the packages, hierarchically, but many programmers click the Index link located at the top of the page to display the entire list alphabetically.

With the Java API Specification open in the browser window, perform the following steps.

1. Use the down scroll arrow in the upper-left frame to display the javax.swing link. Click the javax.swing link.

2. When the javax.swing page is displayed in the lower-left frame, scroll down to display the list of Classes. Click JOptionPane in the list of Classes.

3. When the Class JOptionPane page is displayed in the main frame, read the opening paragraphs that describe the JOptionPane class (Figure 3-54). Read three sections entitled Parameters, Examples, and Direct Use.

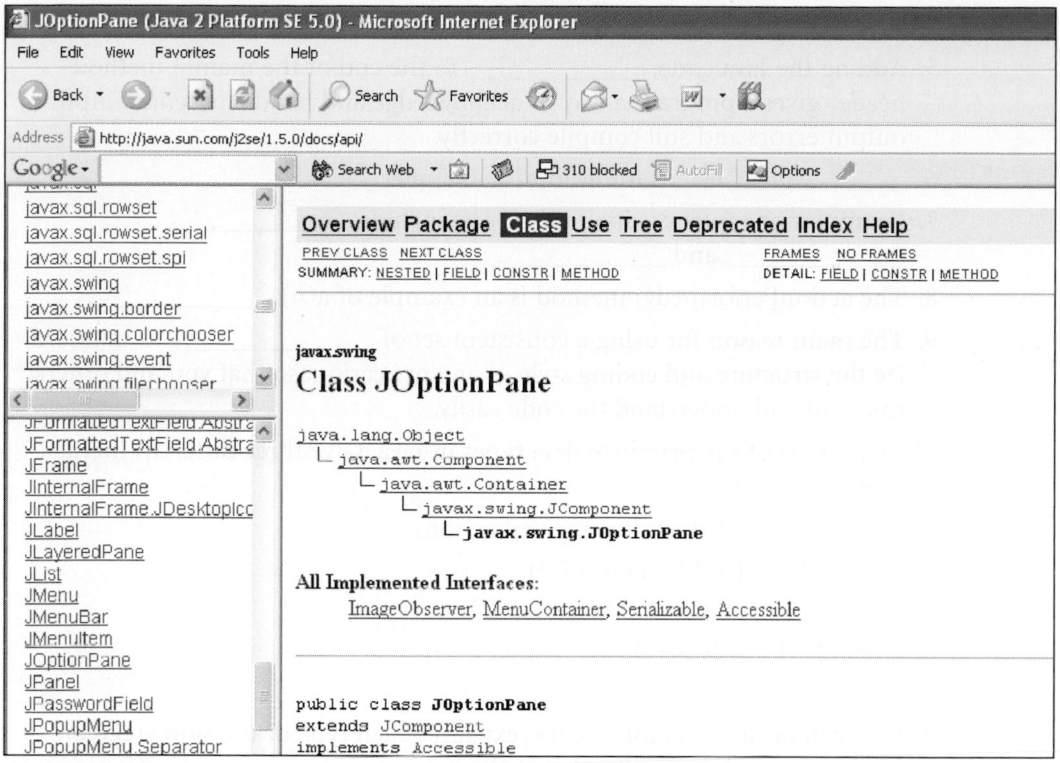

**FIGURE 3-54**

4. Scroll to display the Field Summary table.

5. Chose any three fields in the Field Summary table. One at a time, click each of the three links. When the field definition is displayed, drag through the definition to select it. Print a copy of the field definition by clicking File on the browser's menu bar and then click Print on the File menu. When the Print dialog box is displayed, click Print selection and then click the Print button in the Print dialog box.

6. Click the Back button on your browser's toolbar to return to the JOptionPane page. Scroll to the Method Summary table. Choose any five methods and then click the links and read their descriptions. Make a list of the five methods, their return values, and their argument data types.

7. Write a paragraph describing a computer application that might make good use of a JOptionPane method.

## Short Answer

1. In Java, the process of joining two strings with a plus sign is called _____.

2. Data flowing in or out of a program in Java is called _____.

3. ISR stands for _____.

4. _____ is the process of constructing an instance of a data type or object from a previously defined class.

*(continued)*

**Short Answer** *(continued)*

5. Adding the Java code, _____, to the end of the main() method header gives a program a way to acknowledge and handle potential input or output errors and still compile correctly.

6. _____ listens for events in an applet.

7. Examples of applet component objects include _____, _____, and _____.

8. The actionPerformed() method is an example of a(n) _____.

9. The main reason for using a consistent set of _____ is to standardize the structure and coding style of an application, so that you and others can read and understand the code easily.

10. Make a list of the primitive data types in Java. Give three different literal examples of each.

11. Evaluate each of the following expressions:
    a. 4 * 3 / 6 – 4 + Math.pow(7,2)
    b. (3 + 4 ) * 7 – 3
    c. 9 * 2 / 4 + 5 % 3 + 3
    d. 55 = = 55

12. For each of the situations below, explain which type of division (regular, integer, or modular) will result in the more appropriate answer. Your answer may include more than one type of division.
    a. calculating how many busses will be needed for 350 students
    b. figuring an average grade
    c. determining how many quarters are in 685 cents
    d. testing user input for an even number
    e. rounding down

13. Which arithmetic or comparison operation is performed first in the following expressions?
    a. 144 / (6 * 2)
    b. 25<57 != false
    c. answerA + answerB * answerC
    d. 125 / (result * 4)
    e. true = = true != false
    f. 5 * 3 % 2 + 7 / 2 – 7

14. Which of the following expressions are valid and do *not* require the Java compiler to cast?
    a. double answerA = 12.0 / 4.0;
    b. int answerB = 12 / 7;
    c. int answerC = 3 + 4 + "subtotal";
    d. boolean answerD = 9 * 6;
    e. double answerE = 3answerB;
    f. double answerF = 15 % 5;

15. If necessary, insert parentheses so that each numeric expression results in the value indicated on the left side of the assignment operator (=).

    a. 33 = 3 * 6 – 3 + 2 + 6 * 4 – 4 / Math.pow(2,1);

    b. 22 = 7 * 3 + Math.pow(4,2) – 3 / 13;

    c. 1 = 25 % 6 - 18 + 6 * 3;

    d. 5.0 = 3.0/2.0 + 0.5 + Math.pow(3.0,1.0);

16. Assume each of the following values has been entered by the user and stored as a String. Write a line of code to convert each variable to an appropriate primitive data type.

    a. interestRate

    b. age

    c. *pi*

    d. distanceToMoon

    e. numberOfStudents

17. Describe the differences between JOptionPane message boxes and JOptionPane input boxes.

18. Describe the difference between the getText() method and the setText() method. Give examples of each, including components, arguments, and results.

19. Choose any two numbers and write a formula using each of the arithmetic operators with those two numbers. Solve each formula the way Java would solve it.

20. List five boolean expressions using the relational or conditional operators. Use a variable as one part of your expression. Then, list two variable values that would make your expression true and two that would make your expression false.

21. Write a paragraph describing a situation in which casting might be appropriate. Give examples.

22. Define what is meant by a loss of precision.

23. What does it mean to say that Java is a strongly typed language?

24. Describe the difference between primitive data types and reference data types, and give examples of each.

25. List a variable in the Body Mass Index Calculator program that must have class level scope, and explain why.

## Learn It Online

Start your browser and visit scsite.com/java3e/learn. Follow the instructions in the exercises below.

1. **Chapter Reinforcement TF, MC, and SA**   Click the True/False, Multiple Choice, and Short Answer link below Chapter 3. Print and then answer the questions.

2. **Practice Test**   Click the Practice Test link below Chapter 3. Answer each question, enter your first and last name at the bottom of the page, and then click the Grade Test button. When the graded practice test is displayed on your screen, click Print on the File menu to print a hard copy. Continue to take practice tests until you score 80% or better. Hand in a printout of the final practice test.

3. **Crossword Puzzle Challenge**   Click the Crossword Puzzle Challenge link below Chapter 3. Read the instructions, and then enter your first and last name. Click the Play button. Complete the crossword puzzle. When you are finished, click the Submit button. When the crossword puzzle is redisplayed, click the Print button.

4. **Tips and Tricks**   Click the Tips and Tricks link below Chapter 3. Click a topic that pertains to Chapter 3. Right-click the information and then click Print on the shortcut menu. Construct a brief example of what the information relates to in Java to confirm that you understand how to use the tip or trick. Hand in the example and printed information.

5. **Newsgroups**   Click the Newsgroups link below Chapter 3. Click a topic that pertains to Chapter 3. Print three comments.

6. **Expanding Your Horizons**   Click the Articles for Java link below Chapter 3. Click a topic that pertains to Chapter 3. Print the information. Construct a brief example of what the information relates to in Java to confirm that you understand the contents of the article. Hand in the example and printed information.

7. **Search Sleuth**   Select three key terms from the Key Terms section of this chapter and then use the Google search engine at google.com (or any major search engine) to display and print two Web pages for each key term.

# Debugging Assignment

Start TextPad and open the file, Bert, from the Chapter03 folder on the Data Disk. See the preface of this book for instructions for downloading the Data Disk or see your instructor for information about accessing the files required in this book.

The Bert program is a Java application that calculates the monthly payment on a car by requesting inputs from the user, performing calculations, and displaying output, as shown in Figure 3-55.

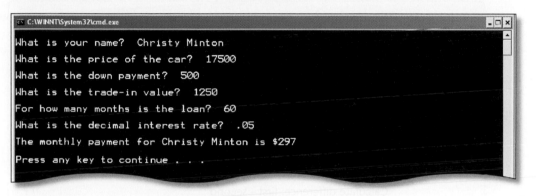

```
C:\WINNT\System32\cmd.exe
What is your name?  Christy Minton
What is the price of the car?  17500
What is the down payment?  500
What is the trade-in value?  1250
For how many months is the loan?  60
What is the decimal interest rate?  .05
The monthly payment for Christy Minton is $297

Press any key to continue . . .
```

FIGURE 3-55

The Bert program has several syntax, semantic, and logic errors in the program code. Perform the following steps to debug the program.

1. Open the file Bert.java in TextPad.
2. Insert your name as the programmer in line 3 of the comment header. Insert the current date in line 4 and write a purpose comment for the program in line 6. Read through the code and fix any errors that you see.
3. Compile the program. As TextPad displays compilation errors, return to the coding window to find the first error, fix it, and then recompile the program.
4. When you have fixed all the syntax and semantic errors so that the program will compile without errors, run the program. Use the following sample data in Table 3-18 to test the program for run-time and logic errors. Fix any errors and compile again.

*Table 3-18   Sample Data for Bert Program*

| Name | Christy Minton |
| --- | --- |
| Price | 17,500 |
| Down payment | 500 |
| Trade-in value | 1250 |
| Number of months of loan | 60 |
| Decimal interest value | .05 |

5. When the program compiles and runs to produce the output as shown in Figure 3-55, print a copy of the source code.

# Programming Assignments

## 1 Writing Java Code from Pseudocode

Start TextPad. Open the Java source code file SimpleMath.java from the Chapter03 folder on the Data Disk. Using the techniques you learned in this chapter, write the lines of code inside the main() method to perform the simple math operations, as outlined by the pseudocode in Table 3-19.

---

**Table 3-19   Pseudocode for Simple Math Program**

---

Begin SimpleMath

    Get Data

        Get first integer from user

        Get second integer from user

    End Get Data

    Perform Math

        Calculate sum: first + second

        Calculate difference: first - second

        Calculate product: first * second

        Calculate quotient: first / second

    End Perform Math

    Display all answers

End

---

1. With the SimpleMath.java source code displayed in the TextPad coding window, insert your name and date in the comments. Insert an appropriate purpose comment. Change the name of the program to MathProgram in the class header and comments.

2. Click inside the main() method braces.

3. Begin by entering the declaration statements to declare the following variables:
   - declare string variables for user input
   - declare integer variables to store the user input after it has been parsed
   - declare integer variables to store the sum, difference, and product
   - declare a double variable to store the quotient

4. After studying the pseudocode in Table 3-19, enter the lines of code necessary to produce the output.

5. Save the file on the Data Disk with the file name MathProgram.

6. Compile the program. If errors occur, fix them in the TextPad coding window and compile again.

7. Run the program. If the program runs correctly, return to TextPad and print a copy of the source code. Otherwise, return to Step 3, review the code, and correct the errors until the program runs error-free.

## 2 Analysis and Design

Figure 3-56 shows a requirements document for a new application, as requested by a small business owner. Using the six phases of the development cycle as shown in Table 3-1 on page 130, perform the following steps:

**REQUEST FOR NEW APPLICATION**

| Date submitted: | November 12, 2007 |
|---|---|
| Submitted by: | Patricia Wolinsky |
| Purpose: | The personnel department often is asked to do a quick computation of an employee's state income tax. Personnel staff would save time and provide more accurate information if members of the staff had a stand-alone application at their disposal to perform the calculation. |
| Application title: | State Tax Computation |
| Algorithms: | State tax is computed as follows:<br>State tax = 0.03 x (Income – (600 x Dependents)) |
| Notes: | 1) The personnel staff is accustomed to the following terminology:<br>**Taxpayer's income** for Income in the above algorithm,<br>**Number of dependents** for Dependents in the above algorithm,<br>**State tax due** for State tax in the above algorithm.<br><br>2) The application should allow the user to enter values for Taxpayer's income and number of dependents, so that state tax due can be computed.<br><br>3) The computation should be designated by the term, Compute. |

**Approvals**

| Approval status: | X | Approved |
|---|---|---|
| | | Rejected |
| Approved by: | Leslie Broda | |
| Date: | November 19, 2007 | |
| Assigned to: | J. Starks, Programmer | |

**FIGURE 3-56**

1. Analyze the requirements. Read the requirements document carefully. Think about the requester, the users, the problem, and the purpose of the application.
2. Design the solution. Draw a storyboard for the program. Pay careful attention to the inputs and outputs. Write either pseudocode or draw a flowchart to represent the sequence of events in your program.

*(continued)*

**2 Analysis and Design** (continued)

3. Validate the design. Have a classmate or your instructor look over your storyboard and make suggestions before you proceed.

4. Implement the design. Translate the design into code for the program.

5. Test the solution. Test the program, finding and correcting errors (debugging) until it is error-free.

6. Document the solution. Print a copy of the source code.

7. Hand in all documents to your instructor.

## 3 Converting from Sample Data to User Input

In order to practice writing interactive programs that require user input, you decide to convert a console application that includes sample data to one that has user prompts and accepts input values. Perform the following steps.

1. Start TextPad. Open the file Money.java from the Chapter03 folder of the Data Disk. The Money.java file contains program code for a program that converts any number of coins into dollars and cents. Change the lines of code that assign sample data into lines of code that prompt the user and store the answers.

2. With the Money.java source code displayed in the TextPad window, insert your name and date in the block comment at the beginning.

3. Use TextPad's Replace dialog box to change each occurrence of the text, Money, to the text, Coins.

4. Save the file on the Data Disk, using Coins as the file name.

5. Add four additional variable declarations for string inputs by typing:

```
String strQuarters;
String strDimes;
String strNickels;
String strPennies;
```

at the appropriate place in the program code.

6. Delete the Assigning Values section of code. Replace it with the following code:

```
System.out.println("Enter the number of quarters.");
    strQuarters = dataIn.readLine();
System.out.println("Enter the number of dimes.");
    strDimes = dataIn.readLine();
System.out.println("Enter the number of nickels.");
    strNickels = dataIn.readLine();
System.out.println("Enter the number of pennies.");
    strPennies = dataIn.readLine();
```

7. Delete the Calculations section of code. Replace the statements that multiply the number of coins by their face value with lines of code that parse the input values and assign the values to variables by typing the following:

quarters = Integer.parseInt(strQuarters) * 25;

dimes = Integer.parseInt(strDimes) * 10;

nickels = Integer.parseInt(strNickels) * 5;

pennies = Integer.parseInt(strPennies) * 1;

8. Compile the program by clicking Tools on the menu bar and then clicking Compile Java. If the compilation results in any errors, correct the errors and recompile the program.

9. Run the program by clicking Tools on the menu bar and then clicking Run Java Application. Enter sample data to test the program. If the program runs correctly, return to TextPad and print a copy of the source code for your instructor. Otherwise, correct any errors and return to step 8.

10. Quit TextPad.

## 4 Interactive Checkbook Balancing Calculator

The local credit union has asked you to develop a simple program to help customers balance their checkbooks. You decide to write a stand-alone Java application that accepts the beginning balance, the total of the checks written, the total of any deposits, and the fees charged by the bank as inputs. The program then calculates and displays what the ending balance should be. Figure 3-57 displays the results from executing the application. Perform the following steps:

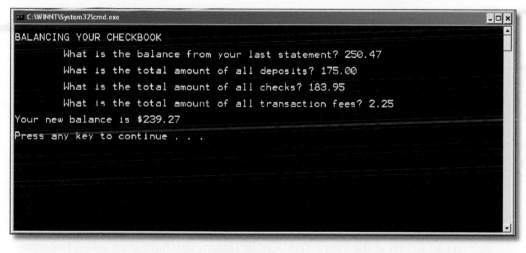

**FIGURE 3-57**

1. Start TextPad. Save the new document as a Java source code file on the Data Disk using the file name Balance.

2. Begin your code by typing a block comment with the Programming Assignment number, your name, the current date, and the program name, Balance.java. Write a description or purpose comment.

3. Type the import statement, class header, and main() method header and their opening braces. Remember to use the phrase, throws IOException, as the program will be interactive.

*(continued)*

**4 Interactive Checkbook Balancing Calculator (continued)**

4. Type a constructor for the BufferedReader, as described in this chapter.

5. Declare both String and float variables for beginning balance, total deposits, total checks, and total fees. Declare a float variable for ending balance. Use user-friendly, unique names for each variable.

6. Using System.out.println() methods, enter lines of code to prompt the user for each of the input variables, as shown in Figure 3-57. Include a readLine() method to accept each input and assign it to its corresponding declared String variable.

7. Enter code to convert each input variable to doubles or floats using the appropriate parse() method.

8. Write a formula that takes the beginning balance plus the total deposits minus the checks and fees, and assigns the value to the ending balance.

9. Write an output section that displays an appropriate message and the ending balance on the display.

10. Label each section with an appropriate line comment.

11. Compile your program by pressing CTRL+1.

12. If there are no compilation errors, execute the program by pressing CTRL+2. Enter the sample input data from Figure 3-57; confirm that the program provides correct output data. Run the program again with your own personal data.

13. In the TextPad window, use the Print command on the File menu to print a copy of the code for your instructor.

14. Quit TextPad.

## 5 Income to Debt Ratio Calculator

Many financial institutions make decisions about extending credit and financing major purchases based on a customer's income to debt ratio. This ratio is the percentage of a customer's income that is spent paying off debts such as mortgages, automobile loans, and other debt, such as credit cards. Typically, all debts are added together and then that total is divided by the customer's monthly income. Customers with a lower income to debt ratio are more likely to qualify for a loan.

As an intern at the Employees' Credit Union, you have been asked to create an interactive income to debt ratio calculation program that can run as a stand-alone application. Input should be via dialog boxes. Table 3-20 on the next page displays the inputs and outputs for the program.

**Table 3-20 Inputs and Outputs for Income to Debt Ratio Calculator**

| INPUTS | OUTPUTS |
|---|---|
| amount of monthly income | Income to Debt Ratio |
| amount of mortgage or rent (or zero) | |
| amount of auto loan (or zero) | |
| amount of other debt (or zero) | |

Perform the following steps.

1. Start TextPad. Save the new document as a Java source code file on the Data Disk. Name the file DebtRatio.

2. Begin your code by typing a block comment with the Programming Assignment number, your name, the current date, and the program name, DebtRatio.java. Write a description or purpose comment.

3. Type a statement to import the javax.swing package.

4. Type the class header and main() method header.

5. Declare the following variables to be Strings: strMonthlyIncome, strMortgage, strAutoLoan, and strOtherDebt.

6. Declare the following variables to be doubles: monthlyIncome, mortgage, autoLoan, otherDebt, and ratio.

7. Create an input section beginning with an appropriate line comment. In order to accept user input, enter showInputDialog() methods to display the prompts and accept user input for monthly income, mortgage, auto loan, and other debt.

8. Create a conversion section, beginning with an appropriate line comment, to parse each of the inputted values.

9. Create a calculation section, beginning with an appropriate line comment, to calculate the income to debt ratio using the following formula: ratio = (mortgage + autoLoan + otherDebt) / monthlyIncome.

10. Create an output section, beginning with an appropriate line comment. Use concatenation to print a message and the variable, ratio, in a JOptionPane dialog or message box.

11. Close both the main() and class methods with closing braces.

12. Compile your program by clicking Tools on the menu bar and then clicking Compile Java.

13. If no compilation errors occur, execute the program by clicking Tools on the menu bar and then clicking Run Java Application. Run the program again with your own personal data.

14. In the TextPad window, use the Print command on the File menu to print a copy of the source code for your instructor.

15. Quit TextPad.

## 6 Creating an Applet

As Webmaster for a chain of appliance stores, you have been asked to create an applet that will display as part of the store's e-commerce site. The applet will calculate the annual cost of running an appliance. Using text boxes, the applet will ask the user for (1) the cost per kilowatt-hour in cents and (2) the number of kilowatt-hours the appliance uses in a year. Perform the following steps to create the applet. Figure 3-58 displays the applet.

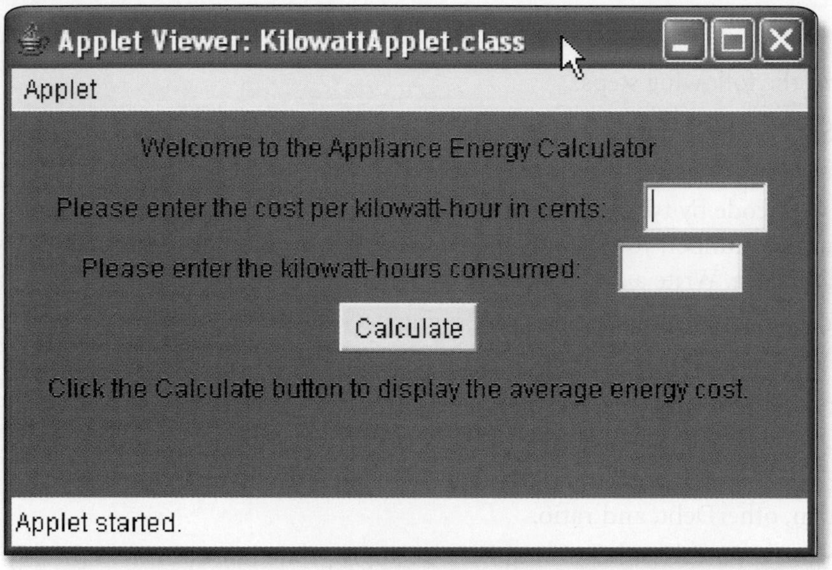

**FIGURE 3-58**

1. Start TextPad. Save the new document as a Java source code file on the Data Disk using the file name KilowattApplet.

2. Begin your code by typing a block comment with the Programming Assignment number, your name, the current date, and the program name, KilowattApplet.java. Write a description or purpose comment.

3. Type lines of code to import all of the classes from the following packages: java.awt, java.applet, and java.awt.event.

4. Type a class header that extends Applet and implements the ActionListener.

5. Construct the components listed in Table 3-21 on the next page.

**Table 3-21    Kilowatt Applet Constructed Components**

| OBJECT | IDENTIFIER | METHOD PARAMETER (CAPTION OR LENGTH) |
|--------|-----------|--------------------------------------|
| Label | welcome | Welcome to the Appliance Energy Calculator |
| Label | costKwhrLabel | Please enter the cost per kilowatt-hour in cents: |
| TextField | costKwhrField | 5 |
| Label | hoursPerYearLabel | Please enter the kilowatt-hours consumed: |
| TextField | hoursPerYearField | 5 |
| Button | calcButton | Calculate |
| Label | outputLabel | Click the Calculate button to display the average energy cost. |

6. Create an init() method to add all of the above components to the applet interface.

7. Enter the code to add the ActionListener to the calcButton and close the init() method with a brace.

8. Create an actionPerformed() method to convert the input and perform the calculations. Enter the code to get the text from each text box, parse it, and assign it to the appropriate declared variable as shown in Table 3-22.

**Table 3-22    KilowattApplet Construction and Conversion Code**

```
double costKwhr = Double.parseDouble(costKwhrField.getText());

double kwHours = Double.parseDouble(hoursPerYearField.getText());
```

9. Declare a double variable named average.

10. Write a line of code to perform the calculation that multiplies the cents by the kilowatt-hours in a year and then assigns it to the variable, average.

11. Enter the code from Table 3-23 to round the average with the Math.round() method and assign it to the text of the output label. The Math.round() method includes a casting of the literal 100 to double in order to retain the decimal places.

**Table 3-23    KilowattApplet Output Code**

```
outputLabel.setText("The average annual cost to operate this appliance is $" +
    Math.round(average* 100)/100D);
```

*(continued)*

## 6 Creating an Applet *(continued)*

12. Close the actionPerformed() method with a closing brace and then close the applet class with a closing brace.

13. Compile your program by clicking Tools on the menu bar and then clicking Compile Java.

14. In the TextPad window, click the New Document button on the Standard toolbar. Type the code from Table 3-24 for the HTML host document.

---

*Table 3-24   HTML Host Document Code*

```
<HTML>
<APPLET CODE = "KilowattApplet.class" WIDTH = 430 HEIGHT = 200>
</APPLET>
</HTML>
```

---

15. Save the HTML file on the Data Disk using the file name KilowattApplet.html.

16. Execute the program. Enter the sample data as shown in Table 3-25. Run the program again with your own personal data.

---

*Table 3-25   Sample Data for Appliance Energy Calculator*

| INPUTS | | OUTPUTS |
|---|---|---|
| Cost per kilowatt-hour | Number of kilowatt-hours consumed | Annual cost |
| .086 | 730 | $62.78 |

---

17. In the TextPad window, use the Print command on the File menu to print a copy of the source code for your instructor; then quit TextPad.

## 7 Bill's Burgers

Bill's Burgers would like an applet that calculates the sales tax for their front counter help. The applet should let the worker enter the total amount of the customer's order and then calculate a six percent (6%) sales tax. When the worker clicks a Calculate button, the applet should display the amount of the customer's order, the tax, and the total of the customer's order and tax added together. *Hint:* Use a method and formula similar to the one in Table 3-23.

## 8 Ohm's Law

Ohm's law relates the resistance of an electrical device, such as a portable heater, to the electric current flowing through the device and the voltage applied to it. The law uses the formula

$$I = V/R$$

where V is the voltage, measured in volts; R is the resistance, measured in ohms; and I is the answer, the electrical current, measured in amps. Write an applet that displays a welcome message, two Label prompts, and TextFields. One Label will ask the user to input the voltage; the other Label will ask the user to input the resistance of a device. The applet then will display the current. Remember that because V and R will be entered as integers, the ActionListener will have to parse the numbers into double values in order to perform the division.

## 9 Calculating the Circumference of a Circle

Your younger brother is studying beginning geometry. He has to calculate the circumference of several different circles and would like to automate the process. Write a stand-alone application for him that calculates the circumference of a circle from the radius. The radius will be an integer value input from the keyboard. Create a method that will accept the integer and perform the calculation using the formula, 2*pi*r — that is, 2 times the value of *pi* times the radius. Use the value 3.14 or the Java variable, Math.PI, in your calculation.

## 10 Dollars and Cents

Write a program that will spell out the number of dollars and cents based on user numeric input. For instance, if the user inputs 925, the program will print out 9 dollars and 25 cents. For this program, you will use integer arithmetic and will need to avoid floating point arithmetic. Review modular division and the modular operator (%), as discussed in the chapter.

## 11 Currency Conversion

Because you are an outstanding student, a local civic organization has awarded you a generous sum of money to pursue your education in England. You also plan to do some sightseeing while you are in Europe. The award money is in U.S. dollars, and you want to know how that will convert to the British pound, the euro, and the Russian ruble. Use the concepts and techniques presented in this chapter to create an application that will accept the U.S. dollar amount, convert the U.S. dollar amount, and display the British pound, euro, and Russian ruble equivalents. Use the Web, a newspaper, or a local financial institution to obtain the conversion rates.

## 12 Using the Sun Microsystems Java Documentation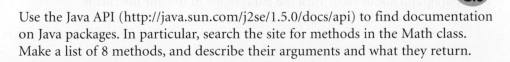

Use the Java API (http://java.sun.com/j2se/1.5.0/docs/api) to find documentation on Java packages. In particular, search the site for methods in the Math class. Make a list of 8 methods, and describe their arguments and what they return.

### 13 Moving from the BufferedReader to Scanner

In Programming Assignment 4, you created an interactive checkbook using the BufferedReader to accept input in the console window. Convert the program so that it uses the J2SE version 5.0 Scanner class described on page 148. Import the java.util.* package. You will change the line of code that constructs an instance of the BufferedReader to construct an instance of the Scanner class. Change the lines of code that use the readLine() method to use the nextFloatFloat() method. Insert comment marks in front of lines that previously parsed the data.

### 14 Moving from Swing to Scanner

In Programming Assignment 5, you created an income to debt ratio calculator with Swing input using dialog boxes. Convert the program so that it uses the J2SE version 5.0 Scanner class described on page 148. Import the java.util.* package. You will construct an instance of the Scanner class. Change the lines of code that use the showInputDialog() method to use the nextDouble() method. Insert comment marks in front of lines that previously parsed the data.

### 15 Input Usability

Many businesses conduct usability tests evaluating user interfaces. Your job is to provide four versions of user input from which a business may select. Choose any program in this chapter and create the following forms of the same program:

- An application with user input from the BufferedReader at the command prompt, parsing the data from the readLine() method.
- An application with user input from the Scanner class at the command prompt, using the nextInt() or nextDouble() method.
- An application with user input from Swing dialog boxes, parsing the data from the showInputDialog() method.
- An applet with user input from Swing dialog boxes, parsing the data from the showInputDialog() method.

Add comments to each program describing the kind of input and the methods used. Print a copy of each program. Demonstrate the program, in execution, to a classmate. On the back of the printouts, write any feedback about speed, usability, or preferences. Turn the printouts in to your instructor.

### 16 The Scanner Methods

The Scanner method, new to J2SE version 5.0, uses several different methods to receive user input based on data types. Visit the Sun Microsystems Java API site at http://java.sun.com/j2se/1.5.0/docs/api/. Use the index to find the Scanner class. Scroll to the Method Summary. Choose any four methods that begin with the word, next, and click each one. Read the information provided and write a brief paragraph about each. Turn the paragraphs in to your instructor.

# 4

# Decision Making and Repetition with Reusable Objects

## Objectives

You will have
mastered the material in
this chapter when you can:

- Design a program using methods
- Code a selection structure to make decisions in code
- Describe the use of the logical AND, OR, and NOT operators
- Define exceptions and exception handling
- Code a try statement and a catch statement to handle exceptions
- Create a user-defined method
- Code a repetition structure using the while statement
- Write a switch statement to test for multiple values in data
- Format numbers using a pattern and the format() method
- Construct a Color object
- Use a Checkbox and a CheckboxGroup in the user interface

# Introduction

Thus far in this book, Java programming examples have included code statements that execute sequentially, from top to bottom, without skipping any code, repeating any code, or branching to another class or method. Realistically, most programs use a **selection structure**, also called an **if...else structure**, to branch to a certain section of code and a **repetition structure** to repeat a certain section of code. Both selection structures and repetition structures are considered to be **control structures,** because the logic of these structures controls the order in which code statements execute. These structures will be covered in detail later in the chapter as you learn how to write code that uses if...else statements, while statements, and switch statements.

You also will learn how to write user-defined methods in Java in order to break tasks into small sections of code that can be reused. You will learn how to write a try statement and a catch statement to handle exceptions, in addition to learning ways to test for validity, reasonableness, and accurate input. Finally, you will learn how to write code to add check boxes and option buttons to an applet.

# Chapter Four — Sales Commission

The programs developed in this chapter create a Commission program that GetOuttaTown Travel, a nationwide travel agency, can use to calculate sales commission for their travel agents. The agents at GetOuttaTown Travel can complete three types of sales — telephone, in-store, and outside — each of which earns a different commission percentage. The travel agency requires a computer program that will accept a sales amount and then, based on a choice of commission codes, will calculate a dollar commission amount using the formula, commission = sales amount * commission rate. The commission code identifies the type of sale and commission rate. Telephone sales receive a 10% commission, in-store sales receive a 14% commission, and outside sales receive an 18% commission. Output will include a formatted message displaying the calculated commission.

Two versions of the Commission program are developed in this chapter, as shown in Figure 4-1. First, the Commission program is developed as an application with two dialog boxes that provide text boxes for user input. Next, the Commission program is developed as an applet that uses a text box and option buttons for user input.

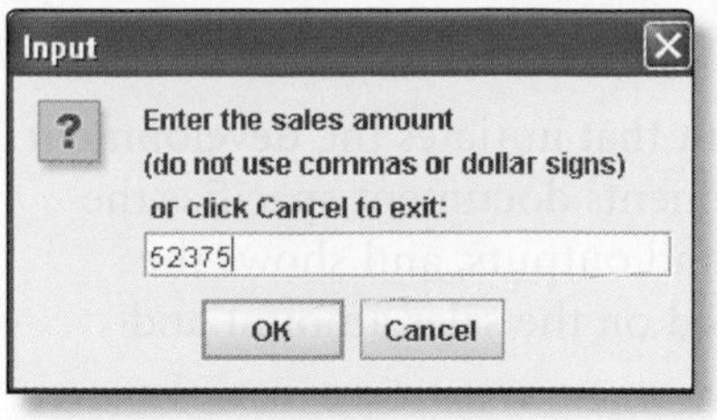

(a) User enters sales amount.

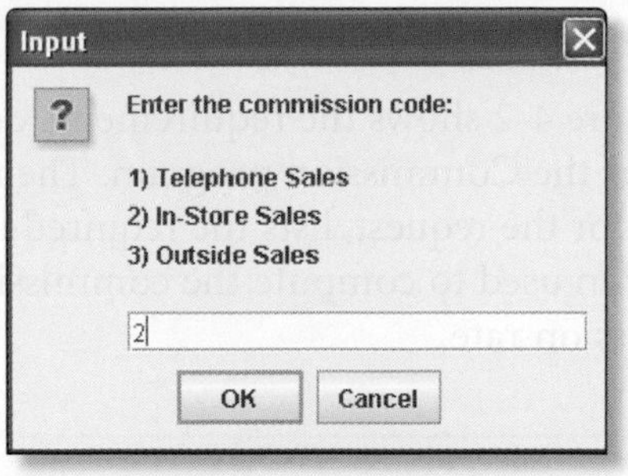

(b) User enters commission code.

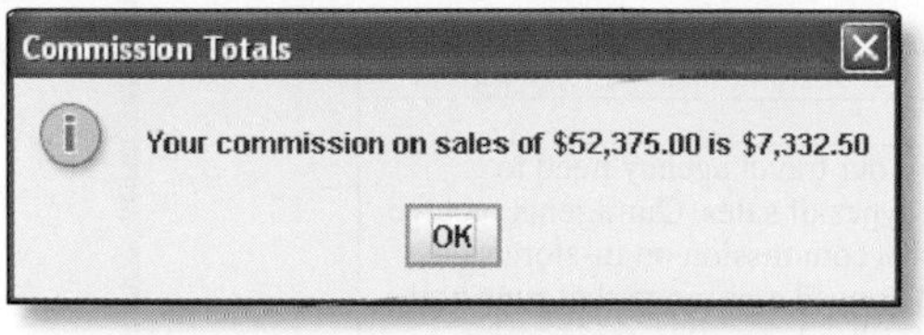

(c) Application calculates commission.

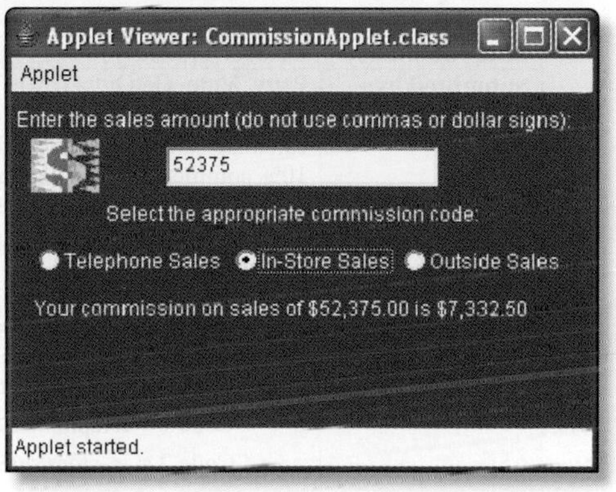

**FIGURE 4-1**

(d) Web user enters sales amount and then clicks an option button to display the sales and commission.

# Program Development

The program development cycle for the Commission program consists of tasks that correspond to the six development cycle phases, as shown in Table 4-1.

**Table 4-1    Commission Program Development Tasks**

| | DEVELOPMENT PHASE | TASK(S) |
|---|---|---|
| 1 | Analyze the requirements | Analyze the Commission problem. |
| 2 | Design the solution | Design the user interface for the console application and the applet, including output data and placement of the applet components and graphic. Design the logic to solve the problem. |
| 3 | Validate the design | Confirm with the user that the design solves the problem in a satisfactory manner. |
| 4 | Implement the design | Translate the design into code. Include internal documentation (comments and remarks) within the code that explains the purpose of the code statements. Create the HTML file to host the applet. |
| 5 | Test the solution | Test the program. Find and correct any errors (debug) until it is error-free. |
| 6 | Document the solution | Print copies of the application code, applet code, applet interface, and HTML code. |

## Analysis and Design

Figure 4-2 shows the requirements document that initiates the development cycle for the Commission program. The requirements document specifies the reason for the request, lists the required inputs and outputs, and shows the algorithm used to compute the commission based on the sales amount and commission rate.

### REQUEST FOR NEW APPLICATION

| | |
|---|---|
| **Date submitted:** | October 11, 2007 |
| **Submitted by:** | Patty Witte, GetOuttaTown Travel |
| **Purpose:** | Many departments and employees within our travel agency need to calculate sales commission for different types of sales. Our agents receive 10% commission for telephone sales, 14% commission on in-store sales, and 18% commission on outside sales. We need a program that runs both locally and over the Web to give quick feedback on sales commission. |
| **Application title:** | Commission |
| **Algorithms:** | Users should be able to type in the total sales, select one of the three types of sales mentioned above and then click a button to display the resulting commission. Each type of sales should have a commission code assigned. Sales commission is calculated as follows:<br><br>• Code 1 = telephone sales amount * .10<br><br>• Code 2 = in-store sales amount * .14<br><br>• Code 3 = outside sales amount * .18 |
| **Notes:** | 1) You may want to help users enter valid data by reminding them to not enter commas or dollar signs when they enter the sales amount.<br><br>2) Please label the commission codes with descriptive words, rather than listing the commission percentages. For example, in the local version running on our desktops, the program should present a simple list with the words, Telephone Sales, In-Store Sales, and Outside Sales, to identify the type of sales. In the Web version, option buttons labeled Telephone Sales, In-Store Sales, and Outside Sales would help users choose the correct commission code.<br><br>3) The application should employ dialog boxes to allow users to enter data. Appropriate error messages should display when users enter invalid information.<br><br>4) The user should be able to exit the application by clicking a Cancel button or by clicking the Close button in the application window.<br><br>5) The attached graphic uses our company colors. Can you try to match the dark red color in the applet? |

**Approvals**

| **Approval status:** | X | Approved |
|---|---|---|
| | | Rejected |
| **Approved by:** | Amir Rubadi | |
| **Date:** | October 18, 2007 | |
| **Assigned to:** | J. Starks, Programmer | |

**FIGURE 4-2**

**PROBLEM ANALYSIS**   The Commission program should accept and test a numeric value from the user, display a list of codes and test for a valid choice, and then calculate and display results. The program also should include appropriate prompts and messages.

Because this program involves making decisions based on user input, the code that executes each decision can be designed, developed, and tested individually as it is added to the program. Programmers commonly create a small portion of code and then thoroughly test it before moving on to the next section. The object-oriented nature of Java lends itself to this kind of component design, creating reusable portions of code and breaking the programming tasks down into simpler, more manageable steps. Throughout the chapter, the code for each decision is designed and tested as it is added to the program.

**DESIGN THE SOLUTION**   Once you have analyzed the problem, the next step is to design the user interface and the logic to solve the problem. The Commission program has two versions: a console application and an applet. The console application uses dialog boxes with prompts and text boxes to accept numeric input, and then displays formatted output in a message box, as shown in the storyboard in Figure 4-3a. The applet uses a prompt, a text box, and option buttons to accept input, and then displays formatted output in the applet window, as shown in the storyboard in Figure 4-3b on the next page.

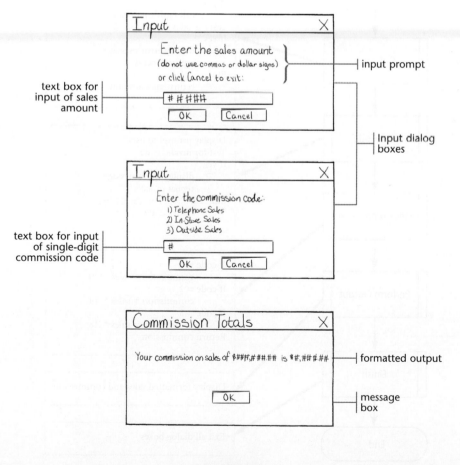

**FIGURE 4-3a**

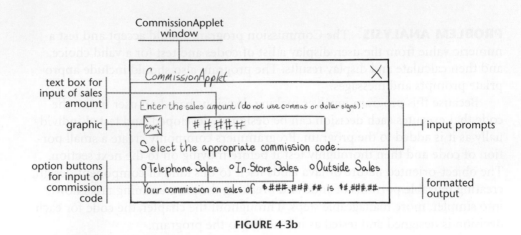

FIGURE 4-3b

**PROGRAM DESIGN**   Once you have designed the interface, the next step is to design the logic to solve the problem and create the desired results. Figure 4-4 shows the flowchart and related pseudocode that represents the logic of the program. Each process symbol references the pseudocode for each of the five methods required in this program. The main() method calls each of these five methods after the program starts.

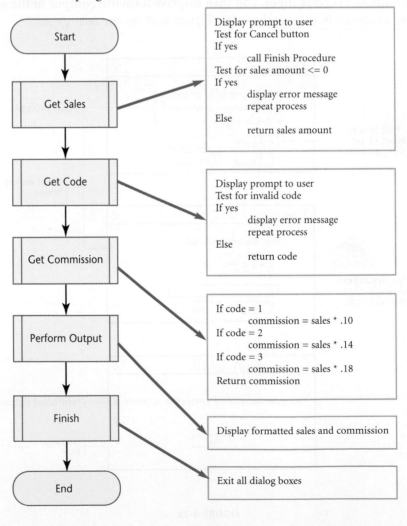

FIGURE 4-4

The getSales() method displays an input dialog box and prompts the user for a sales amount in dollars. If the user clicks the Cancel button or Close button in the user interface, the program will terminate. If not, the getSales() method will make sure the value entered is greater than zero. If the value is not greater than zero, the program will display an error message and allow the user to enter a new value. When a valid value for sales amount is entered, the code returns the value to the main() method for storage.

The getCode() method then displays a list of valid commission codes that the user can enter. The getCode() method also checks for a valid integer between 1 and 3. If an invalid number is entered, the method displays an error message and prompts the user to enter a new value. When a valid value for commission code is entered, the code value is returned to the main() method for storage.

The getComm() method uses the two previous input values to calculate a commission amount using the formula commission = sales amount * commission rate, and then returns it to the main() method for storage.

The output() method displays formatted output with dollar signs, commas, and decimal points. The output message will include the sales amount and the total commission.

The finish() method calls the System.exit() method to close all dialog boxes and then terminate the program.

**VALIDATE DESIGN**   Once you have designed the program, you can validate the design by stepping through the requirements document and making sure that the design addresses each requirement. If possible, you also should step through the solution with test data to verify that the solution meets the requirements. The user also should review the design to confirm that it solves the problem outlined in the requirements. The user may realize that the instructions the programmer was given do not cover all the company's needs, requiring additional features. By comparing the program design with the original requirements, both the programmer and the user can validate that the solution is correct and satisfactory.

Having analyzed the problem, designed the interface, and designed the program logic, the analysis and design of the application is complete. As shown in Table 4-1 on page 219, the next task in the development cycle is to implement the design by creating a new Java program using TextPad. Implementing the design for this program involves creating Java methods to modularize the task of obtaining a sales amount, using Java's ability to catch errors as they occur, and then creating a module to display an appropriate error message. The program code also involves using code statements that will allow the program to make decisions based on user input.

## Starting a New Java Program in TextPad

In Chapter 2, you learned how to start TextPad and save a file using a Java file type. The steps on the next page start TextPad and save the TextPad document using a Java file type.

### To Start TextPad and Save a TextPad Document

1. Start TextPad following the steps outlined on page 53. If necessary, click View on the menu bar and then click Line Numbers on the View menu to display line numbers.

2. Insert the Data Disk in drive A. Click File on the menu bar and then click Save As on the File menu.

3. When the Save As dialog box is displayed, type Commission in the File name text box and then click Java (*.java) in the Save as type list. Click the Save in box arrow and then click 3½ Floppy (A:) in the Save in list.

4. Double-click the Chapter04 folder or a location specified by your instructor.

   *TextPad will save the file named Commission.java as a Java source code file in the Chapter04 folder on the Data Disk in drive A (Figure 4-5). Your list of files may differ.*

Save As dialog box        Chapter04 folder

file name        Java (*.java) file type        Save button

**FIGURE 4-5**

5. Click the Save button in the Save As dialog box.

**OTHER WAYS**

1. To start TextPad, click Start button, click TextPad on Start menu
2. To view line numbers, press CTRL+Q, L
3. To save, press F12
4. To save, press ALT+F, A

## Coding the Program

As you have learned, the implementation phase of the program development cycle involves writing the code that translates the design into a program. During program design, a flowchart and pseudocode were used to outline the logic of the program code used in the Commission program (Figure 4-4 on page 222). As outlined in that pseudocode, the tasks that the program should perform are to accept two inputs of sales amount and commission code, determine which commission code the user selected, calculate commission using the appropriate formula, and then display the commission as formatted output. The coding process starts with entering the beginning program code.

## Entering Beginning Code

Several statements and commands are used as the beginning code in most executable Java programs, including comments, import statements, the class header, and the main method header. In the Commission program, one import statement imports the JOptionPane class from the javax.swing package so that the program can use some of its methods to create and display dialog boxes that display a message or prompt users for an input value. A second import statement imports the DecimalFormat class from the java.text package in order to format the output displayed to the user. The DecimalFormat class will be covered in detail later in the chapter.

The Commission program requires three variables: one to hold the dollar sales amount, one to hold the calculated commission, and one to hold the commission code. Table 4-2 summarizes the data types, variable names, and purposes of the three variables.

**Table 4-2   Variables for the Commission Program**

| DATA TYPE | VARIABLE NAME | PURPOSE |
|-----------|---------------|---------|
| double | dollars | To hold the valid dollar amount of sales |
| double | answer | To hold the answer returned after commission is calculated |
| int | empCode | To hold the commission code for the employee's sales |

Figure 4-6 displays the comments, import statements, headers, braces, and variable declarations used in the Commission program. Even though this program has no code inside the main() method — other than to declare variables — Java can compile and execute the program successfully.

```
1   /*
2         Chapter 4:   Sales Commission
3         Programmer:  J. Starks
4         Date:        October 25, 2007
5         Filename:    Commission.java
6         Purpose:     This program calculates sales commission using five methods:
7                      getSales(), getCode(), getComm(), output(), and finish().
8   */
9
10  import javax.swing.JOptionPane;
11  import java.text.DecimalFormat;
12
13  public class Commission
14  {
15      public static void main(String[] args)
16      {
17          //declare class variables
18          double dollars, answer;
19          int empCode;
20      }
21  }
```

**FIGURE 4-6**

This section of code represents a program **stub**, which is an incomplete portion of code entered to allow the developer to compile and test the program. The stub does not actually implement the details of methods, functions, or other elements of the code, but serves as a template or placeholder, in which the developer can later enter code. Using a program stub allows a developer to compile and test a program incrementally while developing the program, to allow for debugging and refinement of code.

The following step enters beginning code.

## To Enter Beginning Code

**1.** Enter the code as shown in Figure 4-6 on the previous page, replacing the programmer name and date shown with your name and the current date.

*The TextPad window displays the code for the program stub (Figure 4-7).*

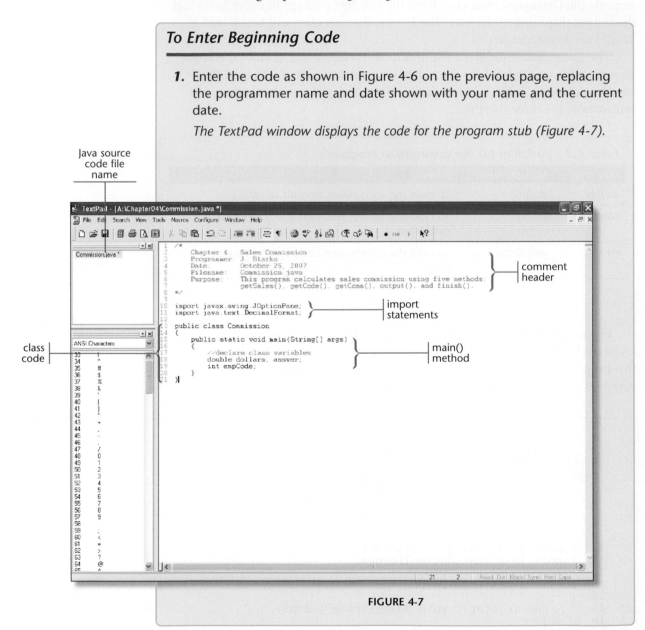

FIGURE 4-7

Remember that the name of the class must match the name of the Java source code file exactly. In the code entered in the previous step, the Java source code file and the class both use the name Commission. The code created a program stub, which provides the basic template or structure for the code to be entered but does not yet include the detailed code. While the program stub can be compiled and run, it needs additional code to provide the functionality specified in the requirements document.

### Compiling and Testing the Program Stub

Recall that the compiler automatically saves the program and then translates the source code into Java bytecode. The following steps show how to test the Commission program stub by compiling the source code and then running the bytecode.

---

#### To Compile and Test the Program Stub

1. With the Data Disk in drive A, compile the program by clicking Compile Java on the Tools menu. If TextPad notifies you of errors, click Commission.java in the Selector window, fix the errors, and then compile again.

2. When the program compiles with no errors, if necessary, click Commission.java in the Selector window to display the code in the TextPad window. Click Run Java Application on the Tools menu.

3. When the command prompt window displays, click the Close button in the title bar.

   *TextPad compiles and runs the program. No output displays unless the code has errors. If TextPad notifies you of errors, fix the errors and then compile the program again.*

---

**OTHER WAYS**

1. To compile, press CTRL+1
2. To compile at command prompt, type javac Commission.java
3. To run, press CTRL+2
4. To run at command prompt, type java Commission

---

Coding, compiling, and then testing a program stub before moving on to the next section of code can provide several benefits. You can check for compilation errors with fewer lines of code, see the results of just one condition or one set of inputs, or debug and look for problems within a narrower framework.

## Writing Methods

The object-oriented nature of Java lends itself to modularity in both the program design and implementation processes. **Modularity** is a characteristic of a program in which a larger program's source code is broken down into smaller sections, or modules, of source code. In Java, these modules include methods and classes.

Breaking a large program's source code down into smaller modules applies to both the design process and implementation. As shown in the previous steps, a Java program needs only one public class and one main() method in order to compile the source code. After that, it does not matter how many other methods you add. In a program with many different methods, good program design involves keeping the code for each method in its own separate and reusable section. Thus, instead of writing all code in the main() method, you can write code to transfer execution from the main() method to a user-defined method. The user-defined method (sometimes called a programmer-defined method) is coded in its own separate and reusable section of code, or module.

Recall that a method is a set of instructions used to manipulate values, generate outputs, or perform actions. Methods have a unique name that usually includes an active verb, such as get or write, followed by a descriptive word such as Tax or Output. As with Java-defined methods, any method you write must follow certain syntax rules.

Creating a method is a two-part process that involves writing a call statement and then writing the code for the method itself.

## Calling a Method

When you reach the place in the program where the method is to perform its service, you must write code to call the method. The **call** is a line of code stating the name of the method, followed by any data needed by the method in the form of arguments enclosed in parentheses. Once the method performs its service, it may return a value, or an answer, to the program.

Table 4-3 shows the general form of the statements used to call a method.

*Table 4-3   Method Call*

| General form: | 1. callMethod(argument); //with one argument<br>2. callMethod(argument1, argument2); //arguments separated by commas<br>3. callMethod(); //no arguments<br>4. firstMethod(secondMethod()); //method used as argument<br>5. returnValue = callMethod(argument); //method returns a value |
|---|---|
| Purpose: | To transfer execution of the program to another method |
| Examples: | 1. `displayOutput(answer);`<br>2. `getCommission(sales, rate);`<br>3. `finish();`<br>4. `System.out.println(output());`<br>5. `salesTax = getTax(sales);` |

In example 1, a method is called and set with one argument, which is enclosed within parentheses. When sending multiple arguments, as in example 2, the arguments are separated by commas. If you have no arguments, as shown in example 3, you still must include the parentheses with nothing inside. As shown in example 4, the method call also can be part of another method or statement. In example 4, the output() method is the argument of the println() method.

In program code, it is quite common to call a method that performs a function designed to return an answer. In that case, the method call becomes part of an assignment statement, as shown in example 5. Example 5 calls a method named getTax(), sends an argument named sales, and receives a return value that the program stores in the variable location named salesTax.

Line 22 in Figure 4-8 shows the line of code that calls the getSales() method in the Commission program. When the method is called, no arguments are sent, but the method returns a value that the program stores in the variable location named dollars.

```
20
21          //call methods
22          dollars = getSales();
23     }
24
25     //The getSales() method asks the user to input a dollar amount and validates it.
26     public static double getSales()
27     {
28          //declare method variables
29          double sales = 0.0;
30
31          String answer = JOptionPane.showInputDialog(null,
            "Enter the sales amount\n(do not use commas or dollar signs)\n or click Cancel to
            exit:");
32
33          sales = Double.parseDouble(answer);
34
35          return sales;
36     }
37 }
```

**FIGURE 4-8**

When a call statement is encountered, the Java compiler looks for a matching method, either a method from an imported package, a method embedded in the application, or a method from an external class. If the call is not accessing a Java-supplied method, the programmer then must write the method header and the section of code statements that define the method.

## Coding a Method

When coding a new user-defined method, start the code with the method header. Recall that the method header includes any modifiers, the return value data type or void, the method name, and any parameters in parentheses.

The beginning code for the getSales() method is shown in lines 25 through 36 in Figure 4-8. The purpose of the getSales() method is to receive a valid sales amount and return it to the main() method to be stored in the variable location, dollars. The method header in line 26 contains an access modifier, a method modifier, and the data type of the return value. These three keywords display before the name of the method, getSales(). Recall that an access modifier specifies the circumstances in which the class can be accessed. The access modifier, public, indicates that the method can be accessed by all objects and can be extended, or used, as a basis for another class. The method modifier enables you to set properties for the method, such as where it will be visible and how subclasses of the current class will interact with the method. The method modifier, **static**, indicates that the getSales() method is unique and can be invoked without creating a subclass or instance.

When a method returns a value, the data type of the return value is the third keyword listed before the method name. In this case, the getSales() method returns a double value. Return value identifiers must be declared in the body of the method, as shown in line 29.

After the return data type, the method header then contains the name of the method, getSales. In this program, the method header accepts no passed parameters, so the call statement has no arguments in the parentheses.

When called, the getSales() method will execute the code inside its braces. Line 31 in Figure 4-8 on the previous page uses the showInputDialog() method of the JOptionPane class to instruct the program to display an input dialog box with a message and a text box for user input. The showInputDialog() method has two arguments. The first argument indicates the placement of the dialog box on the screen. The Java keyword, null, instructs the program to display the dialog box centered within the program's active window. The second argument, which is enclosed in quotation marks in line 31, includes the prompt or message to display inside the dialog box. Unless otherwise specified, the showInputDialog() method displays a dialog box with a text box, an OK button, and a Cancel button.

The getSales() method for the Commission program thus causes an input dialog box to display with a message that prompts the user to enter a sales amount. After the user enters the value in the text box and clicks the OK button, line 31 returns and assigns the value to a String variable named answer. In order for math to be performed on the answer, the parseDouble() method in line 33 converts the value to a double data type and assigns it to a variable location named sales.

To return the value to the main() method, the last line inside the getSales() method (line 35) must be a return statement. The **return statement** indicates to the JVM that the method is finished and that execution may return to the main() method. In this program, line 35 returns the value stored in the variable location, sales, back to the main() method. In the main() method, the returned value is assigned to a variable location named dollars. The return value and its resulting storage location, if any, must be of the same data type, but may have different names. For example, the getSales() method declares and uses the variable location, sales, to store the return value, while the main() method declares and uses the variable location, dollars, to store the same return value. When a method is complete, execution always passes back to the next sequential line that follows the call.

This code does not yet validate or test the value entered by the user in any way other than when Java tries to convert it to a double, but it does serve as a stub to allow you to check the method call in line 22.

The following steps enter the code to call the getSales() method and the stub for the getSales() method.

### To Enter Code for the getSales() Method

*1.* Enter lines 20 through 22 as shown in Figure 4-8 on the previous page.
*The main() method will call the getSales() method during execution (Figure 4-9). Line 20 is a blank line. As you enter new code, the closing braces for the main() method and class automatically will move down.*

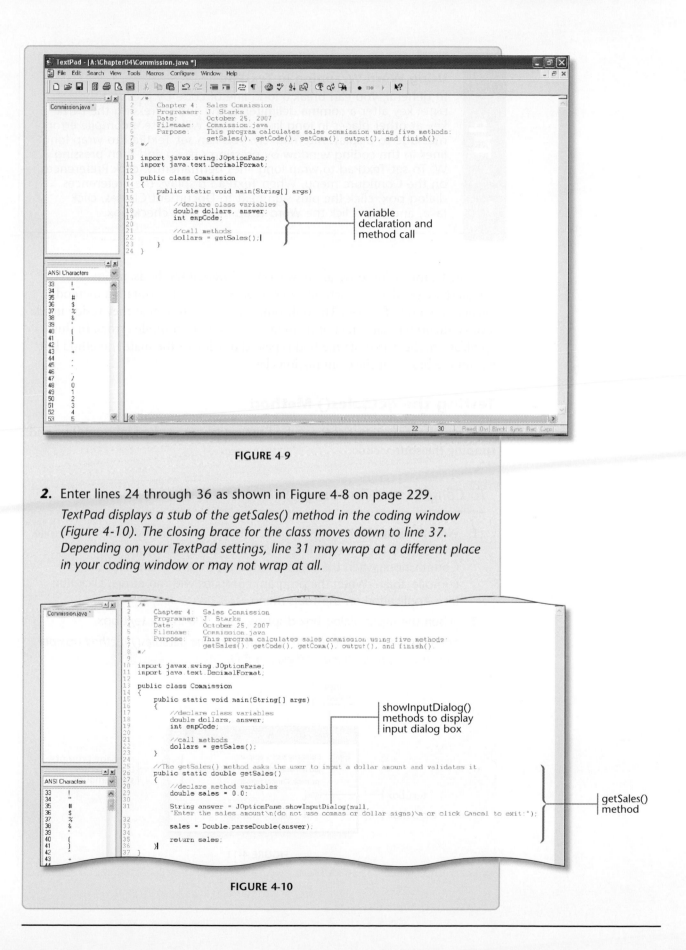

FIGURE 4-9

**2.** Enter lines 24 through 36 as shown in Figure 4-8 on page 229.

*TextPad displays a stub of the getSales() method in the coding window (Figure 4-10). The closing brace for the class moves down to line 37. Depending on your TextPad settings, line 31 may wrap at a different place in your coding window or may not wrap at all.*

FIGURE 4-10

> **Tip**
>
> **Using Word Wrapping in TextPad**
> In general, you can break a long line of code by pressing the ENTER key after a comma delimiter in the code. Pressing the ENTER key at other places in long lines of code will cause a compile error message to display. Alternatively, you can set TextPad to wrap long lines in the coding window by pressing CTRL+Q and then pressing W. To set TextPad to wrap long lines permanently, click Preferences on the Configure menu. When TextPad displays the Preferences dialog box, click the plus sign next to Document Classes, click Java, and then click the Word wrap long lines check box.

The Commission program now has two internal methods, main() and getSales(). User-defined methods such as getSales() must contain a method header and a set of braces. The only other requirement is that they reside inside a class. Incorrect placement of methods will generate compile errors. In this application, the getSales() method is placed outside of the main() method but within the braces of the Commission class.

## Testing the getSales() Method

The following steps test the stub of the getSales() method by compiling and running the source code.

> **To Compile and Test the getSales() Method**
>
> **1.** With the Data Disk in drive A, compile the program by clicking Compile Java on the Tools menu. If TextPad notifies you of errors, click Commission.java in the Selector window, fix the errors, and then compile again. When the program compiles with no errors, click Run Java Application on the Tools menu.
>
> **2.** When the Input dialog box displays, type 500 in the text box.
> *Entering the test value of 500 confirms that the getSales() method accepts the value input by the user (Figure 4-11).*

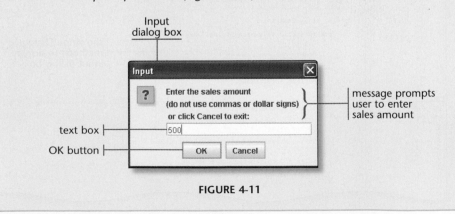

**FIGURE 4-11**

**3.** Click the OK button in the Input dialog box.

**4.** If necessary, click the Close button in the command prompt window title bar.

*The Commission program terminates and the command prompt window closes.*

OTHER WAYS

1. To compile, press CTRL+1
2. To compile at command prompt, type javac Commission.java
3. To run, press CTRL+2
4. To run at command prompt, type java Commission

When the program runs without any errors, line 33 converts the value entered by the user to a data type of double. No other validation of the data takes place. As you will see in the next section, however, Java provides many tools that programmers can use to test or validate data.

# The if...else Statement

The function of the selection structure is to state a condition that allows a program to choose whether to execute one or more lines of code. The selection structure used by Java, also called the **if...else statement**, is used to perform selection or make a decision on whether to execute a particular piece of code based on the evaluation of a condition. The general form of the if...else statement is shown in Table 4-4 on the next page. The if...else logic also is described in detail in Appendix A on page APP 8.

As noted in Table 4-4, the if statement is followed by a condition in parentheses, which is followed by a clause or clauses. A **condition** is a boolean expression that evaluates to true or false. If the condition in an if statement is true, Java acts on the clause or clauses that follow the if statement. A **single-line if statement**, as shown in example 1 in Table 4-4, is used to perform a single task when the condition in the statement is true. A **block if statement**, as shown in example 2, is used to execute more than one command if the condition in the statement is true. Example 3 displays a block if...else specifying that, if the condition in the statement is true, all of the commands in the if clause are executed. If the condition is false, Java acts on the else clause. In either case, after executing the statements in the if clause or else clause, control passes to the statement following the entire if...else statement.

In example 3, if the condition is true, Java takes a path to execute one set of code; if it is false, Java takes a path to execute another set of code. These two paths do not have to have the same number of lines of code; the false condition may result in no action being performed, while the true condition might have many lines of code that execute. The only restriction is that the two paths must come back together after the selection structure, in order to continue processing.

**Tip**

**double vs. Double**

Java requires a lowercase d in double when referring to the primitive data type, as programmers do when they declare variables. An uppercase D is required when referring to its wrapper class the – Double class of objects – and its associated methods such as the Double.parseDouble() method. The same is true for other primitive data types and their wrapper classes, such as int and Integer and float and Float.

*Table 4-4   The if...else Statement*

| | |
|---|---|
| **General form:** | 1. if (condition) clause; //single result<br>2. if (condition)<br>   {<br>     clause 1;<br>     clause 2;<br>   } //used for multiple results<br>3. if (condition)<br>   {<br>     clause(s);<br>   }<br>   else<br>   {<br>     clause(s);<br>   }<br><br>where condition is a relation that is evaluated to be boolean (either true or false) and clause is a statement or series of statements; the else keyword and subsequent clause are optional. |
| **Purpose:** | To perform selection or make a decision on whether to execute a particular piece of code based on the evaluation of a condition. The words, **if** and **else**, are reserved keywords. The condition must evaluate to a boolean expression. If the condition is true, the clause or clauses following the if statement execute. If the condition is false and an else clause is included, Java executes the else clause. After either clause is executed, control passes to the statement following the if statement in the first form (known as a single-line if statement) and to the statement following the corresponding statement in the second and third forms. Either way, execution passes out of the if statement to the next line of code following the statement. |
| **Examples:** | 1. if (age > 65) seniorCount = seniorCount + 1;<br>2. if (tax >= 0)<br>   {<br>     code = "Y";<br>     text = "Gross Pay";<br>   }<br>3. if (marStatus == 1)<br>   {<br>     System.out.println("Married");<br>   }<br>   else<br>   {<br>     System.out.println("Single");<br>   } |

Each of the single-line if statements, block if statements, or if...else statements may be **nested**, or completely included, within another if statement. For example, in the if...else statement in Figure 4-12, the code in line 15 first tests if the age is greater than 21. If that condition is evaluated as true, a second if statement in line 17 is nested within the first if statement to test if the age is greater than 64. Lines 17 through 26 are said to be nested within the block if statement that begins in line 15.

```
15   if (age > 21)
16   {
17        if (age > 64)
18        {
19             seniorCount = seniorCount + 1;
20             System.out.println("Senior");
21        }
22        else
23        {
24             adultCount = adultCount + 1;
25             System.out.println("Adult");
26        }
27   }
28   else
29   {
30        if (age > 12) System.out.println("Teen");
31        else System.out.println("Youth");
32   }
```

**FIGURE 4-12**

Lines 30 and 31 are nested within the else clause that begins in line 28; however, because there is only one clause for each of the if and else clauses in lines 30 and 31, no braces are necessary, and the clauses are coded on one line. Programmers normally indent nested structures to facilitate easy reading. TextPad will indent automatically after you type a brace.

When programming selection structures, be careful to use two equal signs (==) in the condition. Beginning programmers sometimes use only one equal sign (=), forgetting that the condition must be boolean, which requires two equal signs (==) for equality. Using only one equal sign (=) results in a compile error. Another common error is forgetting the braces for a block if or else statement. In those cases, Java considers only the first line as part of the condition, incorrectly executing all of the other lines.

## Using Operators in an if...else Statement

In many instances, a decision to execute one set of code or another is based on the evaluation of one or more conditions. In Chapter 3, you learned that different types of comparison operators are used in conditional expressions to evaluate the relationship between two expressions or values logically. Relational operators are used to compare the relation of two values; equality operators are used to determine if two values are equal. The values may be variables, constants, numbers, strings, or the result of a function or method.

Another type of operator, the **logical operator**, is used to connect two conditional expressions. As shown in Table 4-5 on the next page, the logical **AND operator** (&&) connects two expressions, x and y, so that both conditions individually must be evaluated as true for the entire expression, x && y, to be evaluated as true. The logical **OR operator** (| |) connects two expressions, x and y, so that the whole expression, x | | y, evaluates to true if either x or y evaluates to true, or if they both do. The logical **NOT operator** (!) connects two expressions, x and y, so that if x evaluates to true, then the expression !x evaluates to false, and vice versa.

Table 4-5 shows the equality, relational, and logical operators used in Java, including examples of each and the result of evaluating the condition.

*Table 4-5*    *Operator Results in Selection Structures*

| OPERATOR | MEANING | EXAMPLE | RESULT | TYPE |
|---|---|---|---|---|
| = = | equal to | 2 == 2 <br> 1 == 6 | true <br> false | equality |
| != | not equal to | 7 != 4 <br> 4 != 4 | true <br> false | equality |
| < | less than | 3 < 5 <br> 5 < 3 | true <br> false | relational |
| <= | less than or equal to | 4 <= 6 <br> 7 <= 6 | true <br> false | relational |
| > | greater than | 9 > 7 <br> 7 > 9 | true <br> false | relational |
| >= | greater than or equal to | 8 >= 8 <br> 8 >= 10 | true <br> false | relational |
| && | logical AND (both conditions must be true in order to make the condition true) | (7 > 3) && (0 < 1) <br> (7 > 3) && (1 < 0) | true <br> false | logical |
| \|\| | logical OR (one of the conditions must be true in order to make the condition true) | (7 > 3) \|\| (1 < 0) <br> (3 > 7) \|\| (1 < 0) | true <br> false | logical |
| ! | logical NOT (condition must evaluate to false in order to make the condition true) | ! (5 == 4) <br> ! (a == a) | true <br> false | logical |

## Coding an if Statement to Test the Cancel Button

As shown in the previous steps, when executed, the getSales() method displays a dialog box prompting the user to enter a dollar amount. The dialog box contains a text box for user input and two buttons: an OK button and a Cancel button. If the user clicks the Cancel button, the program should terminate. If the user clicks the OK button, the method validates the user input.

An if statement, as shown in line 33 of Figure 4-13, is used to test if the user clicked the Cancel button. When clicked, the Cancel button in a JOptionPane dialog box returns a blank value to the variable, answer. Line 33 uses the equal to operator (= =) to compare the variable, answer, against a null. In Java, **null** is a constant that represents the presence of no data. If the return value matches, or is equal to, null, the condition is evaluated to be true and the finish() method is called.

```
31                      String answer = JOptionPane.showInputDialog(null,
                          "Enter the sales amount\n(do not use commas or dollar signs)\n or click Cancel to
                          exit:");
32
33                      if (answer == null) finish();
34
35                      sales = Double.parseDouble(answer);
36
37                      return sales;
38              }
39
40      //The finish() method ends the program.
41      public static void finish()
42      {
43              System.exit(0);
44      }
45  }
```

**FIGURE 4-13**

The finish() method, displayed in lines 40 through 44, calls the System.exit() method in line 43 to terminate the program. Note that the if statement in line 33 could call the System.exit() method directly, bypassing the need for the extra finish() method. While that approach might work within the getSales() method, coding the System.exit() method in the finish() method allows it to be called from multiple methods, thus reducing code redundancy and keeping a single exit for the program no matter which method calls it. Other uses for methods such as finish() include opportunities to display a closing message, to save data, or to perform memory clean-up tasks. Later in the chapter, after all data is validated and the commission rate has displayed to the user, an additional call to the finish() method is added to the program.

The following steps enter an if statement to test the Cancel button.

## To Code an if Statement to Test the Cancel Button

**1.** Enter lines 33 and 34 as shown in Figure 4-13.

*The if statement will compare the variable, answer, to the null constant (Figure 4-14). Line 34 is a blank line.*

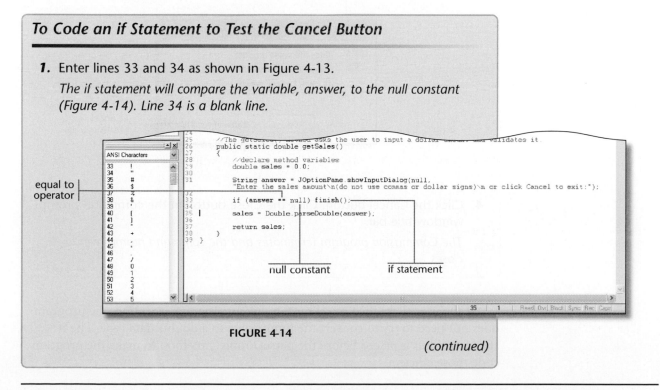

**FIGURE 4-14**

*(continued)*

**2.** Enter lines 39 through 44 as shown from Figure 4-13.

*TextPad displays the finish() method in the coding window. The closing brace for the class moves down to line 45. When called, the finish() method will exit the program (Figure 4-15).*

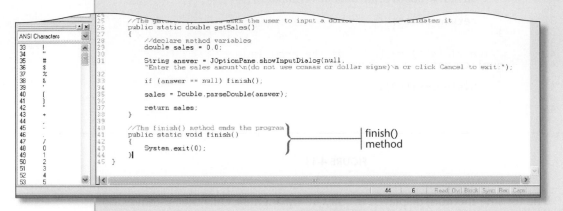

FIGURE 4-15

**3.** With the Data Disk in drive A, compile the program by clicking Compile Java on the Tools menu. If TextPad notifies you of errors, click Commission.java in the Selector window, fix the errors, and then compile again. When the program compiles with no errors, click Run Java Application on the Tools menu.

*TextPad compiles and runs the program. The program displays the Input dialog box (Figure 4-16).*

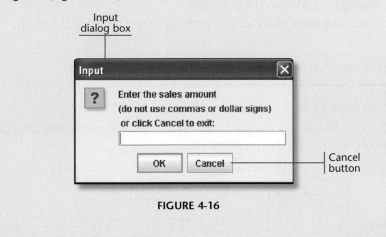

FIGURE 4-16

**4.** Click the Cancel button. Click the Close button in the command prompt window title bar.

*The Commission program terminates and the command prompt window closes.*

If the user clicks the Cancel button during program execution, the program does not need to try to convert the input value to a double data type. The if statement thus is placed before the parseDouble() method to make the program code more efficient.

## Coding an if Statement to Test Multiple Conditions

The previous steps included code that tested for only one condition at a time. While this is common, an if statement or an if...else statement can test more than one possible condition as well. The logical AND operator (&&) typically would be used for situations in which you might want to test more than one piece of data at the same time. For example, a program that checks for adult male students might compare the gender with a code 1 for male and compare the age with a numeric value. In this case, each condition is enclosed in its own set of parentheses, as shown in the following line of code.

```
if ((gender == 1) && (age >= 18))
```

The logical OR operator (||) typically would be used for testing the same piece of data in two different ways. For example, a program that tests an age for possible child or senior discount might compare the age against two different numeric values, as shown in the following line of code.

```
if ((age < 13) || (age > 65))
```

The logical NOT operator (!) typically would be used for testing a boolean piece of data that evaluates to true or false. For example, a programmer might assign a boolean true value to the variable, done, in response to a user's input to quit the program. If done were not set, then processing would continue. The if statement using the NOT operator might display as shown in the following line of code.

```
if (!done)
```

The logical operators produce boolean results – that is, they evaluate to true or false. The values or operands used in the expressions also must be boolean. An important characteristic of the logical AND and OR is that if the left operand can be sufficient to decide the condition, the right side never is evaluated. For example, if the left side of the logical AND operator (&&) evaluates to false, the condition automatically is false and the right side need not be evaluated. The left operand is sufficient to decide that the condition evaluates to false.

# Exception Handling

An **exception** is a Java event resulting from an unusual or erroneous situation which disrupts the normal program flow of instructions. An exception also sometimes is referred to as a **run-time exception** or run-time error, as discussed in Chapter 2. **Exception handling** is the general concept of planning for possible exceptions by directing the program to deal with them gracefully without terminating prematurely. For example, in Chapter 3, possible exceptions were handled by adding the code, throws IOException, to the main() method header. The code gave the program a way to acknowledge and handle potential input or output errors and still compile correctly.

Java has different types of exceptions, including the I/O exceptions covered in Chapter 3, run-time exceptions, and checked exceptions. As you have learned, a run-time exception occurs within the Java run-time system and includes arithmetic exceptions, such as when dividing by zero. Run-time exceptions can occur anywhere in a program and may be quite numerous.

When a run-time exception occurs, the run-time system then looks for a handler, or a way to handle the exception. A **checked exception** is one in which the compiler checks each method during compilation to ensure that each method has a **handler** — the code used to address any possible exceptions.

A method can handle a checked exception in one of two ways: (1) by handling the exception using a catch statement, or (2) by throwing the exception to the code that called the method. By using the keyword, throws, in the method header, the method **claims** the exception; in other words, it lets the compiler know that it may pass along an exception rather than handling it.

Using a checked exception thus allows programmers to catch an exception and handle it in the program. Often programmers write code to catch the exception at the exact point in the program where it might occur, or in other cases, they write code within a calling method, thereby handling it at a higher level.

If the programmer does not code a way to catch the exception, the program may terminate prematurely and display an exception error message. In some cases, Java may throw an exception representing an unrecoverable situation, such as an out of memory error, which is a more serious problem. The object created in response to such an exception can be caught; however, it is not required because it indicates a serious problem that an application should not try to catch.

## Handling Exceptions Using try and catch Statements

Java provides several ways to write code that checks for exceptions. One object-oriented way to handle exceptions is to include the lines of code that might cause exceptions inside a try statement. The **try statement** identifies a block of statements that potentially may throw an exception. If an exception occurs, the try statement transfers execution to a handler. Table 4-6 shows an example of the try statement.

---

**Table 4-6   The try Statement**

| | |
|---|---|
| **General form:** | ```try
{
    . . . lines of code that might generate an exception;
    . . .throw new exceptionName;
}``` |
| **Purpose:** | To enclose the code statements that might throw an exception. **Try** and **throw new** are reserved words. All statements within the braces in the try statement are monitored for exceptions. Programmers may **explicitly**, or purposefully, cause an exception by typing the words, throw new, followed by the name of a standard Java exception object. A try statement must be followed by a catch statement. |
| **Example:** | ```try
{
    answer = 23 / 0; //Java throws exception automatically
    throw new DivideByZeroException(); //programmer explicitly
        throws exception
}``` |

As noted in Table 4-6, all statements within the braces of the try statement are monitored for exceptions. The try statement notifies the JVM that you plan to deal with them as checked exceptions rather than just allowing them to happen. Any exception occurring as a result of code within the try statement will not terminate the program; rather, you as the programmer will handle the exception through coding.

When an exception occurs, a new exception object is created. The exception object contains information about the exception, such as its location and type. If a run-time exception occurs, the program method that creates the exception object automatically throws it to the run-time system.

You also can cause an exception explicitly, or purposefully, by using a throw statement. The **throw statement** transfers execution from the method that caused the exception to the handler that addresses any possible exceptions. The throw statement is followed by the constructor keyword, new, and a single argument, which is the name of the exception object.

If an exception occurs in the try statement, the throw statement transfers execution from the try statement to the catch statement to handle the exception. The try statement thus must be followed by a catch statement. The **catch statement** consists of the keyword, catch, followed by a parameter declaration that identifies the type of exception being caught and an identifier name in parentheses. The identifier name holds a Java-assigned error value that can access more information about the error through the use of messages. Inside the catch statement braces, you can include statements to either describe the error to the user or fix the error through programming. Table 4-7 shows an example of the catch statement.

### Table 4-7  The catch Statement

| General form: | `catch(ExceptionName identifier)`<br>`{`<br>   `. . . lines of code that handle the exception;`<br>`}` |
|---|---|
| Purpose: | To handle an exception generated in the try statement. **Catch** is a reserved word. ExceptionName is the name of a standard Java exception. Identifier is a variable name to hold a Java-assigned error value. A catch statement optionally may be followed by a finally statement to continue more processing. |
| Example: | `catch(ArithmeticException errNum)`<br>`{`<br>   `System.out.println("An arithmetic error has occurred. " +`<br>   `errNum.getMessage());`<br>   `// message prints with Java-generated data`<br>`}` |

Used together in a program, the try statement and catch statement are used to handle exceptions. For example, if a user error causes a program to try to divide by zero, the program normally would abort with the following error message:

```
Exception in thread "main" java.lang.ArthmeticException: / by zero
```

If, however, the code is put in a try statement and the same exception occurs, execution is thrown to the corresponding catch statement. The catch statement then can execute code that instructs the program to display a descriptive message to the user and perhaps let the user reenter the data.

As previously discussed, Java may generate the exception, as in the division by zero example above, or you may use the keywords, throw new, to throw the exception explicitly or intentionally. For example, if Java expects an integer input and the user types a decimal point, a NumberFormatException displays and the program terminates. A **NumberFormatException** indicates an operation attempted to use a number in an illegal format. In another example, as shown in Table 4-6 on page 4.24, you could instruct Java to throw a DivideByZeroException if you tried to divide a value by zero by using the following code:

```
throw new DivideByZeroException();
```

Alternately, you might want to create a new exception type. For example, to handle an exception when a user enters the wrong password, you could enter the following line of code:

```
throw new WrongPasswordException();
```

The program then would call the class, WrongPasswordException, if the user entered the wrong password. That new class must be defined by the programmer, however, and be accessible to the class that contains the throw statement.

The throw statement within the try statement causes execution to be transferred to the catch statement. That way, control passes to the same error-handling routine whether the exception is caught by the JVM, as in a data type error, or caught by the programmer testing for an invalid or unreasonable number.

As with the if statement, the try and catch statements can be nested within any other code statements. In addition, you can have more than one catch statement in the same program, or even within the same method, if you are trying to catch multiple types of exceptions.

### Catching a NumberFormatException in the getSales() Method

In the Commission program, a valid sales amount must be numeric. The JOptionPane input dialog box, however, does not restrict the type of data entered in the text box. As a result, regardless of what data the user enters, the input is stored in the variable location named answer. If, however, the user has entered alphabetic data and the code tries to parse it, the code will generate a NumberFormatException — an exception that must be caught. To catch the exception, you should include the parse code inside a try statement and write a catch statement to handle the exception.

Figure 4-17 displays the try statement and catch statement used to handle the exception. Lines 35 through 38 show the try statement and the braces enclosing the code that parses the answer value. Lines 39 through 42 catch the NumberFormatException and display a JOptionPane message box. The catch statement will execute only if a NumberFormatException occurs in line 37; when it executes, the catch statement handles the error by displaying a message box rather than allowing Java to terminate the program.

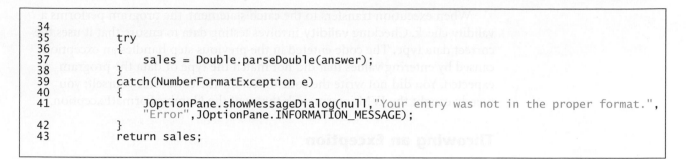

```
34
35        try
36        {
37            sales = Double.parseDouble(answer);
38        }
39        catch(NumberFormatException e)
40        {
41            JOptionPane.showMessageDialog(null,"Your entry was not in the proper format.",
                 "Error",JOptionPane.INFORMATION_MESSAGE);
42        }
43        return sales;
```

FIGURE 4-17

The following step enters the try and catch statements.

## To Code the try and catch Statements

**1.** Enter lines 35 through 36 and lines 38 through 42 as shown in Figure 4-18. Use proper spacing and indentation.

*The try and catch statements are displayed in the TextPad coding window (Figure 4-18). Line 37 is indented within the braces of the try statement. Line 41 wraps. If your display does not wrap, click Word Wrap on the Configure menu.*

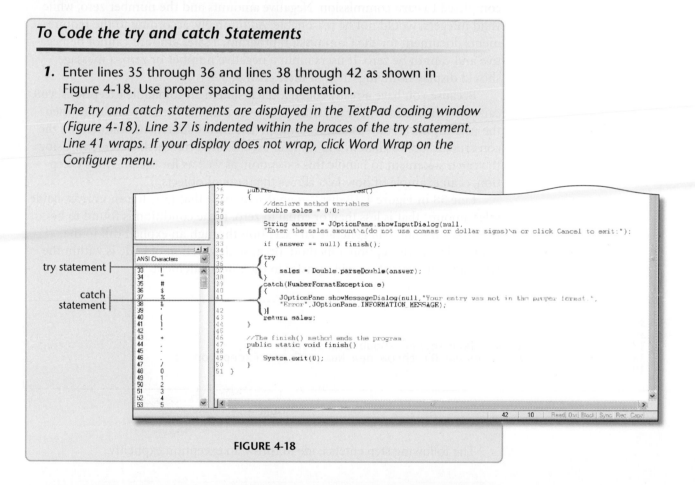

FIGURE 4-18

The try and catch statements may be followed by an optional finally statement, which is placed after the catch statement. The **finally statement** typically contains code to perform any cleanup that might be necessary after executing the try statement and catch statement. The finally statement always is executed, regardless of whether the try statement generates an exception. The most common usage of the finally statement is to release a resource specifically allocated for use by a method, such as an open file.

When execution transfers to the catch statement, the program performs a validity check. Checking **validity** involves testing data to ensure that it uses the correct data type. The code entered in the previous step handles an exception caused by entering values that did not match the type of data the program expected. You did not write the code to test for the condition yourself; you merely caught the JVM interpreter's throw of the NumberFormatException.

## Throwing an Exception

Input from the user also should be checked for **reasonableness** — that is, that the values entered are within reason as expected input. For example, in the Commission program, any positive number might be a reasonable answer for the sales amount, as you do not know how many sales a travel agent may have completed to earn commission. Negative amounts and the number zero, while valid integers, would not be reasonable. Additionally, according to the requirements document for the Commission program, a sales amount cannot be negative and cannot be zero. If users input a negative number or zero, a message should display notifying them of their error.

Because you have already coded a catch statement to handle exceptions, you can use a throw statement to create your own NumberFormatException when the user inputs an unreasonable number. The throw statement, followed by the constructor keyword, new, will transfer execution to the catch statement. Using the catch statement to handle this exception, as well as for the previous exception, is an example of how Java allows the reuse of objects.

Line 38 in Figure 4-19 displays an if statement that tests for an unreasonable sales amount that is less than or equal to zero. If the condition is found to be true, the program will generate an exception through an explicit call to the NumberFormatException() method. Because this section of code is within the try statement, execution will transfer to the catch statement.

```
35          try
36          {
37              sales = Double.parseDouble(answer);
38              if (sales <= 0) throw new NumberFormatException();
39          }
```

FIGURE 4-19

The following step enters code to throw an exception explicitly.

### To Enter Code to Throw an Exception

*1.* Enter line 38 as shown in Figure 4-19.

*TextPad displays the code to throw an exception in the TextPad coding window (Figure 4-20).*

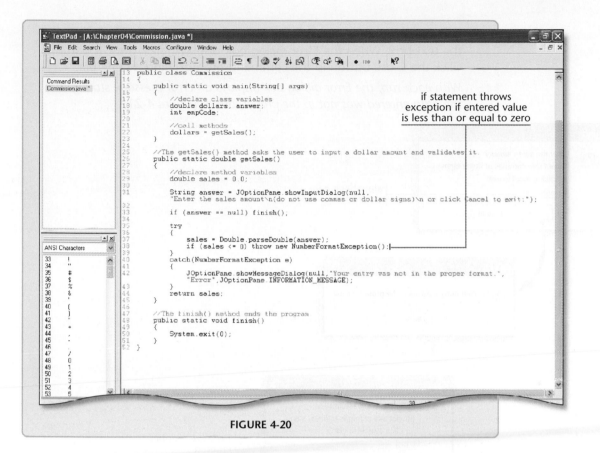

**FIGURE 4-20**

The try and catch statements are ready to be tested. The code can be tested by entering alphabetic data, a negative sales amount, and a zero sales amount in the Input dialog box. The program will catch the exception and display an Error message box with the message coded in line 42. The following steps compile and test the try and catch statements.

## To Compile and Test the try and catch Statements

*1.* With the Data Disk in drive A, compile the program by clicking Compile Java on the Tools menu. If TextPad notifies you of errors, click Commission.java in the Selector window, fix the errors, and then compile again. When the program compiles with no errors, click Run Java Application on the Tools menu.

*2.* When the Input dialog box displays, type seventy-nine in the text box. Click the OK button.

*3.* When the Error dialog box displays, click the OK button. Click the Close button in the command prompt window title bar.

*4.* Run the program again. When the Input dialog box displays, type –382 in the text box. When the Error dialog box displays, click the OK button. Click the Close button in the command prompt window title bar.

*(continued)*

**5.** Run the program again. When the Input dialog box displays, type 0 in the text box. When the Error dialog box displays, click the OK button. Click the Close button in the command prompt window title bar.

*With each run, the Error dialog box displays an error message stating that the data entered was not in the proper format (Figure 4-21).*

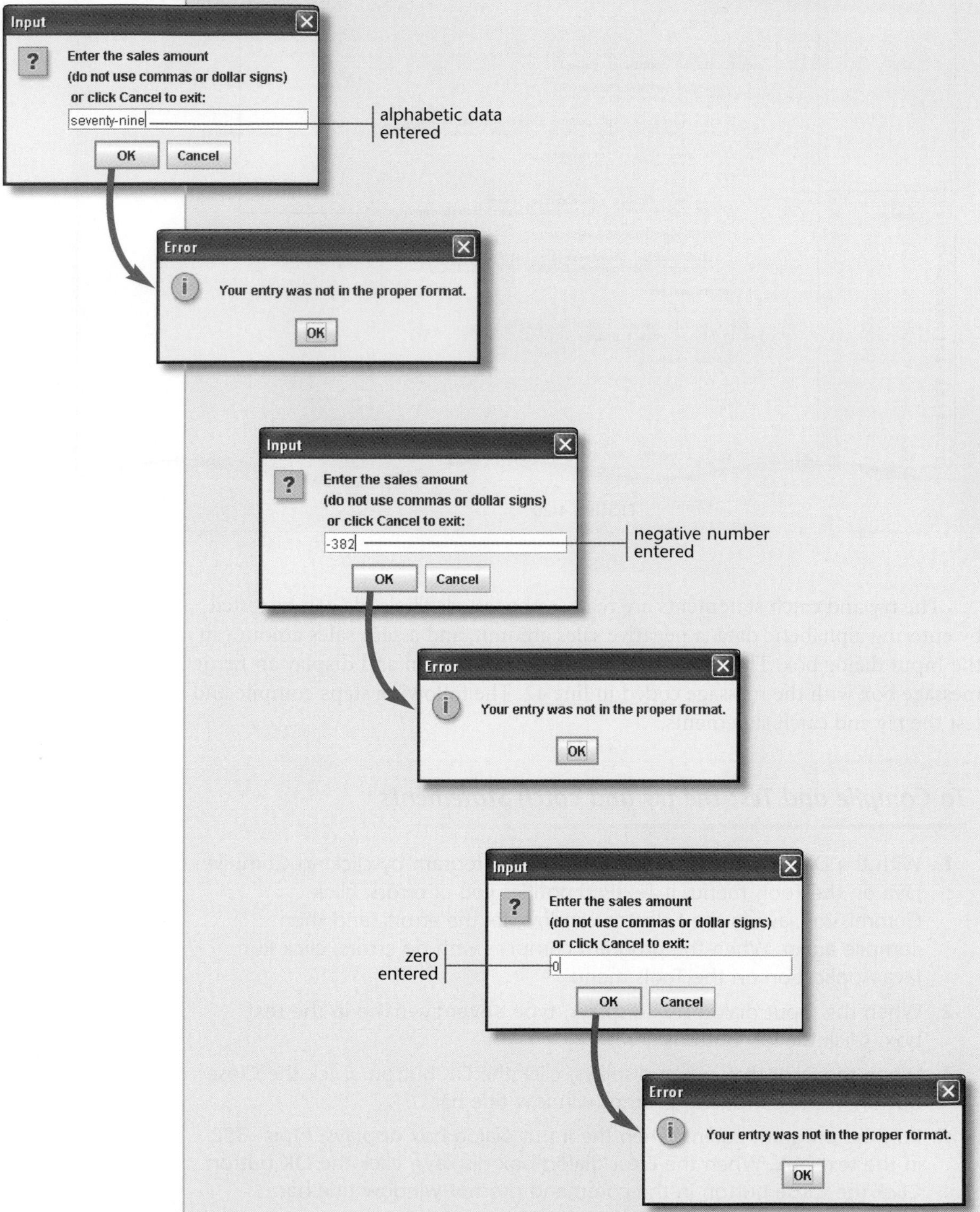

FIGURE 4-21

It is important to have a well thought-out and consistent exception-handling strategy for the sake of efficiency and good programming practice. Exception handling should not be considered an afterthought, but an integral part of the development process. Having a consistent exception-handling strategy helps develop applications that are robust and dependable by design rather than by accident. The Java Language Specification states that "an exception will be thrown when semantic constraints are violated," which implies that an exception throws in situations that ordinarily are not possible or in the event of a violation of normal program behavior. Therefore, sometimes it is easier to address data entry errors with simple if statements that display error messages, rather than by throwing exceptions. On the other hand, if the error is related to a type of exception that Java already is handling in the program, it makes sense to reuse that catch code to validate the data entry.

# Repetition Structure

Thus far in this program code, if the user enters an invalid or unreasonable number, the program terminates. A message displays notifying the user of the error, but it does not allow the user to reenter the data and try again without rerunning the entire program. As previously noted, Java uses a repetition structure to repeat a certain section of code. This repetitive, or iterative, process is referred to as **looping**. The Commission program will use a repetition structure so that if the user enters an invalid or unreasonable number, it again displays the Input dialog box so that the user can try again to enter valid and reasonable data.

## The while Statement

Java uses a special repetition structure, called a **while loop,** for looping when the exact number of repetitions is unknown. To code a while loop, you code a **while statement**, starting with the keyword, while, followed by a condition in parentheses. All of the code that should be repeated, or looped, while the condition evaluates to true is enclosed in braces. Table 4-8 on the next page shows the general form of the while statement. The repetition structure and the while statement also are described in detail in Appendix A on page APP 8.

*Table 4-8  The while Statement*

| General form: | while(condition)<br>{<br>. . . lines of code to repeat while above condition is true;<br>} |
|---|---|
| Purpose: | To create a process that will repeat, or loop through, executing a series of statements while the condition in the while statement is true. The word, **while**, is a reserved keyword. The condition must be a boolean expression that evaluates to true or false. The code repeats as long as the condition is evaluated as true. The condition eventually must evaluate to false in order to exit the loop. |
| Example: | while(!done)<br>{<br>    System.out.println("Are you done (yes or no)");<br>    String answer = dataIn.readLine();<br>    if (answer == "yes") done;<br>} |

The getSales() method requires that its statements continue to be executed while the sales amount data entered by the user is invalid. If the program throws an exception, it should loop back to the JOptionPane input dialog box and allow the user to enter a new sales amount. Figure 4-22 displays the complete getSales() method definition. Lines 30 through 34, line 43, and line 49 are new to the method.

```
25      //The getSales() method asks the user to input a dollar amount and validates it.
26      public static double getSales()
27      {
28          //declare method variables
29          double sales = 0.0;
30          boolean done = false;
31
32          //loop while not done
33          while(!done)
34          {
35              String answer = JOptionPane.showInputDialog(null,
                    "Enter the sales amount\n(do not use commas or dollar signs)\n or click Cancel
                    to exit:");
36
37              if (answer == null) finish();
38
39              try
40              {
41                  sales = Double.parseDouble(answer);
42                  if (sales <= 0) throw new NumberFormatException();
43                  else done = true;
44              }
45              catch(NumberFormatException e)
46              {
47                  JOptionPane.showMessageDialog(null,
                        "Your entry was not in the proper format.", "Error",
                        JOptionPane.INFORMATION_MESSAGE);
48              }
49          }
50          return sales;
51      }
```

**FIGURE 4-22**

Line 30 declares a boolean variable, done, and assigns it a value of false, thus allowing the program to enter the loop structure that begins with the while statement in line 33. The exclamation point is the logical NOT operator, thus causing the code in the while statement to loop when the value of done is not true. Recall that boolean variables may be used as conditions. In this example, the variable serves as a flag to notify the loop whether or not to execute. The braces for the while statement in lines 34 and 49 enclose the code that should repeat until the value of done is true.

Within the body of the while loop, some trigger must cause the loop to stop — in other words, something must happen within the code that changes the state of the boolean variable, done. In line 43, an else clause has been added to the selection structure. The else clause is executed if the entered sales amount did not throw an exception automatically when the sales amount was parsed in line 41, and was not greater than zero in line 42. When execution passes back to line 33, the true value will cause the loop created by the while statement to stop executing. Control then will pass to line 50, outside the while statement.

The following step adds the code for the while loop to the getSales() method.

## To Enter Code for the while Statement

**1.** Within the getSales() method in the Commission program, enter new lines 30 through 34, line 43, and line 49 as shown in Figure 4-22. Use appropriate spacing and indentation.

*The new code is displayed (Figure 4-23). Your lines may wrap differently.*

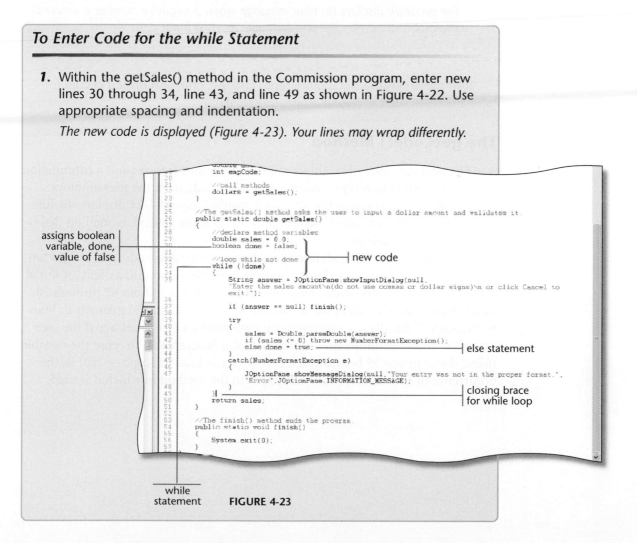

**FIGURE 4-23**

## Testing the while Statement

The following steps compile and test the while statement.

---

### To Compile and Test the while Statement

1. With the Data Disk in drive A, compile the program by clicking Compile Java on the Tools menu. If TextPad notifies you of errors, click Commission.java in the Selector window, fix the errors, and then compile again. When the program compiles with no errors, click Run Java Application on the Tools menu.

2. When the program displays the Input dialog box, type –35000 and then click the OK button.

3. When the program displays the Error dialog box, click the OK button.

4. When the program again displays the Input dialog box, type 35000 and then click the OK button. Click the Close button in the command prompt window title bar.

*The program displays an error message when a negative number is entered. The program accepts the positive value as valid input data.*

---

Run the program several more times and test valid and invalid entries for sales amounts, such as zero or alphanumeric data.

## The getCode() Method

The next step after obtaining a valid sales amount is to request a commission code. The method to accept a valid commission code from the user employs similar logical constructs as the getSales() method. Figure 4-24 displays the line of code to call the getCode() method (line 23) and the getCode() method definition (lines 53 through 80).

In the getCode() method, line 58 declares the variable, code, and assigns an initial value of 0. Line 59 declares a boolean variable, done, and assigns an initial value of false. Execution then enters the while statement in lines 62 through 78, which repeats until a valid code is entered. The try and catch statements in lines 64 through 77 handle any exceptions by displaying an error message if the user enters an invalid commission code. Note that it is acceptable to reuse the variable name, done, in line 59 because each occurrence is local in scope — that is, the occurrence of the variable, done, is unique to the method in which it is used.

```
 23              empCode = getCode();
```

```
 53
 54          //The getCode() method retrieves a code from the user and validates it.
 55          public static int getCode()
 56          {
 57              //declare method variables
 58              int code = 0;
 59              boolean done = false;
 60
 61              //loop while not done
 62              while(!done)
 63              {
 64                  try
 65                  {
 66                      String message = "Enter the commission code:" +
                         "\n\n1) Telephone Sales\n2) In-Store Sales\n3) Outside Sales\n\n";
 67
 68                      code = Integer.parseInt(JOptionPane.showInputDialog(null,message));
 69
 70                      //test for valid codes 1, 2, or 3
 71                      if (code<1 || code>3) throw new NumberFormatException();
 72                      else done = true;
 73                  }
 74                  catch(NumberFormatException e)
 75                  {
 76                      JOptionPane.showMessageDialog(null,"Please enter a 1, 2, or 3.",
                         "Error",JOptionPane.INFORMATION_MESSAGE);
 77                  }
 78              }
 79              return code;
 80          }
```

**FIGURE 4-24**

Line 66 assigns the String data used to define the prompt to a variable named message. The String data includes the user prompt, Enter the commission code:, followed by a numbered list of valid commission codes. Recall that the escape character sequence, \n, will cause the data that follows it to print on a new line. When you convert this program to an applet later in the chapter, you will learn how to create option buttons from which the user can choose a commission code. For this application, however, the numbered list presents an easy to understand set of choices to the user.

In line 68, the variable, message, is included as the second argument of the showInputDialog() method, which will cause the message to display as a prompt in the Input dialog box. The value entered by the user serves as the return value of the method and thus becomes the argument for the parseInt() method. After the input is returned and parsed, it then is assigned to the variable, code. Wrapping a method inside another, as shown in line 68, commonly is used in Java programming because it reduces the number of lines of code.

Line 71 uses the logical OR operator to test for commission codes less than one or greater than three. In either case, a NumberFormatException is explicitly thrown, and execution transfers to the catch statement, which displays a message in an Error dialog box (line 76). The program then loops back to allow the user to reenter a new, valid commission code.

Line 79 returns the valid code to the calling statement in line 23, where it is assigned to the variable, empCode.

The following steps enter code to call and then execute the getCode() method.

### To Enter Code for the getCode() Method

*1.* Enter line 23 as shown in Figure 4-24 on the previous page into the main() method of the Commission program.

*The statement calls the getCode() method and assigns its return value to a variable named empCode (Figure 4-25).*

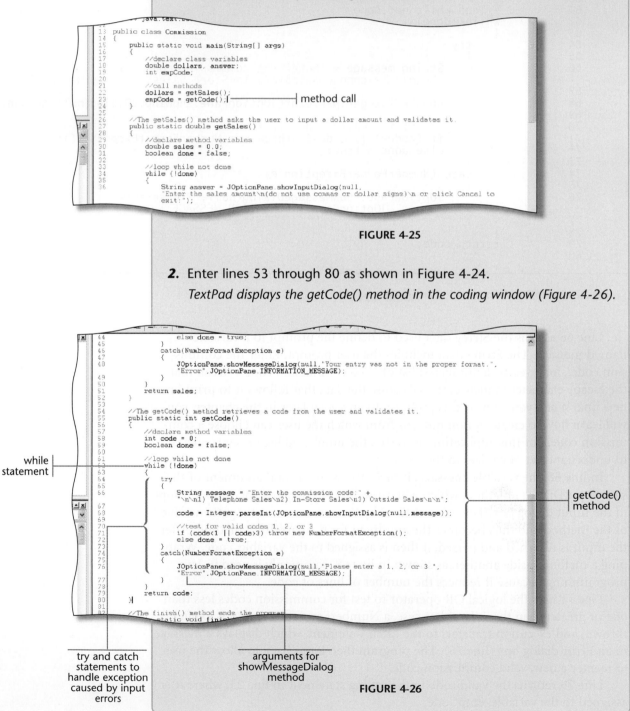

```
 12   > java.text.
 13   public class Commission
 14   {
 15       public static void main(String[] args)
 16       {
 17           //declare class variables
 18           double dollars, answer;
 19           int empCode;
 20
 21           //call methods
 22           dollars = getSales();
 23           empCode = getCode();         ──────────┤ method call
 24       }
 25
 26       //The getSales() method asks the user to input a dollar amount and validates it.
 27       public static double getSales()
 28       {
 29           //declare method variables
 30           double sales = 0.0;
 31           boolean done = false;
 32
 33           //loop while not done
 34           while (!done)
 35           {
 36               String answer = JOptionPane.showInputDialog(null,
                       "Enter the sales amount\n(do not use commas or dollar signs)\n or click Cancel to
                       exit:");
```

**FIGURE 4-25**

*2.* Enter lines 53 through 80 as shown in Figure 4-24.

*TextPad displays the getCode() method in the coding window (Figure 4-26).*

```
 44               else done = true;
 45           }
 46           catch(NumberFormatException e)
 47           {
 48               JOptionPane.showMessageDialog(null,"Your entry was not in the proper format.",
                       "Error",JOptionPane.INFORMATION_MESSAGE);
 49           }
 50       }
 51       return sales;
 52   }
 53
 54       //The getCode() method retrieves a code from the user and validates it.
 55       public static int getCode()
 56       {
 57           //declare method variables
 58           int code = 0;
 59           boolean done = false;
 60
 61           //loop while not done
 62           while (!done)
 63           {
 64               try
 65               {
 66                   String message = "Enter the commission code:" +
                           "\n\n1) Telephone Sales\n2) In-Store Sales\n3) Outside Sales\n\n";
 67
 68                   code = Integer.parseInt(JOptionPane.showInputDialog(null,message));
 69
 70                   //test for valid codes 1, 2, or 3
 71                   if (code<1 || code>3) throw new NumberFormatException();
 72                   else done = true;
 73               }
 74               catch(NumberFormatException e)
 75               {
 76                   JOptionPane.showMessageDialog(null,"Please enter a 1, 2, or 3 ",
                           "Error",JOptionPane.INFORMATION_MESSAGE);
 77               }
 78           }
 79           return code;
 80       }
 81
 82       //The finish() method ends the program
          static void finish
```

while statement

getCode() method

try and catch statements to handle exception caused by input errors

arguments for showMessageDialog method

**FIGURE 4-26**

### Testing the getCode() Method

The following steps compile and test the getCode() method.

---

#### *To Compile and Test the getCode() method*

---

**1.** With the Data Disk in drive A, compile the program by clicking Compile Java on the Tools menu. If TextPad notifies you of errors, click Commission.java in the Selector window, fix the errors, and then compile again. When the program compiles with no errors, click Run Java Application on the Tools menu.

**2.** When the program displays the first Input dialog box, type 20000 as the sales amount and then click the OK button. When the program displays the second Input dialog box, type 5 and then click the OK button.

**3.** When the program displays the Error dialog box, click the OK button.

**4.** When the program again displays the Input dialog box, type 2 and then click the OK button. Click the Close button in the command prompt window title bar.

*The program displays an error message when a number less than one or greater than three is entered for the commission code. The program accepts any number between one and three as valid input data.*

---

Run the program several more times and test valid and invalid entries for commission code, such as negative numbers, zero, or alphanumeric data.

## The Case Structure

Sending a value to a method where it will be tested is a convenient way to make the program easy to read and to test its components. In the case of a menu, for example, there might be many possible, valid choices for the user to input. When there are more than two possible, valid choices, the logical operators become cumbersome and hard to understand, even when the logical AND and OR operators are used.

Most programming languages, including Java, thus contain a variation of the selection structure called a case structure. A **case structure** is a type of selection structure that allows for more than two choices when the condition is evaluated. For example, if a user selects from several choices on a menu, the code evaluates the choice. If a match is found, then the appropriate action is performed. For example, if the user selected Option 1 on the menu, the logic of the code might execute one section of code; if the user selected Option 4 on the menu, an entirely different section of code might execute. Alternatively, if no match is found, the case structure can provide feedback to the user or store the no match result for later use in the program. The case structure is described in detail in Appendix A on page APP 8.

### The switch Statement

Java uses a **switch statement** to evaluate an integer expression or value and then conditionally perform statements. The switch statement evaluates its value and then, depending on the value, transfers control to the appropriate **case statement**. Control is transferred to a case statement that has a value following the case keyword that matches the value evaluated by the switch statement. Table 4-9 displays the general form of the switch statement.

---

**Table 4-9  The switch Statement**

| | |
|---|---|
| **General form:** | ```switch(value)```<br>```{```<br>   ```case value1:```<br>   ```. . . statements to execute if value matches value1```<br>   ```break;```<br><br>   ```case value2:```<br>   ```. . . statements to execute if value matches value2```<br>   ```break;```<br>   ```.```<br>   ```.```<br>   ```.```<br>   ```default:```<br>   ```. . . statements to execute if no match is found```<br>```}``` |
| **Purpose:** | To evaluate an integer expression or value and then conditionally perform statements. The words **switch**, **case**, **break**, and **default** are reserved keywords. The switch value is any valid integer data type, variable, or constant. The case value is any valid integer data type, variable or constant. The switch statement compares the value to the case. If they match, the code following that case statement is executed. The default case is optional and executes only if none of the other, previous cases executes. |
| **Example:** | ```switch(flavor)```<br>```{```<br>   ```case 1:```<br>      ```System.out.println("chocolate");```<br>      ```break;```<br><br>   ```case 2:```<br>      ```System.out.println("vanilla");```<br>      ```break;```<br><br>   ```case 3:```<br>      ```System.out.println("strawberry");```<br>      ```break;```<br><br>   ```default:```<br>      ```System.out.println("Please choose one of our three flavors.");```<br>```}``` |

---

As shown in Table 4-9, each case statement contains a **break statement** at the end, which forces an exit of the structure when a match is found. After the break, no more statements within the structure are evaluated, thereby reducing processing time.

# The getComm() Method

In the Commission program, a method named getComm() will get a commission rate based on the dollar amount of the sales and the employee sales code. Figure 4-27 displays the line of code to call the getComm() method (line 24) and the getComm() method definition (lines 82 through 104).

```
24              answer = getComm(dollars,empCode);
```

```
82
83       //The getComm() method accepts the dollars and code and returns the commission.
84       public static double getComm(double employeeSales, int employeeCode)
85       {
86           double commission = 0.0;
87
88           switch(employeeCode)
89           {
90               case 1:
91                   commission = .10 * employeeSales;
92                   break;
93
94               case 2:
95                   commission = .14 * employeeSales;
96                   break;
97
98               case 3:
99                   commission = .18 * employeeSales;
100                  break;
101          }
102          return commission;
103      }
104
```

**FIGURE 4-27**

When the getComm() method is called from the main() method in line 24, it sends the arguments, dollars and empCode, to the getComm() method itself. The method returns a double value that is stored in a variable named answer.

The method header for the getComm() method displays in line 84. Its two parameters are declared to accept the values sent from the calling statement. Those values do not have to have different names than the arguments, dollars and empCode, used in line 24; however, because Java considers them different storage locations, visible only in their respective methods, most programmers assign the arguments and parameters different — but user-friendly and related — names. The arguments, dollars and empCode, become the parameters, employeeSales and employeeCode, in the getComm() method.

After the return variable, commission, is declared and assigned an initial value of 0.0 (line 86), a switch statement is used to assign a commission rate based on the commission code entered by the user (lines 88 through 101). If the user enters 1, the method call in line 24 sends that value as the argument, emp-Code, to the getComm() method. The getComm() method receives the value and stores it as the parameter, employeeCode, which is local to the getComm() method. The switch statement evaluates the value of employeeCode and, because the value matches the value used in the case statement in line 90, the program assigns the commission variable a commission rate of .10 multiplied by the value for employeeSales. If the user enters a 2, the program assigns a commission rate of .14 multiplied by the value for employeeSales. If a user enters a 3, the program assigns a commission rate of .18 multiplied by the value for employeeSales.

Because the getCode() method already validated the commission code entered by the user to ensure it was in the range of one through three, there is no chance of the switch structure encountering a number outside of the range, which means no default case statement is necessary to handle exceptions.

The following steps enter code to call and execute the getComm() method.

## To Enter Code for the getComm() Method

1. Enter line 24 as shown in Figure 4-27 on the previous page.

   *The main() method of the Commission program includes the statement to call the getComm() method and assign its return value to a variable named empCode (Figure 4-28).*

```
15  public static void main(String[] args)
16  {
17      //declare class variables
18      double dollars, answer;
19      int empCode;
20
21      //call methods
22      dollars = getSales();
23      empCode = getCode();
24      answer = getComm(dollars,empCode);    ──────── method call
25  }                                                  with arguments
26
27  //The getSales() method asks the user to input a dollar amount and validates it
28  public static double getSales()
29  {
30      //declare method variables
31      double sales = 0.0;
32      boolean done = false;
33
34      //loop while not done
35      while (!done)
36      {
37          String answer = JOptionPane.showInputDialog(null,
            "Enter the sales amount\n(do not use commas or dollar signs)\n or click Cancel to
            exit.");
```

FIGURE 4-28

**2.** Enter lines 83 through 104 as shown in Figure 4-27 on page 4.39.

*TextPad displays the getComm() method in the coding window (Figure 4-29).*

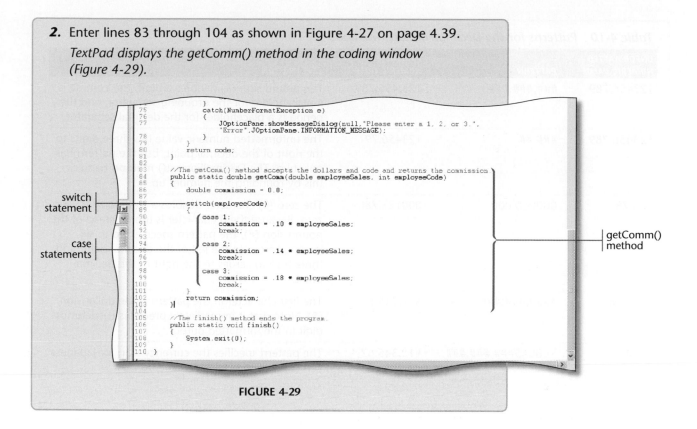

switch statement

case statements

getComm() method

```
 75            }
 76            catch(NumberFormatException e)
 77            {
                   JOptionPane.showMessageDialog(null,"Please enter a 1, 2, or 3.",
                   "Error",JOptionPane.INFORMATION_MESSAGE);
 78            }
 79        }
 80        return code;
 81    }
 82
 83    //The getComm() method accepts the dollars and code and returns the commission
 84    public static double getComm(double employeeSales, int employeeCode)
 85    {
 86        double commission = 0.0;
 87
 88        switch(employeeCode)
 89        {
 90            case 1:
 91                commission = .10 * employeeSales;
 92                break;
 93
 94            case 2:
 95                commission = .14 * employeeSales;
 96                break;
 97
 98            case 3:
 99                commission = .18 * employeeSales;
100                break;
101        }
102        return commission;
103    }
104
105    //The finish() method ends the program
106    public static void finish()
107    {
108        System.exit(0);
109    }
110 }
```

**FIGURE 4-29**

While the getComm() method is complete, it merely returns a commission rate to the main() method. Additional code must be added to the program to display output showing the calculated commission.

## Formatting Numeric Output

As you have learned, both the System.out.println() and the JOptionPane methods can display numeric output, but it is not formatted in any special way. **Formatted numeric output** includes features such as dollar signs, commas, decimal points, leading zeroes, and other formatting symbols, applied automatically to a displayed value.

Java has a special class of methods to handle numeric formatting. For example, the **DecimalFormat class** formats decimal numbers. It has a variety of features designed to make it possible to parse and format numbers in any locale, including support for Western, Arabic, and Indic digits. It also supports different kinds of numbers, including integers (123), fixed-point numbers (123.4), scientific notation (1.23E4), percentages (12%), and currency amounts ($123).

Programmers use the DecimalFormat class to format decimal numbers into Strings for output. This class allows you to control the display of leading and trailing zeroes, prefixes and suffixes, grouping (thousands) separators, and the decimal separator.

A constructor is used to create a named String using the **DecimalFormat() method**. The argument for the DecimalFormat() method is a String called a **pattern**, which determines how the formatted number should be displayed. Table 4-10 on the next page displays some examples of patterns and the resulting output.

*Table 4-10   Patterns for the DecimalFormat() Method*

| UNFORMATTED NUMERIC VALUE | PATTERN | FORMATTED NUMERIC OUTPUT | EXPLANATION |
|---|---|---|---|
| 123456.789 | ###,###.### | 123,456.789 | The pound sign (#) denotes a digit, the comma is a placeholder for the grouping separator, and the period is a placeholder for the decimal separator. |
| 123456.789 | ###.## | 123456.79 | The unformatted numeric value has three digits to the right of the decimal point, but the pattern has only two. The DecimalFormat() method handles this by rounding the number up. |
| 123.78 | 000000.000 | 000123.780 | The zero (0) character denotes a leading or trailing zero. Because the 0 character is used instead of the pound sign (#), the pattern specifies up to six leading zeroes to the left of the decimal point and three trailing zeroes to the right of the decimal point. |
| 12345.67 | $###,###.### | $12,345.67 | The first character in the pattern is the dollar sign ($). Note that it immediately precedes the leftmost digit in the formatted output. |
| 12345.67 | \u00A5###,###.### | ¥12,345.67 | The pattern specifies the currency sign for Japanese yen (¥) with the Unicode value 00A5. |

Once declared and constructed, the **format() method** can be used to assign the formatting pattern to a specific value. Table 4-11 shows the general form of the DecimalFormat class constructor, the DecimalFormat() method and its argument, and the use of the format() method to assign the formatting specified in a pattern to a value.

*Table 4-11   DecimalFormat Class Constructor and DecimalFormat() Method*

| | |
|---|---|
| **General form:** | DecimalFormat patternName = new DecimalFormat("pattern String"); patternName.format(value); |
| **Purpose:** | To provide formatted output of decimal numbers |
| **Examples:** | `DecimalFormat twoDigits = new DecimalFormat("$000.00");`<br>`twoDigits.format(123.45);` |

### Coding the output() Method

The output() method in the Commission program will construct an instance of the DecimalFormat object and assign it a pattern that includes a dollar sign, a comma for a grouping (thousands) separator, a decimal point, and two digits for cents. The DecimalFormat object then is used with the format() method to provide properly formatted numeric output of the sales and commission values in a JOptionPane message dialog box. Figure 4-30 displays the line of code to call the output() method (line 25) and the output() method definition (lines 105 through 113).

```
25              output(answer, dollars);
```

```
105
106         //The output() method displays the commission and sales.
107         public static void output(double commission, double sales)
108         {
109             DecimalFormat twoDigits = new DecimalFormat("$#,000.00");
110
111             JOptionPane.showMessageDialog(null,"Your commission on sales of "+ twoDigits.format
                (sales) + " is " + twoDigits.format(commission),"Commission Totals",JOptionPane.
                INFORMATION_MESSAGE);
112         }
113
```

**FIGURE 4-30**

When the output() method is called from the main() method in line 25, it sends the arguments, answer and dollars, to the output() method itself. It does not receive a return value.

In line 109 in the output() method, an instance of the DecimalFormat object, named twoDigits, is constructed with a pattern allowing for thousands of dollars, formatted with a dollar sign, a comma thousands separator, and two decimal places.

In line 111, the second argument of the showMessageDialog() method represents the message that will display in the dialog box. The argument is composed of a string of characters concatenated, or joined, with the values for the sales amount and the commission amount. As you learned in Chapter 2, the plus sign (+) is a concatenation symbol used to join String values. In line 111, the twoDigits.format() methods take the numeric arguments, sales and commission, and apply the format pattern defined and assigned in line 109.

The following steps enter code for the output() method.

## To Code the output() Method

**1.** Enter line 25 as shown in Figure 4-30.

*TextPad displays the statement to call the output() method and send two arguments (Figure 4-31).*

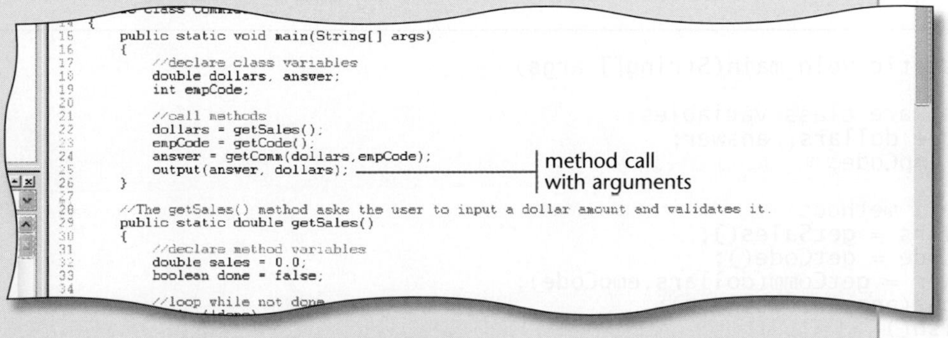

**FIGURE 4-31**

*(continued)*

**2.** Enter lines 106 through 113 as shown in Figure 4-30 on the previous page.

*TextPad displays the output() method in the coding window (Figure 4-32).*

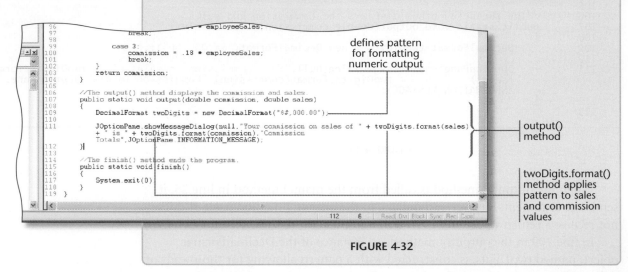

**FIGURE 4-32**

The DecimalFormat class contains many useful methods to change numeric formatting symbols. For example, instead of formatting a number in the form:

4,200,923.25

Some European countries use different numeric conventions, such as using a comma instead of a period to separate decimal values and a period instead of a comma as the grouping or thousands separator, in the form:

4.200.923,25

The DecimalFormat class offers a great deal of flexibility in the formatting of numbers.

### The finish() Method

Finally, the main() method must call the finish() method to exit the system when the program is completed successfully. The complete main() method displays in Figure 4-33, including a call to the finish() method in line 26.

```
15      public static void main(String[] args)
16      {
17          //declare class variables
18          double dollars, answer;
19          int empCode;
20
21          //call methods
22          dollars = getSales();
23          empCode = getCode();
24          answer = getComm(dollars,empCode);
25          output(answer, dollars);
26          finish();
27      }
28
```

**FIGURE 4-33**

The following step enters code to call the finish() method as shown in Figure 4-33.

### To Enter Code for the finish() Method

**1.** Enter line 26 as shown in Figure 4-33.

The application now is complete. The following steps compile and run the application, testing the application using sample data.

### To Compile and Test the Application

**1.** With the Data Disk in drive A, compile the program by clicking Compile Java on the Tools menu. If TextPad notifies you of errors, click Commission.java in the Selector window, fix the errors, and then compile again. When the program compiles with no errors, click Run Java Application on the Tools menu.

**2.** When the Input dialog box displays, type 52375 and then click the OK button.

**3.** When the second Input dialog box displays, type 2 and then click the OK button.

*The Commission Totals dialog box displays the formatted sales and the commission (Figure 4-34).*

Commission Totals dialog box

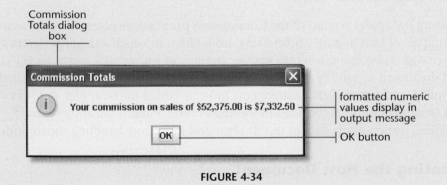

formatted numeric values display in output message

OK button

**FIGURE 4-34**

**4.** Click the OK button in the Commission Totals dialog box. Click the Close button in the command prompt window title bar.

*The Commission program terminates and the command prompt window closes.*

The Commission class now contains six working methods: main(), getSales(), getCode(), getComm(), output(), and finish(). You may want to print a copy of the Commission.java source code for reference, as you modify the code to create different versions of the program.

In J2SE version 5.0, the **printf() method** may be used to format numeric output. After importing the java.io.* package, programmers may embed one of several special **conversion characters** that will insert data into a string, as shown in Table 4-12.

**Table 4-12   The printf() Method**

| Conversion Character | sample code |
|---|---|
| General form: | System.out.printf(String format, Object arguments) |
| Purpose: | To write a formatted string to an output stream using the specified format string and arguments |
| Examples: | |
| %b – Boolean value | System.out.printf("The Boolean value is %b\n", true); |
| %c – character | System.out.printf("The character %c\n", 'A'); |
| %d – decimal integer | System.out.printf("An integer %d displays from a declared variable, num\n", num); |
| %f – floating-point number | System.out.printf("%f is a floating-point number representation of 3.1415929\n", 3.1415929); |
| %e – number in standard scientific notation | System.out.printf("The scientific notation is %e\n", 3.1415929); |
| %s – String | System.out.printf("The string %s displays\n", "Hi There"); |

# Moving to the Web

Creating the applet version of the Commission program involves using the same techniques of building the applet using modularity, in which a larger program's source code is broken down into smaller sections of source code. First, an HTML host document to call the applet must be created; then the applet stub is created, compiled, and tested. Next, components must be added to the applet and selection structures must be included in the applet code. Finally, the applet should be tested, using sample data to test its error and exception-handling capabilities.

## Creating the Host Document

Recall from previous chapters that because an applet is initiated and executed from within another language or run as part of a Web page, you must identify a host, or reference program, to execute the applet. The host document often is a Web page created as an HTML file with an applet tag.

The code to create an HTML file to access the CommissionApplet program is shown in Figure 4-35.

```
1   <HTML>
2   <APPLET CODE = "CommissionApplet.class" WIDTH = "350" HEIGHT = "200">
3   </APPLET>
4   </HTML>
```

**FIGURE 4-35**

The following steps create the HTML file and save it on the Data Disk in Drive A.

### To Create the HTML Host Document

1. With the TextPad window displayed, click File on the menu bar and then click New.
2. Click File on the menu bar and then click Save As on the File menu. When the Save As dialog box is displayed, click the Save in box arrow and then click 3½ Floppy (A:) in the Save in list.
3. Double-click the Chapter04 folder or a location specified by your instructor.
4. Type CommissionApplet in the File name text box and then click HTML (*.htm*, *.stm*) in the Save as type list.
5. Click the Save button in the Save As dialog box.
6. In the coding window, type the code as shown in Figure 4-35.

   *TextPad displays the HTML code (Figure 4-36).*

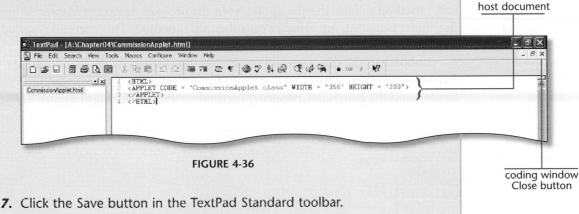

FIGURE 4-36

7. Click the Save button in the TextPad Standard toolbar.
8. Click the coding window Close button.

## Coding an Applet Stub

As you may recall from previous chapters, creating an applet typically involves importing two class packages that Java will need to support the applet-related methods. First, the java.applet package is imported to lay the foundation for an applet by allowing the applet to inherit certain attributes and manipulate classes.

Programmers commonly enter an import statement to import the Abstract Window Toolkit (AWT), which provides resources that implement rich, attractive, and useful interfaces in Java applets. As you learned in Chapter 2, the java.awt package is included with the SDK and contains all of the classes for creating user interfaces and for painting graphics and images, as well as container classes to add components such as Buttons, TextFields, and Labels. The AWT's Graphics class is quite powerful, allowing you to create shapes and display images.

The other imported package used in many interactive applets is the java.awt.event package. The java.awt.event package provides interfaces and classes for dealing with different types of events triggered by AWT components. The java.awt.event package is not a subset of the java.awt package; rather, it is a separate package enabling you to implement interfaces, such as the ActionListener and the ItemListener.

As you learned in Chapter 3, ActionListener listens for events that occur during execution of the program, such as a user clicking a mouse button or pressing the ENTER key. **ItemListener** can be added to an applet to listen for when the user clicks components such as check boxes. ItemListener has several methods, such as addItemListener() and itemStateChanged(), that enable you to test whether or not items in the user interface are selected. These packages — java.awt, java.applet, and java.awt.event, as well as the java.text.DecimalFormat used in the Commission application — can be imported in any order.

Recall that applets do not have a main() method. Instead, applets use the init() method to initialize the applet from the browser or Applet Viewer. When the applet is loaded, the browser calls the init() method. This method is called only once, no matter how many times you might return to the Web page.

Stubbing in the program will involve typing the general block comments; importing the four classes; and entering the class header, the init() method header, and the itemStateChanged() method header, as shown in Figure 4-37.

```
1   /*
2       Chapter 4:    Sales Commission
3       Programmer:   J. Starks
4       Date:         October 25, 2007
5       Filename:     CommissionApplet.java
6       Purpose:      This applet calculates sales commission using a sales amount
7                     (input by the user) and a sales code (chosen from among option buttons).
8   */
9
10  import java.awt.*;
11  import java.applet.*;
12  import java.awt.event.*;
13  import java.text.DecimalFormat;
14
15  public class CommissionApplet extends Applet implements ItemListener
16  {
17      public void init()
18      {
19      }
20
21      //This method is triggered by the user clicking an option button
22      public void itemStateChanged(ItemEvent choice)
23      {
24      }
25  }
```

**FIGURE 4-37**

The following steps code the program stub for the Commission applet.

## To Code the Applet Stub

**1.** With the TextPad window displayed, click File on the menu bar and then click New.

**2.** With the Data Disk in drive A, click File on the menu bar and then click Save As on the File menu. When the Save As dialog box is displayed, type CommissionApplet in the File name text box and then click Java (*.java) in the Save as type list. Click the Save in box arrow and then click 3½ Floppy (A:) in the Save in list. Double-click the Chapter04 folder. Click the Save button.

**3.** Enter the code as shown in Figure 4-37, using your name and the current date in the block comment.

*TextPad displays the code for the applet stub in the coding window (Figure 4-38).*

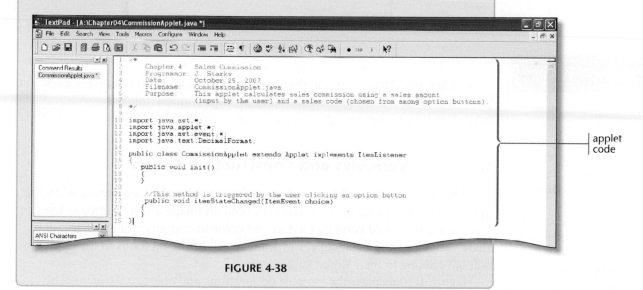

applet code

**FIGURE 4-38**

You can test the applet stub, even without any commands or data components in the applet code. The following steps compile and test the applet stub.

## To Compile and Test the Applet Stub

**1.** With the Data Disk in drive A, compile the program by clicking Compile Java on the Tools menu. If TextPad notifies you of errors, click CommissionApplet.java in the Selector window, fix the errors, and then compile again. When the program compiles with no errors, click Run Java Applet on the Tools menu.

**2.** When the Choose File dialog box displays, if necessary, click the box arrow and then click CommissionApplet.html in the list.

*(continued)*

3. Click the Yes button in the Choose File dialog box.

*Applet Viewer displays the applet with no components (Figure 4-39). The program stub has no active statements or commands.*

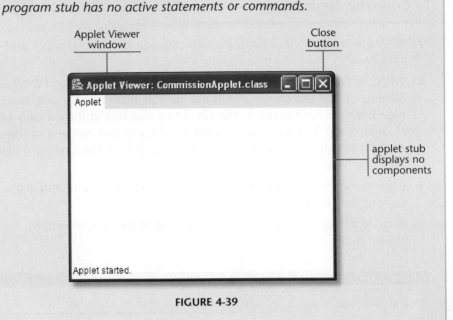

FIGURE 4-39

4. Click the Close button in the Applet Viewer title bar. If necessary, click the Close button in the command prompt window title bar.

## OTHER WAYS

1. To compile, press CTRL+1
2. To compile at command prompt, type javac CommissionApplet.java
3. To run, press CTRL+3
4. To run at command prompt, type appletviewer CommissionApplet.html

## Declaring Variables and Constructing Colors

The code for the applet must declare the same variables as those used in the application, along with a new variable to hold an image for the company logo. The code also should construct a dark red color to complement the logo. All of these variables have class scope, which means all of the methods in the applet will have access to their stored values.

Figure 4-40 displays the variable declarations and color constructor. The variables, dollars and answer, will store dollar amounts using the double data type. In line 19, the variable, empCode, will hold the commission code of 1, 2, or 3 using an integer data type. Line 20 declares an Image object named dollarSign. Line 21 constructs a **Color object** named darkRed. As shown in Line 21, the **Color() method** takes three arguments, each of which is a number in the range from 0 to 255 that corresponds to a specified red, green, and blue color. When combined, these three red, green, and blue colors can create a wide range of different colors, including darkRed.

```
17    //declare variables and construct a color
18    double dollars, answer;
19    int empCode;
20    Image dollarSign;
21    Color darkRed = new Color(160, 50, 0);
22
```

FIGURE 4-40

The following step enters code to declare the variables and construct the darkRed color.

## To Enter Code to Declare Variables and Construct a Color

**1.** Enter lines 17 through 22 as shown in Figure 4-40.

*TextPad displays the declared variables, including the constructed Color object, in the coding window. All methods in the class will be able to use the declared variables (Figure 4-41).*

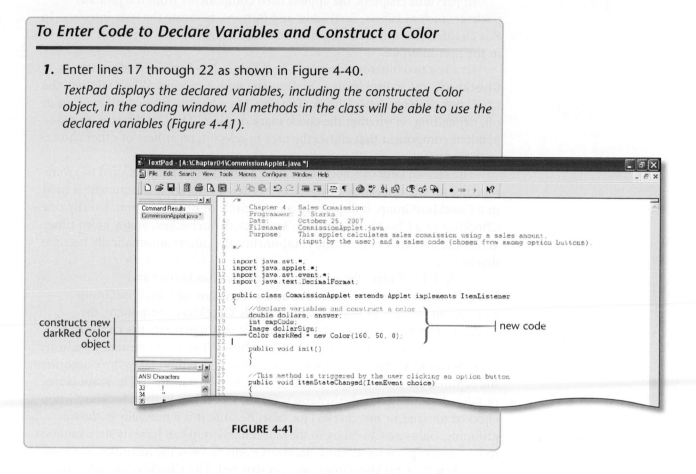

**FIGURE 4-41**

# Making Decisions in Applets

As with the Commission program created in the previous sections, a Java applet also may need to execute a specific section of code based on the actions of the user. For example, if the user enters an invalid number, the applet should display an error message and then give the user a chance to enter another number. Alternatively, if the user makes a choice from a list of options, a Java applet should switch or branch to a certain set of code statements based on that choice.

Through the use of check boxes, Java applets can allow the user to make choices that are evaluated by the applet. For instance, a user can click a check box to select it. The applet uses the ItemListener to listen for that click and then performs a unique set of instructions associated with that component.

Java applets also support the traditional if...else statements as well as the switch statement, to make a decision or determine which code to execute based on a user or program action.

## Constructing Checkboxes

In previous chapters, the applets used components from the java.awt package, such as Labels, TextFields, and Buttons, to create the user interface. In this chapter, you will create a constructor for a Checkbox component that is used in the user interface.

Java has two different kinds of Checkboxes. The first is a traditional **Checkbox**, which displays as a small square with a caption. When selected, the Checkbox displays a check mark. The Checkbox has the toggled value of on or off, depending on whether the check mark displays. The Checkbox is an independent component that allows the user to select it, regardless of other choices in the interface.

The second kind of Checkbox, called a **CheckboxGroup,** is used to group together several Checkbox components. When a Checkbox component is used in a CheckboxGroup, it displays as a small circle or option button. Exactly one Checkbox in a CheckboxGroup can be selected, or checked, at any given time. When the user clicks one of the components, the others automatically become deselected.

Table 4-13 displays the general form of the Checkbox() and CheckboxGroup() methods used to add a Checkbox or CheckboxGroup component to the user interface. For a single Checkbox component, the Checkbox() method takes a String argument that represents the **caption**, or label, you want to display beside the Checkbox. When using mutually exclusive Checkboxes in a CheckboxGroup, the Checkbox() method takes three arguments: the caption, the state, and the name of the CheckboxGroup(). The **state** is true or false, depending on whether you want the Checkbox in the CheckboxGroup checked for true, or not checked for false. Because it is a mutually exclusive grouping, only one Checkbox in the CheckboxGroup can have its state value set to true at any given time. The CheckboxGroup name is the identifier previously used when the CheckboxGroup was constructed. The CheckboxGroup name assigns the Checkbox as a member of the particular CheckboxGroup.

*Table 4-13 Checkbox() and CheckboxGroup() Methods*

| General form: | ```//Checkbox```<br>```Checkbox variableName = new Checkbox("caption");```<br>```//grouped Checkbox```<br>```CheckboxGroup variableName = new CheckboxGroup();```<br>```    Checkbox variableName = new Checkbox("caption", state, GroupName);``` |
| --- | --- |
| Purpose: | Component allows user to select on or off in a non-grouped Checkbox or to select one from many in a grouped Checkbox. Checkboxes toggle checked and unchecked based on a user's click. Grouped Checkboxes are mutually exclusive. Selecting one from among the group deselects all others. |
| Examples: | 1. ```Checkbox mayoBox = new Checkbox("Mayo");```<br>   ```Checkbox ketchupBox = new Checkbox("Ketchup");```<br>   ```Checkbox mustardBox = new Checkbox("Mustard");```<br>2. ```CheckboxGroup sizeGroup = new CheckboxGroup();```<br>   ```    Checkbox smallOpt = new Checkbox("Small", false, sizeGroup);```<br>   ```    Checkbox mediumOpt = new Checkbox("Medium", false, sizeGroup);```<br>   ```    Checkbox largeOpt = new Checkbox("Large", true, sizeGroup);``` |

## Constructing Applet Components

Next, code must be added to the applet to construct Labels for the prompts and output, a TextField in which the user will enter the sales amount, and a CheckboxGroup for the three sales code options. Figure 4-42 displays the code used to construct the applet components.

```
22
23          //Create components for applet
24          Label promptLabel = new Label(
            "Enter the sales amount (do not use commas or dollar signs):");
25               TextField salesField = new TextField(20);
26
27          Label codeLabel = new Label("Select the appropriate commission code:");
28
29          CheckboxGroup codeGroup = new CheckboxGroup();
30               Checkbox telephoneBox = new Checkbox("Telephone Sales",false,codeGroup)
31               Checkbox inStoreBox = new Checkbox("In-Store Sales",false,codeGroup);
32               Checkbox outsideBox = new Checkbox("Outside Sales",false,codeGroup);
33               Checkbox hiddenBox = new Checkbox("",true,codeGroup);
34
35          Label outputLabel = new Label(
            "Click an option button to calculate the sales commission.");
36
```

**FIGURE 4-42**

Line 29 in Figure 4-42 constructs an instance of the CheckboxGroup, thus directing the Java compiler that only one Checkbox in the group can be checked at one time. Lines 30 through 33 then construct individual instances of the Checkboxes with unique identifiers. The hidden Checkbox coded in line 33 will not be added to the applet's user interface, as you will see in later steps. Instead, the hidden Checkbox is included so that if you want to clear all the other Checkboxes in the CheckboxGroup, the code can set the hidden Checkbox to true, thus changing the others to false automatically. Because you want none of the visible options to be selected when the applet starts, the hidden Checkbox is set to true, and all other members of the CheckboxGroup are set to false.

The step on the next page enters the code to construct the applet components.

## To Construct Applet Components

**1.** Enter lines 23 through 36 as shown in Figure 4-42 on the previous page.

*TextPad displays the code to construct the components (Figure 4-43).The Checkbox constructors use the variable, codeGroup, to include the four Checkboxes as members of the CheckboxGroup named codeGroup.*

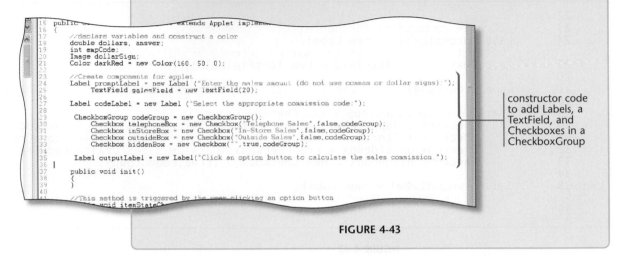

```
15  public          extends Applet implem
16  {
17    //declare variables and construct a color
18    double dollars, answer;
19    int empCode;
20    Image dollarSign;
21    Color darkRed = new Color(160, 50, 0);
22
23    //Create components for applet
24    Label promptLabel = new Label ("Enter the sales amount (do not use commas or dollar signs):");
25      TextField salesField = new TextField(20);
26
27    Label codeLabel = new Label ("Select the appropriate commission code:");
28
29    CheckboxGroup codeGroup = new CheckboxGroup();
30      Checkbox telephoneBox = new Checkbox("Telephone Sales",false,codeGroup);
31      Checkbox inStoreBox = new Checkbox("In-Store Sales",false,codeGroup);
32      Checkbox outsideBox = new Checkbox("Outside Sales",false,codeGroup);
33      Checkbox hiddenBox = new Checkbox("",true,codeGroup);
34
35    Label outputLabel = new Label("Click an option button to calculate the sales commission.");
36
37    public void init()
38    {
39    }
40
41    //This method is triggered by the user clicking an option button
        void itemStateC
```

constructor code to add Labels, a TextField, and Checkboxes in a CheckboxGroup

**FIGURE 4-43**

Table 4-14 displays some of the methods used with a Checkbox. For information on other methods, the Java API contains a table associated with each component.

*Table 4-14   Methods Used with the Checkbox Component*

| METHOD | PURPOSE | EXAMPLE |
|---|---|---|
| setState()<br>getState() | To set or determine whether the Checkbox is selected | `boolean answer = myOption.getState();` |
| setLabel()<br>getLabel() | To set or determine the caption of a Checkbox | `myOption.setLabel("This is the new caption");` |
| addItemListener() | Allows the Checkbox to become a trigger for an event | `myCheckbox.addItemListener();` |

### Adding Color, Components, Focus, and Listeners to the Applet

You may recall that the add() method takes an argument of a declared component and adds it to the Applet Viewer window when the applet is initiated. The **addItemListener event** then causes the applet to listen for clicks initiated by the user. When the click occurs, a series of associated objects and methods change, including the getState() method, the itemStateChanged() method, and the ItemEvent() object. Table 4-15 describes the general form of the addItemListener event.

*Table 4-15   The addItemListener Event*

| | |
|---|---|
| **Syntax:** | component.addItemListener(ItemListener object) |
| **Comment:** | Causes the applet to listen for clicks initiated by the user. The component must be declared with a constructor before triggering the event. The ItemListener object may be self-referential, using the argument, this, or a constructor of a new ItemListener object. |
| **Example:** | `optBlue.addItemListener(this);` |

Applets can use graphics and color to keep users interested and provide ease of use. Two methods help you change the color of your applet: the setBackground() method and the setForeground() method. As you learned in Chapter 2, the setBackground() method changes the background color of the applet window or other component. The **setForeground() method** changes the color of the text used in the applet window. You may want to change the foreground (text) color to draw attention to a certain component or use a lighter color to make the text display more clearly on darker backgrounds. Table 4-16 displays the general form of the setBackground() and setForeground() methods.

*Table 4-16   The setBackground() and setForeground() methods*

| METHOD | PURPOSE | EXAMPLE |
|---|---|---|
| setBackground() | Set the background color of an applet or other component | 1. `setBackground(Color.blue);`<br>2. `myLabel.setBackground(Color.cyan);` |
| setForeground() | Set the foreground color of an applet or other component | 3. `setForeground(darkRed);`<br>4. `myTextField.setForeground(Color.cyan);` |

Example 1 sets the background of the entire applet window to blue. If you want to set the background color for a specific Label or Checkbox, you must precede the command with the name of the object, as shown in example 2.

The argument of both methods uses a Color object. In example 3, the color darkRed was declared and assigned previously, so the attribute does not need to be preceded by the name of the Color object. In example 4, the Color object is followed by a period delimiter followed by a valid color attribute. The preset color attributes used for most components are medium gray for the background and black for the foreground or text. To review a list of valid attributes for the Color object, see Table 2-9 on page 99.

Another method associated with applets that use TextFields is the requestFocus() method. The **requestFocus() method** moves the insertion point to the component that calls it. In the case of TextFields, when the TextField has the focus, the insertion point displays as a vertical flashing line in the text box. A command button, such as OK or Cancel, may display focus with a dotted rectangle displayed around the button's caption. Displaying the insertion point helps users focus on the appropriate spot to enter the next item of text and commonly is used when clearing an incorrect entry to let the user try another entry.

## Coding the init() Method

Figure 4-44 displays the code for the init() method. Lines 39 and 40 set the background and foreground colors of the applet window, and lines 41 and 42 add the promptLabel and salesField to accept user input. Line 43 sets the focus to the salesField and line 44 sets the foreground color of the salesField component to black. Lines 45 through 52 use the add() method to add the components to the applet and to add the ItemListener to each of the Checkbox components.

```
37      public void init()
38      {
39           setBackground(darkRed);
40           setForeground(Color.white);
41           add(promptLabel);
42           add(salesField);
43           salesField.requestFocus();
44           salesField.setForeground(Color.black);
45           add(codeLabel);
46           add(telephoneBox);
47           telephoneBox.addItemListener(this);
48           add(inStoreBox);
49           inStoreBox.addItemListener(this);
50           add(outsideBox);
51           outsideBox.addItemListener(this);
52           add(outputLabel);
53      }
54
```

**FIGURE 4-44**

It is a common coding practice to set the applet background and foreground colors first and then add additional components and set their background and foreground colors as they are added to the applet interface. The applet components will display in the order they are added. The code to add the ItemListener for each Checkbox component typically is coded directly after the code used to add each Checkbox component.

The following step codes the init() method in the applet.

### To Code the init() Method

*1.* Enter the code from lines 39 thorugh 52 as shown in Figure 4-44.

*The init() method code will execute at run time (Figure 4-45). The code completes the init() method by adding the components to the user interface, defining the foreground and background colors for the applet window and components, setting the corresponding ItemListener for each Checkbox, and setting the focus to the salesField TextField component.*

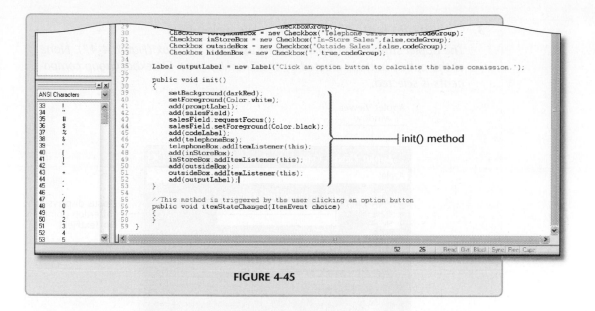

```
29
30      Checkbox telephoneBox = new Checkbox("Telephone Sales",false,codeGroup);
31      Checkbox inStoreBox = new Checkbox("In-Store Sales",false,codeGroup);
32      Checkbox outsideBox = new Checkbox("Outside Sales",false,codeGroup);
33      Checkbox hiddenBox = new Checkbox("",true,codeGroup);
34
35      Label outputLabel = new Label("Click an option button to calculate the sales commission.");
36
37      public void init()
38      {
39          setBackground(darkRed);
40          setForeground(Color.white);
41          add(promptLabel);
42          add(salesField);
43          salesField.requestFocus();
44          salesField.setForeground(Color.black);
45          add(codeLabel);
46          add(telephoneBox);
47          telephoneBox.addItemListener(this);
48          add(inStoreBox);
49          inStoreBox.addItemListener(this);
50          add(outsideBox);
51          outsideBox.addItemListener(this);
52          add(outputLabel);
53      }
54
55      //This method is triggered by the user clicking an option button
56      public void itemStateChanged(ItemEvent choice)
57      {
58      }
59  }
```

init() method

**FIGURE 4-45**

## Compiling and Testing the init() Method

With the init() method complete, the applet will display its Labels, TextField, and Checkboxes, allowing the user to click one Checkbox in the CheckboxGroup. The following steps compile the applet and test the init() method.

### To Compile and Test the init() Method

**1.** With the Data Disk in drive A, compile the program by clicking Compile Java on the Tools menu. If TextPad notifies you of errors, click CommissionApplet.java in the Selector window, fix the errors, and then compile again. When the program compiles with no errors, click Run Java Applet on the Tools menu.

**2.** When the Choose File dialog box displays, if necessary, click the box arrow and then click CommissionApplet.html in the list.

*TextPad displays the Choose File dialog box (Figure 4-46).*

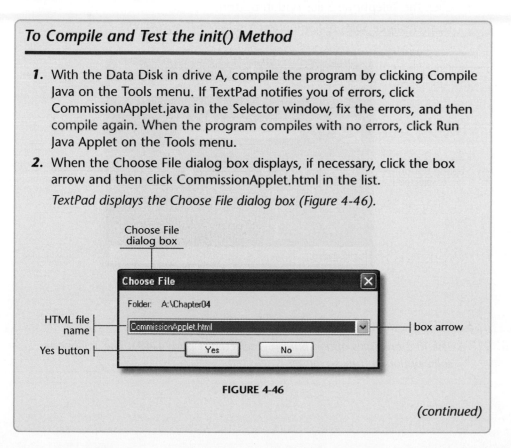

**FIGURE 4-46**

*(continued)*

**3.** Click the Yes button in the Choose File dialog box.

*The applet starts and displays the focus in the text box (Figure 4-47). None of the option buttons created by the Checkbox and CheckboxGroup components is selected.*

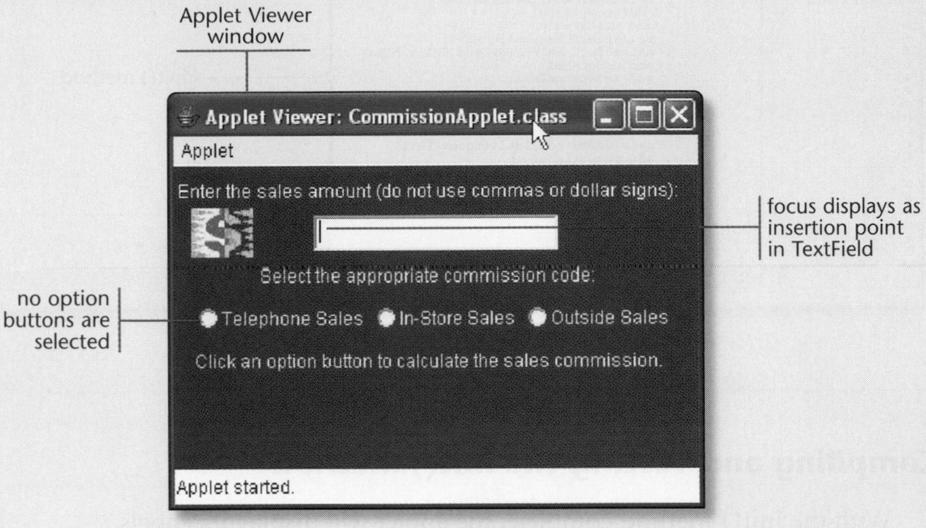

Applet Viewer window

focus displays as insertion point in TextField

no option buttons are selected

**FIGURE 4-47**

**4.** Click the Telephone Sales option button.

*The Telephone Sales option button is selected (Figure 4-48).*

Telephone Sales option button is selected

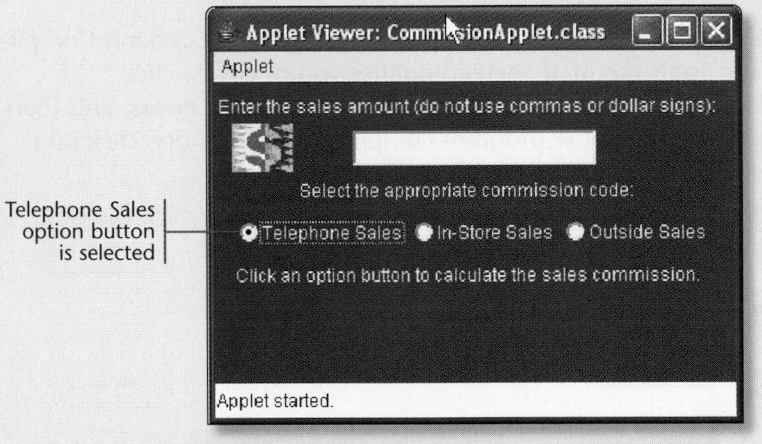

**FIGURE 4-48**

**5.** Click the In-Store Sales option button.

*The In-Store Sales option button is selected (Figure 4-49). The Telephone sales option button no longer is selected.*

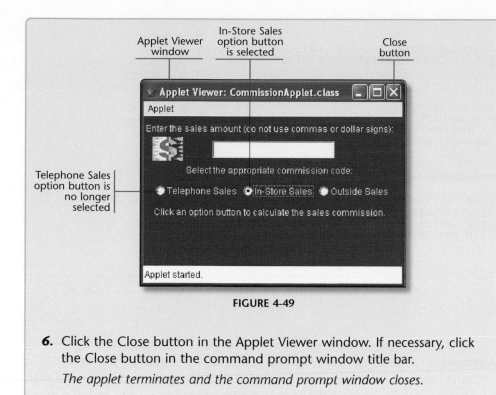

Applet Viewer window

In-Store Sales option button is selected

Close button

Telephone Sales option button is no longer selected

**FIGURE 4-49**

6. Click the Close button in the Applet Viewer window. If necessary, click the Close button in the command prompt window title bar.
   *The applet terminates and the command prompt window closes.*

**OTHER WAYS**

1. To compile, press CTRL+1
2. To compile at command prompt, type javac CommissionApplet.java
3. To run, press CTRL+3, choose file, click Yes button
4. To run at command prompt, type appletviewer CommissionApplet.html

Setting the hidden Checkbox to true, as part of the CheckboxGroup, means that when the applet starts, none of the option buttons displayed on the user interface are selected. The hidden Checkbox allows you to control the selection when the applet starts rather than letting a default selection dictate the course of the program.

## Handling Exceptions in the Applet Using try and catch Statements

When one of the Checkboxes in the CheckboxGroup is selected by a user during run time, the ItemListener changes the state of the component. That means when a user clicks an option button, the itemStateChanged() method is triggered.

In the applet, the code in the itemStateChanged() method includes a try and catch statement to call the methods used to test for valid data and to handle exceptions. The try and catch statements are shown in Figure 4-50 on the next page.

```
54
55          //This method is triggered by the user clicking an option button
56          public void itemStateChanged(ItemEvent choice)
57          {
58              try
59              {
60                  dollars = getSales();
61                  empCode = getCode();
62                  answer = getComm(dollars,empCode);
63                  output(answer, dollars);
64              }
65
66              catch(NumberFormatException e)
67              {
68                  outputLabel.setText("You must enter a dollar amount greater than zero.");
69                  hiddenBox.setState(true);
70                  salesField.setText("");
71                  salesField.requestFocus();
72              }
73          }
```

**FIGURE 4-50**

Lines 58 through 64 show the try statement and the braces enclosing the statements to call the getSales() method that returns a sales amount, the getCode() method that returns a commission code, the getComm() method that calculates a commission, and the output() method used to format and display the output. The try statement is similar to the main() method in the application, except it does not have to call the finish() method to terminate the program. Applets are controlled by their calling programs; therefore, Applet Viewer's Close button will be used to close the applet.

The catch statement, which executes when the try statement encounters an exception, uses the setText() method to display an error message. The message is displayed in line 68 in the outputLabel component on the applet interface. The setState() method in line 69 is used to set the state of the hidden Checkbox to true, thus deselecting the other Checkboxes. The setText() method in line 70 is used to clear the salesField TextField. Finally, in line 71, the requestFocus() method moves the insertion point to the salesField TextField so that the user can reenter a value for the sales amount.

The following step codes the try and catch statements for the applet. As you enter the code for this and the remaining methods in the applet, you may use cutting and pasting techniques to copy appropriate code from the application to the applet.

## To Enter Applet Code for the try and catch Statements

**1.** Enter the code in lines 58 through 72 as shown in Figure 4-50.

· *TextPad displays the try and catch statements in the coding window (Figure 4-51).*

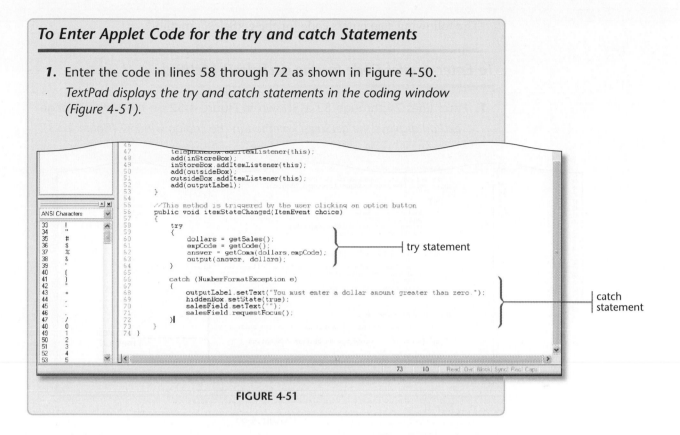

FIGURE 4-51

If the catch statement executes, a message will display in the applet window, the TextField will be cleared of any invalid input data, focus will be reset to that TextField, and any option buttons selected via the user interface will be cleared.

## Coding the getSales() Method for the Applet

The getSales() method used in the applet, as shown in Figure 4-52, is similar to that used in the application. The getSales() method parses the data from the TextField to a double data type and stores it in a declared variable named sales (line 77). Then, in line 79, it tests to see if sales is less than or equal to zero. If it is, the getSales() method throws an exception back to the calling init() method. If the sales amount is valid, line 81 returns the valid sales amount to the init() method.

```
74
75    public double getSales()
76    {
77        double sales = Double.parseDouble(salesField.getText());
78
79        if (sales <= 0) throw new NumberFormatException();
80
81        return sales;
82    }
```

FIGURE 4-52

The following step enters code for the getSales() method.

### To Enter Applet Code for the getSales() Method

***1.*** Enter lines 74 through 82 as shown in Figure 4-52 on the previous page. *TextPad displays the getSales() method in the coding window (Figure 4-53).*

```
//This method is triggered by the user clicking an option button
public void itemStateChanged(ItemEvent choice)
{
    try
    {
        dollars = getSales();
        empCode = getCode();
        answer = getComm(dollars,empCode);
        output(answer, dollars);
    }

    catch (NumberFormatException e)
    {
        outputLabel.setText("You must enter a dollar amount greater than zero.");
        hiddenBox.setState(true);
        salesField.setText("");
        salesField.requestFocus();
    }
}

public double getSales()
{
    double sales = Double.parseDouble(salesField.getText());

    if (sales <= 0) throw new NumberFormatException();

    return sales;
}
```

getSales() method

**FIGURE 4-53**

## Coding the getCode() Method for the Applet

The getCode() method, as shown in Figure 4-54, is slightly different than that of the application. Line 86 declares a variable named code and assigns the initial value of 0. The getCode() method uses an if statement with the getState() method to assess the state of each of the Checkboxes in the CheckboxGroup, one after the other. If the getState() method evaluating the first Checkbox returns a true value, the program sets the variable code to 1. Otherwise, the else statement is followed by another if statement, which evaluates the state of the next Checkbox. If the second getState() method returns a true value, the program sets the variable code to 2. The process is repeated for the third Checkbox. The appropriate variable code is returned to the calling init() method in line 92.

```
83
84          public int getCode()
85          {
86              int code = 0;
87              if (telephoneBox.getState()) code = 1;
88              else
89                  if (inStoreBox.getState()) code = 2;
90                  else
91                      if (outsideBox.getState()) code = 3;
92              return code;
93          }
```

**FIGURE 4-54**

The following step enters code for the getCode() method.

## To Enter Applet Code for the getCode() Method

**1.** Enter the code in lines 83 through 93 as shown in Figure 4-54.
*TextPad displays the getCode() method in the coding window (Figure 4-55).*

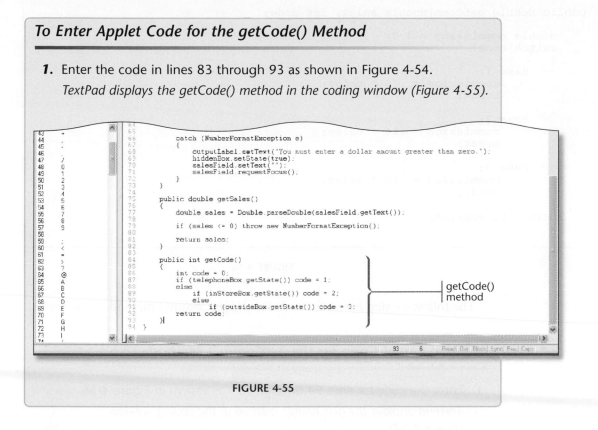

```
catch (NumberFormatException e)
{
    outputLabel.setText("You must enter a dollar amount greater than zero.");
    hiddenBox.setState(true);
    salesField.setText("");
    salesField.requestFocus();
}
}

public double getSales()
{
    double sales = Double.parseDouble(salesField.getText());

    if (sales <= 0) throw new NumberFormatException();

    return sales;
}

public int getCode()
{
    int code = 0;
    if (telephoneBox.getState()) code = 1;
    else
        if (inStoreBox.getState()) code = 2;
        else
            if (outsideBox.getState()) code = 3;
    return code;
}
```
getCode() method

**FIGURE 4-55**

In the application, the code uses a switch statement to evaluate the value entered by the user and then transfers control to the appropriate case statement. The switch statement, however, can accept only an integer value as an argument, which means it cannot accept the boolean value of true or false required to test the state of a Checkbox. Because of this, the applet uses nested if statements to determine which Checkbox the user selected. You will learn other ways to check the state of components in a later chapter.

## Coding the getComm() Method for the Applet

The getComm() method used in the applet is identical to the getComm() method used in the application. When the getComm() method is called from the init() method, it sends the arguments, dollars and empCode, along to the getComm() method itself. As shown in line 95 in Figure 4-56 on the next page, the arguments, dollars and empCode, become the parameters, sales and code, in the getComm() method. As with the getComm() method in the application, the getComm() method in the applet receives the value of the argument, empCode, and stores it as the parameter, code, which is local to the getComm() method. The switch statement evaluates the value of code, and if the value matches the value used in the case statement in line 100, the program assigns the commission variable a commission rate of .10 multiplied by the value for sales. If the user enters a 2, the program assigns a commission rate of .14 multiplied by the value for sales. If a user enters a 3, the program assigns a commission rate of .18 multiplied by the value for sales.

```
94
95      public double getComm(double sales, int code)
96      {
97          double commission = 0.0;
98          switch(code)
99          {
100             case 1:
101                 commission = .10 * sales;
102                 break;
103
104             case 2:
105                 commission = .14 * sales;
106                 break;
107
108             case 3:
109                 commission = .18 * sales;
110                 break;
111         }
112         return commission;
113     }
```

**FIGURE 4-56**

The following step enters the code for the getComm() method in the applet.

### To Enter Applet Code for the getComm() Method

**1.** Enter the code for lines 94 through 113 as shown in Figure 4-56.

*TextPad displays the getComm() method in the coding window (Figure 4-57).*

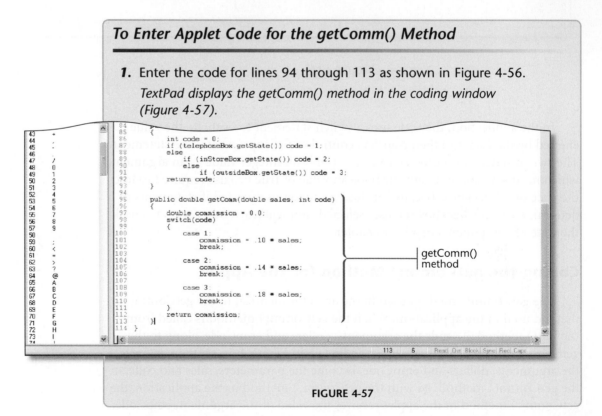

**FIGURE 4-57**

## Coding the output() Method for the Applet

The output() method, shown in Figure 4-58, causes the output to display in the applet. The output() method accepts the commission and sales values (line 115) from the calling method, constructs an instance of the DecimalFormat object with a pattern of dollars and cents (line 117), and then uses the setText() method to send the output to the Label in the applet interface (line 118).

```
114
115       public void output(double commission, double sales)
116       {
117           DecimalFormat twoDigits = new DecimalFormat("$#,000.00");
118           outputLabel.setText("Your commission on sales of " + twoDigits.format(sales) +
              " is " + twoDigits.format(commission));
119       }
```

**FIGURE 4-58**

The following step enters code for the output() method in the applet.

### To Enter Applet Code for the output() Method

***1.*** Enter the code for lines 114 through 119 as shown in Figure 4-58.
   *TextPad displays the output() method in the coding window (Figure 4-59).*

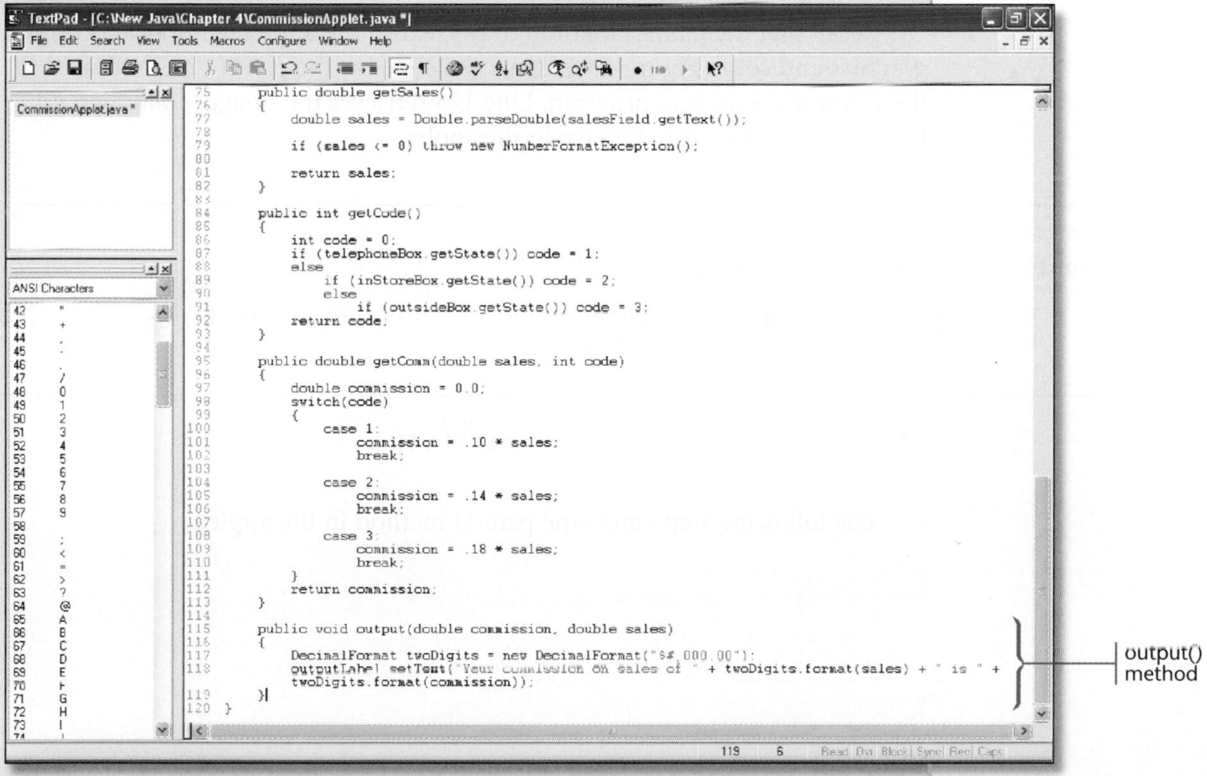

**FIGURE 4-59**

When used in a pattern for the DecimalFormat method, most characters, both numeric and alphabetic, are taken literally — that is, they are unchanged during formatting. On the other hand, special characters, such as those listed in Table 4-17, stand for other characters, strings, or classes of characters; they are replaced with the appropriate value when the method is called.

### Table 4-17  Special Characters Used in Patterns

| SYMBOL | PATTERN LOCATION | MEANING |
| --- | --- | --- |
| 0 | Number | Digit; zero shows as leading or trailing zero |
| # | Number | Digit; zero shows as absent |
| . | Number | Decimal separator or monetary decimal separator |
| − | Number | Minus sign |
| , | Number | Grouping separator |
| E | Number | Separates mantissa and exponent in scientific notation |
| ; | Subpattern boundary | Separates positive and negative subpatterns |
| % | Prefix or suffix | Multiply by 100 and show as percentage |

## Coding the paint() Method

Recall that the paint() method draws text in the applet window and displays graphics and color. Figure 4-60 shows the code for the paint() method used in the CommissionApplet program. Line 123 retrieves the image, dollarSign.gif; line 124 draws the stored image in the applet.

```
120
121     public void paint(Graphics g)
122     {
123         dollarSign = getImage(getDocumentBase(), "dollarSign.gif");
124         g.drawImage(dollarSign,12,28,this);
125     }
```

FIGURE 4-60

The following step enters the paint() method in the applet.

## To Enter Applet Code for the paint() Method

**1.** Enter the code for lines 120 through 125 as shown in Figure 4-60.

*TextPad displays the paint() method in the coding window (Figure 4-61).*

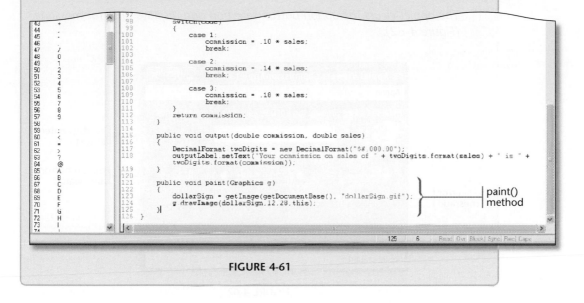

```
switch(code)
{
    case 1:
        commission = .10 * sales;
        break;

    case 2:
        commission = .14 * sales;
        break;

    case 3:
        commission = .18 * sales;
        break;
}
return commission;
}

public void output(double commission, double sales)
{
    DecimalFormat twoDigits = new DecimalFormat("$#,000.00");
    outputLabel.setText("Your commission on sales of " + twoDigits.format(sales) + " is " +
    twoDigits.format(commission));
}

public void paint(Graphics g)
{
    dollarSign = getImage(getDocumentBase(), "dollarSign.gif");
    g.drawImage(dollarSign, 12, 28, this);
}
```

paint() method

**FIGURE 4-61**

The image file is located in the Chapter04 folder of the Data Disk that accompanies this book; you also can contact your instructor for additional information on how to obtain the image. Remember that the image file and the source code file need to be in the same folder for the applet to compile and run successfully.

## Compiling and Testing the Applet

The code for the applet now is complete. You declared variables; constructed components; and wrote code for the init(), itemStateChanged(), and several user-defined methods that were similar to the user-defined methods in the Commission program. Now the applet can be compiled, and then run and tested using test data.

The following steps compile and then test the applet.

## To Compile and Test the Applet

**1.** With the Data Disk in drive A and the image file located in the same folder as the source code, compile the program by clicking Compile Java on the Tools menu. If TextPad notifies you of errors, click CommissionApplet.java in the Selector window, fix the errors, and then compile again. When the program compiles with no errors, click Run Java Applet on the Tools menu.

*(continued)*

**2.** When the Choose File dialog box displays, if necessary, click the box arrow and then click CommissionApplet.html in the list. Click the Yes button.

**3.** When the applet displays, do not enter any data in the text box. Click any one of the option buttons.

*The applet clears the option button selection and displays an error message (Figure 4-62).*

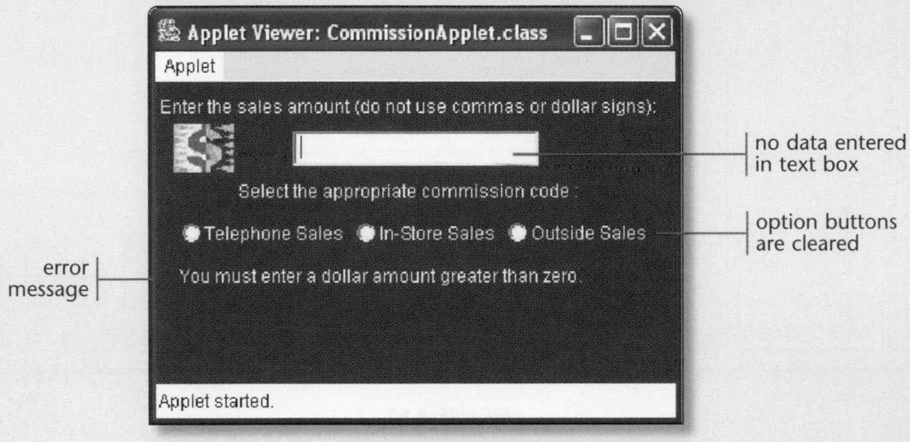

FIGURE 4-62

**4.** Type two thousand in the text box.

*The invalid alphabetic data is displayed in the text box (Figure 4-63).*

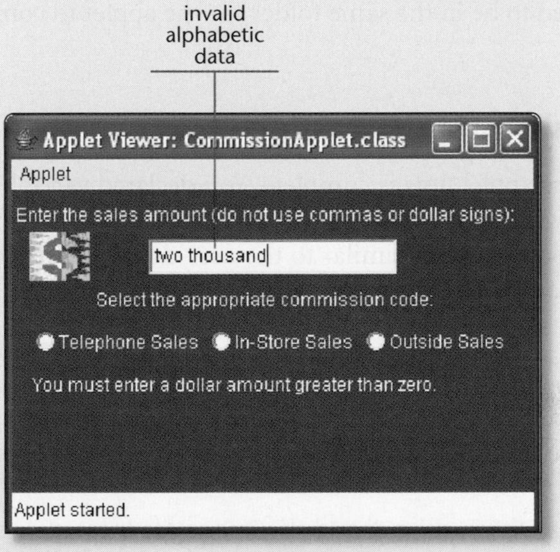

FIGURE 4-63

**5.** Click any of the option buttons. When the applet displays an error message and clears the alphabetic data, type 52375 in the text box.

*The applet clears the invalid alphabetic data and the option buttons. A valid sales amount is displayed in the text box (Figure 4-64).*

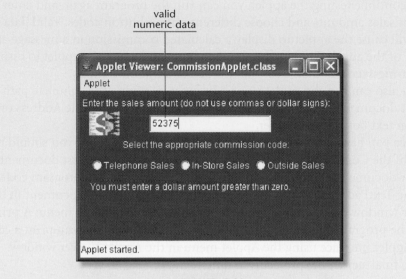

valid
numeric data

FIGURE 4-64

**6.** Click the In-Store Sales option button.

*The itemStateChanged() method, which is triggered by the click of the option button, causes the commission calculation to be performed. The applet displays the answer in an output message (Figure 4-65).*

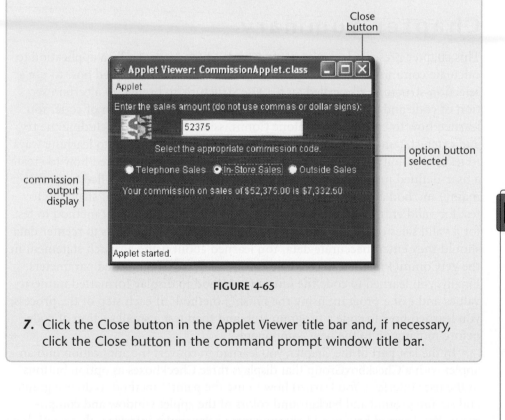

Close button

option button
selected

commission
output
display

FIGURE 4-65

**7.** Click the Close button in the Applet Viewer title bar and, if necessary, click the Close button in the command prompt window title bar.

## OTHER WAYS

1. To compile, press CTRL+1
2. To compile at command prompt, type javac Commission.java
3. To run, press CTRL+3, choose file, click Yes button
4. To run at command prompt, type appletviewer CommissionApplet. html

To continue testing the applet, you can run the program again and enter different sales amounts and choose different option button codes. Valid data input will cause the applet to display a calculated commission in a message at the bottom of the applet window; invalid data input will cause the applet to display an error message and then clear the text box and option buttons.

You also can run the applet using a browser by typing the complete path of the host document, a:\Chapter04\CommissionApplet.html, in the Address or Location text box of the browser.

Once you have determined that the program runs correctly, you should print a copy of the CommissionApplet source code and the HTML host document code for documentation purposes. You can print a copy of the program code from the TextPad coding window by selecting the appropriate document in the Selector window and then using the Print command on the File menu. A print-out of the program code will be sent to the default printer. You can print a copy of the applet interface using the Applet menu in the Applet Viewer window.

The final step in the project is to quit TextPad.

---

### To Quit TextPad

---

*1.* Click the Close button in the TextPad title bar.

---

# Chapter Summary

This chapter presented a series of steps and a discussion of a Java application to calculate commission based on a dollar sales amount. You learned how to use a selection structure, also called an if…else structure, to branch to a certain section of code and a repetition structure to repeat a certain section of code. You learned how to create a stand-alone Commission application, including the try and catch statements to handle possible exceptions, in addition to learning ways to test for validity, reasonableness, and accurate input. You learned how to create a user-defined method, called the getSales() method, which is called from the main() method and obtains a sales amount after employing an if structure to test for valid entries. You also learned how to code the getCode() method to test for a valid sales code, along with a while statement to allow users to reenter data should they enter inaccurate data. You learned about using a switch statement in the getComm() method to calculate commission based on passed parameters. Finally, you learned to code the output() method to display formatted numeric values and exit a program using the finish() method. At each step of the process, you learned how to code a program stub and then test a small section of code before moving on to the next component.

In the last part of the chapter, you learned to convert the application into an applet with a CheckboxGroup that displays three Checkboxes as option buttons in the user interface. You learned how to use the paint() method to draw a graphic and set foreground and background colors of the applet window and components. You learned how to add components to the applet interface, along with how to code an ItemListener event to listen for the user's click of the option button and to perform the corresponding event code. In both the application and the applet, you learned to use code to perform data validation and display error messages.

# What You Should Know

Having completed this chapter, you now should be able to perform the tasks shown in Table 4-18.

**Table 4-18  Chapter 4 What You Should Know**

| TASK NUMBER | TASK | PAGE |
|---|---|---|
| 1 | Start TextPad and Save a TextPad Document | 224 |
| 2 | Enter Beginning Code | 226 |
| 3 | Compile and Test the Program Stub | 227 |
| 4 | Enter Code for the getSales() Method | 230 |
| 5 | Compile and Test the getSales() Method | 232 |
| 6 | Code an if Statement to Test the Cancel Button | 237 |
| 7 | Code the try and catch Statements | 243 |
| 8 | Enter Code to Throw an Exception | 244 |
| 9 | Compile and Test the try and catch Statements | 245 |
| 10 | Enter Code for the while Statement | 249 |
| 11 | Compile and Test the while Statement | 250 |
| 12 | Enter Code for the getCode() Method | 252 |
| 13 | Compile and Test the getCode() Method | 253 |
| 14 | Enter Code for the getComm() Method | 256 |
| 15 | Code the output() Method | 259 |
| 16 | Enter Code for the finish() Method | 261 |
| 17 | Compile and Test the Application | 261 |
| 18 | Create the HTML Host Document | 263 |
| 19 | Code the Applet Stub | 265 |
| 20 | Compile and Test the Applet Stub | 265 |
| 21 | Enter Code to Declare Variables and Construct a Color | 267 |
| 22 | Construct Applet Components | 270 |
| 23 | Code the init() Method | 272 |
| 24 | Compile and Test the init() Method | 273 |
| 25 | Enter Applet Code for the try and catch Statements | 277 |
| 26 | Enter Applet Code for the getSales() Method | 278 |
| 27 | Enter Applet Code for the getCode() Method | 279 |
| 28 | Enter Applet Code for the getComm() Method | 280 |
| 29 | Enter Applet Code for the output() Method | 281 |
| 30 | Enter Applet Code for the paint() Method | 283 |
| 31 | Compile and Test the Applet | 283 |
| 32 | Quit TextPad | 286 |

# Key Terms

addItemListener event *(270)*

AND operator *(235)*

block if statement *(233)*

break *(254)*

break statement *(254)*

call *(228)*

caption *(268)*

case *(254)*

case statement *(254)*

case structure *(253)*

catch *(241)*

catch statement *(241)*

Checkbox *(268)*

CheckboxGroup *(268)*

checked exception *(240)*

claims *(240)*

Color object *(266)*

Color() method *(266)*

condition *(233)*

control structures *(218)*

conversion characters *(262)*

DecimalFormat class *(257)*

DecimalFormat() method *(257)*

default *(254)*

else *(234)*

exception *(239)*

exception handling *(239)*

explicitly *(240)*

finally statement *(243)*

format() method *(258)*

formatted numeric output *(257)*

handler *(240)*

if *(234)*

if...else statement *(233)*

if...else structure *(218)*

ItemListener *(264)*

logical operator *(235)*

looping *(247)*

modularity *(227)*

nested *(234)*

NOT operator *(235)*

null *(236)*

NumberFormatException *(242)*

OR operator *(235)*

pattern *(257)*

printf() method *(262)*

reasonableness *(244)*

repetition structure *(218)*

requestFocus() method *(271)*

return statement *(230)*

run-time exception *(239)*

selection structure *(218)*

setForeground() method *(271)*

single-line if statement *(233)*

state *(268)*

static *(229)*

stub *(226)*

switch *(254)*

switch statement *(254)*

throw new *(240)*

throw statement *(241)*

try *(240)*

try statement *(240)*

validity *(244)*

while *(248)*

while loop *(247)*

while statement *(247)*

# Homework Assignments

## Label the Figure

In Figure 4-66, arrows point to components of a Java applet running on the desktop. Identify the various components of the applet in the spaces provided.

1. _____   4. _____

2. _____   5. _____

3. _____

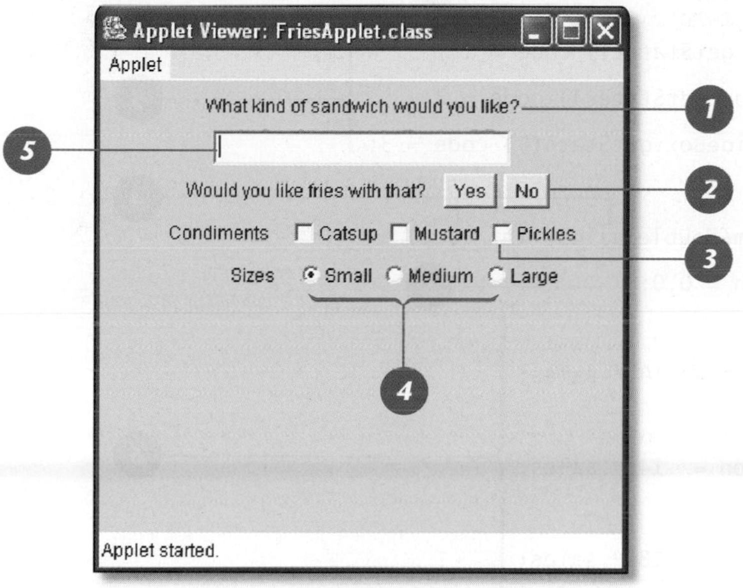

FIGURE 4-66

## Identify Code

In Figure 4-67 on the next page, arrows point to sections of Java source code. Identify the code in the spaces provided using the appropriate word from the following list.

| | | |
|---|---|---|
| arguments | case structure | initialization |
| concatenation | constructor | exception |
| data type | selection structure | while loop |
| header | method | object |
| pattern | package name | parameters |

*(continued)*

## Identify Code (continued)

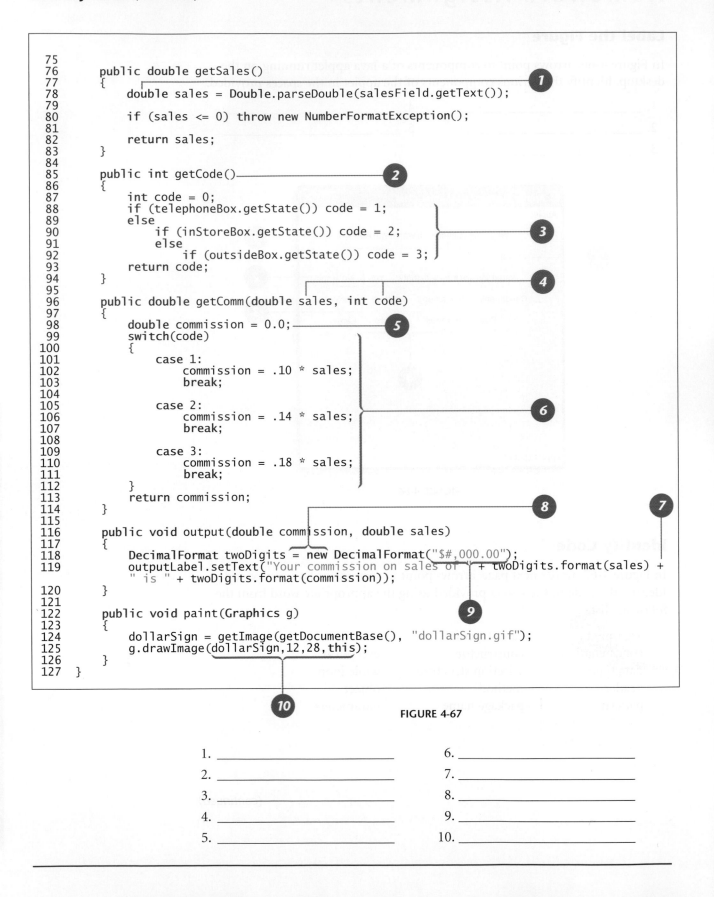

```
75
76      public double getSales()
77      {
78          double sales = Double.parseDouble(salesField.getText());
79
80          if (sales <= 0) throw new NumberFormatException();
81
82          return sales;
83      }
84
85      public int getCode()
86      {
87          int code = 0;
88          if (telephoneBox.getState()) code = 1;
89          else
90              if (inStoreBox.getState()) code = 2;
91              else
92                  if (outsideBox.getState()) code = 3;
93          return code;
94      }
95
96      public double getComm(double sales, int code)
97      {
98          double commission = 0.0;
99          switch(code)
100         {
101             case 1:
102                 commission = .10 * sales;
103                 break;
104
105             case 2:
106                 commission = .14 * sales;
107                 break;
108
109             case 3:
110                 commission = .18 * sales;
111                 break;
112         }
113         return commission;
114     }
115
116     public void output(double commission, double sales)
117     {
118         DecimalFormat twoDigits = new DecimalFormat("$#,000.00");
119         outputLabel.setText("Your commission on sales of " + twoDigits.format(sales) +
                " is " + twoDigits.format(commission));
120     }
121
122     public void paint(Graphics g)
123     {
124         dollarSign = getImage(getDocumentBase(), "dollarSign.gif");
125         g.drawImage(dollarSign,12,28,this);
126     }
127 }
```

**FIGURE 4-67**

1. _____    6. _____

2. _____    7. _____

3. _____    8. _____

4. _____    9. _____

5. _____    10. _____

## Understanding Error Messages

Locate the file named Errors in the Chapter04 folder on the Data Disk. Start TextPad and open the file. Compile the program. Using what you know about coding and error messages, list the possible coding errors that might cause TextPad to display the error messages. Or, if your instructor directs you to do so, fix the errors and submit a copy of the program to your instructor.

## Short Answer

1. A(n) _____ Checkbox in a CheckboxGroup can be used to clear others in the mutually exclusive set.

2. A statement is referred to as _____ when it is located completely within another statement.

3. Java uses a(n) _____ statement to evaluate a value for the case statement.

4. You can use the _____ method to position the insertion point in a TextField.

5. If the left side of the _____ operator evaluates to false, then the right side is not evaluated. If the left side of the _____ operator evaluates to true, then the right side is not evaluated.

6. The _____ typically contains code to perform any cleanup that might be necessary after executing the try statement and catch statement.

7. A(n) _____ displays as option buttons in the user interface of a Java applet.

8. An operation that attempts to use a float value in a location declared to be an integer is an example of a(n) _____.

9. A(n) _____ check might be used to ensure that data input by the user fits the program's specifications for a correct data type.

10. Conditions in Java are _____ expressions that evaluate to true or false.

11. A control structure that allows for more than two choices when a condition is evaluated is called a(n) _____.

12. When a Checkbox is clicked, the _____ method is called.

13. Study the following conditions and determine whether they evaluate to true or false. In those examples that display more than one condition, tell which condition confirms the true or false state.

    a. 25 == 25
    b. (18 < 19) && (12 > 14)
    c. (18 < 19) || (12 > 14)
    d. 31 <= 31
    e. !(5 == 5)
    f. (a == a) || (b == b) || (c == c)
    g. !((14 > 12) && (27 >= 26))
    h. (45 < 55) && (55 > 45)

*(continued)*

**Short Answer** *(continued)*

13. *(continued)*

    i. (100 + 5) != (40 + 65)

    j. (a == a) || !( == a)

14. Given the expression E = 450, S = 670, J = 1, T = 56, I = 34, determine the truth value of the following compound conditions:

    a. ((E < 400) || (J == 1))

    b. ((S == 700) && (T == 400))

    c. ((I == S) || J == 0))

    d. ((S < 300) && ((I < 50) || (J == 1)))

    e. ((S < 300) && (!(I < 50) || (J == 1)))

15. Determine a value of Q that will cause the condition in the if statements below to be true:

    a. if ((Q > 8) || (Q = 3) || (Z / 10))

    b. if ((Q >= 7) && (Q > 0)) strMessage = "Maximum
       number exceeded."

    c. if (Q / 3 < 9) intCount = intCount + 1

    d. if ((Q > 3) && !(Q == 3)) dblSum = dblSum + dblAmt

16. Given the conditions S == 0, Y == 4, B == 7, T == 8, and X == 3, determine the action taken for each of the following:

    a. if (S > 0) JOptionPane.showMessageDialog(null,
       "Computation complete.");

    b. if ((B == 4) || (T > 7))
       if (X > 1) JOptionPane.showMessageDialog(null,
       "Computation complete.");

    c. if ((X == 3) || (T > 2))
       if (Y > 7) JOptionPane.showMessageDialog(null,
       "Computation complete.");

    d. if ((X + 2) < 5)
      if (B < (Y + X))
       JOptionPane.showMessageDialog(null, "Computation
       complete.");

17. Given five variables with previously defined values intA, intB, intC, intD, and intE, write an if statement to increment the variable, intTotal, by 1 if all five variables have the exact value of 10.

18. Given the following code, what will display if the variable, answer, is set to 2? What will display if the variable, answer, is set to 4?

```
switch(answer)
{
    case 1:
        System.out.println("true");
        break;
```

```
        case 2:
            System.out.println("false");
            break;
        default:
            System.out.println("unknown");
            break;
    }
```

19. Given the following code, state five appropriate test values for the variable, dollars, that would cause the catch statement to be executed.

```
    try
    {
        double dollars = getSales();
        if (dollars < 0) throw new NumberFormatException;
    }

    catch (NumberFormatException e)
    {
        outputLabel.setText("You must enter a valid dollar amount greater than zero.");
    }
```

20. Assuming correct variable declaration and assignment, write a while statement for each of the following conditions.

    answer is equal to yes
    done is set to false
    moreRecords is set to true
    sex is male and age is greater than or equal to 21

21. Write a try statement and catch statement that will test a value entered by the user into a TextField named myAge. If the value is not a valid age, the catch statement should display a message in a Label named errorLabel. *Hint:* the error message should display for errors in range, validity, and data type.

22. Given two positive integer variables, intA and intB, write a sequence of statements to assign the variable with the larger value to intBig and the variable with the smaller value to intSmall. If intA and intB are equal, assign either to intSame. Be sure to show variable declarations.

23. The values of three variables, intU, intV, and intW, are positive and not equal to each other. Using if and else statements, determine which has the smallest value and assign this value to intLittle. Be sure to show variable declarations.

24. Write a partial program to display a message that reads, "Amanda Hefner, you may be the winner of $10,000.00!" in a JOptionPane dialog box. The message should use the proper concatenation and formatting. The title of the dialog box should be, Amanda Hefner, Lucky Winner. Properly declare any necessary variables. Use the corresponding variables listed below for the first name, last name, and winnings amount, but do not code those values directly into the statements.

```
    String firstName = "Amanda"
    String lastName  = "Hefner"
    double winnings = 10000.00
```

25. Write a partial program that creates a color called purple using RGB values and then displays the color as the background of an applet.

## Learn It Online

Start your browser and visit scsite.com/java3e/learn. Follow the instructions in the exercises below.

1. **Chapter Reinforcement TF, MC, and SA**   Click the True/False, Multiple Choice, and Short Answer link below Chapter 4. Print and then answer the questions.

2. **Practice Test**   Click the Practice Test link below Chapter 4. Answer each question, enter your first and last name at the bottom of the page, and then click the Grade Test button. When the graded practice test is displayed on your screen, click Print on the File menu to print a hard copy. Continue to take practice tests until you score 80% or better. Hand in a printout of the final practice test.

3. **Crossword Puzzle Challenge**   Click the Crossword Puzzle Challenge link below Chapter 4. Read the instructions, and then enter your first and last name. Click the Play button. Complete the crossword puzzle. When you are finished, click the Submit button. When the crossword puzzle is redisplayed, click the Print button.

4. **Tips and Tricks**   Click the Tips and Tricks link below Chapter 4. Click a topic that pertains to Chapter 4. Right-click the information and then click Print on the shortcut menu. Construct a brief example of what the information relates to in Java to confirm that you understand how to use the tip or trick. Hand in the example and printed information.

5. **Newsgroups**   Click the Newsgroups link below Chapter 4. Click a topic that pertains to Chapter 4. Print three comments.

6. **Expanding Your Horizons**   Click the Articles for Java link below Chapter 4. Click a topic that pertains to Chapter 4. Print the information. Construct a brief example of what the information relates to in Java to confirm that you understand the contents of the article. Hand in the example and printed information.

7. **Search Sleuth**   Select three key terms from the Key Terms section of this chapter and then use the Google search engine at google.com (or any major search engine) to display and print two Web pages for each key term.

# Programming Assignments

## 1 Multiplication Quiz

Start TextPad. Open the file named Multiply from the Chapter04 folder of the Data Disk. Review the program. This Multiplication Quiz application asks students to enter the multiplication table they wish to practice and then prompts them to enter each answer, multiplying their table value by each integer from 0 to 12. Although the program tells students whether they are right or wrong, it does not provide error checking to handle exceptions caused by the input of non-integer values, such as decimal or String values.

Using techniques learned in this chapter, write the try and catch statements to display appropriate messages if students try to enter non-integer numbers. Also write a while statement to create a loop that repeats the input prompt if a student enters invalid data.

1. With the Multiply.java code displayed in the TextPad window, substitute your name and date in the block comment. Type Quiz as the new class name. Edit the name of the class in the class header as well.

2. Save the file on your Data Disk with the file name Quiz.java. If you wish, print a copy of the source code to reference while completing this lab.

3. Compile the program by pressing CTRL+1.

4. Run the program by pressing CTRL+2. When the program executes in the command prompt window, enter an integer value, such as 8, as the value for the multiplication table you wish to practice. Respond to the prompts by entering the correct answers as integers. When you have completed the multiplication table, press any key or click the Close button in the command prompt window to quit the program.

5. Run the program again. Enter 8 as the value for the multiplication table you wish to practice. Respond to the first prompt by entering an incorrect answer, such as 80. Notice that the program tells you the answer is incorrect but does not allow you to try again. Click the Close button on the command prompt window to quit the program.

6. Run the program again. Enter a non-integer value, such as 7.5, as the value for the multiplication table you wish to practice. Java throws an exception, and a NumberFormatException message displays in the command prompt window.

7. Use TextPad to edit the program source code. In the main() method, enclose the section of code starting with the line, //Calling the user-defined methods, in a try statement. Remember to enter the try statement and an opening brace before and a closing brace after that section of code.

8. Below the try statement, enter a catch statement for a NumberFormatException. Write code to print an appropriate error message using the System.out.println() method or a JOptionPane message box.

9. Compile and run the program again, testing with both integer and non-integer values. Notice that an appropriate message now displays, but students must run the program again to answer any additional questions.

*(continued)*

**1 Multiplication Quiz** (continued)

10. Edit the program to enclose the section of code including the try and catch statements in a while loop. To do this, enter the code:

    ```
    while(!done)
    ```

    and an opening brace before and a closing brace after that section of code.

11. Before the closing brace of the try statement, enter the line of code:

    ```
    done = true;
    ```

    to terminate the loop during execution. Save the file by clicking Save on the File menu.

12. Compile and run the program again, testing with both integer and non-integer values. Notice that users now are directed back to the beginning of the program after the error message displays.

13. Edit the program again. In the takeQuiz() method, find the statement, while (count <= 12). Click below the while statement's opening brace. Enclose all the code within the while statement in a try statement. Include all the code statements in the try statement but not the opening or closing braces of the while statement itself. Move the line

    ```
    count = count + 1;
    ```

    up to position it inside the if statement braces, at approximately line 80.

14. Below the try statement, enter a catch statement for a NumberFormatException. Print an appropriate message using the System.out.println() method or a JOptionPane message box. Compile and run the program again, testing with both integer and non-integer values. Notice that the program now displays an error message if a user enters an incorrect answer and then gives the user a chance to enter a different answer.

15. Print a copy of the revised source code for your instructor.

## 2 Using switch and try Statements to Validate User Input

You would like to write a program to help beginning Java programmers understand data types. You have noticed that students have trouble differentiating among doubles, ints, Strings, and other data types. You decide to create an application, such as the one in Figure 4-68, that uses input boxes to test their knowledge. Beginning with a try statement, the program should allow users to choose a data type. Then, based on a switch statement and several case statements, the program should prompt the user to enter a value that would fit that specific data type. If the user inputs valid data — that is, data that matches the chosen data type and parses correctly — the program should display positive feedback. If the inputted data does not match the chosen data type, the parse statement will throw a NumberFormatException. The program then should use a catch statement to display an appropriate error message and then allow the user to try again.

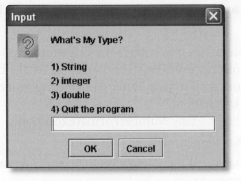

**FIGURE 4-68**

1. Start TextPad. Save the program as a Java source code file with the file name, MyType.

2. Enter general documentation comments, including the name of this lab, your name, the date, and the file name.

3. Import the java.io.* package and the javax.swing.JOptionPane package.

4. Type the class header and an opening brace to begin the class.

5. Type `public static void main(String[] args)` and an opening brace to begin the main() method header.

6. Declare the following variables using the code:

   `String strChoice, strTryString, strTryInt, strTryDouble;`

   `int choice, tryInt;`

   `double tryDouble;`

   `boolean done = false;`

7. Begin a while(!done) loop to repeat as long as the user does not click the Cancel button.

8. Inside a try statement, enter code to display an input box with three choices, as shown in Figure 4-68.

9. Type `choice = Integer.parseInt(strChoice);` on the next line to parse the value for the choice entered by the user.

10. Create a switch statement to test for each of the three choices. Type `switch(choice)` as the header and then press the ENTER key. Type an opening brace.

11. Enter a case statement for each of the three choices, using pages 254 through 257 as a guide for coding the switch, case, and break statements.

    • Case 1: If the user enters a 1, display a message that informs users they are correct, as any input can be saved as a String. Enter the break statement.

    • Case 2: If the user enters a 2, parse the value into tryInt. Display a message that informs users they are correct. Enter the break statement.

*(continued)*

**2 Using switch and try Statements to Validate User Input**
*(continued)*

- Case 3: If the user enters a 3, parse the value into tryDouble. Display a message that informs users they are correct. Enter the break statement.
- Case 4: Set done equal to true. Enter code to display a closing message. Enter the break statement.
- Case default: throw a new NumberFormatException.

12. Close the switch statement with a closing brace.

13. Create a catch statement by typing `catch(NumberFormatException e)` and then an opening brace.

14. Display an appropriate message directing the user to try again and then close the catch statement with a closing brace.

15. Close the try statement, the while statement, and the main() method with closing braces.

16. Save the file on the Data Disk using the file name MyType.java.

17. Compile the program. If necessary, fix any errors in the TextPad window, save, and then recompile.

18. Run the program. Enter various values for each menu choice. Check your answers.

19. Print a copy of the source code for your instructor.

20. As an extra credit assignment, add choices for long, byte, and boolean data types.

## 3 Writing User-Defined Methods

A small proprietary school that offers distance-learning courses would like an application that calculates total tuition and fees for their students. Users will input the number of hours; the program then will calculate the total cost. For full-time students taking greater than 15 hours of courses, the cost per credit hour is $44.50. For part-time students taking 15 hours or fewer, the cost per credit hour is $50.00.

1. Start TextPad. Save the file on your Data Disk with the file name Tuition.java.

2. Enter general documentation comments, including the name of this lab, your name, the date, and the file name.

3. Import the java.io.* package and the java.text.DecimalFormat package.

4. Type the class header and opening brace for the public class, Tuition.

5. Enter the main() method header.

6. Declare an integer variable named hours. Declare double variables named fees, rate, and tuition.

7. Enter the following method calls and then close the main() method with a closing brace.

```
displayWelcome();
hours = getHours();
```

```
rate = getRate(hours);
tuition = calcTuition(hours, rate);
fees = calcFees(tuition);
displayTotal(tuition + fees);
```

8. Code the corresponding methods:

   • Type `public static void displayWelcome()` and then, within that method block, code the statements to display a welcome message.

   • Type `public static int getHours()` and then, within that method block, declare strHours as a String and hours as an int, setting hours to an initial value of zero. Display a prompt that allows the user to enter a string value, strHours, for the total number of hours. Parse that value into the integer, hours. The getHours() method also should include a try and catch statement for non-integer input. This method will return the int, hours, to main.

   • Type `public static double getRate(int hours)` and then, within that method block, include an if...else statement for hours greater than 15, which will calculate a rate per credit hour. This method will return the double value, rate, to main() method.

   • Type `public static double calcTuition(int hours, double rate)` and then, within that method block, code the statements to accept two values, multiply them, and return a double value, tuition, to main.

   • Type `public static double calcFees(double tuition)` and then, within that method block, code the statements to accept the double value, tuition, multiply it by .08, and then return a double value, fees, to the main method.

   • Type `public static void displayTotal(double total)` and then, within that method, construct a DecimalFormat pattern for currency. Use the System.out.println method to display the value passed by adding tuition and fees, along with a closing message.

9. Compile the program. If necessary, fix any errors in the TextPad window, save, and then recompile.

10. Run the program. Test the program by entering values both less than and greater than 15. Check your answers.

11. Print a copy of the source code for your instructor.

## 4 User Decisions

CandleLine is a business that sells designer candles and personal gifts. They cater to customers who want to send gifts for birthdays, holidays, and other special occasions. CandleLine's e-commerce site is an interactive Web site that uses a shopping cart to allow customers to purchase items. As customers choose the candles and gifts they wish to purchase, the items are added to an electronic shopping cart. Approximately 300 people per day are accessing CandleLine's Web site, but many customers have complained that the shipping charges become a hidden cost when they are placing an order. In order to improve customer relations, the company would like to give its customers a choice in shipping methods and would like to create a way for customers to calculate their shipping costs before finalizing their order.

*(continued)*

**4 User Decisions** *(continued)*

Create a Java applet similar to the one shown in Figure 4-69 that calculates the shipping cost for customer purchases. Eventually, the program will read the total price of purchases as data from the Web page; for now, the user will be able to enter the total price as an input value and then have the program calculate shipping charges. If a customer wants priority delivery (overnight), then the shipping charge is $16.95. If the customer prefers express delivery (2 business days), then the shipping charge is $13.95. If the customer wants standard delivery (3 to 7 business days) and the total cost of the order is more than $100.00, then CandleLine ships the items to the customer free; if the order is less than $100.00, then CandleLine charges $7.95 for standard delivery.

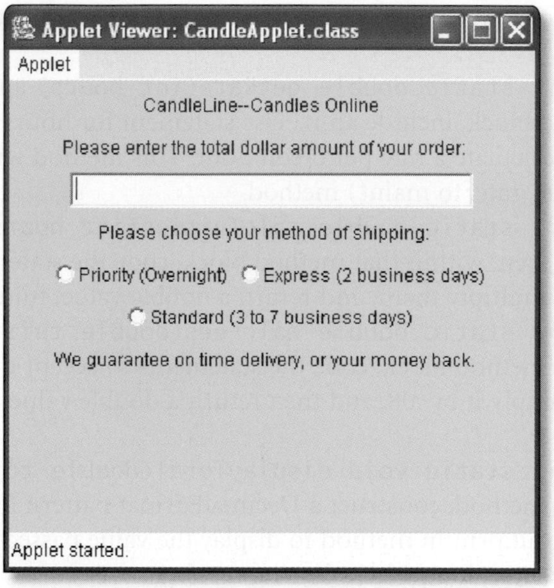

FIGURE 4-69

## 5 Freddie's Fast Food

Create an applet that displays an interface related to fast-food sandwiches created at Freddie's Fast Food. Using the techniques you learned in Chapter 4, add user interface components, including Checkboxes for the condiments and a CheckboxGroup with Checkboxes for the sizes. Add enough code to the program to make the selection of both the CheckboxGroup and Checkboxes work.

1. Start TextPad. Save the file on the Data Disk using the file name Freddie.java.
2. Enter general documentation comments, including the name of this lab, your name, the date, and the file name.
3. Import the following packages: java.awt.*, java.applet.*, and java.awt.event.*. Remember to use the import statement and conclude each line with a semicolon.

4. Enter a public class header for Freddie that extends Applet and implements ItemListener.

5. Create each of the following components using a constructor: sandwichPromptLabel, sandwichInputField, sizePromptLabel, catsupBox, mustardBox, picklesBox, sizeGroup, smallBox, mediumBox, largeBox. Set all the condiment Checkboxes to false. Set the first size Checkbox in the CheckboxGroup to true and the other sizes to false.

6. Create an init() method by typing `public void init()` as the header and adding an opening brace.

7. Set the background color of the applet window to red.

8. Enter add() methods for each of the components created in Step 5. Use an addItemListener(this) for each of the boxes and buttons. Type the closing braces for the init() method.

9. Type `public void itemStateChanged(ItemEvent choice)` as the header of the itemStateChanged() method. Type an opening brace and closing brace to stub in the event.

10. Compile the program and fix any errors.

11. In TextPad, click New on the File menu and then enter the HTML code to create an HTML host document to display the applet. Be sure to include the beginning and ending HTML and APPLET tags. Use a width of 350 and a height of 300.

12. Save the HTML host document on the Data Disk using the file name Freddie.html.

13. Run the applet. Click each of the buttons and boxes. Notice the Checkboxes toggle on and off, individually, while the grouped Checkboxes are mutually exclusive.

14. Print a copy of the source code for your instructor.

15. As an extra credit assignment, code the itemStateChanged() method to print out a confirmation dialog box of the customer's order.

## 6 Traffic Violations

You are serving an internship with the traffic court in the city where you live. The clerks in the traffic court office want a simple application that will allow them to enter the actual speed limit, the speed at which the offender was traveling, and the number of previous tickets that person has received. The application should provide interface options to allow users to calculate charges and exit the application. The application should calculate and display how many miles over the speed limit the offender was traveling, the cost of the speeding ticket, and court costs. The program should calculate a charge of $20.00 for each mile per hour over the speed limit. The program should calculate court costs beginning at $74.80 for the first offense and increasing by $25.00 for each subsequent offense up to the third offense (that will represent the maximum court cost).

## 7 We Love Pets

We Love Pets is a pet clinic with several locations. The office manager has asked you to create an applet that could run from a browser at all the offices. The applet should be designed with individual check boxes for users to select various services such as office visits, vaccinations, hospitalization, heartworm prevention, boarding, dentistry, x-rays, laboratory work, and prescriptions. As each service is selected, the charge for the service should display. After all selections have been made, the charges should be added together to arrive at a total amount due that displays when the user clicks the Calculate button. The office manager also has requested that when the user clicks the Calculate button, the program will clear all the check boxes for the next user.

## 8 Reasonable Computers Corporation

Reasonable Computers Corporation would like an applet to calculate the cost of adding peripherals to a basic computer system. Use at least six single check boxes for various types of peripheral devices, including printers, monitors, modems, and other devices with which you are familiar. Assume a basic computer system price of $575 and then add appropriate prices based on user checks. Add a button that tells the program to perform the calculation and display the final price. Try various width and height values in your HTML code to help align components.

## 9 Wright's Garage

Wright's Garage wants an interactive program that requires the mechanic to enter the tire pressure from four tires on any given car that comes into the garage. The program should first display three options to select a driving type: normal, hauling, and rugged terrain. After the mechanic chooses a driving type, the program should prompt the user to enter the tire pressure for each of the four tires. Finally, the program should tell the mechanic what adjustments to make. Assume the following:

- For normal driving, all four tires should be inflated between 33 and 43 pounds per square inch (psi).
- For hauling, rear tire pressure should be approximately 10% greater.
- For rugged terrain, rear tire pressure should be approximately 15% greater.

## 10 Overdue Books

Your city library has hired you on a consulting basis to provide them with an application to calculate overdue charges. The overdue charges apply to hardcover or paperback books, records, tapes, CDs, and videos. The librarians want an easy way to calculate the overdue charges, keeping in mind that a borrower could be returning multiple overdue items. Some method of looping to enter the next item is necessary. The total number of overdue items and the total amount due should display.

## 11 Stockbroker's Commission

Draw a flowchart and then develop an application that allows a user to enter a stock purchase transaction and determine the stockbroker's commission. Each transaction includes the following data: the stock name, price per share, number of shares involved, and the stockbroker's name. Assuming price per share = P, the stockbroker's commission is computed in the following manner:

If P (price per share) is less than or equal to $75.00, the commission rate is $0.19 per share; if P is greater than $75.00, the commission rate is $0.26 per share. If the number of shares purchased is less than 150, the commission is 1.5 times the rate per share.

Write code so that the program displays a message box that includes the stock transaction data and the commission paid the stockbroker in a grammatically correct set of sentences. After the message box displays, reset the input values to their original state.

## 12 Volume Computations

Use good design and programming techniques to develop a program to compute the volume of a box, cylinder, cone, and sphere. The user interface should provide option buttons to allow the users to select a shape. The interface also should include four input fields that allow a user to enter numbers with two decimal places; each input field should indicate that the input value is measured in feet. Label the four input fields as Length, Width, Height, and Radius.

When the user clicks a button to perform the calculation, the button's event procedure first should determine that the user selected a shape type. Next, the event procedure should ensure that only nonzero, positive values have been entered for the measurements required for the particular formula being used. Finally, the program should perform the calculation and display a message box listing the inputs, output, and calculated volume in a suitable format:

For example, the volume of a box with a length of 1.00 feet, a width of 2.00 feet, and a height of 3.00 feet is 6.00 cubic feet.

Use the following formulas to determine the volumes of the various shapes:

1. Volume of a box: $V = L \times W \times H$, where L is the length, W is the width, and H is the height of the box

2. Volume of a cylinder: $V = pi \times R \times R \times H$, where R is the radius and H is the height of the cylinder

3. Volume of a cone: $V = (pi \times R \times R \times H)/3$, where R is the radius of the base, and H is the height of the cone

4. Volume of a sphere: $V = (4/3) \times pi \times R \times R \times R$, where R is the radius of the sphere

In all of the above formulas, use either 3.14 or the Java constant, Math.PI, for the value of pi. You may use the Math.Pow() method for exponentiation.

### 13 What's My Color

Write an applet that allows the user to enter three positive integers between 0 and 255, each of which corresponds to a specified red, green, and blue color. Then, when the user clicks a Button object, the background color of the applet changes to match the color created by the red, green, and blue colors. Invalid numbers, less than zero or greater than 255, should display error messages.

### 14 Formatting Output

Write an application that accepts a double number and then displays it in five different ways, using a combination of dollar signs, thousands separators, decimal places, and other formats. Use the Java API to look up DecimalFormat and discover some formatting patterns that were not covered in this chapter. Use at least two patterns from the API.

### 15 Using the API  Java 2 v5.0

The printf() method, new to J2SE Version 5.0, uses several special characters to provide formatted output based on data types, similar to the C++ programming language. Visit the Sun Microsystems Java API Web site at http://java.sun.com/j2se/1.5.0/docs/api/io/PrintStream.html. Use the index to find the printf() method. Click the link, Format string Syntax. Scroll to display the conversion characters, flags, and their definitions. Using a word processing program, create a table with three columns that lists each character or flag, its definition in your own words, and a sample usage or code. Print the table and turn it in to your instructor.

### 16 Using the printf() Method  Java 2 v5.0

In Programming Assignment 6, you created an application to calculate traffic violation charges. Convert the program to use the J2SE 5.0 printf() method. Use dialog boxes for input, but convert all output to display in the console using forms of the printf() method. Table 4-12 on page 262 displays the various special characters used in the format string to embed data within the output rather than concatenating it to display in a dialog box.

# A

# Flowcharting, Pseudocode, and the Unified Modeling Language (UML)

Appendix A explains how to prepare, use, and read program flowcharts, pseudocode, and basic Unified Modeling Language (UML) diagrams. Chapter 1 includes an introduction to flowcharting and flowchart symbols beginning on page 16. Pseudocode is introduced on page 18, and the UML is discussed briefly on page 25.

# Guidelines for Preparation of Flowcharts

Before the flowchart can be drawn, a thorough analysis of the problem, the input data, and the desired output results must be performed. The program logic required to solve the problem also must be determined. On the basis of this analysis, a **general flowchart** illustrating the main path of the logic can be sketched. This flowchart can be refined until the overall program logic is fully determined. This general flowchart is used to make one or more **detailed flowcharts** of the various branches of and detours from the main path of the program logic. After each detailed flowchart has been freed of logical errors and other undesirable features, such as unnecessary steps, the actual coding of the program in a computer language can be undertaken.

## Straight-Line Flowcharts

Figure A-1 illustrates a general, straight-line flowchart. A **straight-line flowchart** is one in which the symbols are arranged sequentially, without any deviations or looping, until the terminal symbol that represents the end of the flowchart is reached. Once the operation indicated in any one symbol has been performed, that operation is never repeated.

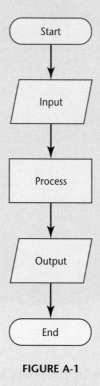

**FIGURE A-1**

## Flowcharts with Looping

A general flowchart that illustrates an iterative, or repeating, process known as **looping** is shown in Figure A-2. The logic illustrated by this flowchart is in three major parts: initialization, process, and wrap-up. A flowline exits from the bottom symbol in Figure A-2 and enters above the diamond-shaped decision symbol that determines whether the loop is to be executed again. This flowline forms part of a loop inside which some operations are executed repeatedly until specified conditions are satisfied. This flowchart shows the input, process, and output pattern; it also uses a decision symbol that shows where the decision is made to continue or stop the looping process.

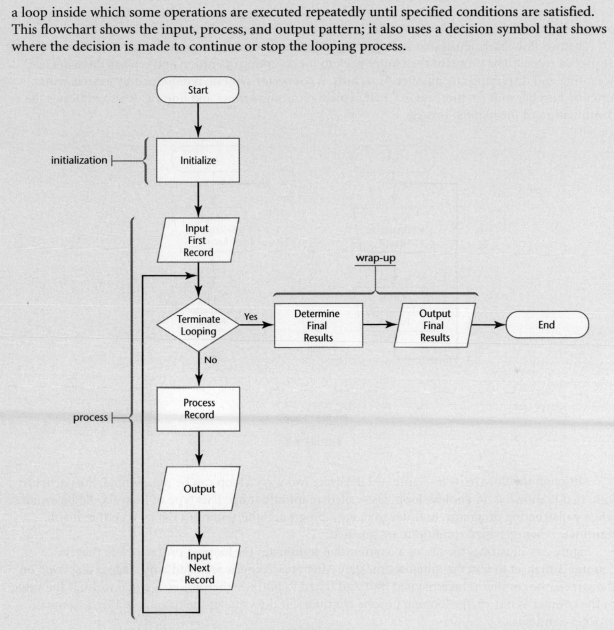

**FIGURE A-2**

Figure A-2 contains three braces that show the initialization, process, and wrap-up operations. For example, setting the program counters to 0 may represent an initialization operation and displaying the values of counters may represent a wrap-up operation.

Like the straight-line flowchart, a flowchart with looping may not have all the symbols shown in Figure A-2, or it may have many more symbols. For example, the process symbol within the loop in Figure A-2, when applied to a particular problem, may expand to include branching forward to bypass a process or backward to redo a process. It is also possible that, through the use of decision symbols, the process symbol in Figure A-2 could be expanded to include several loops, some of which might be independent from each other and some of which might be within other loops.

A flowchart shows a process that is carried out. Flowcharts are flexible; they can show any logical process no matter how complex it may be, and they can show it in whatever detail is needed.

The two flowcharts illustrated in Figure A-3 represent the same program, which accepts and then displays a record. The program then loops back to the accepting operation and repeats the sequence, accepting and displaying any number of records. A connector symbol, represented by a circle with a letter or number in it (in this case, A), may replace returning arrows and lines, as it also indicates the continuation of the looping process.

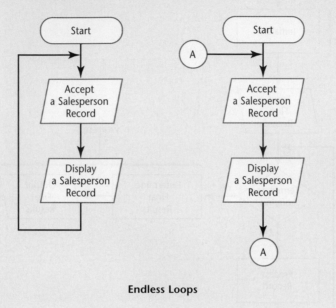

**Endless Loops**

**FIGURE A-3**

Although the flowcharts in Figure A-3 illustrate two ways a loop can be represented, the particular loop that is shown is an **endless loop**, also called an **infinite loop**. This type of loop should be avoided when constructing programs. In order to make a program finite, you must define it so that it will terminate when specified conditions are satisfied.

Figure A-4 illustrates the use of a counter that terminates the looping process. Note that the counter is first set to 0 in the initialization step. After an account is read and a message is displayed on the screen, the counter is incremented by 1 and tested to find whether it now is equal to 15. If the value of the counter is not 15, the looping process continues. If the value of the counter is 15, the looping process terminates.

For the flowchart used in Figure A-4, the exact number of accounts to be processed must be known beforehand. In practice, this will not always be the case because the number of accounts may vary from one run to the next.

```
                        ┌─────────┐
                        │  Start  │
                        └─────────┘
                             │
                             ▼
                     ┌───────────────┐
                     │      Set      │
                     │  Counter to 0 │
                     └───────────────┘
         ┌───┐               │
         │ A │──────────────▶│
         └───┘               ▼
                     ┌───────────────┐
                     │    Accept     │
                     │   an Aging    │
                     │    Account    │
                     └───────────────┘
                             │
                             ▼
            No          ◇─────────◇          Yes
       ┌───────────────  Age of   ───────────────┐
       │              Account ≥ 90               │
       │                  ◇─────◇                 │
       ▼                                          ▼
┌───────────────┐                      ┌───────────────────┐
│    Display    │                      │      Display      │
│ "Send Credit  │                      │  "Turn Over to    │
│    Memo"      │                      │ Collection Agency"│
└───────────────┘                      └───────────────────┘
       │                                          │
       └──────────────────┬───────────────────────┘
                          ▼
                  ┌───────────────┐
                  │     Add 1     │
                  │  to Counter   │
                  └───────────────┘
                          │
                          ▼
                      ◇─────────◇        Yes     ┌─────────┐
                      Counter = 15  ─────────────▶│   End   │
                      ◇─────────◇                 └─────────┘
                          │
                          │ No
                          ▼
                        ┌───┐
                        │ A │
                        └───┘
```

**FIGURE A-4**

A way to solve this type of problem is shown in Figure A-5, which illustrates the use of an end-of-file test to terminate the looping process. The value –999999 has been chosen to be the last account number. This kind of value sometimes is known as the **sentinel value** because it guards against continuing past the end-of-file. Also, the numeric item chosen for the last value cannot possibly be confused with a valid item because it is outside the range of the account numbers. Programs using an end-of-file test, such as the one shown in Figure A-5, are far more flexible and less limited than programs that do not, such as those illustrated in Figures A-3 and A-4 on pages A.04 and A.05.

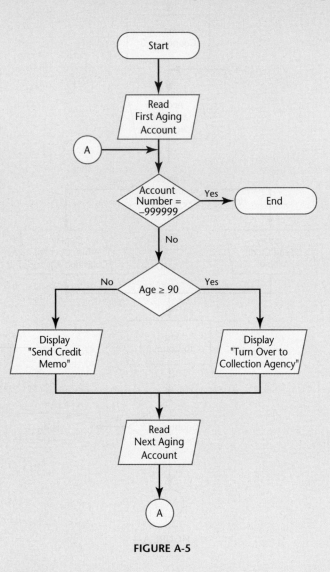

**FIGURE A-5**

Another flowchart with a loop is shown in Figure A-6, which illustrates the concept of counting. The flowchart incorporates the end-of-file test.

Simple computer programs do not require complex flowcharts and sometimes do not require flowcharts at all. As programs become more complex with many different paths of execution, however, a flowchart not only is useful but usually is a prerequisite for successful analysis and coding. Indeed, developing the problem solution by arranging and rearranging the flowchart symbols can lead to a more efficient solution.

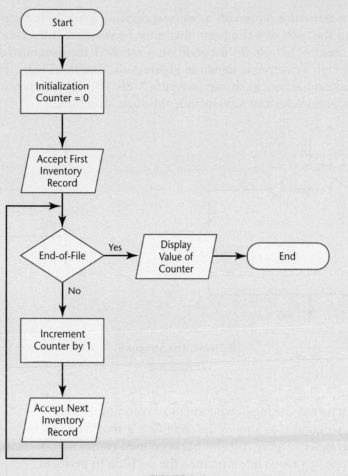

**FIGURE A-6**

# Control Structures

The logic of almost any procedure or method can be constructed from the following three basic logic structures:

1. Sequence structure
2. If...Then...Else or Selection structure
3. Do While or Repetition structure

The following are two common extensions to these logic structures:

Do Until (an extension of the Repetition structure)

Select Case (a multiple choice extension of the Selection structure)

The **Sequence structure** is used to show one action or one action followed by another, as illustrated in Figures A-7a and A-7b. Every flowchart in this book includes this control structure.

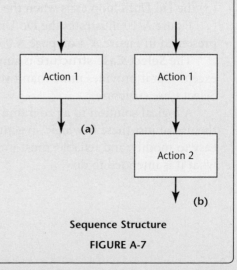

Sequence Structure

**FIGURE A-7**

The **If...Then...Else structure** represents a two-way decision made in the logic of the program. The decision is made on the basis of a condition that must be satisfied. If the condition is not satisfied, the program logic executes one action. If the condition is satisfied, the program logic executes a different action. This type of logic structure is shown in Figure A-8a. The If...Then...Else structure also can result in a decision to take no action, as shown in Figure A-8b. The flowcharts presented in Figures A-4 and A-5 on pages A.05 and A.06 include this logic structure.

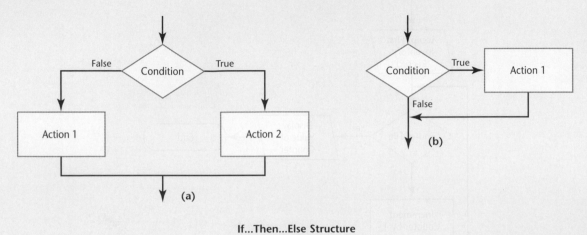

If...Then...Else Structure

FIGURE A-8

The **Do While structure** is the logic structure most commonly used to create a process that will repeat as long as the condition is true. The Do While structure is illustrated in Figure A-9 and has been used earlier in Figures A-2, A-5, and A-6. In a Do While structure, the decision to perform the action within the structure is at the top of the loop; as a result, the action will not occur if the condition is never satisfied.

The **Do Until structure** (Figure A-10) also is used for creating a process that will be repeated. The major differences between the Do Until and the Do While structures are that (1) the action within the structure of a Do Until always will be executed at least once, (2) the decision to perform the action within the structure is at the bottom of the Do Until loop, and (3) the Do Until loop exits when the condition is true.

Figure A-10 illustrates the Do Until structure, and the flowchart presented in Figure A-4 on page A.05 includes a Do Until structure.

The **Select Case structure** is similar to the If...Then...Else structure except that it provides more than two alternatives. Figure A-11 illustrates the Select Case structure.

A logical solution to a programming problem can be developed through the use of just these five logic structures. The program will be easy to read, easy to modify, and reliable; most important of all, the program will do what it is intended to do.

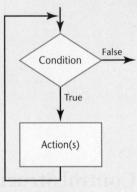

Do While Structure

FIGURE A-9

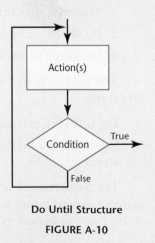
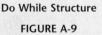

Do Until Structure

FIGURE A-10

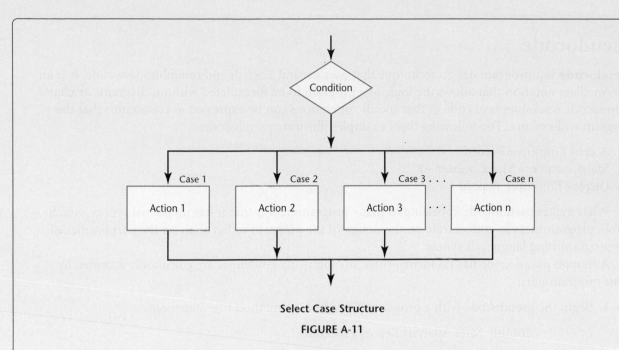

**Select Case Structure**

**FIGURE A-11**

# Flowcharting Tips

The following recommendations can help make flowcharts more efficient and easier for others to understand. These suggestions assume that the input, processing, and output of the problem are defined properly in a requirements document.

1. Sketch a general flowchart and the necessary detail flowcharts before coding the problem. Repeat this step until you are satisfied with your flowcharts.

2. Use the control structures described on pages A.07 and A.08.

3. Put yourself in the position of the reader, keeping in mind that the purpose of the flowchart is to improve the reader's understanding of the solution to the problem.

4. Show the flow of processing from top to bottom and from left to right. When in doubt, use arrowheads as required to indicate the direction of flow.

5. Draw the flowchart so that it is neat and clear. Use the connector symbols to avoid excessively long flowlines.

6. Choose labels for each symbol that explain the function of the symbols in a clear and precise manner.

7. Avoid endless loops; construct loops so that they will be terminated when specific conditions are satisfied.

The reason that flowcharts are so important is simple: the difficulties in programming lie mostly in the realm of logic, not in the syntax and semantics of the computer language. In other words, most computer errors are mistakes in logic, and a flowchart aids in detecting these types of mistakes. For an additional example of a flowchart, see Figure 1-14 on page 18.

# Pseudocode

**Pseudocode** is a program design technique that uses natural English and resembles Java code. It is an intermediate notation that allows the logic of a program to be formulated without diagrams or charts. Pseudocode resembles Java code in that specific operations can be expressed as commands that the program will execute. The following three examples illustrate pseudocode:

Accept Employee Record
MaleCounter = MaleCounter +1
Display Employee Record

What makes pseudocode appealing to many programmers is that it has no formal syntax, which allows programmers to concentrate on the design of the program rather than on the peculiarities of the programming language's syntax.

Although pseudocode has no formal rules, the following guidelines are commonly accepted by most programmers:

1. Begin the pseudocode with a program, procedure, or method title statement.

   Monthly Sales Analysis Report Procedure

2. End the pseudocode with a terminal program statement.

   End

3. Begin each statement on a new line. Use simple and short imperative sentences that contain a single transitive verb and a single object.

   Accept EmployeeNumber
   Subtract 10 From Quantity

4. Express assignments as a formula or as an English-like statement.

   WithholdingTax = 0. 20 $\times$ (GrossPay – 38.46 $\times$ Dependents)

   or

   Compute WithholdingTax

5. To avoid errors in the design, avoid using logic structures not available in the programming language being used.

6. For the If…Then…Else structure, use the following conventions:

   a. Indent the true and false tasks.

   b. Use End If as the structure terminator.

   c. Vertically align the If, Else, and End If statements.

The conventions for the If…Then…Else structure are illustrated in Figures A-12 and A-13. (Java implements the structure in code with the keywords, if and else.)

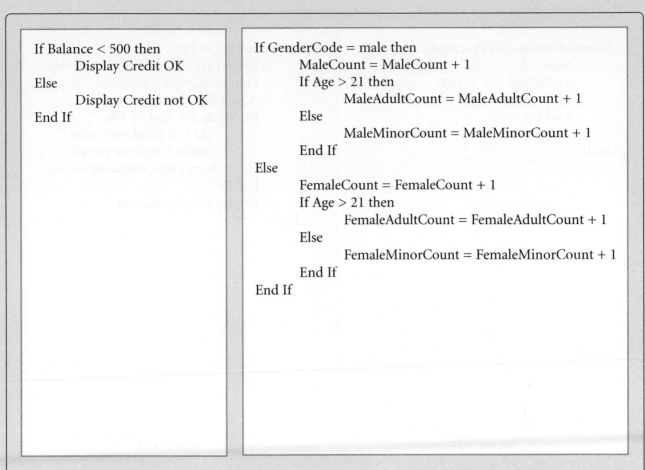

If Balance < 500 then
        Display Credit OK
Else
        Display Credit not OK
End If

If GenderCode = male then
      MaleCount = MaleCount + 1
      If Age > 21 then
           MaleAdultCount = MaleAdultCount + 1
      Else
           MaleMinorCount = MaleMinorCount + 1
      End If
Else
      FemaleCount = FemaleCount + 1
      If Age > 21 then
           FemaleAdultCount = FemaleAdultCount + 1
      Else
           FemaleMinorCount = FemaleMinorCount + 1
      End If
End If

**FIGURE A-12**

**FIGURE A-13**

7. For the Do While structure, use the following conventions:

   a. If the structure represents a counter-controlled loop, begin the structure with Do.

   b. If the structure does not represent a counter-controlled loop, begin the structure with Do While.

   c. Specify the condition on the Do While or Do line.

   d. Use End Do as the last statement of the structure.

   e. Align the Do While or Do and the End Do vertically.

   f. Indent the statements within the loop.

The conventions for the Do While structure are illustrated in Figures A-14 and A-15 on the next page. (Java implements the structure in code with the keywords, do and while.)

8. For the Do Until structure, use the following conventions:

   a. Begin the structure with Do Until.

   b. Specify the condition on the Do Until line.

   c. Use End Do as the last statement of the structure.

   d. Align the Do Until and the End Do vertically.

   e. Indent the statements within the loop.

```
SumFirst100Integers Procedure
       Sum = 0
       Do Integer = 1 to 100
              Sum = Sum + Integer
       End Do
       Display sum
End
```

FIGURE A-14

```
EmployeeFileList Procedure
       Display report and column headings
       EmployeeCount = 0
       Accept first Employee record
       Do While Not End-of-File
              Add 1 to EmployeeCount
              Display Employee record
              Accept next Employee record
       End Do
       Display EmployeeCount
   End
```

FIGURE A-15

The conventions for the Do Until structure are illustrated in Figure A-16. (Java implements the structure in code with the keywords, do and until.)

```
SumFirst100Integers Procedure
       Sum = 0
       Integer = 1
       Do Until Integer >100
              Sum = Sum + Integer
              Integer = Integer + 1
       End Do
       Display Sum
   End
```

FIGURE A-16

9. For the Select Case structure, use the following conventions:

   a. Begin the structure with Select Case, followed by the variable to be tested.

   b. Use End Case as the structure terminator.

   c. Align Select Case and End Case vertically.

   d. Indent each alternative.

   e. Begin each alternative with Case, followed by the value of the variable that equates to the alternative.

   f. Indent the action of each alternative.

These conventions are illustrated in Figure A-17. (Java implements the structure in code with the keyword, switch.)

```
Select Case CustomerCode
        Case 100
                HighRiskCustomerCount = HighRiskCustomerCount + 1
        Case 200
                LowRiskCustomerCount = LowRiskCustomerCount + 1
        Case 300
                RegularCustomerCount = RegularCustomerCount + 1
        Case 400
                SpecialCustomerCount = SpecialCustomerCount + 1
End Case
```

**FIGURE A-17**

For an additional example of pseudocode, see Figure 1-15 in Chapter 1 on page 19.

# The Unified Modeling Language (UML)

Just as flowcharts describe algorithms, object-oriented design (OOD) has a standard method to depict, or diagram, concepts for design purposes. The Unified Modeling Language (UML) is a notation used to describe object behaviors and interaction. The UML is a graphical language used to represent how a system behaves or should behave. The UML is a relatively new language, having been developed in the 1990s from a number of competing object-oriented design tools.

In OOD, each class can have one or more lower levels, called **subclasses**, or one or more higher levels, called **base classes** or **superclasses**. For example, a class for Secretaries is a subclass of the Employee class. Person is a base class or superclass of Employee. The relationship among the classes, subclasses, and base classes is called the **hierarchy**. A **high-level class diagram** is a UML diagram used to show the hierarchical relationships among classes (Figure A-18).

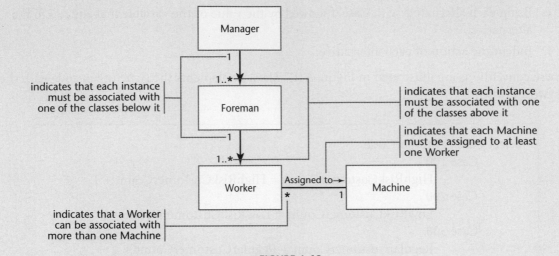

**FIGURE A-18**

**Associations** describe the manner in which instances of a class, or objects, are related. For example, two instances of a Worker class can have the association of being coworkers. This type of association is **bidirectional**, meaning each instance is associated with the other. Some associations are **unidirectional**, which means that only one class is associated with the other. For example, a Worker instance can be assigned to operate an injection molder machine, which is an instance of the class Machines. The Worker is associated with the injection molder instance because a Worker must know how to operate the injection molder, but the injection molder does not have any information about or relationship to the Worker. In this way, the association between the Worker and Machine class is unidirectional.

The high-level class diagram shown in Figure A-18 depicts a hierarchy in which an instance of the Manager class can have several instances of the Foreman class associated with it; each instance of the Foreman class can have several workers associated with it; and each instance of the Worker class can be assigned to exactly one machine. Each class is represented by a box with the class name inside the box. Relationships are designated by lines between the classes.

The 1 below the Manager class indicates that each Manager class must have at least one Foreman class associated with it; the 1 below the Foreman class indicates that each Foreman class must have at least one Worker class associated with it. The 1..* above the Foreman class indicates that each Foreman class must be associated with at least one Manager class above it; the 1..* above the Worker class indicates that each Worker class must be associated with at least one Foreman class above it. The Assigned to label indicates that each Worker class is assigned to one Machine class. The 1 next to the Machine class indicates that each Machine class must be assigned at least one Worker class. The * next to the Worker class indicates that a worker can be associated with more than one Machine class.

Object-oriented programming (OOP) and OOD use many unique terms to describe program elements. In object-oriented terminology, the data stored about an object is called an attribute or property. An **attribute** or **property** is an identifying characteristic of individual objects, such as a name, weight, or color. An **operation** is an activity that reads or manipulates the data of an object. In OOD, an operation is a type of service. In OOP, the code that may be executed to perform a service is called a **method**.

A **detailed class diagram** is used to provide a visual representation of a class, its attributes, and its methods (Figure A-19 and Figure A-20). Figure A-19 shows the general form of a detailed class diagram. Figure A-20 shows a specific example of a detailed class diagram for the Foreman class. The Foreman class contains six attributes and five methods. The rules of the UML prescribe that each attribute and method begin with lowercase letters and that each method name is followed by parentheses. The parentheses indicate that the methods are procedures in the class. A detailed class diagram also can have additional notations.

| **Class name** |
| --- |
| Class attributes |
| Class methods |

**FIGURE A-19**

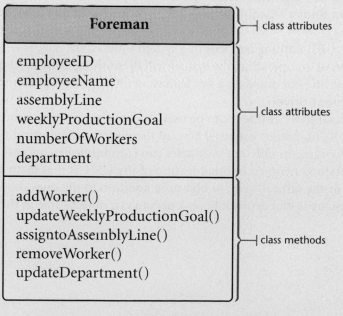

| **Foreman** | class attributes |
| --- | --- |
| employeeID<br>employeeName<br>assemblyLine<br>weeklyProductionGoal<br>numberOfWorkers<br>department | class attributes |
| addWorker()<br>updateWeeklyProductionGoal()<br>assigntoAssemblyLine()<br>removeWorker()<br>updateDepartment() | class methods |

**FIGURE A-20**

## Messages and Events

Message sending is a key component of object-oriented design because it describes how objects work together. For an object to do something, it must be sent a message. The **message** must have two parts: (1) the name of the object to which the message is being sent, and (2) the name of the operation that will be performed by the object. As you have learned, an operation is an activity that reads or manipulates the data of an object. An operation also can send additional messages while it performs its task.

Messages are sent through an interface to the object. Just as a user interface allows a program to accept data and instructions from the user, the **interface** is the way that an object receives messages.

As an example, suppose each time an assembly-line worker turns on a machine (an object), the machine tracks how many times it has been turned on by incrementing a counter. To turn on the machine, the worker presses a button on a panel to send a message to the machine. The button on the panel is the interface to the on() method of the machine, and pressing the button is the event that sends a message to execute the on() method. When the on() method executes, part of its operation is to increment the numberTimesOn counter, which is an attribute of the machine. Suppose that the shop also uses an automated system to operate its machines, so that the machines can be turned on remotely using a computer. The interface that the computer uses to turn on the machine is different from the one the worker uses. The on() method that executes on the machine, however, remains the same and the on() method still increments the numberTimesOn counter attribute when it executes.

In OOD terminology, the operation, increment counter, is a service and the message, turn machine on, is called a **request for service**. Remember that in OOP terminology, the service is called a method and the message is what is sent when an event, such as a user pressing the on button, occurs. **Sequence diagrams** are used to represent the relationships among events and objects. In a sequence diagram, messages or events are shown as lines with arrows, classes are shown across the top in rectangles, and class names are underlined and prefaced by a colon (Figure A-21). As you read the sequence diagram, time progresses from top to bottom, and the time the object is active is shown by vertical rectangles.

Figure A-21 illustrates a sequence diagram for a Foreman assigning a Worker to a Machine. The Foreman object in the first column interacts with other objects through the Foreman Interface. The Foreman sends a message through the Foreman Interface to find a Worker based on the worker's name. Next, the Foreman finds a Machine to assign the Worker based on the worker's skill. Finally, the assignment is made.

As shown in Figure A-21, nothing happens in a system unless a message is sent when an event occurs. At the conclusion of an operation, the system will do nothing until another event occurs. This relationship of events causing operations is a key feature of OOP, and programs that are constructed in this way are said to be **event driven**.

The UML is a powerful tool because it can be used to describe any item, process, or concept in the real or imagined world. Its usefulness goes well beyond the programming world. People working in different disciplines or working in different industries can communicate concepts using the UML in a standard and well-understood manner. Another feature of the UML is that many types of diagrams provide different views of the same system, or object, in addition to the ones shown here. Different views of the same system are useful depending on a person's or object's role in the system.

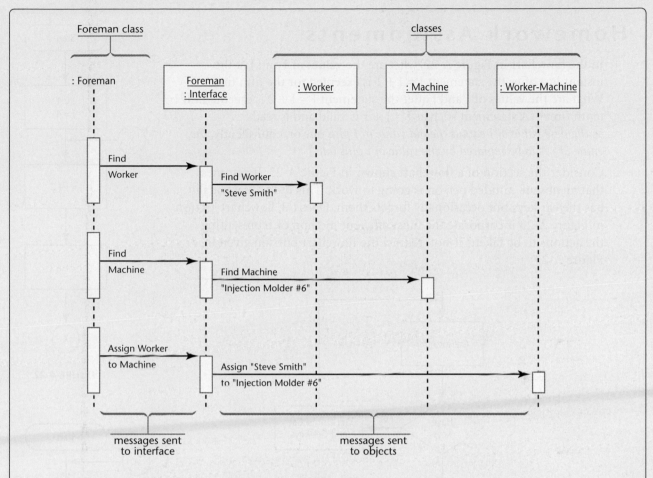

**FIGURE A-21**

# Homework Assignments

1. In the flowchart in Figure A-22, what are the values of I and J at the instant just after the statement J = J + 1 is executed for the fifth time? What are the values of I and J after the statement I = I + 2 is executed the tenth time? (A statement such as J = J + 1 is valid and is read as *the new value of J equals the old value of J plus one* or, equivalently, *the value of J is to be replaced by the value of J plus one*.)

2. Consider the section of a flowchart shown in Figure A-23. It assumes that an absent-minded person is going to work. This individual usually has the car keys but occasionally forgets them. Does the flowchart section in Figure A-23 incorporate the most efficient method of representing the actions to be taken? If not, redraw the flowchart portion given in Figure A-23.

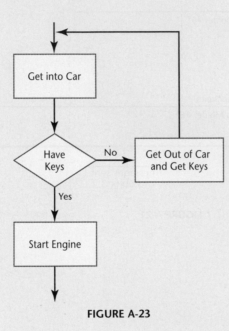

**FIGURE A-23**

3. In the flowchart shown in Figure A-24, what values of I and J are printed when the output symbol is executed for the fiftieth time?

4. An opaque urn contains three diamonds, four rubies, and two pearls. Construct a flowchart that describes the following events: Take a gem from the urn. If it is a diamond, lay it aside. If it is not a diamond, return it to the urn. Continue in this fashion until all the diamonds have been removed. After all the diamonds have been removed, repeat the same procedure until all the rubies have been removed. After all the rubies have been removed, continue in the same fashion until all the pearls have been removed.

5. In the flowchart represented by Figure A-25, what are the values of I and J at the instant the terminal symbol with the word End is reached?

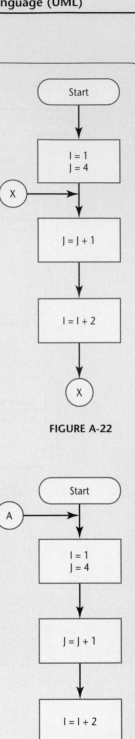

**FIGURE A-22**

**FIGURE A-24**

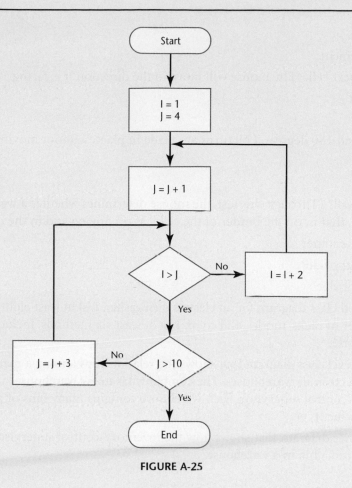

**FIGURE A-25**

6. Draw one flowchart, and only one, that will cause the mechanical mouse to go through any of the four mazes shown in Figure A-26. At the beginning, a user will place the mouse on the entry side of the maze, in front of the entry point, facing up toward the maze. The instruction Move to next cell will put the mouse inside the maze. Each maze has four cells. After that, the job is to move from cell to cell until the mouse emerges on the exit side. If the mouse is instructed to *Move to next cell* when a wall is in front of it, it will hit the wall and fall apart. Obviously, the mouse must be instructed to test whether it is *Facing a wall* before any *Move*. The physical movements and logical tests the mechanical mouse can complete are listed following Figure A-26.

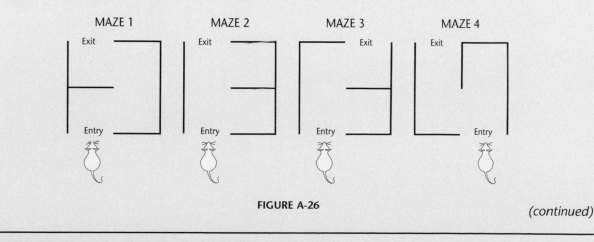

**FIGURE A-26**

*(continued)*

6. (*continued*)

   a. Physical movement:

     (1) Move to next cell. (The mouse will move in the direction it is facing.)

     (2) Turn right.

     (3) Turn left.

     (4) Turn around 180 degrees. (All turns are made in place, without moving to another cell.)

     (5) Halt.

   b. Logic:

     (1) Facing a wall? (Through this test, the mouse determines whether a wall is immediately in front of it, that is, on the border of the cell it is occupying and in the direction it is facing.)

     (2) Outside the maze?

     (3) On the entry side?

     (4) On the exit side?

7. Develop a detailed class diagram for an electric dishwasher. List at least eight attributes, including number of racks, model, and color. List at least six methods, including addDishes() and addDetergent().

8. Develop a high-level class diagram that shows the relationships among a manufacturer's inventory of finished products in its warehouses. The company has many warehouses that are managed by the inventory-control supervisor. Each warehouse contains many bins of products. Each bin contains one product type.

9. Develop a sequence diagram that shows how the inventory-control supervisor in assignment 8 assigns a product to a bin in a warehouse.

# B

# Installing the Java™ 2 SDK, TextPad, and Tomcat

This appendix explains how to install the three software applications used in this text: the Java™ 2 Software Development Kit (SDK), which provides the tools to compile and execute Java programs; the text editor software, TextPad, which provides an environment to create and modify programs; and Tomcat, which provides the server software needed to run servlets and JavaServer Pages™ (JSP). These resources are available free at their respective Web sites, as well as on the CD-ROM that accompanies this text. To install this software on your computer system, you must be logged in to an account or system that gives you the authority to make the necessary modifications to the environment.

# Installing the Java™ 2 Software Development Kit (SDK)

The Java™ 2 SDK can be obtained by downloading the required software from Sun Microsystems at java.sun.com or from the CD-ROM that accompanies this text. The following steps show how to install the SDK from the CD-ROM to a location on your hard drive (C:). If necessary, substitute the destination location with one specified by your instructor.

## To Install the Java Software Development Kit (SDK)

1. Insert the CD-ROM into your CD-ROM drive. If the CT Resources Licensing Agreement dialog box is displayed, click the Yes button. When the Course Technology dialog box is displayed, click Software. When the software files are displayed, click Sun Java™ SDK, Standard Edition 1.5.0_02.

   *The Course Technology dialog box is displayed with Software and Sun Java™ SDK, Standard Edition 1.5.0_02.*

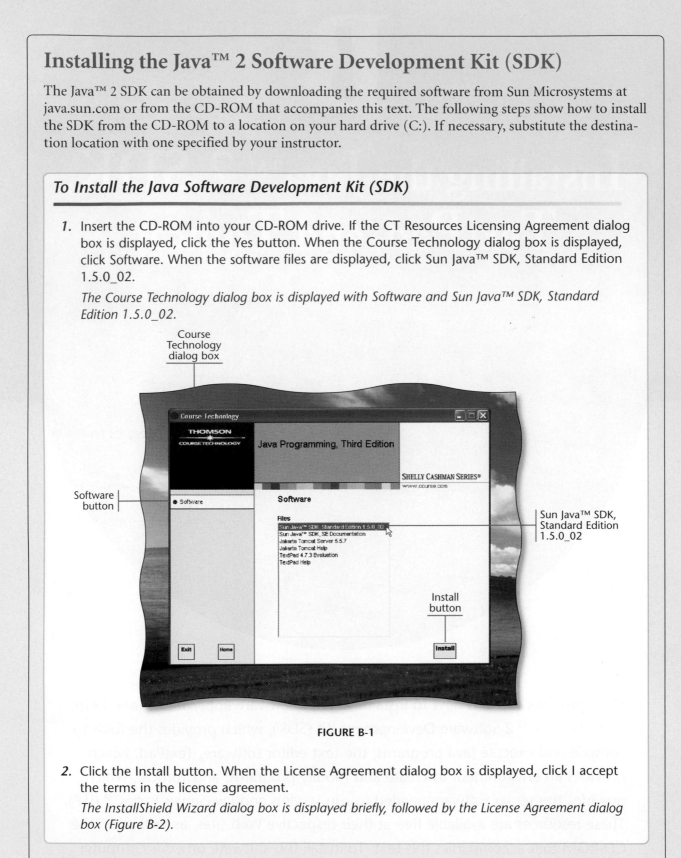

**FIGURE B-1**

2. Click the Install button. When the License Agreement dialog box is displayed, click I accept the terms in the license agreement.

   *The InstallShield Wizard dialog box is displayed briefly, followed by the License Agreement dialog box (Figure B-2).*

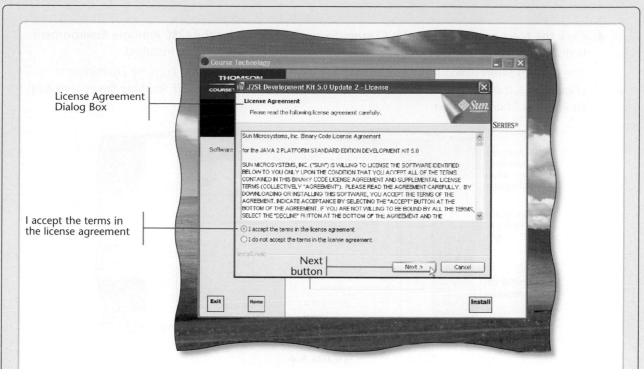

**FIGURE B-2**

3. Click the Next button. When the Custom Setup dialog box for the J2SE Development Kit is displayed, verify the location to which the program features will be installed.

*The Custom Setup dialog box displays the choice of features and the default destination for the J2SE Development Kit installation (Figure B-3). The default folder location includes the version name. If desired, you can change the location for installing the J2SE Development Kit by clicking the Change button. By default, all program features are installed. To save disk space, you can select the icon of individual features, such as Demos or Source Code, to prevent their installation.*

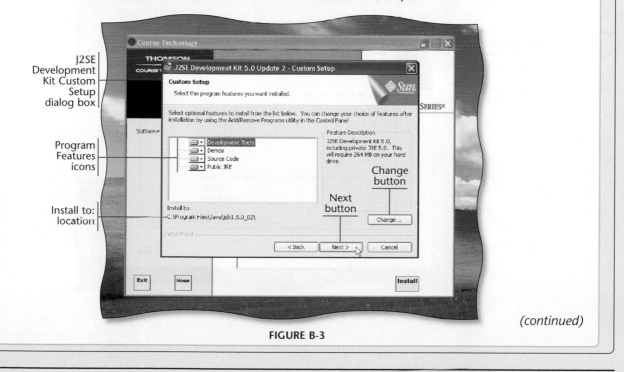

*(continued)*

**FIGURE B-3**

4. Click the Next button. When the Custom Setup dialog box for the J2SE Runtime Environment is displayed, verify the location to which the program features will be installed.

*The Custom Setup dialog box displays the program features for the J2SE Runtime Environment (Figure B-4). If desired, you can change the location for installing the J2SE Runtime Environment by clicking the Change button.*

J2SE Runtime Environment Custom Setup dialog box

Program Features icons

Change button

Next button

Install to: location

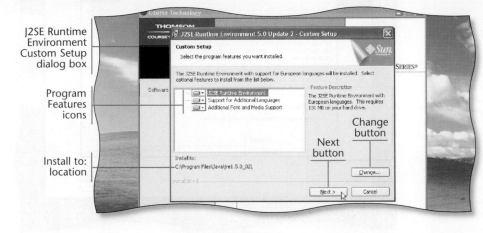

**FIGURE B-4**

5. Click the Next button. When the Browser Registration dialog box is displayed, verify that the check box next to the browser you want to use for applets is checked.

*The Browser Registration dialog box displays the browser(s) available on your system (Figure B-5). The Java™ Plug-in, which is necessary to run applets in a browser, will install for the checked browser(s).*

Browser Registration dialog box

available browsers

Next button

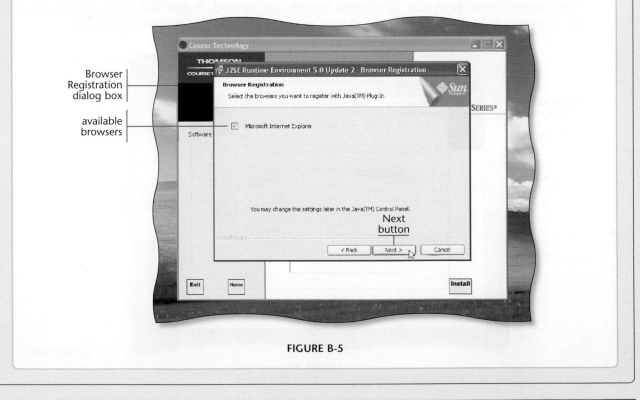

**FIGURE B-5**

6. Click the Next button. When the installation is complete, the Installation Completed dialog box is displayed.

   *The SDK installs to the previously indicated folder location (Figure B-6).*

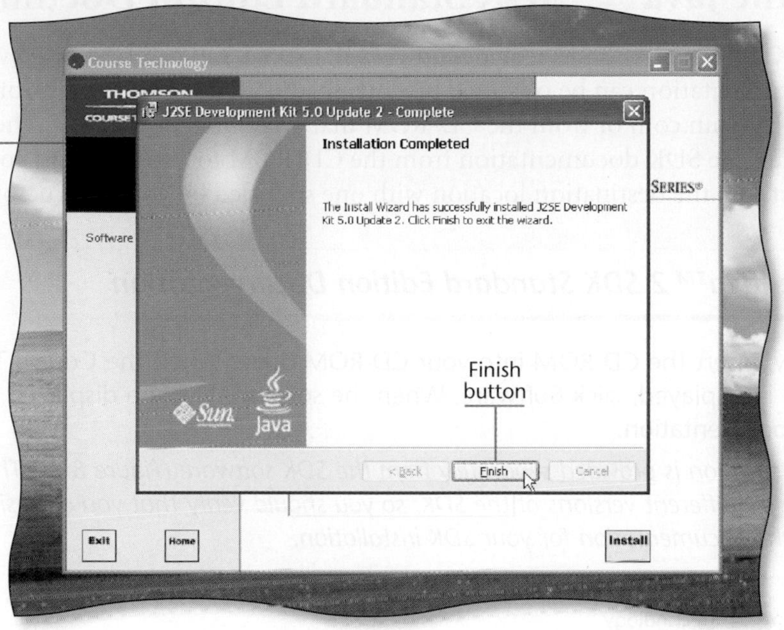

Installation
Completed
dialog box

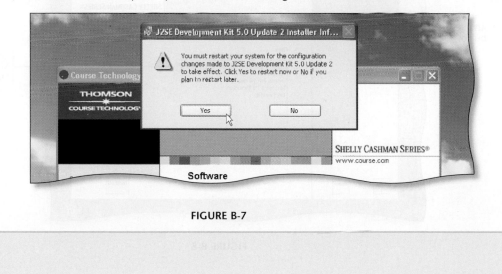

**FIGURE B-6**

7. Click the Finish button.

   *After the SDK installation is complete, you may need to restart your system for the configuration changes to take effect. If so, a dialog box displays, prompting you to restart now or later (Figure B-7). You should restart your system before installing additional software.*

**FIGURE B-7**

If you need to uninstall the Java™ 2 SDK, you can use the Add or Remove Programs utility in the Control Panel.

## Installing the Java™ 2 SDK Standard Edition Documentation

The Java™ 2 SDK documentation is provided in HTML format and can be viewed with a Web browser. The documentation can be obtained by downloading the required files from Sun Microsystems at java.sun.com or from the CD-ROM that accompanies this text. The following steps show how to install the SDK documentation from the CD-ROM to a location on your hard drive (C:). If necessary, substitute the destination location with one specified by your instructor.

### To Install the Java™ 2 SDK Standard Edition Documentation

1. If necessary, insert the CD-ROM into your CD-ROM drive. When the Course Technology dialog box is displayed, click Software. When the software files are displayed, click Sun Java™ SDK, SE Documentation.

   *The documentation is provided separately from the SDK software (Figure B-8). The documentation is available for different versions of the SDK, so you should verify that you are using the correct version of the documentation for your SDK installation.*

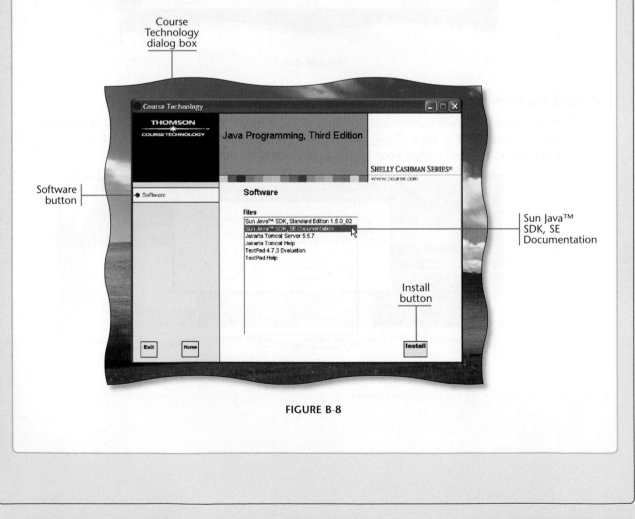

FIGURE B-8

**2.** Click the Install button.

*The WinZip Self-Extractor dialog box is displayed with the default installation location in the Unzip to folder: text box (Figure B-9). If desired, you can modify the text in the Unzip to folder: text box to install the documentation to a location other than the default location. The documentation files are zipped, or compressed into a single archive file, to save space. The zipped file is self-extracting, so no additional software is needed to extract the files from the archive file.*

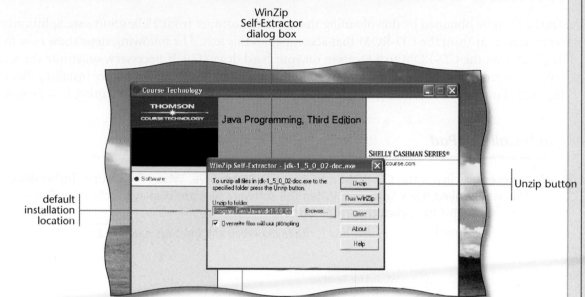

FIGURE B-9

**3.** Click the Unzip button.

*The WinZip Self-Extractor message box is displayed, indicating that the files were successfully unzipped (Figure B-10).*

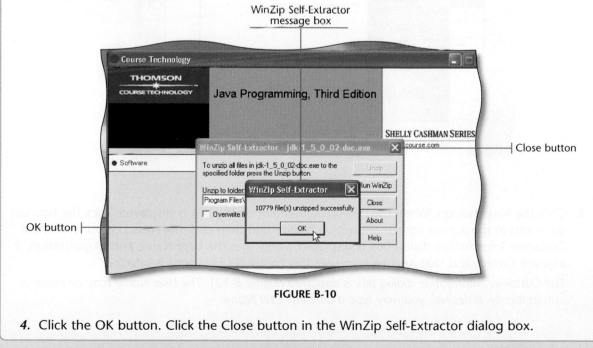

FIGURE B-10

**4.** Click the OK button. Click the Close button in the WinZip Self-Extractor dialog box.

Having the Java™ 2 SDK documentation installed locally may be useful; however, it is not required, as the same pages may be accessed over the Web from Sun Microsystems. The documentation is a series of hypertext documents which may require access to the Web even when accessing a local copy, as some links will refer to pages on Sun Microsystems's Web site.

## Installing TextPad

TextPad can be obtained by downloading the required software from Helios Software Solutions at textpad.com or from the CD-ROM that accompanies this text. The following steps show how to install TextPad from the CD-ROM to a location on your hard drive (C:). If necessary, substitute the location with one specified by your instructor. You should install the Java™ 2 SDK before installing TextPad, as this will allow TextPad to configure itself automatically for compiling and executing Java programs.

### To Install TextPad

1. If necessary, insert the CD-ROM into your CD-ROM drive. When the Course Technology dialog box is displayed, click Software. When the software files are displayed, click TextPad 4.7.3 Evaluation and then click the Install button.

   *The InstallShield Wizard dialog box is displayed when the install is ready to begin (Figure B-11).*

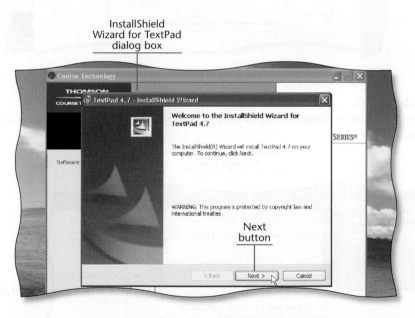

**FIGURE B-11**

2. Click the Next button. When the License Agreement dialog box is displayed, click the I accept the terms in the license agreement option button and then click the Next button. When the Customer Information dialog box is displayed, verify that the User Name and Organization, if any, are correct and that Anyone who uses this computer (all users) is selected.

   *The Customer Information dialog box is displayed (Figure B-12). The User Name may be entered automatically. If desired, you may type a different User Name.*

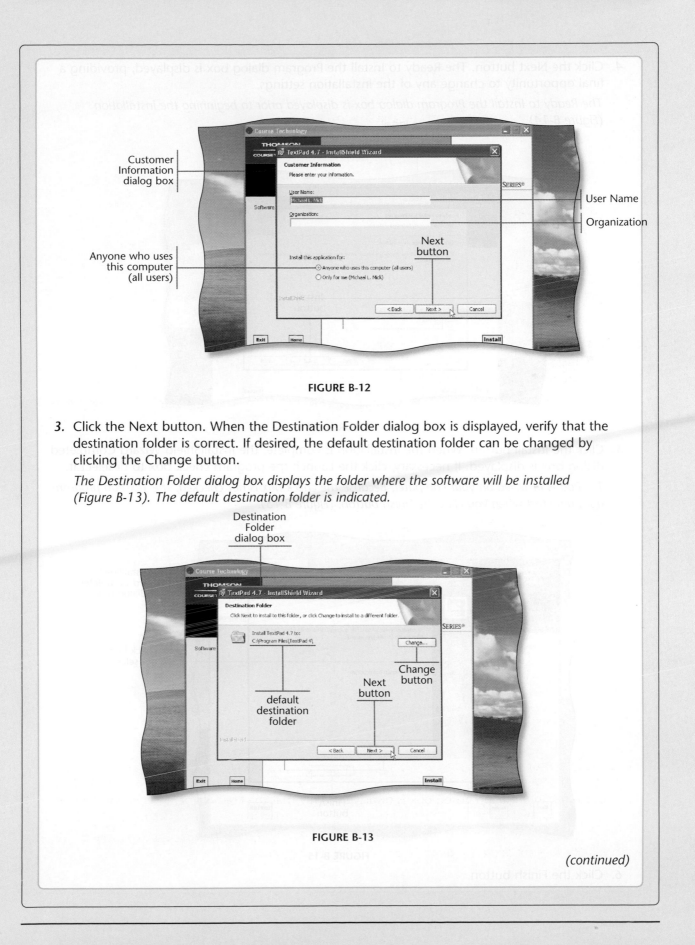

Customer
Information
dialog box

User Name

Organization

Anyone who uses
this computer
(all users)

Next
button

**FIGURE B-12**

3. Click the Next button. When the Destination Folder dialog box is displayed, verify that the destination folder is correct. If desired, the default destination folder can be changed by clicking the Change button.

*The Destination Folder dialog box displays the folder where the software will be installed (Figure B-13). The default destination folder is indicated.*

Destination
Folder
dialog box

Change
button

Next
button

default
destination
folder

**FIGURE B-13**

*(continued)*

4. Click the Next button. The Ready to Install the Program dialog box is displayed, providing a final opportunity to change any of the installation settings.

*The Ready to Install the Program dialog box is displayed prior to beginning the installation (Figure B-14).*

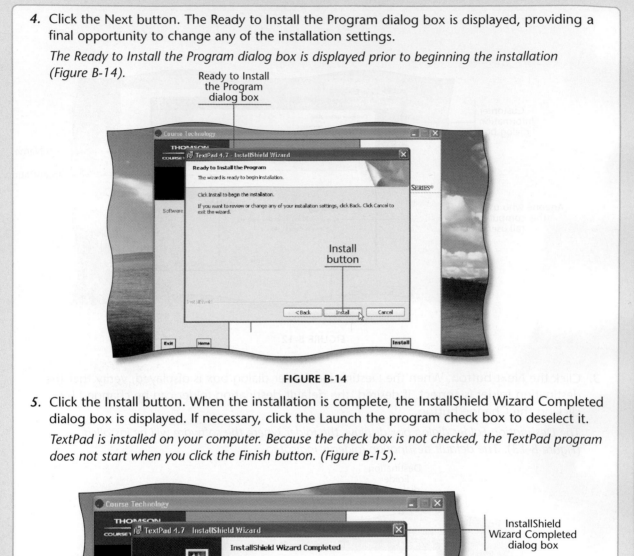

**FIGURE B-14**

5. Click the Install button. When the installation is complete, the InstallShield Wizard Completed dialog box is displayed. If necessary, click the Launch the program check box to deselect it.

*TextPad is installed on your computer. Because the check box is not checked, the TextPad program does not start when you click the Finish button. (Figure B-15).*

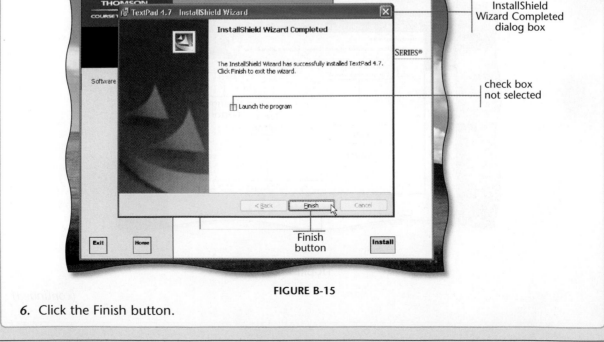

**FIGURE B-15**

6. Click the Finish button.

After the TextPad installation is complete, the TextPad icon is displayed on the All Programs submenu when you click the Windows Start button. TextPad documentation recommends that you have 3 MB of free disk space before attempting to install the TextPad software.

You can customize the TextPad window to display line numbers, use various colors for code elements, and provide other features to help you develop Java programs. Appendix C contains information about setting properties in TextPad to match the figures in this text.

## Installing Tomcat

Tomcat is a Web server software program that supports Java servlets and Java Server Pages (JSP). The Jakarta Project from Apache Software manages the development of Tomcat and makes it freely available to users.

Tomcat is available on the Web at jakarta.apache.org/site/downloads/index.html or on the CD-ROM that accompanies this text. If you download Tomcat from the Web, be sure to download the .exe file version. The following steps show how to install Tomcat from the CD-ROM to a location on your hard drive (C:). If necessary, substitute the location specified by your instructor. Note: If you downloaded the ZIP file version, before installing you should set the JAVA-HOME environment variable first. See page APP 34.

### To Install Tomcat

1. If necessary, insert the CD-ROM into your CD-ROM drive. When the Course Technology dialog box is displayed, click Software. When the software files are displayed, click Jakarta Tomcat Server 5.5.7.

    *For additional information on running Jakarta Tomcat Server 5.5.7, and known issues with this version, you may open the Jakarta Tomcat help selection (Figure B-16).*

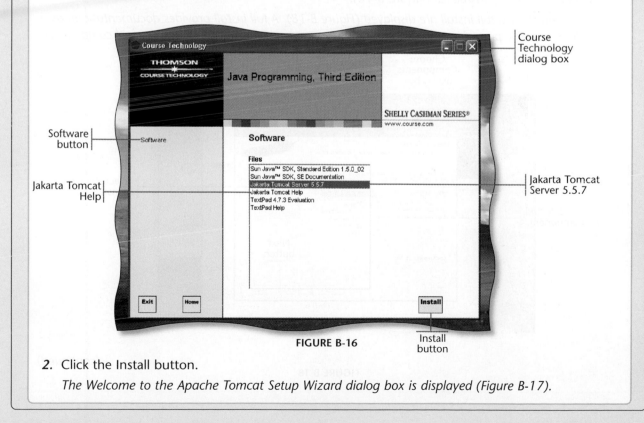

FIGURE B-16

2. Click the Install button.

    *The Welcome to the Apache Tomcat Setup Wizard dialog box is displayed (Figure B-17).*

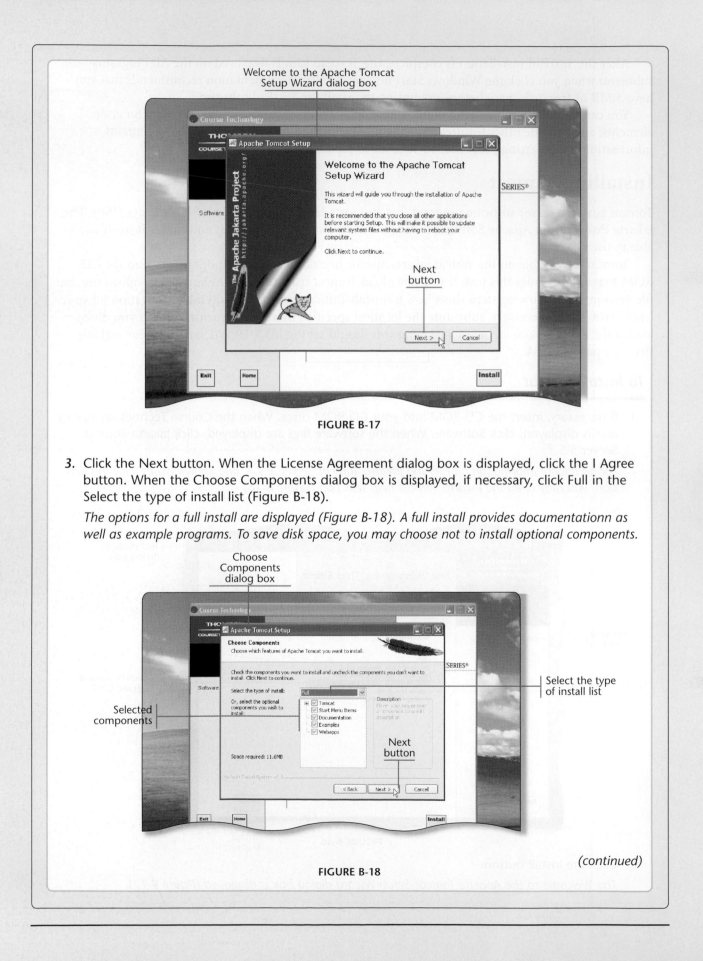

**FIGURE B-17**

3. Click the Next button. When the License Agreement dialog box is displayed, click the I Agree button. When the Choose Components dialog box is displayed, if necessary, click Full in the Select the type of install list (Figure B-18).

*The options for a full install are displayed (Figure B-18). A full install provides documentationn as well as example programs. To save disk space, you may choose not to install optional components.*

**FIGURE B-18**

*(continued)*

*4.* Click the Next button. When the Choose Install Location dialog box is displayed, verify the location where Tomcat should be installed.

*The Choose Install Location dialog box displays the default location of \Program Files\Apache Software Foundation\Tomcat 5.5 on drive C (Figure B-19).*

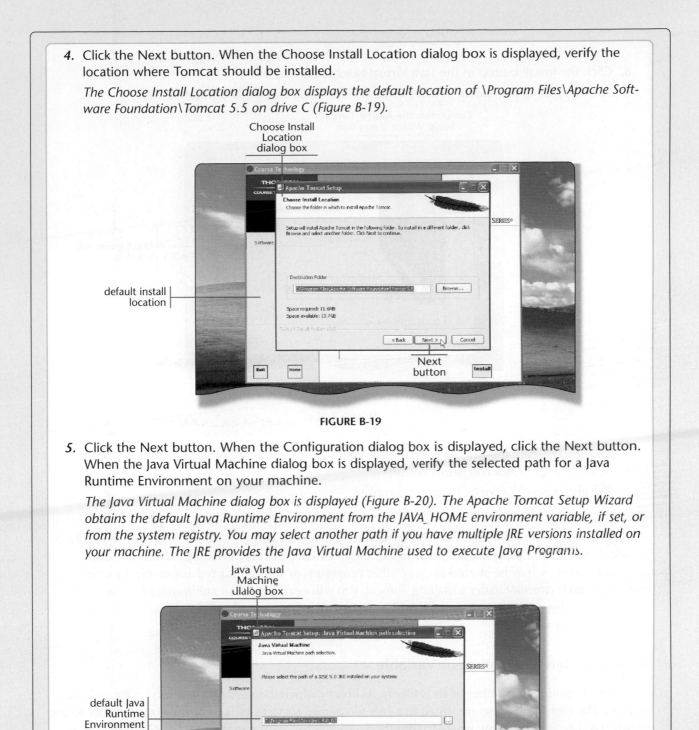

**FIGURE B-19**

*5.* Click the Next button. When the Configuration dialog box is displayed, click the Next button. When the Java Virtual Machine dialog box is displayed, verify the selected path for a Java Runtime Environment on your machine.

*The Java Virtual Machine dialog box is displayed (Figure B-20). The Apache Tomcat Setup Wizard obtains the default Java Runtime Environment from the JAVA_HOME environment variable, if set, or from the system registry. You may select another path if you have multiple JRE versions installed on your machine. The JRE provides the Java Virtual Machine used to execute Java Programs.*

**FIGURE B-20**

6. Click the Install button in the Java Virtual Machine dialog box.

*The Completing the Apache Tomcat Setup Wizard dialog box displays (Figure B-21).*

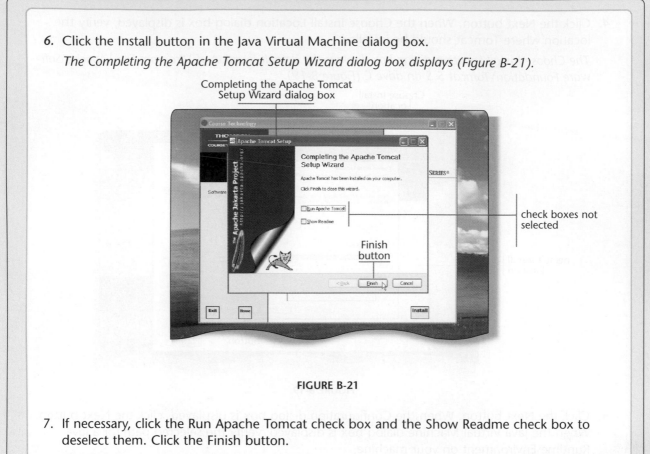

Completing the Apache Tomcat
Setup Wizard dialog box

check boxes not
selected

Finish
button

**FIGURE B-21**

7. If necessary, click the Run Apache Tomcat check box and the Show Readme check box to deselect them. Click the Finish button.

*The installation of Apache Tomcat is complete.*

The Tomcat server software installs as a service under Windows XP and will start automatically. A **Windows service** is a program intended to run for an extended time, providing services to other programs. Services may be started like any other programs, or may be started automatically when the computer starts running. After installing Tomcat, you will need to add an environment variable on your system. This environment variable will be used by the Java compiler to locate certain class files when compiling servlets.

## Adding a New Environment Variable

Tomcat provides a number of class files in its library which are needed when you create and use servlets. The files in this case are stored in a JAR file named servlet-api.jar. For the Java compiler to use these class files, it must know where to find them. An environment variable, named CLASSPATH, is used to identify one or more additional locations where the compiler can search for needed class files. An **environment variable** is a string that lists information about the system environment, such as a drive, path, or file name. The compiler will search for class files in the order of the locations listed in the CLASSPATH environment variable. Perform the following steps to add a new environment variable.

## *To Add a New Environment Variable*

*1.* Click the Start button on the Windows taskbar and then right-click My Computer on the Start menu.

*The My Computer command is selected on the Start menu, and a shortcut menu is displayed (Figure B-22). The Start menu selections on your system may differ from those displayed.*

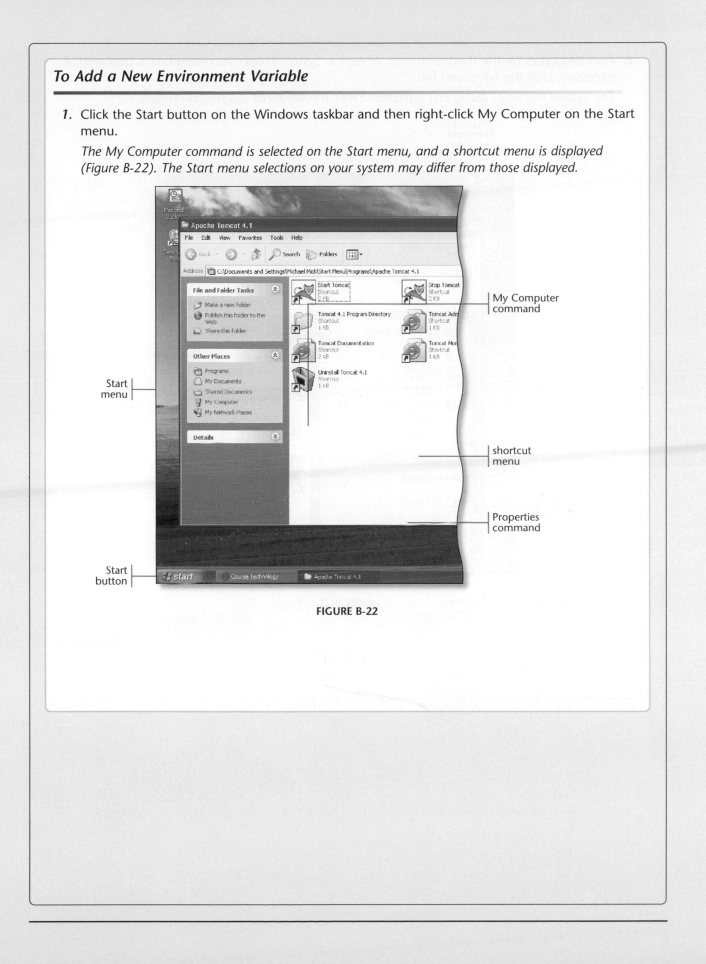

FIGURE B-22

**2.** Click Properties on the shortcut menu. When the System Properties dialog box is displayed, if necessary, click the Advanced tab.

*The System Properties dialog box is displayed with the Advanced tab selected (Figure B-23).*

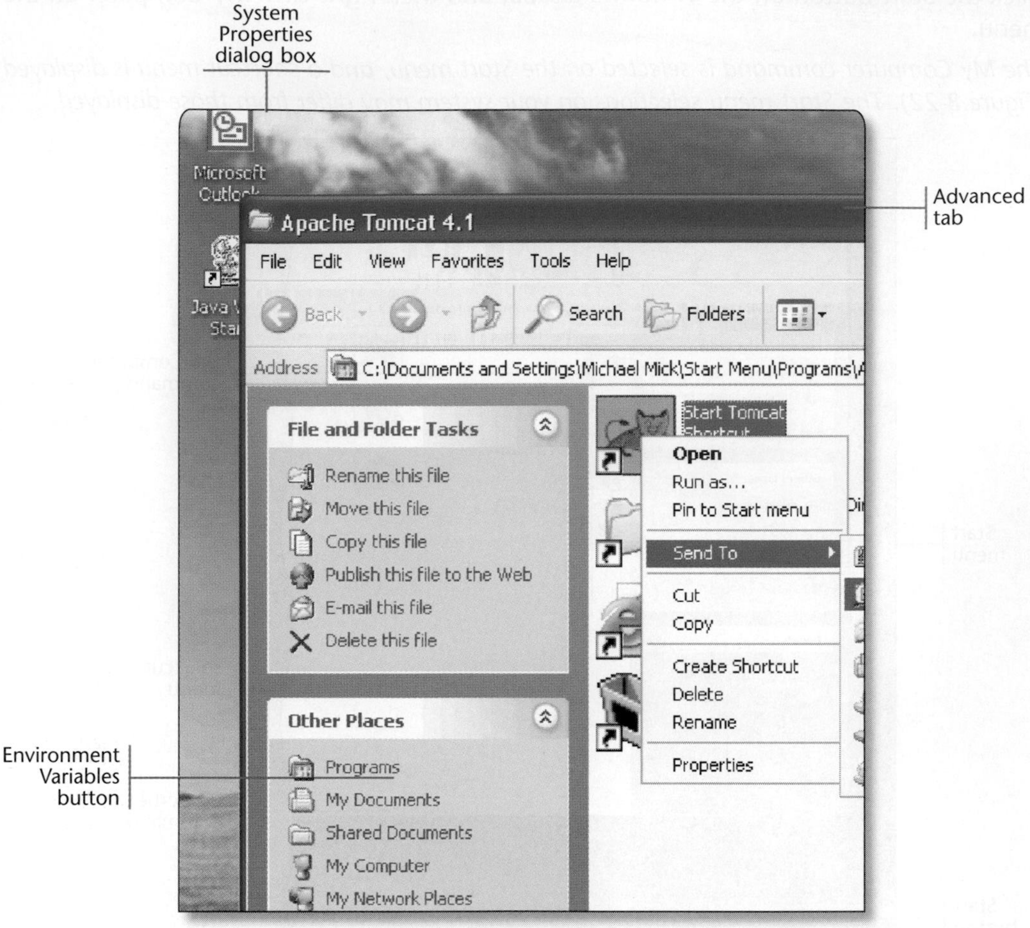

**FIGURE B-23**

*(continued)*

3. Click the Environment Variables button. When the Environment Variables dialog box is displayed, click the New button in the System variables area. When the New System Variable dialog box is displayed, type CLASSPATH in the Variable name text box and then type .;C:\Program Files\Apache Group\Tomcat 5.5\common\lib\jsp-api.jar; C:\Program Files\Apache Group\Tomcat 5.5\common\lib\servlet-api.jar in the Variable value text box (or append \common\lib\jsp-api.jar and then also \common\lib\servlet-api.jar to the location where you installed Tomcat). *The New System Variable dialog box displays the environment variable name and value (Figure B-24). Because we want the compiler to search first in the current folder and then in the servlet-api.jar file for needed servlet classes and in the jsp-api.jar for needed jsp classes, the CLASSPATH variable must indicate all of these locations. The current folder is indicated by a period. Multiple locations are separated by a semicolon.*

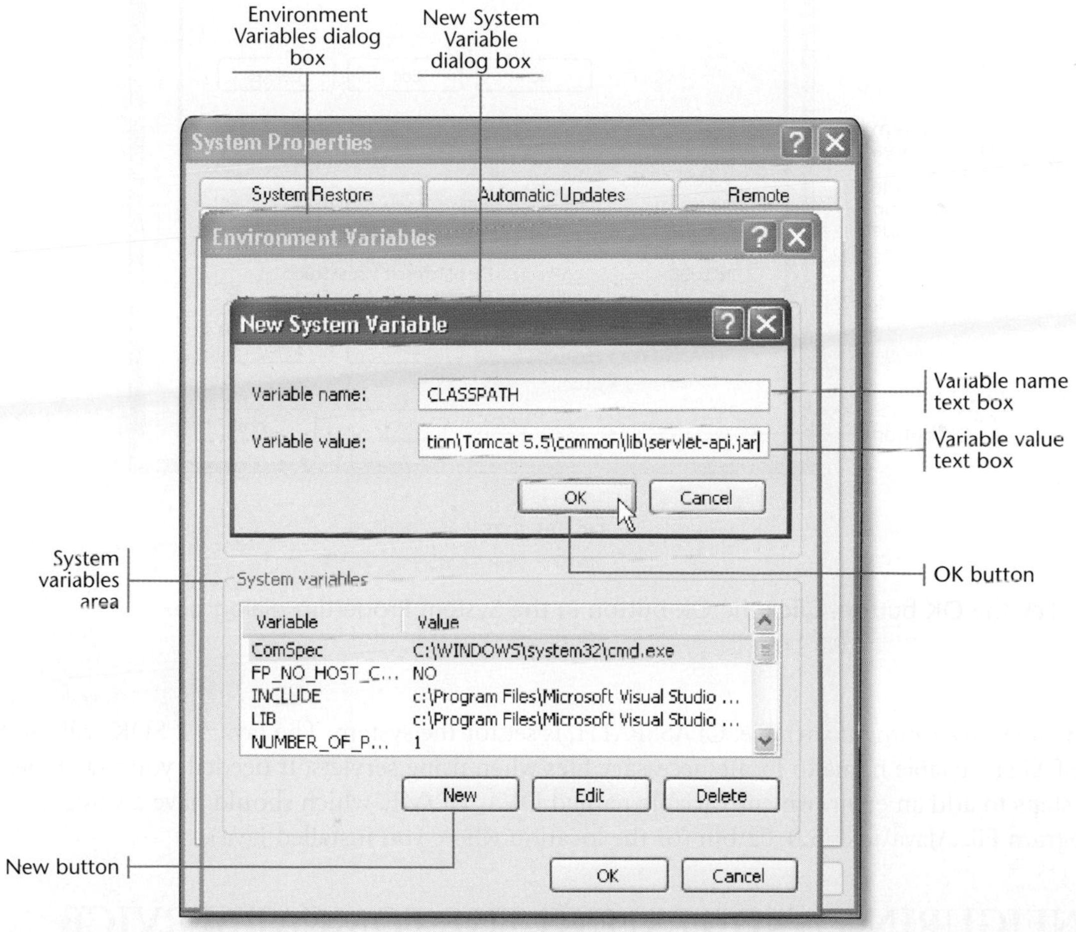

**FIGURE B-24**

*4.* Click the OK button in the New System Variable dialog box.

*The Environment Variables dialog box displays the new variable name and value in the System variables area (Figure B-25).*

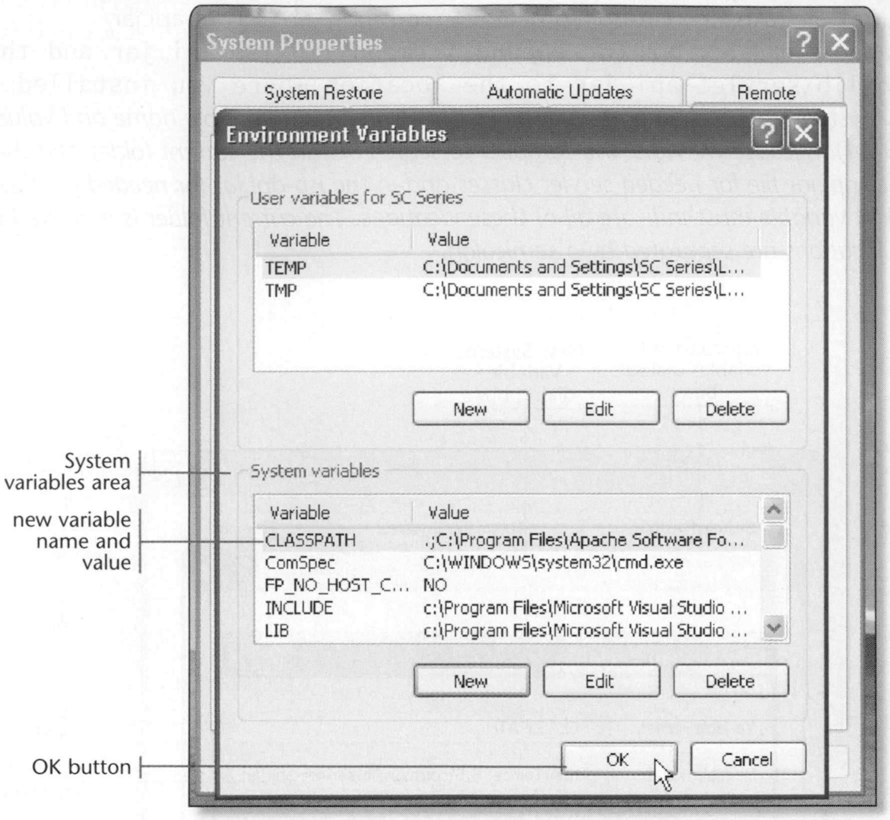

System variables area

new variable name and value

OK button

**FIGURE B-25**

*5.* Click the OK button. Click the OK button in the System Properties dialog box.

The new environment variable, CLASSPATH, is set for the system. The Java™ 2 SDK will use the CLASSPATH variable name to locate necessary files when using servlets. If needed, you may repeat the above steps to add an environment variable named JAVA_HOME, which should have a value of C:\Program Files\Java\jdk1.5.0_02\bin (or the location where you installed Java).

## CONFIGURING AND TESTING THE TOMCAT SERVICE

When you use the Apache Tomcat Setup Wizard under Windows XP, Tomcat installs as a Windows service configured to run automatically. Because services do not have a user interface, it can be difficult to know when the Tomcat service is running.

The Apache Service Manager provides an easy way to determine if the Tomcat service is started or stopped. The Apache Tomcat Setup Wizard automatically installed the Apache Service Manager, which displays in the system tray when running (see Figures B-27a and B-27b). If necessary, perform the following steps to start the Apache Service Manager.

## To Start the Apache Service Manager

*1.* Verify that all system tray icons are displayed. If the Apache Service Manager icon is not present, click the Start button on the taskbar and then point to All Programs on the Start menu. Point to Apache Tomcat 5.5 on the All Programs submenu. Point to Monitor Tomcat on the Apache Tomcat 5.5 submenu.

*The Apache Tomcat 5.5 submenu is displayed (Figure B-26). Only start the Apache Service Manager if it is not already displayed in the system tray.*

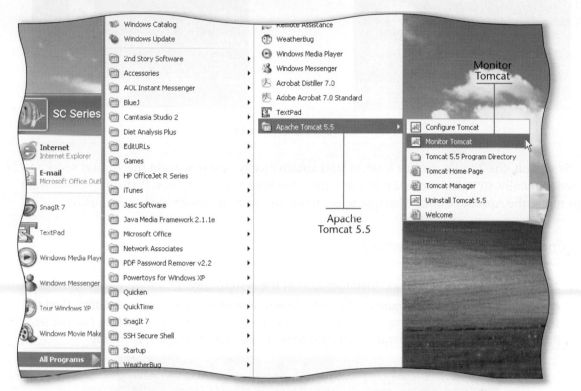

**FIGURE B-26**

*2.* Click Monitor Tomcat.

*The Apache Service Manager displays as an icon in the system tray with a green arrow on the icon indicating that the Tomcat service is running (Figure B-27a). A red square on the icon indicates that the Tomcat service is stopped (Figure B-27b). If an Application System Error dialog box is displayed, then the Apache Service Manager was already running. Only one copy of the program can run at a time.*

FIGURE B-27(a) and (b)

By default, the Tomcat service is set to start automatically. You may want the Tomcat service to be started manually, so it does not execute every time you boot your computer. Perform the following steps to use the Apache Service Manager to configure the Tomcat service to start manually.

## To Configure the Tomcat Service

*1.* Right-click the Apache Service Manager icon in the system tray.

*A shortcut menu displays (Figure B-28). If the Stop service menu item is not selectable, then the service is not running. You may click About to view the license agreement. Clicking Exit will terminate the Apache Service Manager, causing it to no longer display in the system tray.*

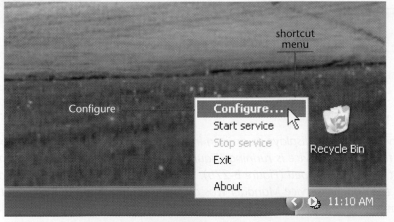

FIGURE B-28

*2.* Click Configure... on the shortcut menu. When the Apache Tomcat Properties dialog box is displayed, if necessary, click the General tab. In the Startup type list, click Manual.

*The Apache Tomcat Properties dialog box is displayed (Figure B-29). A startup type of Manual is selected.*

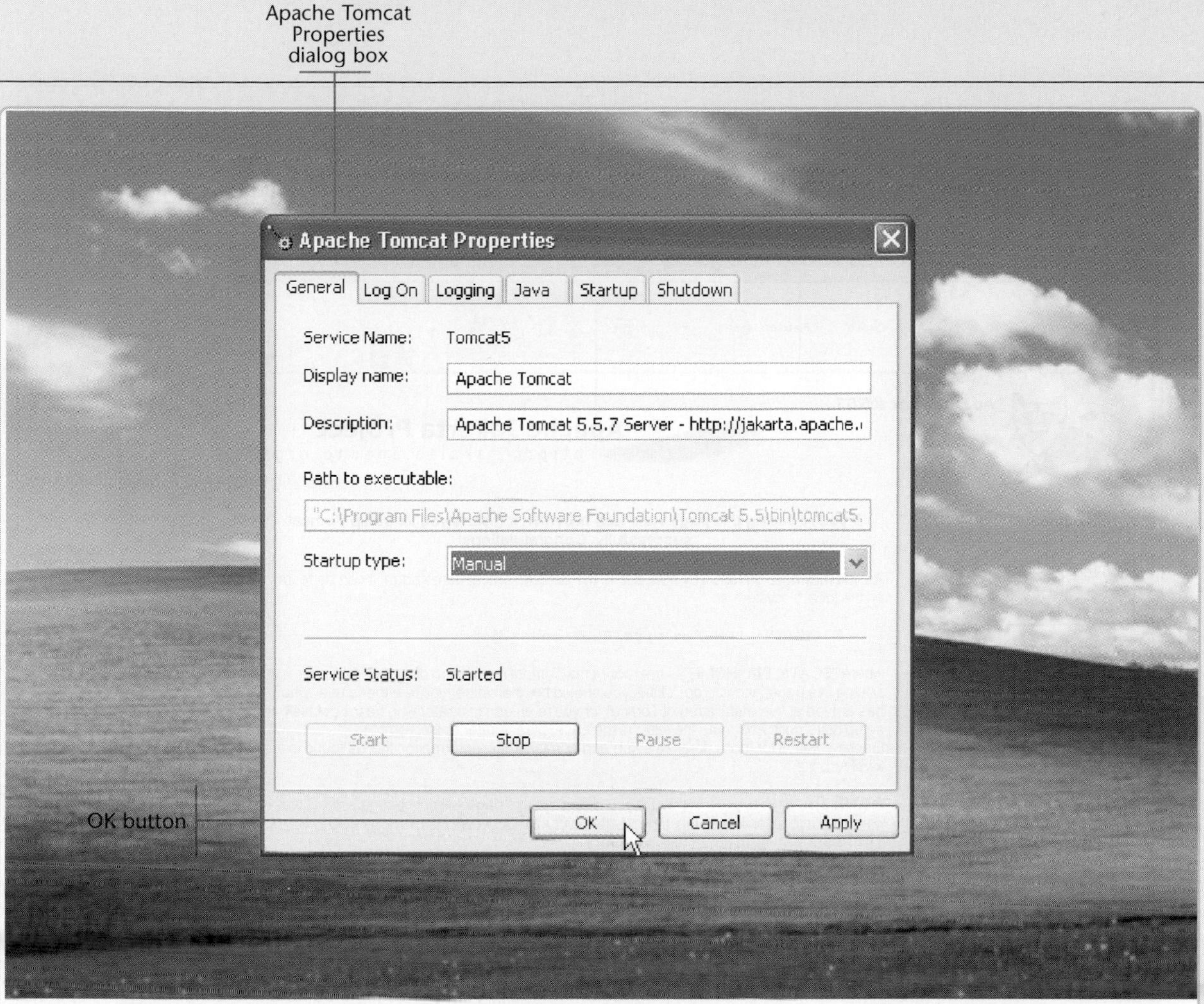

Apache Tomcat
Properties
dialog box

**Apache Tomcat Properties**

General | Log On | Logging | Java | Startup | Shutdown

Service Name: Tomcat5

Display name: Apache Tomcat

Description: Apache Tomcat 5.5.7 Server - http://jakarta.apache.

Path to executable:

"C:\Program Files\Apache Software Foundation\Tomcat 5.5\bin\tomcat5.

Startup type: Manual

Service Status: Started

Start | Stop | Pause | Restart

OK button

OK | Cancel | Apply

**FIGURE B-29**

3. Click the OK button.

*The Apache Tomcat Properties dialog box closes.*

Although Tomcat now is configured to start manually, the Apache Service Manager still should display as an icon in the system tray whether the Tomcat service is running or not. By the color and shape of the icon, you know quickly whether the Tomcat service is running. Perform the following steps to test the Tomcat service.

## To Test the Tomcat Service

1. If necessary, right-click the Apache Service Manager icon in the system tray and then click Start service on the shortcut menu. Start your Web browser. When the Web browser window opens, type http://localhost:8080/ in the Address box and then press the Enter key.

*If Tomcat is running successfully, the browser displays the Web page shown in Figure B-30. The Apache Service Manager also displays a green arrow, indicating that the service is running.*

**FIGURE B-30**

2. Close the browser. Right-click the Apache Service Manager icon in the system tray. Click Stop service on the shortcut menu.

   *The Apache Service Manager is displayed with a small red square in the center indicating that the service is stopped (see Figure B-27b).*

   To view the documentation for Tomcat, use your Web browser to open the file, index.html, in the folder C:\Program Files\Apache Software Foundation\Tomcat 5.5\webapps\tomcat-docs\.

# C

# Changing Screen Resolution and Setting TextPad Preferences

Appendix C explains how to change your screen resolution to the resolution used in this book. The appendix also explains how to set basic preferences in TextPad, so that it is better suited to your preferred work habits.

# Screen Resolution

Screen resolution determines the amount of information that appears on your screen, measured in pixels. A low resolution, such as 640 by 480 pixels, makes the overall screen area small, but items on the screen, such as windows, text, and icons, appear larger on the screen. A high resolution, such as 1024 by 768 pixels, makes the overall screen area large, but items appear smaller on the screen.

## Changing Screen Resolution

The following steps show how to change your screen's resolution from 800 by 600 pixels to 1024 by 768 pixels, which is the screen resolution used in this book.

### To Change Screen Resolution

1. Click the Start button on the Windows taskbar and then point to Control Panel on the Start menu.

   *The Start menu is displayed and Control Panel is highlighted on the Start menu (Figure C-1). Your menu options may differ.*

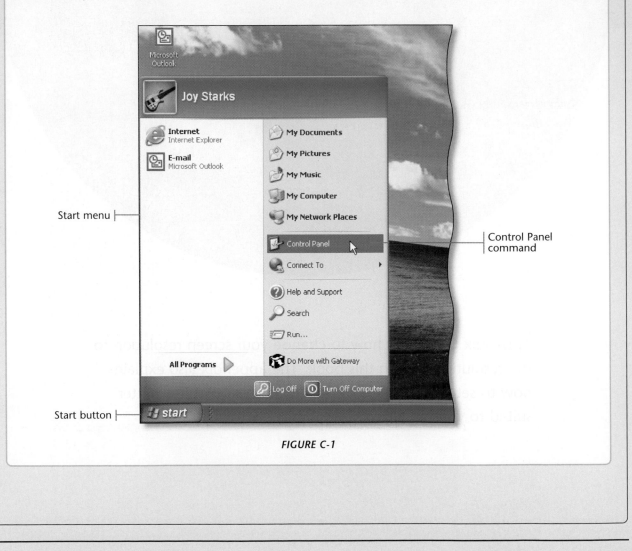

*FIGURE C-1*

**2.** Click Control Panel. If necessary, click Switch to Category View in the Control Panel area.

*The Control Panel window opens (Figure C-2).*

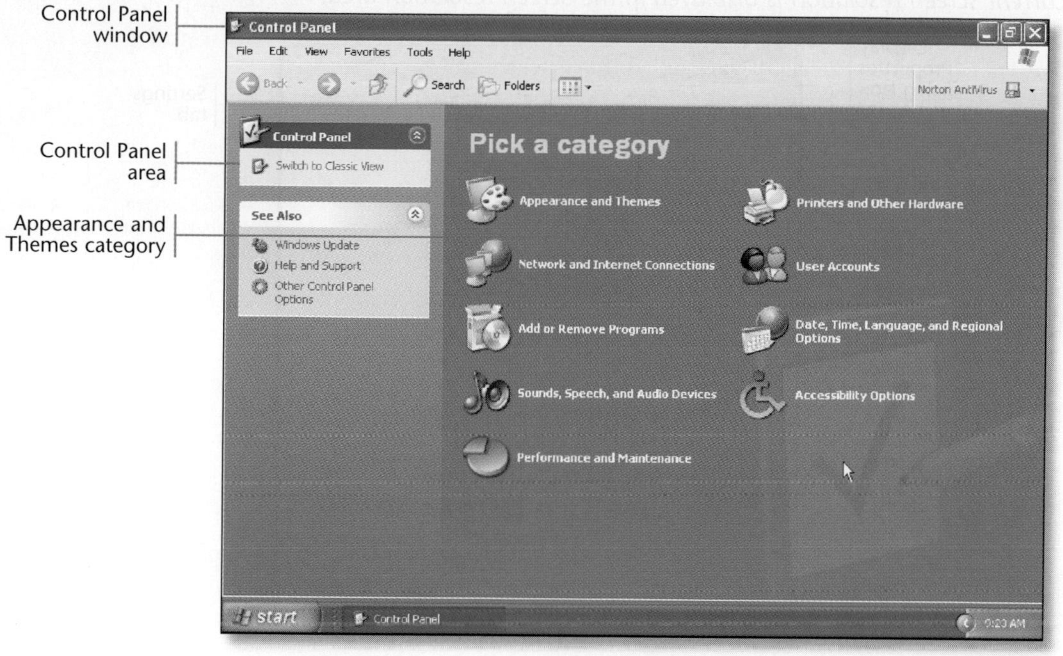

Control Panel window

Control Panel area

Appearance and Themes category

FIGURE C-2

**3.** Click the Appearance and Themes category.

*The Appearance and Themes window opens (Figure C-3).*

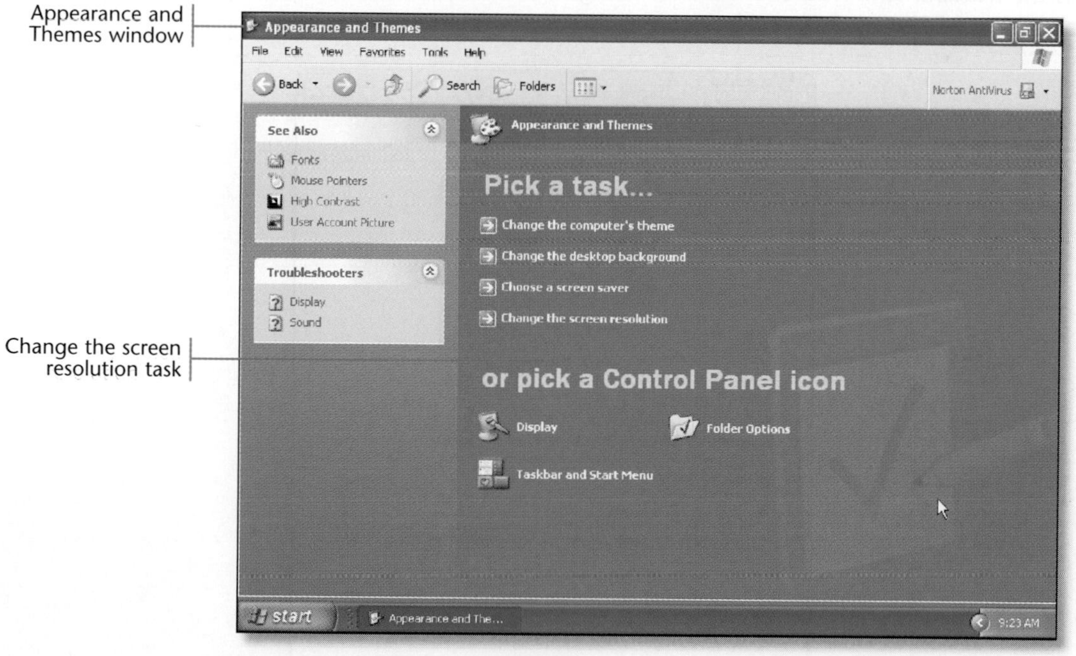

Appearance and Themes window

Change the screen resolution task

FIGURE C-3

**4.** Click the Change the screen resolution task.

*The Display Properties dialog box is displayed, with the Settings tab selected (Figure C-4). The current screen resolution is displayed in the Screen resolution area.*

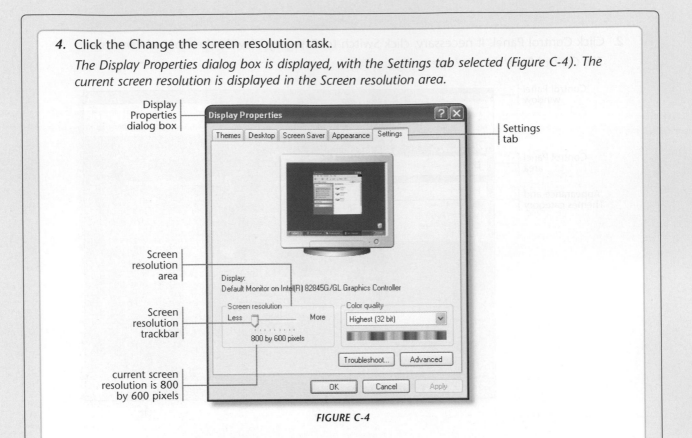

Display Properties dialog box

Settings tab

Screen resolution area

Screen resolution trackbar

current screen resolution is 800 by 600 pixels

**FIGURE C-4**

**5.** Drag the Screen resolution trackbar one tick mark to the right or until the screen resolution below the trackbar reads 1024 by 768 pixels.

*As the trackbar is moved one mark to the right, the screen resolution displayed below the trackbar changes to 1024 by 768 pixels (Figure C-5).*

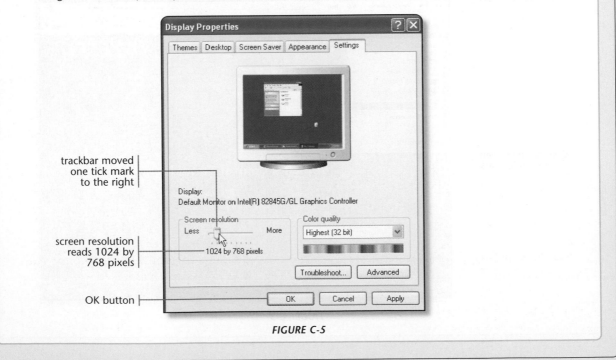

trackbar moved one tick mark to the right

screen resolution reads 1024 by 768 pixels

OK button

**FIGURE C-5**

**6.** Click the OK button.

*The Display Properties dialog box closes. The Windows desktop is displayed at a screen resolution of 1024 by 768 pixels (Figure C-6). Your screen may flicker while the resolution change takes place.*

screen resolution
changed to 1024
by 768 pixels

Close
button

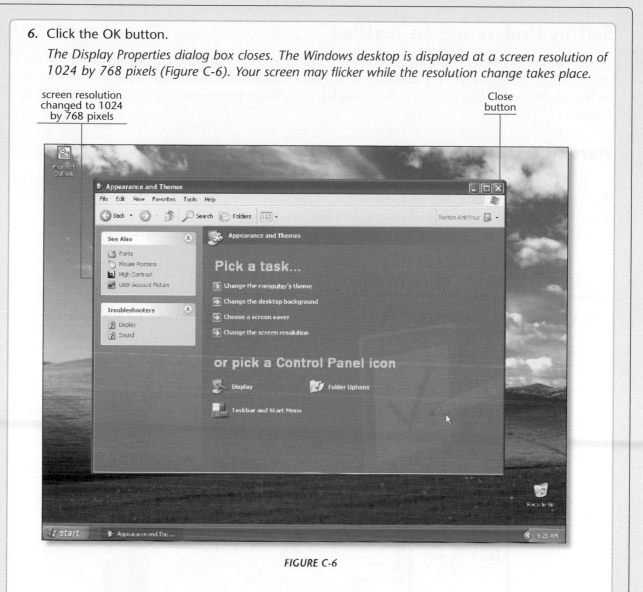

*FIGURE C-6*

**7.** Click the Close button on the Appearance and Themes window title bar.

*The new screen resolution is set.*

Compare Figure C-6 with Figure C-3 on page C.03 to see the difference in the display when screen resolution is set to 800 by 600 pixels or 1024 by 768 pixels. As shown in these figures, using a higher resolution allows more items, such as windows, text, and icons, to fit on the screen, but the items display at a smaller size. In Figure C-6, the Appearances and Themes window does not fill the entire screen.

You can experiment with various screen resolutions. Depending on your monitor and the video adapter installed in your computer, the screen resolutions available on your computer will vary.

When designing a user interface in Java, remember to take into consideration the screen resolutions available to the majority of users of the application. A good rule of thumb is to test your application in all of the screen resolutions in which users are likely to use the application.

# Setting Preferences in TextPad

TextPad allows you to set many preferences to customize and arrange the contents and display of the coding window. This section explains how to add the available Java commands to the Tools menu; turn on line numbering so line numbers always display; and change preferences for color, font, and tabs in TextPad.

## Starting TextPad and Displaying Preferences

To set preferences in TextPad, you use the Preferences command on the Configure menu to display the Preferences dialog box. Any preferences you set are saved when you quit TextPad, which means that the settings still will be in effect when you start TextPad again.

The following steps illustrate how to start TextPad and display the Preferences dialog box.

### To Start TextPad and Display Preferences

1. Click the Start button on the Windows taskbar. Point to All Programs on the Start menu. When the All Programs submenu is displayed, point to TextPad.

   *The All Programs submenu is displayed (Figure C-7).*

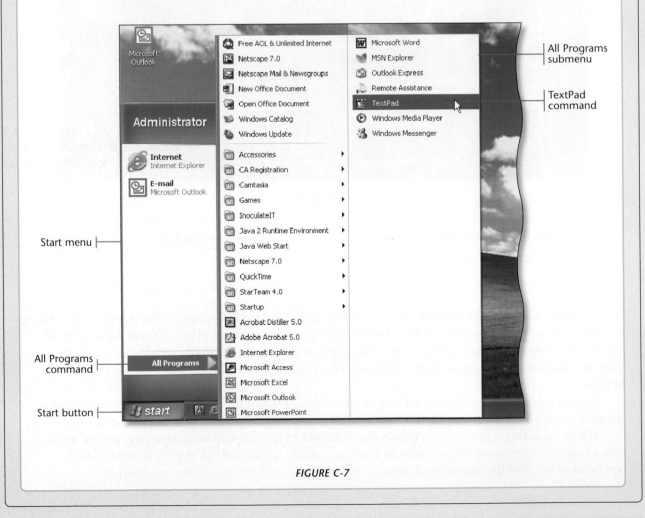

*FIGURE C-7*

2. Click TextPad. If a Tip of the Day dialog box is displayed, click its Close button. On the TextPad menu bar, click Configure.

   *TextPad displays the Configure menu (Figure C-8).*

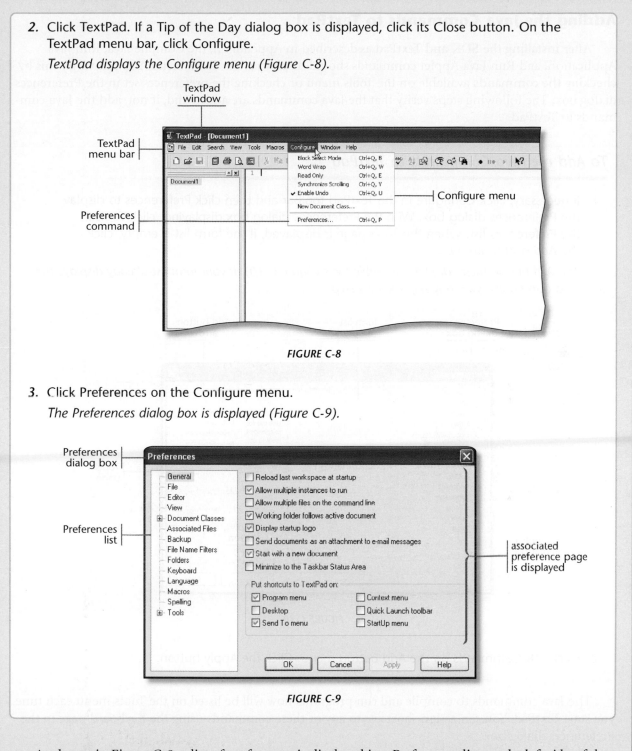

FIGURE C-8

3. Click Preferences on the Configure menu.

   *The Preferences dialog box is displayed (Figure C-9).*

FIGURE C-9

   As shown in Figure C-9, a list of preferences is displayed in a Preferences list on the left side of the Preferences dialog box. When you select a preference in the Preferences list, the associated preference page is displayed on the right.

## Adding the Java Commands to TextPad

After installing the SDK and TextPad as described in Appendix B, the Compile Java, Run Java Application, and Run Java Applet commands should display on the Tools menu. You can verify this by checking the commands available on the Tools menu or checking the preferences set in the Preferences dialog box. The following steps verify that the Java commands are added and, if not, add the Java commands to TextPad.

### To Add the Java Commands to TextPad

1. If necessary, click Configure in the TextPad toolbar and then click Preferences to display the Preferences dialog box. With the Preferences dialog box displaying, click Tools in the Preferences list. When the Tools page is displayed, if the form list is empty, click the Add button arrow.

   *The Add button menu displays available tools (Figure C-10). If your form list already displays the Java commands, you may skip the next step.*

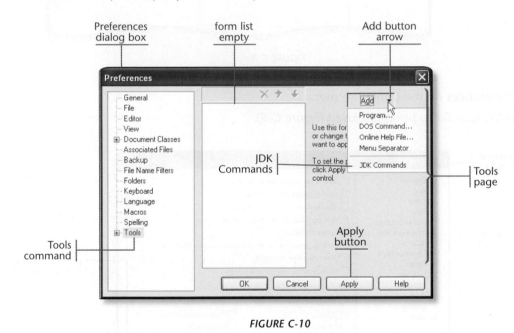

*FIGURE C-10*

2. Click JDK Commands on the Add button menu. Click the Apply button.

The Java commands to compile and run programs now will be listed on the Tools menu each time you start TextPad. You can assign shortcuts to any of these commands using the Keyboard page in the Preferences dialog box.

## Turning on Line Numbers

Line numbers assist programmers in referencing code and fixing errors. TextPad users can set a preference to turn on line numbers so that they always display and print. The following steps show how to turn on line numbers that display on the screen as well as on printouts.

## *To Turn on Line Numbers*

1. With the Preferences dialog box displaying, click View in the Preferences list. When the View page is displayed, click the Line numbers check box. If you want your screen to match the screens in this book exactly, click the Highlight the line containing the cursor check box so that the check mark does not display.

   *The Line numbers check box displays a check mark (Figure C-11). Line numbers automatically will display in the coding window each time you start TextPad.*

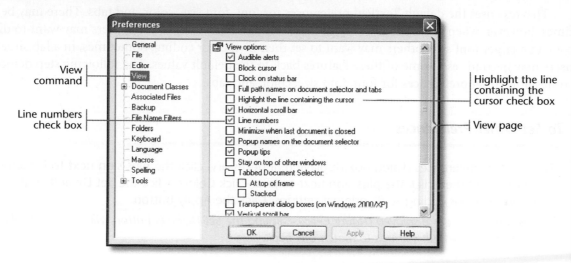

*FIGURE C-11*

2. In the Preferences list, click the plus sign next to Document Classes and then click the plus sign next to Java. Click Printing. When the Printing page is displayed, click Line numbers.

   *The Line numbers check box displays a check mark (Figure C-12). Line numbers automatically will display on all printouts printed using TextPad.*

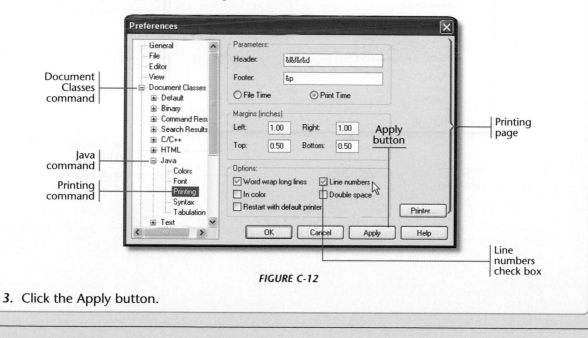

*FIGURE C-12*

3. Click the Apply button.

Other preferences available on the View page include turning on and off alerts, scroll bars, and tabbed document selectors or sheets. Other preferences available on the Printing page include setting print margins and setting TextPad to print in color. For example, if you want your HTML host files to print with line numbers or in color, click the plus sign next to Document Classes in the Preferences list. Click the plus sign next to HTML and then click Printing in the Preferences list. Click the In color and Line numbers check boxes and then click the OK button to set the preferences.

## Setting Other Preferences

This text uses the default TextPad preferences for font, font size, color, and tabs. There may be times, however, when users need to change these settings. For example, some users may want to display code in a larger font size; others may want to set their own color coding. Sometimes, in a lab situation, users may need to reset some of these features back to the default values. The following step demonstrates how to set preferences for font, font size, color, and tabs.

### To Set Other Preferences

1. With the Preferences dialog box displaying, if necessary, click the plus sign next to Document Classes and then click the plus sign next to Java. Click Colors. Click the Set Defaults button to return all color coding to its original settings. Click the Apply button.

   *The Colors page is displayed (Figure C-13). Clicking the Set Defaults button will restore all colors back to their default settings to match this book.*

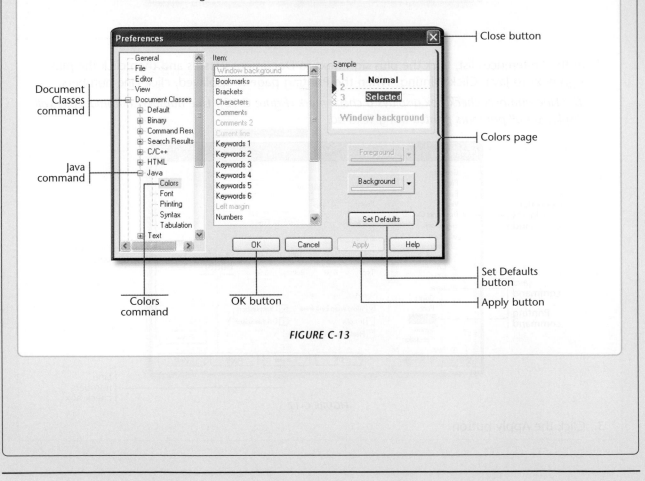

FIGURE C-13

You can change additional settings such as font, font size, and tabs using similar steps. To change font and font size, if necessary, click the plus sign next to Document Classes and then click the plus sign next to Java in the Preferences list. Click Font. When finished making changes to these preferences, click the Apply button. To change tab settings, if necessary, click the plus sign next to Document Classes and then click the plus sign next to Java in the Preferences list. Click Tabulation. When finished making changes to these preferences, click the Apply button.

For more information about changing additional settings, click Help on the TextPad menu bar and then click Help Topics. When the Help window opens, click the Contents tab and then click the plus sign next to How To to display the topic list.

The final step is to close the Preferences dialog box and quit TextPad.

### To Close the Preferences Dialog Box and Quit TextPad

1. In the Preferences dialog box, click the OK button.
2. Click the Close button on the TextPad title bar.

## TextPad Editing Techniques

TextPad supports many of the same editing commands as popular word processing programs. Table C-1 displays TextPad commands to navigate through the coding window. Table C-2 on the next page displays different ways to select text in TextPad.

### Table C-1  Commands to Move through the Coding Window

| TO MOVE THE INSERTION POINT | PRESS THIS KEY |
| --- | --- |
| to the beginning of the document | CTRL+HOME |
| to the end of the document | CTRL+END |
| to first non-space character on a line | HOME |
| to the left margin | HOME twice |
| to the end of a line | END |
| forward one word | CTRL+W or CTRL+RIGHT ARROW |
| back one word | CTRL+B or CTRL+LEFT ARROW |
| back to the end of the previous word | CTRL+D |
| to the start of the next paragraph | ALT+DOWN ARROW |
| to the start of the previous paragraph | ALT+UP ARROW |
| to the start of the first visible line | ALT+HOME |
| to the start of the last visible line | ALT+END |
| scroll display down one line | CTRL+DOWN ARROW |
| scroll display up one line | CTRL+UP ARROW |
| to a specified line, column, or page number | CTRL+G |

*Table C-2   Selecting Text in TextPad*

| TO SELECT | PERFORM THIS ACTION |
|---|---|
| a word | Double-click |
| a line | Double-click left margin or triple-click line |
| all code | On Edit menu, click Select All or press CTRL+CLICK in left margin |
| text using the mouse | Hold the left mouse button and then drag across text, click at the start of text, press SHIFT+CLICK at the end of text |
| text using the keyboard | Press SHIFT+ARROW, using arrow key to move in correct direction |

# D

# Compiling and Running Java Programs Using the Command Prompt Window

Some programmers compile and run Java programs in the Command Prompt window. Unlike the TextPad software used in this book, many text editors — such as Microsoft's Notepad program — can be used to edit Java source code but have no command to compile source code or run programs. In that case, after saving the program in Notepad with the extension .java, you would enter the Java SDK compile and run commands explicitly using the Command Prompt window. In some cases, programmers must set environmental variables in order to successfully compile and run Java programs using the Command Prompt window.

# Using the Command Prompt Window

This appendix describes how to open the Command Prompt window and then set properties to define how the Command Prompt window displays. It also discusses how to change to the proper drive and directory. Finally, it covers how to set the environmental variables in order to compile and run a sample program found on the Data Disk that accompanies this book.

## Opening and Setting Properties of the Command Prompt Window

In Windows, the **Command Prompt window** (Figure D-1) is a way to communicate with the operating system and issue commands without using a program with a graphical user interface. Most versions of Windows contain a Command Prompt command on the Accessories submenu, which allows you to open a Command Prompt window. Opening a Command Prompt window on the desktop facilitates moving between editing programs and running them.

**FIGURE D-1**

As shown in Figure D-1, the Command Prompt window displays a **command prompt** that includes a disk drive location, followed by a subdirectory location (if any), followed by a greater-than sign (>), and finally a flashing insertion point. The insertion point designates the place where users type commands and enter responses.

The Command Prompt window normally displays light gray text on a black screen, with a default font size of 8 × 12 pixels or a similar size. In order to make the screens easier to read in this book, the Command Prompt window properties were set to use a font color of white and a font size of 12 × 16 pixels. The following steps open the Command Prompt window and set its properties to match the figures in this book.

## *To Open and Set Properties of the Command Prompt Window*

1. Click the Start button on the taskbar and then point to All Programs on the Start menu. When the All Programs menu is displayed, point to Accessories and then point to Command Prompt on the Accessories submenu.

   *Windows displays the Accessories submenu (Figure D-2). Your menu options may differ.*

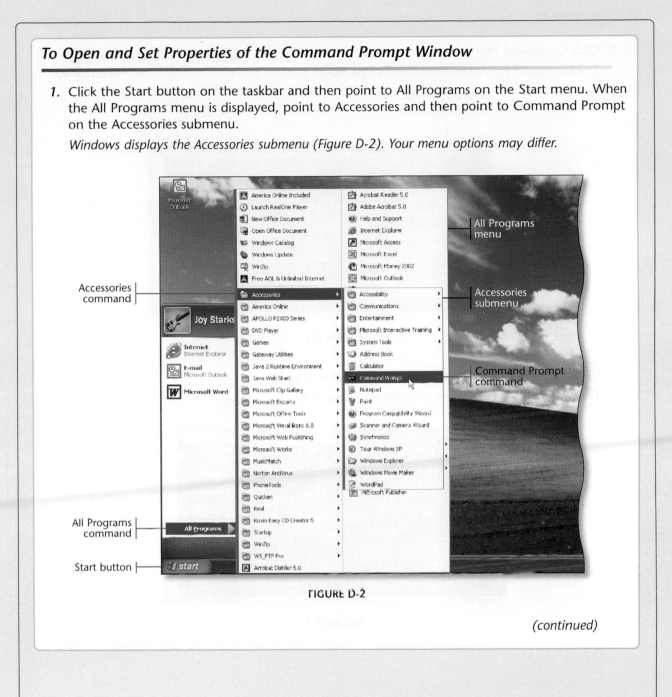

FIGURE D-2

*(continued)*

**2.** Click Command Prompt.

*The Command Prompt window opens (Figure D-3). An icon and title are displayed in the title bar.*

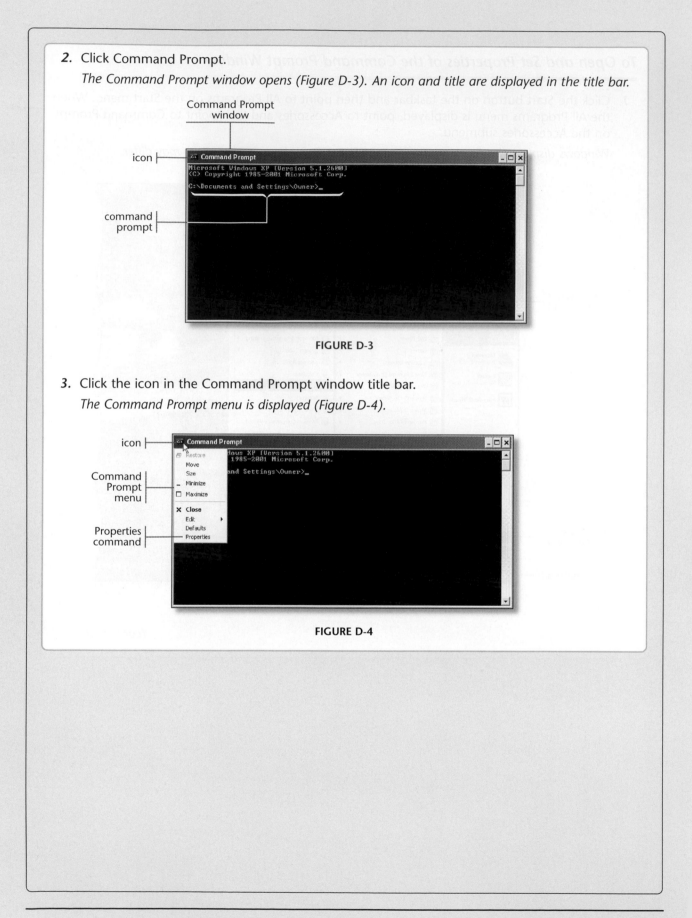

Command Prompt
window

icon

command
prompt

**FIGURE D-3**

**3.** Click the icon in the Command Prompt window title bar.

*The Command Prompt menu is displayed (Figure D-4).*

icon

Command
Prompt
menu

Properties
command

**FIGURE D-4**

**4.** Click Properties on the Command Prompt menu. When the "Command Prompt" Properties dialog box is displayed, if necessary, click the Font tab.

*The "Command Prompt" Properties dialog box contains options to configure how the Command Prompt window will display (Figure D-5).*

"Command Prompt" Properties dialog box

Font tab

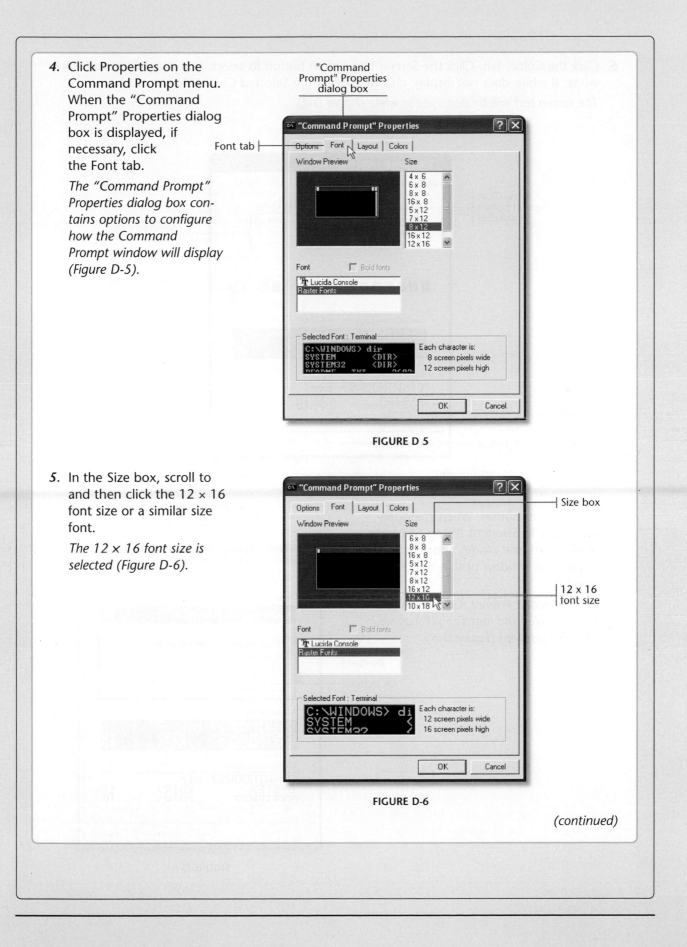

**FIGURE D 5**

**5.** In the Size box, scroll to and then click the 12 × 16 font size or a similar size font.

*The 12 × 16 font size is selected (Figure D-6).*

Size box

12 × 16 font size

**FIGURE D-6**

*(continued)*

6. Click the Colors tab. Click the Screen Text option button to select it. In the color panel, click white. If white does not display, change each of the Selected Color Values to 255.

*The screen text will be displayed in white (Figure D-7).*

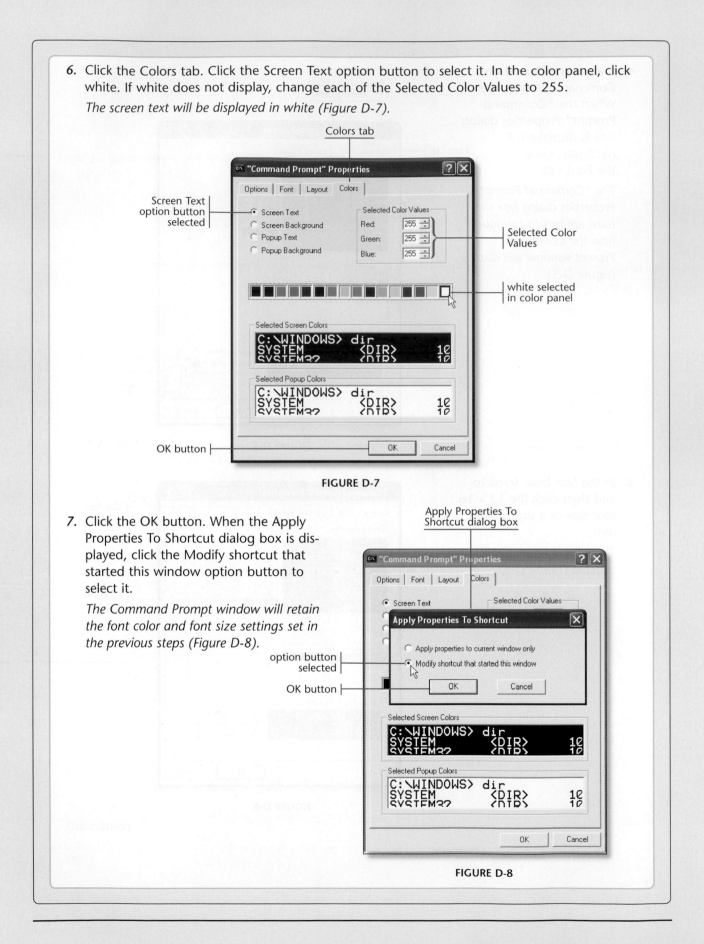

FIGURE D-7

7. Click the OK button. When the Apply Properties To Shortcut dialog box is displayed, click the Modify shortcut that started this window option button to select it.

*The Command Prompt window will retain the font color and font size settings set in the previous steps (Figure D-8).*

FIGURE D-8

**8.** Click the OK button.

*The Command Prompt window displays white text with a font size of 12 × 16 pixels (Figure D-9).*

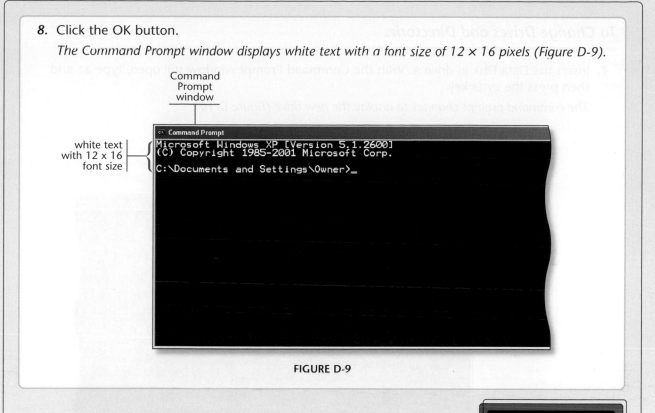

Command
Prompt
window

white text
with 12 × 16
font size

```
Command Prompt

Microsoft Windows XP [Version 5.1.2600]
(C) Copyright 1985-2001 Microsoft Corp.

C:\Documents and Settings\Owner>_
```

FIGURE D-9

## Changing Drives and Directories

Operating system commands help programmers with file maintenance, peripheral control, and other system utilities. When you compile and run programs using the Command Prompt window, you need to issue some commands to the operating system, so that the Java SDK can find your files. If you save your programs on the Data Disk in drive A, for example, you will need to **log on** or instruct the operating system to access drive A. To change to a specific drive, users type the drive letter followed by a colon (:) at the command prompt. To change to a specific **directory** or folder on the drive, users type the command, cd, followed by the folder name. On most systems, the command prompt changes to reflect access to the new storage location.

The steps on the next page change the drive and directory to drive A and the Appendices folder created when you download the Data Disk. See the preface of this book for instructions for downloading the Data Disk or see your instructor for information about accessing the files required in this book.

> **OTHER WAYS**
>
> 1. Click Start button, click Run, type cmd, click OK button

## To Change Drives and Directories

1. Insert the Data Disk in drive A. With the Command Prompt window still open, type a: and then press the ENTER key.

   *The command prompt changes to display the new drive (Figure D-10).*

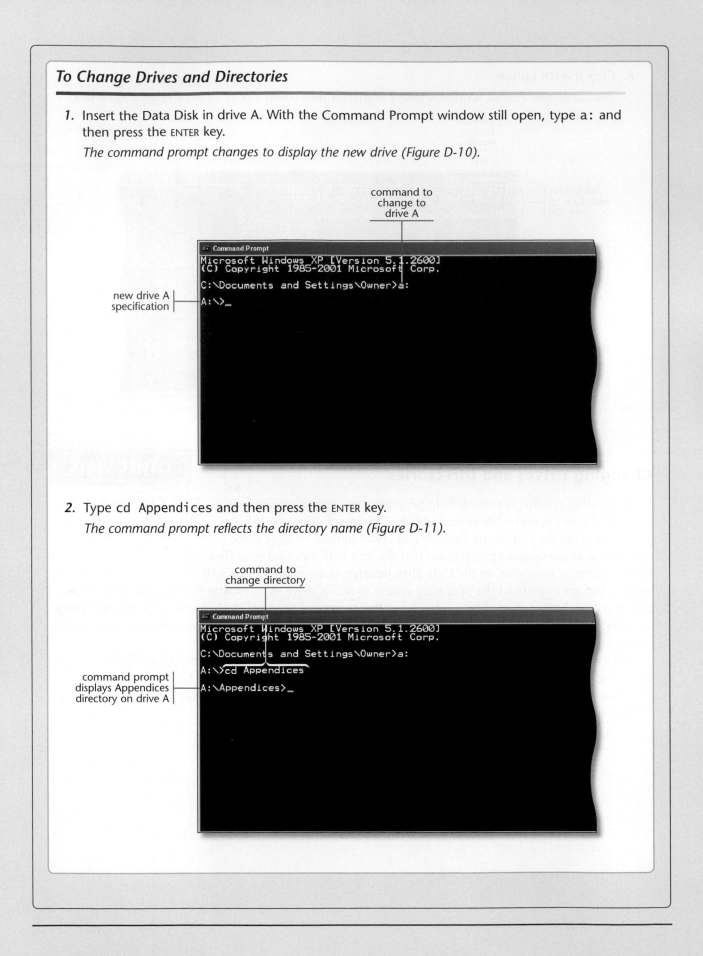

command to change to drive A

new drive A specification

2. Type cd Appendices and then press the ENTER key.

   *The command prompt reflects the directory name (Figure D-11).*

command to change directory

command prompt displays Appendices directory on drive A

Operating system commands such as cd are helpful when compiling and running programs or performing maintenance activities using the Command Prompt window. Table D-1 displays some useful operating system commands you can use in the Command Prompt window to interact with the Windows operating system.

**Table D-1  Useful Operating System Commands**

| COMMAND | PURPOSE |
|---|---|
| cd *directory name* | Changes directory. |
| cls | Clears screen of previous commands. |
| copy *path/filename path/filename* | Copies one or more files *from* one directory *to* another directory. |
| date | Displays or sets the date. |
| del *filename* | Deletes a file or files. |
| dir | Displays a list of all files and subdirectories in the current directory. |
| help | Displays a listing of available operating system commands. |
| md *directory name* | Makes a new directory. |
| move *path/filename path/filename* | Moves one or more files *from* one directory *to* another directory. |
| path *path* | Clears all search path settings and directs Windows to search only in the current directory. |
| rd *directory name* | Removes an existing directory. |
| ren *oldfilename newfilename* | Renames a file. |
| set classpath=*path* | Directs the Java SDK to look for classes in the specified path. |
| type *filename* | Displays the contents of a text file. |

Pressing CTRL+C halts execution of any currently running command.

## Setting the Path and Classpath Environment Variables

Recall that an environment variable is a string that lists information about the system environment, such as a drive, path, or file name. When compiling and executing from the command prompt, no IDE or VATE software has direct control over compiling and executing; only the operating system has direct control over compiling and executing. Therefore, it may be necessary to set a **path** to notify the operating system where the Java SDK is located in order to compile programs. It also may be necessary to set the **classpath** to specify the location of the Java classes in order to run the program.

The steps on the next page set the environment variables for the path and classpath at the command prompt. The steps set the path to the installed location of the Java SDK, as discussed in Appendix B. The classpath will be set to the Appendices directory on drive A.

## To Set the Path and Classpath Environment Variables

1. With the Command Prompt window still open, type path = c:\Program Files\Java\ jdk1.5.0_02\bin (or enter the location of your installation of the Java SDK) and then press the ENTER key.

   *The bin folder contains executable programs related to compiling and executing Java source code (Figure D-12).*

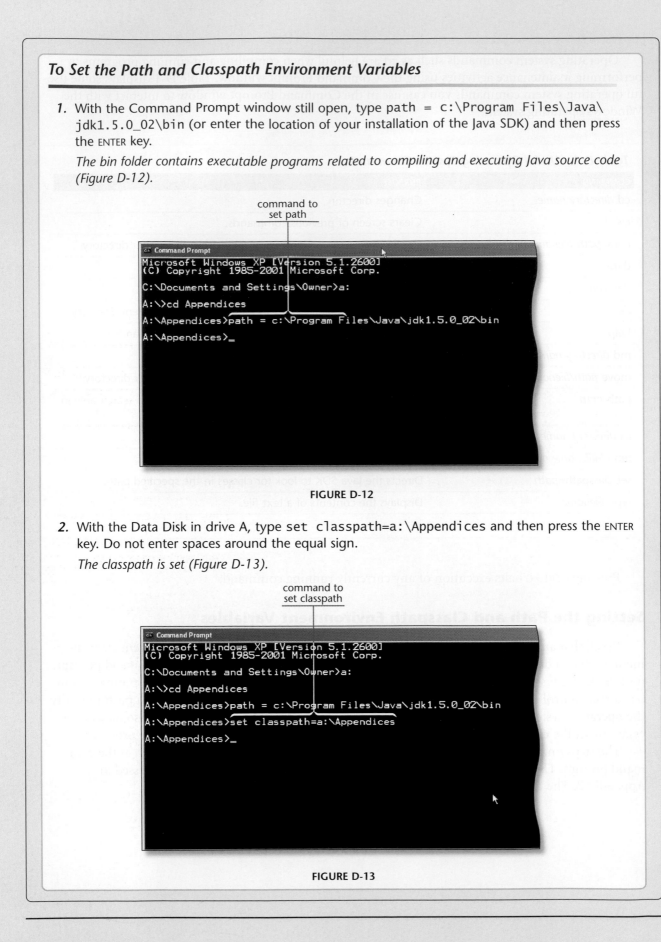

**FIGURE D-12**

2. With the Data Disk in drive A, type set classpath=a:\Appendices and then press the ENTER key. Do not enter spaces around the equal sign.

   *The classpath is set (Figure D-13).*

**FIGURE D-13**

The path and classpath now are set for the system. When compiling and executing in the Command Prompt window, the operating system will use these variables to obtain the value of the location where the SDK was installed on your system and to locate Java class files.

**Tip**

**Permanently Changing the Path**

If you want to permanently include the path of the Java SDK on your system, click the Start button on the Windows taskbar and then right-click My Computer. On the shortcut menu, click Properties. When the System Properties dialog box is displayed, click the Advanced tab. Click the Environment Variables button. In the System variables list, click Path and then click the Edit button. When the Edit System Variable dialog box is displayed, press the RIGHT ARROW to position the insertion point at the end of the Variable Value text box and then type ;C:\Program Files\Java\jdk1.5.0_02\bin (or the location where you installed the SDK) to append the text to the end of the existing string of characters. Click the OK button in each dialog box to accept the new settings.

## Compiling Source Code and Running Programs at the Command Prompt

Programmers enter the **javac** command followed by the full name of the Java source code file in order to compile the source code into bytecode. You must enter the .java extension when compiling. Once compiled, the **java** command will run the bytecode.

The following steps compile and run the Sample Java program located in the Appendices folder using the Command Prompt window.

### To Compile Source Code and Run Programs at the Command Prompt

1. With the Command Prompt window still open, type javac Sample.java and then press the ENTER key.

   *The program compiles (Figure D-14). You must enter the .java extension when compiling.*

compile command

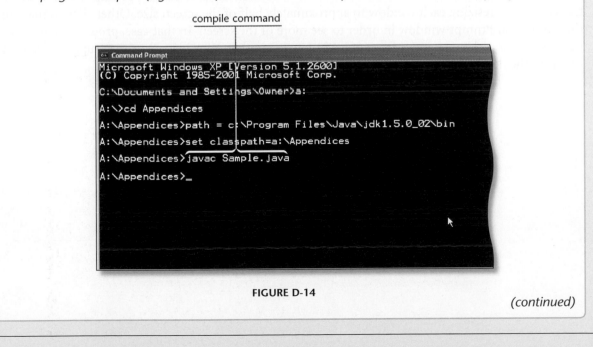

```
Command Prompt
Microsoft Windows XP [Version 5.1.2600]
(C) Copyright 1985-2001 Microsoft Corp.

C:\Documents and Settings\Owner>a:

A:\>cd Appendices

A:\Appendices>path = c:\Program Files\Java\jdk1.5.0_02\bin

A:\Appendices>set classpath=a:\Appendices

A:\Appendices>javac Sample.java

A:\Appendices>_
```

**FIGURE D-14**

*(continued)*

**2.** Type `java Sample` and then press the ENTER key.

*The program runs (Figure D-15). You do not enter an extension when executing. The output from the Sample program displays.*

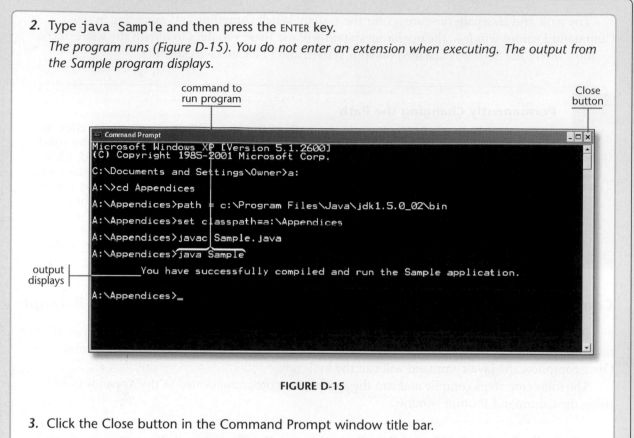

**FIGURE D-15**

**3.** Click the Close button in the Command Prompt window title bar.

*The Command Prompt window closes.*

When programming, compiling, and testing code, Java programmers set up their desktops in a variety of ways. Some like to have both their text editor and their Command Prompt window open at the same time, resizing each window to approximately half of the screen size. Others like to maximize the Command Prompt window in order to see more of the screen. In that case, programmers click the buttons on the taskbar to move from one window to another. Your instructor may suggest other ways to set up the desktop.

# APPENDIX

# E

# Creating Documentation with Javadoc

Appendix E explains how to use the Javadoc utility to create HTML documentation for Java programs. The appendix also describes the various Javadoc tags used in Javadoc comments, as well as how to view and navigate the generated files.

# Using the Javadoc Utility

The Java SDK contains a utility called **Javadoc**, which is used to create Java program documentation as HTML files, such as those shown in Figure E-1a and Figure E-1b. The Javadoc tool parses the special documentation comments and declarations inserted in Java source code to produce a set of HTML files that describe a package, class, interface, constructor, method, field, or any combination of those objects.

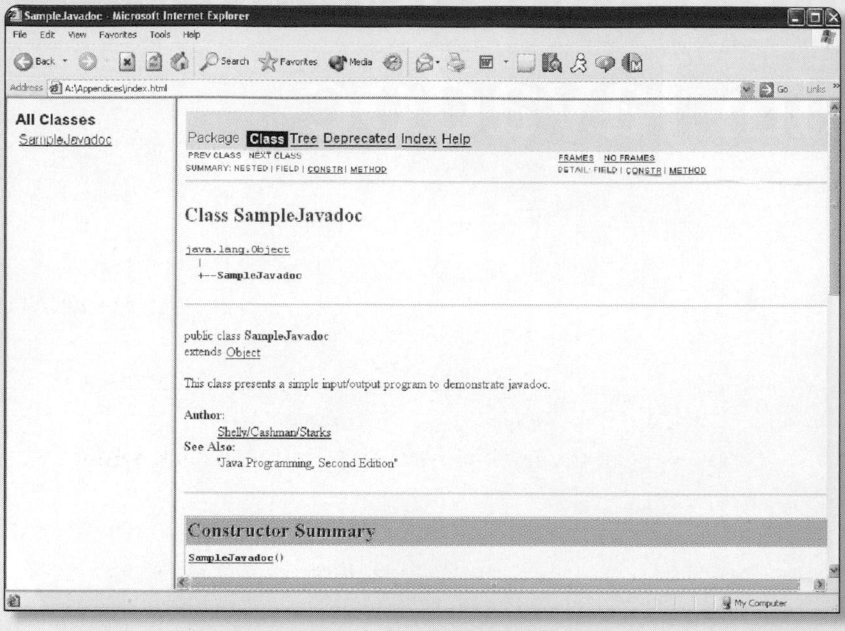

(a)

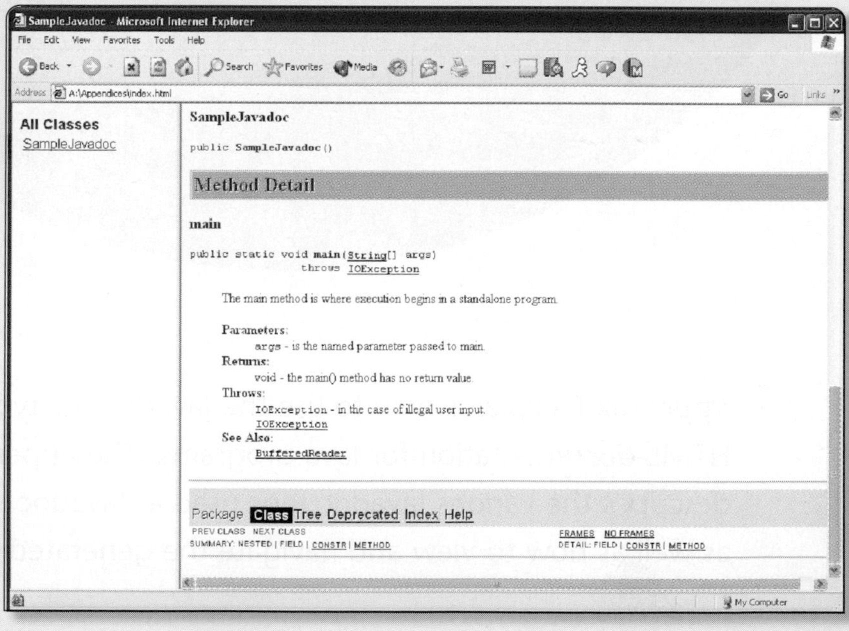

(b)

FIGURE E-1

Generating program documentation using Javadoc is a two-step process. First, you insert special comments in the source code; then, you execute the Javadoc command to create HTML-formatted program documentation.

This appendix illustrates how to use Javadoc to create HTML-formatted program documentation based on comments inserted into Java source code. This appendix uses a sample file on the Data Disk to illustrate this process; however, you can insert Javadoc comments into any existing Java source code file.

## Starting TextPad and Opening an Existing File

The following steps open a program called Sample2.java, included on the Data Disk that accompanies this book. See the preface of this book for instructions for downloading the Data Disk or see your instructor for information about accessing the files required in this book.

### To Start TextPad and Open an Existing File

1. Click the Start button on the taskbar, point to All Programs, and then click TextPad on the All Programs submenu.
2. When the TextPad window opens, if necessary, click the Close button in the Tip of the Day window. Click the Open button on the TextPad toolbar.
3. When the Open dialog box is displayed, click the Look in box arrow and then click 3½ Floppy (A:) in the list.
4. Double-click the Appendices folder.
5. When the list of files displays, double-click the file Sample2.java. If necessary, click View on the menu bar and then click Line Numbers to display line numbers.

*TextPad displays the Java source code for the Sample2.java file in the coding window (Figure E-2).*

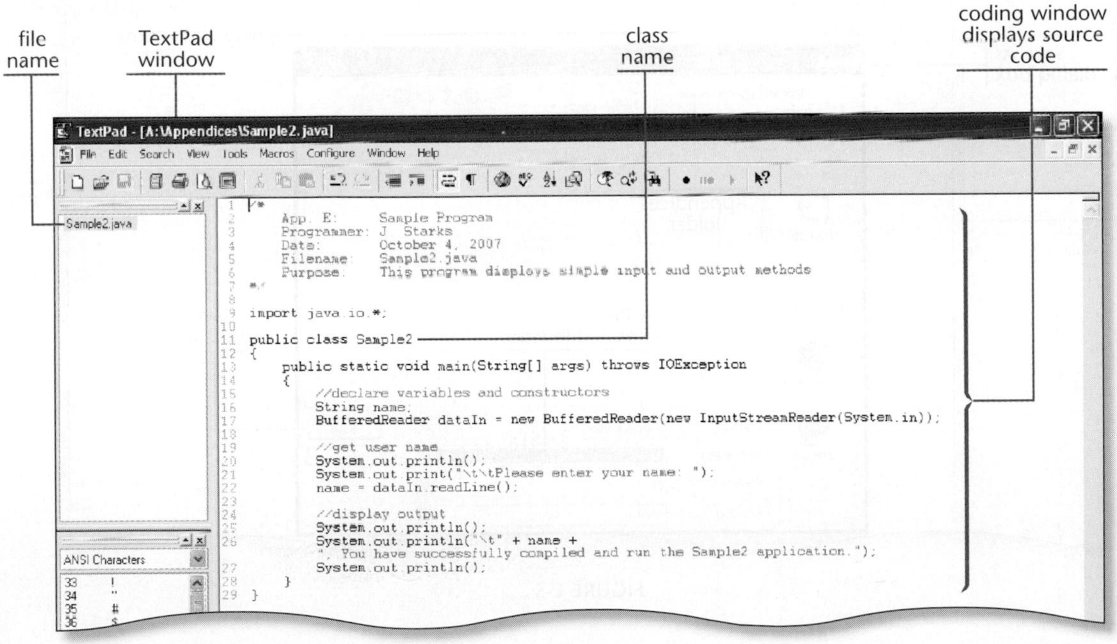

FIGURE E-2

## Editing a Class Name and Saving a File with a New File Name

The program coded in the Sample2.java file asks the user for his or her name and then prints a message in the Command Prompt window. Its purpose is not to show any new coding techniques, but to illustrate how to create program documentation in HTML format.

Before editing an existing file that you may want to use again, it is a good idea to save the file with a different name. Recall that in Java, the class name must match the file name. The following steps edit the class name and then save the Sample2.java file with a new name.

### To Edit a Class Name and Save a File with a New File Name

1. With the Sample2.java source code displaying in the coding window, change the file name in line 5 to SampleJavadoc.java. Change the class name in line 11 to SampleJavadoc.

2. Click File on the menu bar and then click Save As on the File menu. When the Save As dialog box is displayed, if necessary, click the Save in box arrow and then click 3½ Floppy (A:) in the Save in list. Double-click the Appendices folder or a location specified by your instructor.

3. Type SampleJavadoc in the File name text box and then, if necessary, click Java (*.java) in the Save as type list.

*The Save As dialog box displays the new file name in the File name text box (Figure E-3). The comments and class name have been edited to reflect the new file name.*

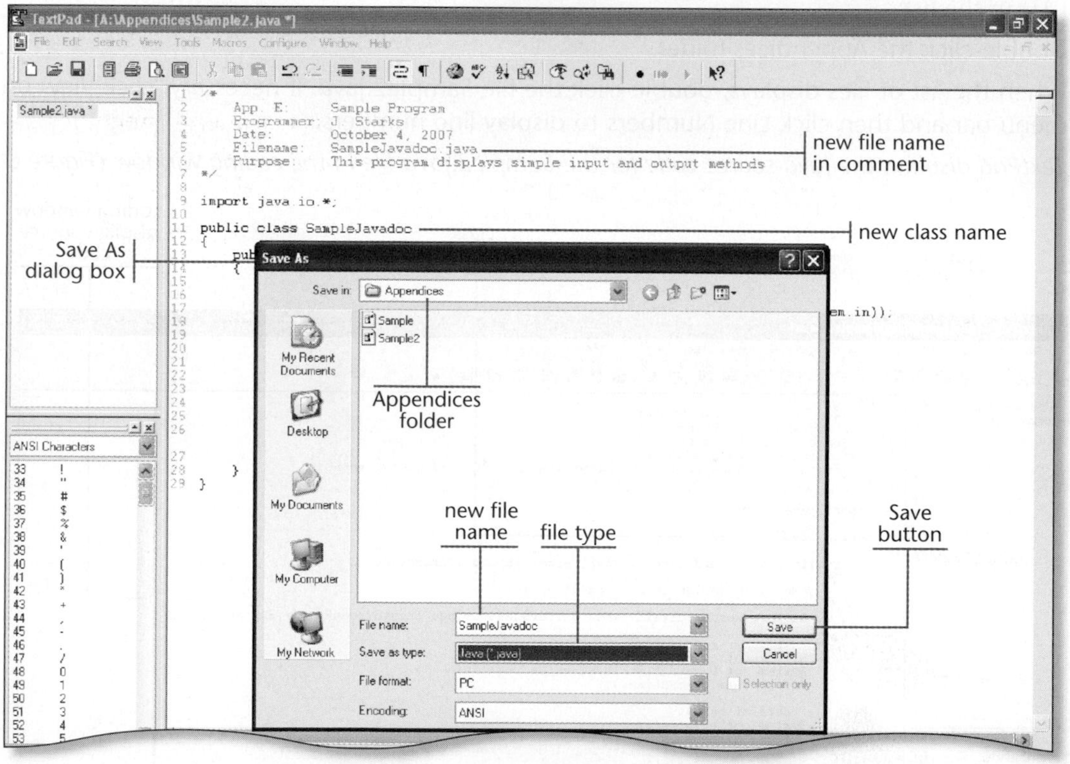

FIGURE E-3

4. Click the Save button in the Save As dialog box.

# Writing Doc Comments

Recall from Chapter 2 that two types of comments are used in Java programming: line comments and block comments. Line comments are used to provide documentation for single lines of code or for short descriptions and documentation comments. A line comment, as shown in line 15 of Figure E-2 on page E.03, begins with two forward slashes (//) that cause the line to be ignored during compilation and execution. Line comments have no ending symbol.

Block comments are used as headers at the beginning of the program or when long descriptions are appropriate. As shown in lines 1 through 7 of Figure E-2 on page E.03, a block comment begins with a forward slash followed by an asterisk (/*) and ends with the symbols reversed, an asterisk followed by a forward slash (*/).

A second type of block comment — called a **doc comment,** or a documentation comment — uses special notation that allows programmers to create HTML-formatted program documentation. A doc comment is placed in the code just before the declaration of the package, class, or method it describes; the doc comment begins with a forward slash followed by two asterisks (/**) and ends with an asterisk followed by a forward slash (*/).

The doc comments then can be extracted to HTML files using the Javadoc tool. Using doc comments does not mean you are required to generate HTML files using the Javadoc tool. By using doc comments, however, you leave the option open in the event that you later decide to create program documentation in HTML using the Javadoc tool. Moreover, because doc comments follow a standard style, other programmers will have an easier time reading code with doc comments than reading code with a non-standard style of comments.

## Writing Doc Comments for the SampleJavadoc Class

Figure E-4 displays the doc comments for the SampleJavadoc class. The doc comment is placed in the code just before the class declaration and begins with a forward slash followed by two asterisks (/**) on a line with no other code (line 11). The doc comment ends with the */ symbol (line 15). The doc comment can span as many lines as necessary within the beginning and ending marks. Typically, each line within a block comment begins with an asterisk and is indented for ease of reading.

```
11   /**
12    * This class presents a simple input/output program to demonstrate javadoc.
13    * @see "Java Programming, Third Edition"
14    * @author <A HREF="http://www.scsite.com/">Shelly/Cashman/Starks</A>
15    */
16   public class SampleJavadoc
17   {
```

**FIGURE E-4**

**Tip**

**Placement of Doc Comments**

In order for the Javadoc command to read the doc comments and convert them to program documentation, you must place doc comments directly above the package, class, or method declaration. For example, if you want to document a method named getCost(), you must place the doc comments in the code just before the getCost() method header. That way, Javadoc can associate the description and tags with the correct method. If you place other code between the doc comment and the method header, the documentation will not display the description and may generate an error.

Within the beginning and ending marks, each doc comment is made up of two parts: a description followed by block tags. A **description** is a short summary or definition of the object, as shown in line 12 of Figure E-4 on the previous page. A **tag**, or **block tag**, is an HTML notation that uses a keyword to send information to an HTML file, as shown in lines 13 and 14 of Figure E-4.

## Javadoc Tags

A Javadoc tag begins with the @ sign, followed by a keyword that represents a special reference understood by Javadoc. A tag provides structure that Javadoc can parse into text, font styles, and links in the HTML files generated as program documentation.

Tags come in two types: stand-alone tags and inline tags. **Stand-alone tags** can be placed only in the tag section that follows the description in a doc comment. These tags are not set off with curly braces. **Inline tags** can be placed anywhere in the comment description or in the comments for stand-alone tags. Inline tags are set off with curly braces. Table E-1 lists commonly used Javadoc tags.

*Table E-1   Commonly Used Javadoc Tags*

| TAG NAME | DOCUMENTATION RESULT | SYNTAX |
|---|---|---|
| @author | Adds an Author section with the specified name to the generated documents when the author parameter is used. A doc comment may contain multiple @author tags. | @author *name-text* |
| @deprecated | Adds a comment indicating that this API is deprecated and should no longer be used. | @deprecated *deprecated-text* |
| @exception | Is a synonym for @throws. | @exception *class-name description* |
| {@link} | Inserts a link that points to the specified name. This tag accepts the same syntax as the @see tag, but generates an inline link. This tag begins and ends with curly braces to separate it from the rest of the inline text. | {@link *name*} |
| @param | Adds a Parameter section that lists and defines method parameters. | @param *parameter-name description* |
| @return | Adds a Returns section with the description text. This text should describe the return type and permissible range of values. | @return *description* |

**Table E-1   Commonly Used Javadoc Tags** (continued)

| TAG NAME | DOCUMENTATION RESULT | SYNTAX |
|---|---|---|
| @see | Adds a See Also section with a link or text entry. A doc comment may contain any number of @see tags, which are all grouped under the same heading. | @see *reference* |
| @throws | Adds a Throws section to describe the kind of data returned to the method. It is a synonym for @exception. | @throws *class-name description* |

In line 13 of Figure E-4 on page E.05, the @see tag instructs the Javadoc tool to add a See Also heading to the program documentation, with a text entry that refers the user to the textbook, Java Programming, Third Edition.

Line 14 in Figure E-4 shows a @author tag that instructs the Javadoc tool to add an Author heading, followed by the specified name, to the program documentation. The HTML tag, HREF, instructs the Javadoc tool to include a link to the Web site www.scsite.com.

## Writing Doc Comments for the main() Method

Figure E-5 displays the doc comments for the main() method of the SampleJavadoc program. In line 20, the @param tag is used to define the parameters that the main() method may use. In this example, the parameter, args, is the parameter passed to the main() method. For multiple parameters, you can list multiple @param tags. When the Javadoc tool executes, the @param tag tells it to add a Parameter heading to the resulting HTML files.

```
18      /**
19       *
20       * The main method is where execution begins in a standalone program.
21       * @param args is the named parameter passed to main.
22       * @throws <code>IOException</code> in the case of illegal user input.
23       * @see BufferedReader
24       */
25      public static void main(String[] args) throws IOException
26      {
```

FIGURE E-5

The @throws tag in line 22 allows you to document what kind of exception is thrown and when that exception might occur. The @throws tag also uses a general HTML tag, <**code**>, and its closing tag, </**code**>, to create a link to the API documentation. In the case of @throws, if the exception is a Java-defined exception, you can enter the exception name between the opening and closing <code> tags; Javadoc will convert the text into a link when it generates HTML-formatted documentation.

The @see tag, as shown in line 23 of Figure E-5, is used to enter other Java keywords, methods, and data types that are related to the class or method. Again, Javadoc automatically will create a link to the API documentation for these keywords, methods, or data types when it generates HTML-formatted documentation.

## Coding Doc Comments

As previously noted, doc comments should be placed directly above a definition for a class, an interface, a constructor, or a method. The following steps show how to code doc comments for the SampleJavadoc class and the main() method.

### *To Code Doc Comments*

1. Enter lines 11 through 15 from Figure E-4 on page E.05 into the SampleJavadoc.java coding window.

   *TextPad displays the doc comments for the SampleJavadoc class in the coding window (Figure E-6).*

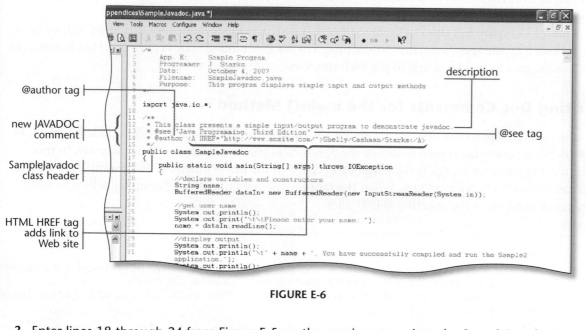

FIGURE E-6

2. Enter lines 18 through 24 from Figure E-5 on the previous page into the SampleJavadoc.java coding window.

   *TextPad displays the doc comments for the main() method in the coding window (Figure E-7).*

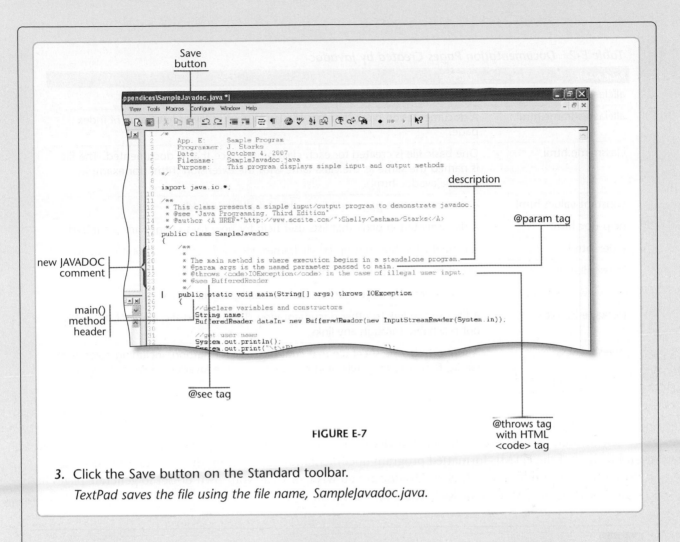

FIGURE E-7

3. Click the Save button on the Standard toolbar.

   *TextPad saves the file using the file name, SampleJavadoc.java.*

The @see tag can take one of three different forms. The first form, as shown in line 13 in Figure E-7, tells Javadoc to display a string of text, such as a reference to a textbook; no link is created. The second form, as shown in line 22 in Figure E-7, tells Javadoc to create a link that points to the documentation for the specified keyword, method, or data type, as referenced in the Java Language Specification on the Sun Microsystems Web site. The third form tells Javadoc to create a link to a specific Web page URL, much like the @author tag in line 14.

## Generating Documentation Using Javadoc

The documentation generated by the Javadoc tool consists of a number of HTML-formatted pages in the same style as the Java API Specification. These HTML-formatted pages, which include cross-reference pages, an index page, and a style sheet, use frames to display information in the Web browser window. When creating these pages, Javadoc automatically includes links to relevant Web pages in the Java API Specification based on the description and tags used in the doc comments.

Table E-2 on the next page lists some of the documentation pages created by Javadoc.

*Table E-2   Documentation Pages Created by Javadoc*

| PAGE NAME | PURPOSE |
|---|---|
| allclasses-noframe.html | A documentation page that lists all classes using no frames. |
| allclasses-frame.html | A documentation page that lists all classes used in lower-left frame of index page. |
| classname.html | One basic file is created for each class or interface that is documented. The file is named the same as the classname with the extension .html (for example, SampleJavadoc.html). |
| constant-values.html | A documentation page that lists values of all static fields. |
| help-doc.html | A documentation page that lists user help for how these pages are organized. |
| index.html | An initial page that sets up HTML frames; file itself contains no text content. |
| index-all.html | The default alphabetical index of all classes and methods. |
| overview-tree.html | A cross-reference page that lists class hierarchy for all packages. |
| package-list.txt | A file used to link to other documentation. This is a text file, not HTML, and is not reachable through any links. |
| stylesheet.css | A supporting style sheet file that controls basic formatting, including color, font family, font size, font style, and positioning on the Javadoc-generated pages. |

By default, Javadoc uses a standard **doclet** file provided by Sun Microsystems to specify the content and format of the HTML-formatted program documentation. You can modify the standard doclet, however, to customize the output of Javadoc as you wish, or write your own doclet to generate pages in other formats, such as XML or Rich Text Format (RTF).

**Tip**

**Writing Doclets**
You can write a new doclet from scratch using the doclet API, or you can start with the standard doclet and modify it to suit your needs. For more information on writing doclets, visit the Sun Microsystems Web site.

The Javadoc tool will generate either two or three HTML frames, based on whether you use Javadoc to document only one or multiple packages. When you pass a single package name or source file as an argument into Javadoc, it will create two frames: a main frame with an overview page and a left frame listing classes. When you pass two or more package names into Javadoc, it will create three frames: a main frame with an overview page, an upper-left frame listing all packages, and a lower-left frame listing all classes. A user viewing the documentation can remove the frames by clicking the No Frames link at the top of the overview page.

## Using the Javadoc Tool

TextPad provides functionality to allow users to run Javadoc by clicking Run on the Tools menu and then entering the correct commands in the Run dialog box. When you run Javadoc, certain parameters can be used to help Javadoc link to the appropriate files. The following steps show how to run the Javadoc tool and enter required parameters to generate HTML-formatted program documentation.

### To Use the Javadoc Tool

*1.* Click Tools on TextPad's menu bar and then click Run.

*TextPad displays the Run dialog box (Figure E-8). The Run dialog box includes text boxes for input of a command, parameters, and an initial folder.*

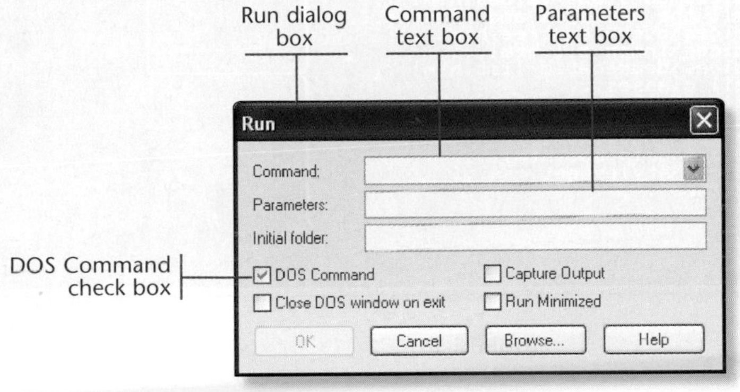

Run dialog box    Command text box    Parameters text box

DOS Command check box

**FIGURE E-8**

*2.* Type javadoc A:\Appendices\SampleJavadoc.java in the Command text box. Press the TAB key. Type -link http://java.sun.com/j2se/1.5.0/docs/api -author -d A:\Appendices\ in the Parameters text box. Press the TAB key. Type C:\Program Files\Java\jdk1.5.0_02\bin in the Initial folder text box.

If necessary, click the DOS Command check box to select it.

*The Run dialog box displays the entered data (Figure E-9). The DOS Command check box is selected.*

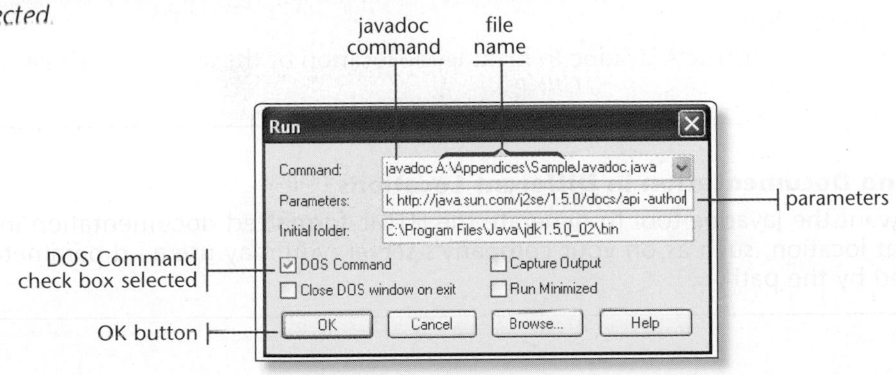

javadoc command    file name

DOS Command check box selected

OK button

parameters

**FIGURE E-9**

*(continued)*

**3.** Click the OK button.

*The Command Prompt window displays messages about the Javadoc-generated files (Figure E-10). If your file location has changed or if your system currently is not connected to the Web, you may be prompted to connect. If you do not connect, your output may display an error or warning message, but still will generate the HTML-formatted documentation pages.*

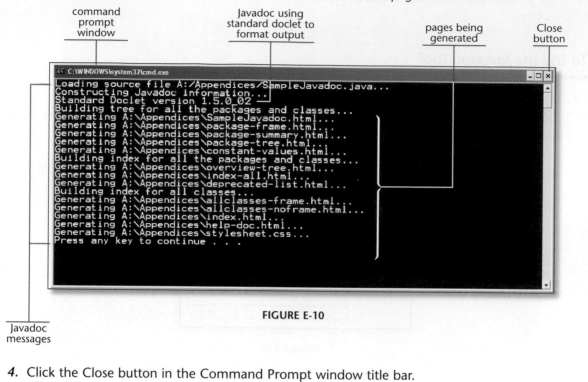

command prompt window

Javadoc using standard doclet to format output

pages being generated

Close button

Javadoc messages

FIGURE E-10

**4.** Click the Close button in the Command Prompt window title bar.

*The Command Prompt window closes.*

The –link parameter (Figure E-9 on the previous page) specifies the location of the Java API on the Sun Microsystems Web site. Using the –link parameter ensures that any links to the Java API documentation will be accessible to all users. For the documentation links to work, however, the user must be connected to the Web.

The –author parameter instructs javadoc to include the location of the author's Web page.

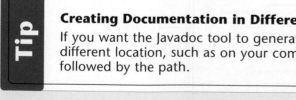

**Tip**

**Creating Documentation in Different Locations**

If you want the Javadoc tool to generate the HTML-formatted documentation in a different location, such as on your company's server, you may use a –d parameter, followed by the path.

## Viewing Javadoc-Generated Documentation

Once Javadoc has generated the HTML-formatted documentation for your Java program, it can be viewed using a Web browser. The following steps show how to view and navigate through Javadoc-generated documentation using a Web browser.

### To *View Javadoc-Generated Documentation*

1. Start Internet Explorer or your Web browser. When the browser window opens, type
   A:\Appendices\index.html in the Address text box. Press the ENTER key.

   *The browser displays the documentation created for the SampleJavadoc program (Figure E-11).*

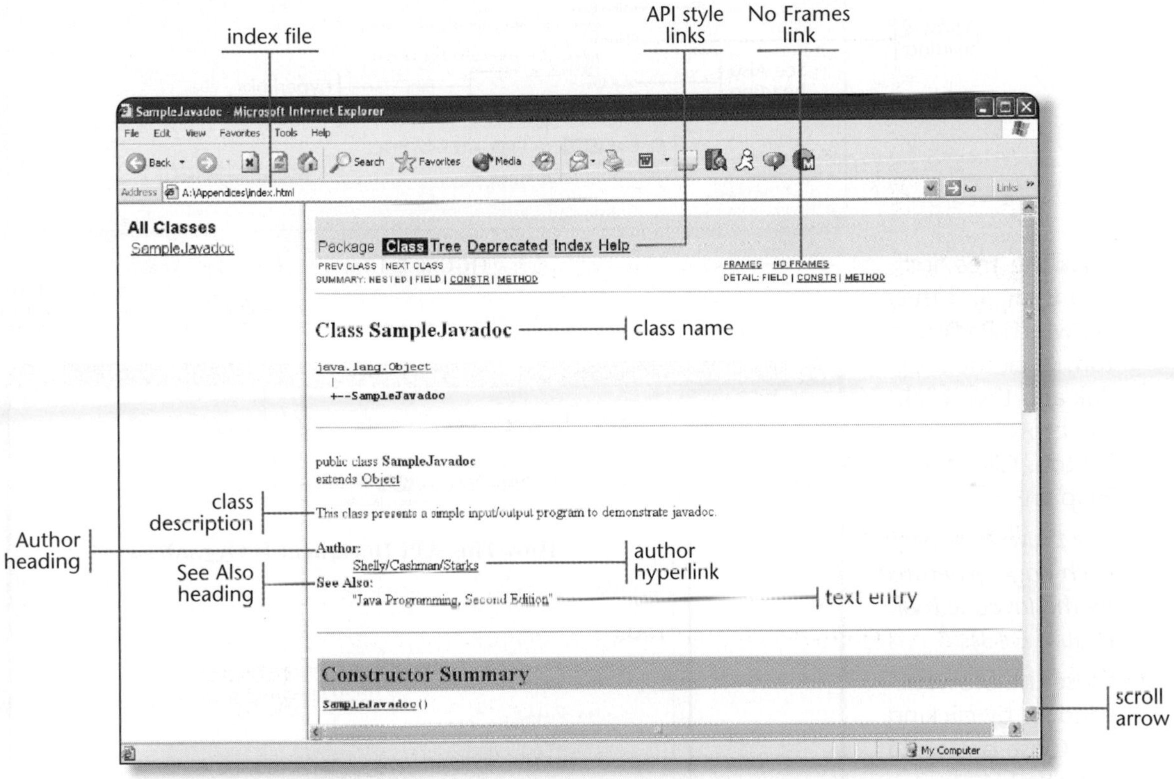

FIGURE E-11

*(continued)*

2. Use the down scroll arrow to display the Method Detail.

   *The frame scrolls to display the Method Detail (Figure E-12).*

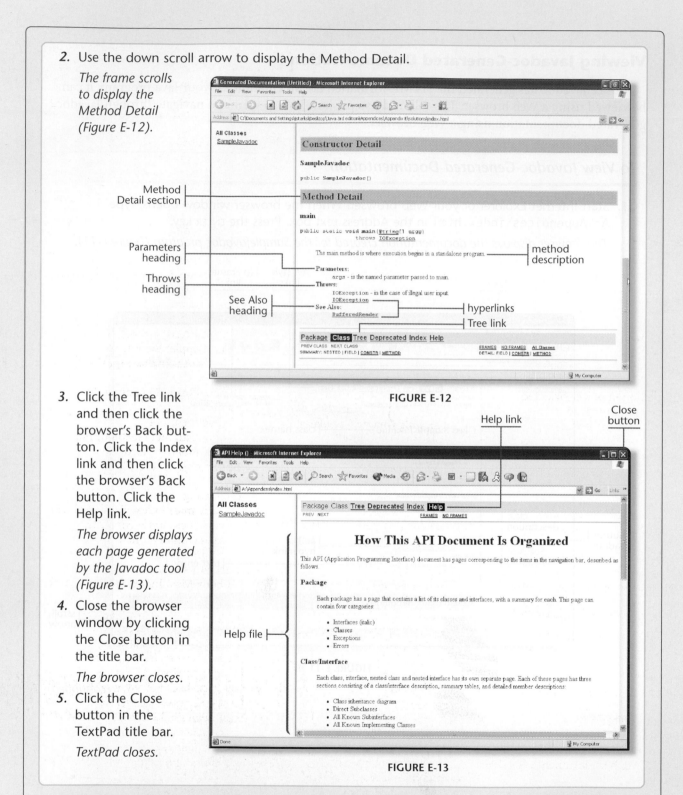

**FIGURE E-12**

3. Click the Tree link and then click the browser's Back button. Click the Index link and then click the browser's Back button. Click the Help link.

   *The browser displays each page generated by the Javadoc tool (Figure E-13).*

4. Close the browser window by clicking the Close button in the title bar.

   *The browser closes.*

5. Click the Close button in the TextPad title bar.

   *TextPad closes.*

**FIGURE E-13**

Businesses and programmers use Javadoc to provide documentation to users of their source code. For example, the Javadoc tool is used by Sun Microsystems to create all API documentation. For these businesses and programmers, the HTML files created by the Javadoc tool are a convenient and platform-independent way of distributing documentation online from a Web site or intranet, via CD-ROM or other media, or even as hard-copy printouts.

# Index